THE
SECOND COMING
OF THE
NEW AGE

THE SECOND COMING OF THE

NEW AGE

THE HIDDEN DANGERS OF ALTERNATIVE SPIRITUALITY IN CONTEMPORARY AMERICA AND ITS CHURCHES

STEVEN BANCARZ
JOSH PECK

Foreword by Dr. Michael S. Heiser

DEFENDER
CRANE, MO

The Second Coming of the New Age: The Hidden Dangers of Alternative Spirituality in Contemporary America and Its Churches
By Steven Bancarz & Josh Peck

Defender Publishing: Crane, MO 65633
© 2018 Thomas Horn, Defender Publishing. All rights reserved.
Published 2018.
Printed in the United States of America.

ISBN: 978-1-948014-11-3

A CIP catalog record of this book is available from the Library of Congress.

Cover Illustration and design by Jeffrey Mardis.

All Scripture quotations from the English Standard Version unless otherwise noted.

Dedication and Acknowledgments

*This book is dedicated to any and all out there seeking
answers to the mysteries of life, death, and beyond.*

As is always the case when I write a new book, the list of people I'd love to thank individually lengthens to the point of being the length of a book all its own. I will just say here, first, I thank my Lord and Savior Jesus Christ, without whom I would be nothing. I'd also like to thank my incredible wife, Christina, and our beautiful children, Jaklynn, Nathan, and Adam. I owe a very big thank-you to my friend and coauthor Steven Bancarz, who is a constant inspiration and source of hope for the Church and young Christians of our generation. Another big thank-you goes out to Tom Horn, Defender Publishing, and my entire SkyWatchTV family (far too many to name individually here, but you all know who you are) for many more reason than can be listed. I like to thank all of my personal friends and family who have kept me in prayers over the years and who have been instrumental in my being where I am today. Last, but certainly not least, I would like to thank my amazing audience, who has been a never-ending source of prayer, support, encouragement, constructive criticism, and above all, love, and who has helped me in more ways than they would ever be able to imagine.

—Josh Peck

Jesus Christ is the only reason my life is not broken beyond repair. He is my life now. I thank Him for saving me from the penalty of my sin, the power of my sin, my own self, and the forces of deception that were at work in my life keeping me away from the truth. I would also like to thank my Patreon supporters and all those who have been supporting me as I made the transition from New Age to Christianity. Without their generosity, I simply would not be able to serve the Lord as I do. My thanks also to the people online who have subscribed or followed my social media pages, as this has been extremely encouraging and edifying to me. In addition, I thank the people I am in ministry with for their continued support of me in Christ and the covering of prayer they have put over my head; my parents—for raising me in a Christian home, being compassionate toward me during my rebellion, and always believing in me as a person; Josh Peck, for presenting me with an opportunity as a brother in Christ to write my first published book; Skywatch TV and Tom Horn for influencing me early on in my walk with the Lord; my home church (Evangel) in Brantford, Ontario; and my pastor, Craig McKibbon, for being an instrument of the Lord to bring healing in my life. Thanks, too, to everyone who has ever taken the time to pray for God to move in my life.

    —Steven Bancarz

CONTENTS

FOREWORD

Dr. Michael S. Heiser

MANY WHO PICK UP THIS book may be inclined to ask the questions I did when I read the manuscript. What's new about the New Age? It's been around since the '70s. If you're like me, you're old enough to remember that. Why talk about its second coming? It never really left.

All true.

But times have indeed changed, especially within the professing Church.

In 1985, I was finishing college. I can remember laughing with my roommates about Bhagwan Shree Rajneesh, a self-professed god-man from India who had come to the United States to celebrate and popularize things like mindfulness, meditation, Eastern mysticism and, in particular, free sex. The Bhagwan came to the United States in 1981 and pretty much got into legal trouble immediately. At first the issue was public resistance over allowing the Bhagwan and his followers to build an ashram (think monastic community) in the state of Oregon. Opposition and countermeasures escalated to the point of death threats and an aborted assassination plot against a state official. The Bhagwan was eventually deported. My friends and I wanted one of the T-shirts that said "We bagged the Bhagwan."

If you don't recall the Bhagwan, you probably remember Shirley MacLaine. By the time Americans had seen the last of the Bhagwan on our soil, we had been treated to two of her New Age bestsellers: *Out on a Limb* (1983) and *Dancing in the Light* (1986). MacLaine did more than any foreign guru in spreading New Age teachings on past lives, transcendental meditation, mediumship, and the mystical smorgasbord that is New Age spirituality. *Out on a Limb* became a five-hour mini-series (1987) in which MacLaine played herself. It was nominated for a Golden Globe award.

What's the point? The Bhagwan was a national joke. What he taught was considered inane psychobabble by the vast majority of Americans, especially those within the Church. MacLaine's books were reviewed by mainstream critics, who described them with terms like "exasperating" and "fatuous." She was publicly poked on late night shows like David Letterman. For Americans at the time, New Age spirituality was at best peripheral.

Times have changed.

If you're old enough to remember the Bhagwan and Shirley MacLaine, you might presume the New Age never really went away. You'd be correct. *The Second Coming of the New Age* isn't trying to prove otherwise. Rather, Steven Bancarz and Josh Peck draw our attention to the fact that not only is the New Age still here and even more entrenched in popular culture, but it's alive and well *in our churches*.

You might think most Christians can clearly distinguish the claims and practices of the New Age from biblical Christianity. If that's you, it's time to look beyond your own immediate circle of friends and family. Times have indeed changed. So has the average Christian's ability to think with theological clarity. Translation: Clear theological thinking is on life support in many congregations. What else can you conclude when, according to a recent Barna research study entitled *Translating the Great Commission*, 51 percent of American churchgoers do not know what the Great Commission is?[1] The same study notes that 41 percent of Millennials "do not know the Great Commission," while just 10 percent of the same demographic "have heard of and remember [the words to] the Great Commission."

Contemporary theological illiteracy manifests in other ways as well. Many people who grow up in Christian contexts cannot see why there would be any tension between the Bible and New Age beliefs. A blend of the two worldviews is inconsequential to them. Many aren't patient enough for the Church to catch up to enlightenment and simply leave. Others who see differences a bit more clearly leave the Christian faith when Church leadership cannot probe New Age thinking for incoherence or who can't have a discussion about New Age spirituality without talking down to people attracted by it.

This set of circumstances does not bode well for our culture, which is already transitioning out of the current post-Christian phase into an anti-Christian phase. The difference between those two cultural phases is subtle but real. The former speaks of tipping the scales from the dominance of a biblical/Christian worldview to a neopagan (New Age) worldview. The latter is concerned with displacing or eliminating Christianity from cultural relevance, not coexistence. This process is underway. It is just as dangerous as militant secularism when it comes to the security of the believing Church with respect to religious freedom. When New Age thought permeates the last bastion of opposition to its ideas, the Church at large, cultural resistance against demonizing Christianity weakens precisely because New Age thinking casts any religion that claims to be the exclusive way to eternal life (i.e., Christianity; cf. John 14:6) irrational and dangerous.

The Second Coming of the New Age provides an overview of some of the prominent beliefs of New Age spirituality and introduces readers to how these beliefs are surfacing in churches—even those in the evangelical tradition. For readers from Generation X or Millennials, the book's examination of these ideas will provide new information. For most readers of any age, what's going on in churches will very likely be a disturbing surprise.

Both authors have deep experience in New Age spirituality. Their knowledge is not merely theoretical or research-based. Rather, they are former practitioners and devotees of New Age spirituality. In other words, when it comes to what the New Age is and says, they know what they're talking about and deserve a hearing. My hope is that anyone attracted by New Age beliefs will take the path of enlightenment and engage in conversation with the authors.

—Dr. Michael S. Heiser

PhD, Hebrew and Semitic Studies, University of Wisconsin-Madison

Host of the *Naked Bible* podcast, *PEERANORMAL* podcast, and FringePop321 YouTube Channel

INTRODUCTION

THE PURPOSE OF THIS BOOK is not to demean or insult individuals within the New Age movement. Rather, it is to help New Age believers by exposing the lies within the movement while providing a better alternative: Christianity. Both authors of this book were heavily involved in New Age practices prior to coming to the saving knowledge of Jesus Christ. Rather than preaching at the readers, authors Steven Bancarz and Josh Peck hope to put forth a persuasive argument against New Age theology and in defense of Christianity. Throughout this book, Peck and Bancarz will provide both objective evidence and subjective experience to present their case. The goal is to provide readers with the necessary facts and arguments to make an informed choice about their own spirituality.

What Is the New Age Movement?

The New Age movement is a spiritual system of thought and practice composed of beliefs, values, and traditions from various schools and religions throughout the world. "New Age movement" is really an umbrella term covering a wide range of topics, including:

- Buddhism
- Hinduism
- Mysticism
- Transcendentalism
- Gnosticism
- Paganism
- Pantheism
- Occultism
- Esotericism
- Witchcraft
- Meditation
- Yoga
- Psychedelics
- Channelling
- Divination
- Sorcery
- Mind science
- Reincarnation
- Astral projection
- Ufology
- Spiritual psychology (Law of Attraction, manifestation , etc.)

The "New Age" is a collection of beliefs and practices aimed at bringing enlightenment. The goal, at an individual level, is to "raise the consciousness" to a "higher density" or a "higher vibration," meaning that knowledge of self, combined with divination and occult practices, can elevate our spiritual condition to a level of self-divinity. This movement teaches that we don't *become* divine, but that we already *are* divine in and of ourselves, such that the enlightenment the New Age movement seeks to bring about is arrived at by leaving a state of self-ignorance and realizing that the inner self is ultimately God. We are a spark of the Creator suffering from amnesia, so the pursuit of the New Age is to bring people into contact with and discovery of their own divinity so they can be liberated from the limitations and sufferings of ego-consciousness and live from a state of "universal consciousness." Supernatural practices are used to cultivate self-realization, the expansion of one's own mind, and contact with the spirit world.

The goal, at a global level, is to initiate world peace by uniting the religions of the world under an impersonal, universal god, restoring the forgotten wisdom traditions of ancient cultures and incorporating them into our civilization. A "Golden Age of Enlightenment" is in mind, wherein mankind will finally recognize the inherent sacredness of all things and his connectedness with fellow man, causing him to live from a heightened state of consciousness in which a world of peace and unity will be a byproduct. As we "awaken" individually, the result is a world system shaped around the principles of individual enlightenment.

Cherry-picking bits of information from whatever its adherents please, the New Age movement is broad in scope as far as what its followers accept and narrow in the scope of what they reject. This means the modern New Age movement accepts everything under the sun, from the mystery teachings of Ancient Babylon and modern-day witchcraft to the *New York Times* best-selling spiritual psychology books available at your local Walmart. Being so broad in scope, its practitioners are encouraged to draw from whatever principle or worldview they feel may serve them, regardless of whether it is true.

Lack of a Common Doctrine

While most people active in the New Age movement have a loose, generally agreed-upon set of beliefs, no official standard or set of core doctrines determines the difference between New Age and something else. No single book or teacher holds a monopoly on New Spirituality. By contrast, Christianity has the Bible to describe its set of core doctrines. For a person to become a Christian, he or she must dedicate his or her life to Jesus Christ by accepting Him as the one and only Savior described in the Bible. New Age theology, on the other hand, has no official rule of faith and practice. No New Age founding document is accepted as the go-to text of the main teachings of New Age theology. In short, there is no official New Age Bible.

New Agers draw on many ancient and modern texts to define what exactly they believe, though that text varies from person to person. To some, New Age is all about sharpening one's astral travel or remote-viewing skills (terms we will describe in full detail in a later chapter). To others, it is about personal enlightenment in the context of Eastern mysticism wherein one moves up the ranks of deification. To others still, it is about having a personal experience with a god or spirit guide. There is no single objective to New Age thought and practice. In fact, it is pretty much open to everything—except, that is, Jesus Christ and His plan of salvation as described in the Holy Bible.

No Christians Allowed in the New Age Clubhouse

Basically every perspective in New Age thinking is considered a valid source of spiritual truth that can be incorporated into one's pursuit of enlightenment. People seek to be "spiritual" but not "religious," giving themselves permission to extract wisdom and experience from all spiritual avenues without epistemic restriction. Since unity is revered as the highest virtue, firm disagreement with anyone else's views is said to "cause separation" or "constrict the flow of Spirit." The free-flowing nature of the movement is preserved by taking in every spiritual teaching without intellectual discrimination (unless, of course, the teachings of the Bible are introduced). Every opinion is accepted—in most cases, dogmatically and uncritically, without need for philosophical cohesiveness or evidence. In one breath, the New Age movement affirms that all religions are aimed at one underlying truth about God and humanity, and in the next breath, it explicitly rejects the Bible as a source of authority on God and shuns those who cite Scripture in its proper context.

The Tao Te Ching, the Tibetan Book of the Dead, the Vedas, the Bhagavad Gita, the Mahayana Sutras, and the other works of mystics and occultists are frequently referenced as sources of wisdom and truth, but if the Bible is quoted from, New Ager teachers are quick to say it is a corrupt book invented by the Church to keep people in fear. All of a sudden, New Age's universal embrace turns into dogmatic rejection. Biblical truths are dismissed without being examined, and the only justifications given are the recycled talking points about its corrupt origin (though it is prophetically divine), its unreliability (though it is far more reliable than any other ancient text), and its abuse throughout history (though this does not determine whether or not its contents are true).

The New Age movement simply does not tolerate ideological intolerance, holding that everything is true except for the belief that not everything is true. It accepts all viewpoints as valid except the one that says only the Gospel is valid.

Why Does the New Age Reject Jesus?

The teachings of Jesus and the belief system of the first-century Church are antithetical to New Age theology. The biggest difference is their Christology, their view of Jesus Himself. Christianity teaches that Jesus is God in the flesh who died on the cross as a sacrifice to atone for the sins of anyone who will believe in Him. After His death and burial, Jesus was resurrected from the dead, thereby proving that He conquered death itself and securing for us the hope of eternal life. After this, Jesus ascended to Heaven with a promise to return one day. He was a monotheistic Jew who claimed to be the only sacrifice for human sin, and that we must believe He is the risen Messiah in order to be saved from the penalty and power of our sins.

The New Age version of Jesus is quite different. It considers Jesus as either merely a wise, human teacher or something quasi-divine, such as an Ascended Master, spirit guide, or even an extraterrestrial being who came here to teach us how we can ascend and reach the same level of consciousness He had. Consider this quote from one popular website:

> "Jesus Christ the same yesterday, today and forever"! (Hebrews 13:8) Worshippers of the Christ have taken this declaration of the Holy Scriptures and have used it as a powerful affirmation to know and feel that Jesus as the Living Christ is here with us today—loving us, raising us upward, and moving us Christ-ward to help us claim the empowerment as God's freewill gift to all; to become that same living Christ that is in Jesus now and always. "Therefore, if any man be in Christ, he is a new creature: old things are passed away: behold, all things are become new." (II Corinthians 5:17) And yet the Jesus of today remarks that few among us choose to be who we truly are as Christed beings as many would rather be something else. And so he gives us this commission: Yes, it is up to each of you as Christed beings to carry forward my message—the message of my mission two thousand years ago and my message of today—that each one is the living Christ, created in God's image and likeness and must choose to be that light, that Reality now and ever through free-will.... And so you must teach them the art and science of kno-wingness, acceptance and beingness as a trilogy of perfection; for when they can feel, know and sense God's Presence within, everything changes, a new universe opens, divine possibilities may be engaged in and further insights ensue.[2]

A common tactic of New Age teachers is to quote a Bible verse, remove it from the context of the surrounding verses, twist the intended meaning of the author, and use it to support their own antibiblical teach-ings. The section quoted above uses Hebrews 13:8 (see below for con-text) and 2 Corinthians 5:17 to promote the idea that Jesus wants each of us to realize we are Christ ourselves just as much as He is. Since Jesus Himself never taught that, the New Age teacher must pervert a statement from "Jesus" to support this teaching. The statement, of course, reads nothing like the words of the true Jesus described in the Bible.

The real Jesus Christ taught a clear distinction between God and mankind. He also taught that He is the only way to God; there is nothing we mere humans can do to attain salvation for ourselves; and we certainly cannot ascend to His level by our own merit, practice, or understanding. Rather, Jesus taught that only through faith in Him can we truly be saved from the penalty and power of sin.

> Jesus said to him, "I am the way, and the truth, and the life. No one comes to the Father except through me." (John 14:6, ESV)

> When the disciples heard this, they were greatly astonished, saying, "Who then can be saved?"
> But Jesus looked at them and said, "With man this is impossible, but with God all things are possible. (Matthew 19:25–26, ESV)

> Because, if you confess with your mouth that Jesus is Lord and believe in your heart that God raised him from the dead, you will be saved. For with the heart one believes and is justified, and with the mouth one confesses and is saved. (Romans 10:9–10, ESV)

> Remember your leaders, those who spoke to you the word of God. Consider the outcome of their way of life, and imitate their faith. Jesus Christ is the same yesterday and today and forever. Do not be led away by diverse and strange teachings, for it is good for the heart to be strengthened by grace, not by foods, which have not benefited those devoted to them. (For context; Hebrews 13:7–9, ESV)

The New Age movement rejects the real Jesus Christ as described in the Bible on the grounds that He did not teach New Age theology. What He actually taught on sin, salvation, and God implies that any other spiritual endeavor is both erroneous and dangerous. His world-view opposes, contradicts, and confronts everything taught and practiced in the New Age movement. No one can be true to the biblical text and derive anything New Age from it. One either has to twist and completely undo the original meaning of the biblical text or simply not teach New Age, but Christianity instead.

Defining the Popularity of the New Age Movement

New Age thought is exceedingly popular, dominating Western civilization. A survey conducted by Pew Research Center found that 26 percent of Americans believe spiritual power exists within mountains, trees, and crystals; 25 percent believe in astrology; 24 percent believe in reincarnation; 23 percent believe that yoga is a spiritual (not just physical) practice; and 15 percent have consulted a psychic or fortune teller. Supernatural and mystical experiences are also on the rise: "This year's survey finds that religious and mystical experiences are more common today among those who are unaffiliated with any particular religion (30%) than they were in the 1960s among the public as whole (22%)."[3]

A study from Pew Research Center in 2017 found that 27 percent of Americans identify themselves as being "spiritual, but not religious," a number that has gone up by 8 percent over the previous five years.[4] People are quick to embrace a form of spirituality with no borders or guidelines, which is the soil underlying New Age philosophy. Many in our culture are becoming more open to seeking spiritual fulfillment within themselves, and they are using supernatural means by which to get there.

Another recent survey found that 40 percent of Americans practice meditation at least once a week,[5] making it so prevalent that it has turned into a billion-dollar industry.[6] More than thirty-six million Americans practice yoga, the Hindu spiritual practice involving stretching, contemplation, and trance, and an additional thirty-one million have at least tried it. Yoga, much like meditation, has ballooned in the last few decades and is now a $10 billion industry.[7] The hidden practices of the occult are becoming not so hidden, turning New Age services, including psychic readings, palmistry (palm reading), cartomancy (fortune-telling or divination using a deck of cards), mediumship, aura readings, and astrology, into a multibillion-dollar industry.[8]

Bookstores are pervaded with New Age books, many of which occupy the all-time best-sellers list. *The Celestine Prophecy*, a classic in the field, has sold over twenty-three million copies,[9] and *The Secret*, based on the Law of Attraction, has sold more than twenty million copies.[10] Sales of *Life after Life*, which details alleged near-death experiences of people in the spirit world, have exceeded thirteen million copies.[11] And more than ten million copies of the *Conversations with God* series, which includes alleged messages from God teaching "New Spirituality," have been sold.[12]

Additionally, works by authors such as Deepak Chopra and Eckhart Tolle have sold tens of millions of copies, having become near staples on the bookshelves of the average American home thanks to publicity from Oprah Winfrey (who has frequently featured New Age teachers on her programs). This only scratches the surface of the pervasiveness of the movement in our culture, but it is clear that New Age thought, practice, and industry are at an all-time high in the West—and they show no signs of slowing down.

The Reason Behind the Popularity of New Age

How could a movement like New Age gain so much footing in our world today? A fundamental truth about human beings is that we are, by nature, image-bearers of God. When God said, "Let us make man in our image, and after our likeness" in Genesis 1:26, He made people to be rational, emotional, personal, and self-aware moral agents even as God is. We are also endowed with knowing that there is more to our existence than the physical realm.

When God made us in His image, He "put eternity into [our] heart," as stated in Ecclesiastes 3:11. He stamped eternity into our very souls, which means that we have an intrinsic awareness that there is something beyond this world. C. S. Lewis once said, "The fact that our heart yearns for something Earth can't supply is proof that Heaven must be our home." This turns out to be more than poetic theology.

Information released in 2011 concerning a three-year international study conducted at Oxford University involving almost sixty experts from twenty different countries found that children are naturally predisposed to supernatural concepts, while natural, atheistic concepts come unnaturally. Humans, from birth, favor supernatural ideas not only in a general sense, but in the specific sense of instinctively believing that the human soul carries on after physical death.[13]

We are made by God, in the image of God, for relationship with God, for the glory of God, with a God-shaped hole in our hearts. As creations of God, we were made to live in fellowship with Him, enjoying His presence—that alone can satiate us. But, rather than being introduced to the supernatural relationship with God in Christ Jesus, too many people are brought up in a hedonistic society revolving around finance, entertainment, and the affairs of the world. Our culture is metaphysically dry and despiritualized. It is mechanic, corporate, and redundant. The lusts of the flesh, the lusts of the eyes, and the pride of life are sometimes seen as the only game in town for human fulfillment.

The education system also contributes to this sense of lack by reinforcing the loathsome idea that people are ultimately nothing: they arose from nothing and one day will return to nothing. We're taught that in the big picture of the universe, we don't matter one bit. Naturalism is the philosophical worldview that nature is all there is, and this is foundational to Western public education.

The physical world alone exists, and it can be explained entirely by natural, unguided mechanisms such as the Big Bang, abiogenesis, and Darwinian evolution. The very mention of God in an explanatory context is looked down upon as being flat-out immature. What does this naturalistic worldview imply? That we are highly developed pond scum who will one day become extinct in the burnout of our sun. We are relatively evolved primates who arose through a series of cosmic accidents doomed to ruin in the heat death of the universe. As Richard Dawkins has written: "There is, at bottom, no design, no purpose, no evil, no good, nothing but pitiless indifference."[14]

What of religion as a means by which to find fulfillment and satisfaction? The religions of this world often get lumped into one big category and treated as if they are equal in their believability and evidence. Islam, Christianity, Hinduism, and other major religions are seen to be equally as childish in their aspirations: They are a primitive means to account for the unexplained natural phenomena in our world. Religions are seen as a comfort pillow by which the desperate and weak can give themselves a sense of value and security.

People often grow up going to church but never come to see it as anything more than a crutch to give people structure and purpose. The Christian life is viewed as being lifeless rule-keeping: *Do the good things you don't want to do and avoid the bad things you want to do so that you can go to Heaven.*

In reality, the Christian's experience is filled with communion with God through the Holy Spirit. It is supernatural interaction with Him on a constant basis. The world, however, is often unaware of this aspect of walking with Christ. The person of the Holy Spirit is as foreign to the discussion of religion as can be, giving people the impression that there is nothing more to be found in the Church than a fear-driven cult revolving around behavior modification.

It is in this deprived, secularized arena where New Age spirituality establishes its appeal and erects itself as our savior. It capitalizes on this gap in our lives by holding out eternal life in one hand and supernatural experiences in the other—both of which are advertised as being available without a need for faith or repentance from sin. It offers a counterfeit form of spiritual nourishment to a culture of image-bearers who are spiritually starved, parched, and anemic because they do not understand or know the God who made them.

Place image-bearers of God in a culture like this, and a class on yoga or a book on astral projection will catch their attention almost immediately. A sense of curiosity sparks when they are told that there is something more to their existence than chemical reactions and random processes, and that there is more to spirituality than sitting in a church pew and trying to follow a list of rules to avoid Hell. Not only are they told there is something more; they are showed how to alter their consciousness to experience more. Supernatural experiences are advertised as common and accessible, without the need for "religion." But one of the most enticing ploys of the New Age movement is to give people meaning and purpose in their lives through the worldview that is taught.

More specifically, they are told that they are God. They are the Creator experiencing itself in human form. While different types views of God exist in the New Age movement (which we will look at in upcoming chapters), the same idea is always reinforced: God is not outside of you; God is not separate from you; God is your ultimate identity. Far from being told they are a random accident, they are introduced to the idea that they are at the very center of the universe—and all this without having to be held morally accountable to a holy and righteous God.

The Tragedy of Being One's Own God

On the surface, the message of New Age theology might sound enticing, but it is in fact a lonely, depressing tragedy. At first, the thought of getting to be your own god might sound great. However, it quickly crumbles once you follow that line of thinking through.

If you are your own god, you are as good as it gets for you. No one can help you spiritually, because no one else is your god; only you are. Your limited experience on Earth is all you have to guide you through the mysteries of the universe, death, and beyond. You have to figure out how to provide your own afterlife without even really knowing what happens when you die. Choosing to be your own god means you are worshipping a being who cannot create anything new, cannot save you from death, cannot provide you any answers you don't already know, cannot tell you what will happen for you, cannot provide a divine meaning or plan for your life, and cannot understand anything about reality outside of a human perspective. In fact, if you are your own god, then your god cares so little for you that he or she believes you deserve nothing better than to worship a flawed and finite god who will die someday and cannot offer any firsthand perspective on life after death.

You are left as the only strength, the only source of wisdom, and the only lifeline you really have. Sure, you can appeal to "spirit guides" or "the universe," but you can't step outside of your own subjectivity to even confirm that what you are reaching out to is even real or reliable in the first place. You are betting your entire existence on being able to navigate the mysteries of the universe through cognitive limitations, sensory limitations, and geographic limitations in time and space. Your three-pound brain is the only real reference point you have. How do you know that your brain even evolved to think accurately about philosophical questions? Independent of the existence of an all-knowing, transcendent mind, how do you know your own reasoning process is valid? How do you know your cognitive processes can be trusted, that the laws of logic are objective, or that anything exists outside of your own mind? You don't. So why make yourself the god over your own life when you are fundamentally unable to give any definitive answers about who you are, why you are here, and where you are going? Why exalt yourself if, in the absence of a creator, you have no good reason to trust your own brain's ability to give you the very answers you are seeking?

If we are honest with ourselves, we would not place that level of importance, responsibility, and worship on any human being. We would not worship one of our friends, family members, or any other human as God. Why, then, would we want ourselves to fill that role?

Wouldn't it be better to submit to a power higher than ourselves? Wouldn't it make sense to trust the One who created everything to give us the answers we seek? Wouldn't it be far more comforting to worship the God who has proven Himself throughout His Word, His actions, and His sacrifice for each of us? To me (Josh), the answers to those questions are easy. I don't have enough faith to believe I can carry myself through this life or into the next one alone. I would rather follow a God who knows what He is talking about and who loves me more than I could ever possibly understand. I would rather deny myself and follow Jesus.

1

THE SUPERNATURAL REALITY
OF THE NEW AGE

IMAGINE YOU WERE TOLD THAT every major experience you have had, every memory you hold dear, and everything you are striving for are hallucinations—fabrications of your own imagination. Regardless of what these experiences may be (whether spiritual, romantic, etc.), you would not take someone seriously if he or she tried to convince you that you had imagined the whole experience. Maybe this person was confused, trying to offend you, or was joking, but you certainly would not take anyone who said that seriously.

Perhaps someone tried to convince you that you really did not feel love for your wife or husband on your wedding day, or experience mystery and awe when you star-gaze, or sense existential marvel when your first child was born. You, of all people, would know whether your experiences were real. You have access to your own memory stream. Sure, you might forget minor details, but you didn't generate these internal experiences out of thin air. You did not hallucinate your wedding day or the feelings of love. You did not make up the stars or the mystery and wonder you felt when you looked at them.

Often, those in the New Age movement feel put off by those within religious circles because the New Agers are dismissed from the get-go as being delusional about their own experiences. Rather than being listened to, they are given a lecture on how naive they are for believing their own experiences were legitimate, or how the human mind can be prone to hallucinations.

Those on the outside looking in aren't finding answers to the questions they're asking or explanations for the experiences they are having, and are off-put by the responses they receive. The wide range of spiritual encounters people have in various religious systems cannot be reduced to: "You're making it all up." People are having at least *some* kind of experience, aren't they? How could they all be hallucinating the same internal and external stimuli from different sides of the world? Is "you're making it up in your head" really the best explanation?

Before we can have any meaningful discussion on the history, thought, and practice of the New Age movement, we should establish some undergirding principles as an interpretative framework by which we can assess the movement's content.

There are three primary points to consider when examining anything pertaining to the New Age movement:

The experiences people have in the New Age movement (whether brought about through occult/pagan ritual, the alteration of their own consciousness, or any other practice) are indeed real.

These experiences fall into two primary categories: a) transpersonal, natural experiences, and b) actual supernatural experiences.

The supernatural experiences people have in the New Age movement are demonic in nature.

In a transpersonal experience, the ordinary experience of "self" shifts to a more expansive state of awareness wherein a person becomes the observer of himself or herself. Rather than being identified with the thought-stream running through our minds, a transpersonal experience pulls a person from the activity of the mind into a state of "pure awareness." These experiences are defined as "experiences in which the sense of identity or self extends beyond (trans) the individual or personal to encompass wider aspects of humankind, life, psyche or cosmos."[15] Practices used to bring about such experiences include certain forms of meditation, contemplation, the practice of mindfulness, listening to certain frequencies, and practicing certain kinds of breathing and stretching techniques that are usually focused on the application of Eastern mysticism.

The goal in these experiences is to reach deeper, more unified levels of consciousness whereby the individual "I" merges into pure "being." While these experiences can be misleading and can become dangerous springboards into the demonic (as we shall explore), they are not supernatural in and of themselves. The alteration of brainwaves and self-observation from deeper levels of awareness do not require us to appeal to anything outside of nature, though they often open doors to the supernatural.

When it comes to alleged supernatural experiences in the New Age movement, there are only two possible interpretations:

1) These experiences might be natural ones that are misinterpreted through a supernatural lens, in which case the individuals are mistaken and delusional about the nature of the experience. They are misreading a supernatural ideology into a totally natural experience and are self-deceived. This is how the majority of the world seems to respond to matters of the occult.

2) The experience might be real, but demonic in nature.

These are the only options in light of the Word of God. We know this because the Bible describes only two spiritual kingdoms in which there is no middle playing field. God has His heavenly kingdom and Satan has his kingdom (Matthew 12:26). We either follow God in Christ Jesus or we follow the prince of the power of the air (Ephesians 2:2). We either gather with the kingdom of God or we scatter with the kingdom of Satan (Matthew 12:30). We either operate under the Spirit of Christ or we operate under the spirit of the Antichrist (1 John 4:3).

Any supernatural encounters or practices in the New Age movement must be understood in light of the exceedingly dualistic worldview that God describes in His Word. There is no spiritually neutral fence on which we can sit to explore higher dimensions with religiously disinterested beings from another realm. Just like we, as human beings, are either for or against Christ (Luke 11:23), interdimensional beings are either for or against Christ. Supernatural experiences have their origin either in the soil of Heaven or the soil of Hell. If they are not from or pointing towards the biblical Jesus of the New Testament, they are, by default, classified as having their origin in the kingdom of Satan. There is no other possible source of origin.

So, if those in the New Age movement are indeed experiencing something supernatural, the Bible only offers one possible interpretation: These experiences are demonically guided deceptions. The real question is this: Do New Agers experience real, supernatural experiences that fall under this category? Let's look briefly at some of the alleged supernatural experiences within New Age circles to see how the Bible classifies them.

Channeling, Mediumship, and Fortune-telling

Channeling is the practice whereby a human taps into an interdimensional being of some kind (believed to be a deceased person, alien, spirit guide, etc.), usually by entering a trance-like state of consciousness before attempting to make contact by reaching out to the being. Once the person makes contact, he or she then acts as a conduit for the being to convey specific messages to the human race. In other words, the person becomes a "vessel" through which a foreign consciousness can speak. Channeled material, also known as "automatic writing," is literature produced by a human subject who writes down the information as it comes from the interdimensional or alien being.

Mediumship is a similar practice wherein, rather than acting as a "channel" for another entity to speak through, the "medium" initiates direct contact with those in the spirit world in the hopes of receiving wisdom and insight (usually about future events). Undoubtedly, sometimes people are deceived into thinking that untapped areas of their own psychology are foreign beings from other dimensions, and some people are con artists looking to make a quick buck—but what does the Bible have to say about such practices? Are they legitimate in some instances, or are they all delusions?

In 1 Samuel 28, we read that King Saul gets impatient with God and reaches out to a medium to help him contact Samuel, the recently deceased judge of Israel, for insight about an upcoming battle. To the surprise of the medium (v. 12), Samuel comes through and delivers a word of rebuke to Saul, explaining why the Lord has forsaken the king (v. 15–19). This is a special instance when God intervenes via a forbidden practice to deliver a prophetic word by His decree and under His guidance.

Normally, this kind of practice did not bring about actual contact with the dead. How do we know this? This woman "cried with a loud voice" and mistook Samuel for being a "god coming up out of the earth" (v. 12–13), which indicates that she had never before initiated contact with a crossed-over spirit like that of Samuel. Her shock and confusion indicates this is unprecedented in her experience. If she had seen dead people before, she would have no reason to be alarmed. Additional evidence that she had never made contact with the dead comes from the New Testament, where Jesus gives a parable of the rich man in Hell who wants to contact those on earth to warn them of the coming judgment. The rich man is not allowed to do so, because, Jesus says, God's revelation in Scripture is sufficient for knowledge of the afterlife (Luke 16:31). Jesus' response was essentially, "You don't get to communicate with the living once you've passed over. If they won't believe Moses, they won't believe you."

In other words, the testimony of the Old Testament Scriptures contains sufficient warning of the upcoming judgment of God, so there's no need for the dead to bring warnings to the living. If God's revelation is sufficient, and God in His sovereignty doesn't permit the dead to communicate with the living, what did the medium of 1 Samuel expect would come through the veil? What was she used to interacting with? Why did Saul approach her with the belief that she would be able to offer supernatural insight? The best explanation is that both she and Samuel believed this method of divination facilitated contact with supernatural beings.

Since the Bible tells us that Satan masquerades as an angel of light (2 Corinthians 11:14), it can be argued that the spiritual powers behind the mediums and the channelers are demonic entities impersonating deceased persons, spirits, and other beings—demons putting on a show to lead people into spiritual darkness and confusion, away from the true God. This is why God considers consulting psychics and mediums to be spiritual adultery (Leviticus 20:6). It wouldn't make sense to be guilty of committing adultery with something that doesn't have any background reality. The Bible commands over and over that we should turn away from consulting mediums and fortune-tellers, but nowhere does it indicate that their practice is empty. Counterfeit and sinful, yes, but not entirely imaginary.

The strongest evidence that such practices are both real and demonic comes from Acts 16:16, where we read of a woman possessed by a spirit of "divination" who brought her owners financial gain through fortune-telling. The word used for "divination" in Greek is πύθωνα, transliterated as "Pythones" or "Python." The word has its origin in the name of a Greek god named Python, an oracle-giving, monstrous serpent living in the center of the Earth guarding the oracle Gaea.[16] Python was killed with arrows shot by Apollo for causing mischief and chaos to man and god alike, the spirit of whom now enters people and gives them supernatural prophetic ability. So when the woman is said to have "a spirit of divination," we can read those words literally as "a spirit of a python." Greek essayist Plutarch gives us a Greco-Roman understanding of this scenario:

Certainly it is foolish and childish in the extreme to imagine that the god himself after the manner of ventriloquists (who used to be called "Eurycleis," but now "Pythones") enters into the bodies of his prophets and prompts their utterances, employing their mouths and voices as instruments.[17]

A first-century Greek would conclude that this woman was being used as an instrument by a fortune-telling spirit of Python, the soothsaying monster of Greek mythology. The *Anchor Yale Bible Dictionary* summarizes:

According to Greek myth, the pythōn was the serpent or dragon that inspired and guarded the oracle at Delphi; the creature was slain by the god Apollo. The word pythōn came to mean a divining spirit, and ventriloquists were called Pythōnes (BAGD, 728–29). In antiquity, ventriloquists (Gk engastrimythoi) were thought to have in their stomachs a mantic spirit that spoke oracles (Festugière 1947:133). The writer of the account in Acts undoubtedly viewed the slave girl as possessed; the exotic quality of pythōn possession enhances the literary appeal of the passage.[18]

The *Lexham Biblical Encyclopedia* states:

This slave girl is described as having a "python spirit" (πνεῦμα πύθωνα, "pneuma pythōna") or "the spirit of a python." According to Greek mythology, "python" refers to the snake or dragon that guarded a shaft at Delphi and was destroyed by Apollo. This creature later became associated with soothsaying, divination, or even ventriloquism (Acts 13:6; Fitzmyer, Acts, 586; Bock, Acts, 535). People often brought inquiries to female seers at Delphi who entered the temple of Apollo and divined answers by the power of this spirit (Klauck, Magic, 65).[19]

Additionally, the early Church may have read the python reference of Acts:16:16 against the backdrop of Genesis 3, where the spirit of Satan animated the serpent to tempt Eve to sin. Later, in Revelation 12:9, we read more about the nature of "the great dragon [who was] was thrown down, that ancient serpent, who is called the devil and Satan, the deceiver of the whole world" (Revelation 12:9).

Both Jew and Gentile would have understood this as a reference to a dark, sinister, serpentine spirit who had possessed the woman and had given her ability to predict the future. The correct historical context demands that we believe in a real, spiritual power that operates through and alongside channels, mediums, and fortune-tellers (in at least some circumstances). In this light, it makes more sense why the Bible condemns the practice of mediumship, channeling, and contact with the dead as sins worthy of the death penalty (Leviticus 19:31, 20:27; Exodus 22:18). The Bible teaches that these practices have a demonic reality to them.

Magik and Sorcery

In Exodus 7–8, God commissioned Moses and Aaron to perform signs and wonders before Pharaoh in Egypt to demonstrate that the Israelites (who were enslaved in Egypt at the time) belonged to the one true God. As divine confirmation of who they represented, Moses and Aaron were given miracle-working power from on high so that Pharaoh might let God's people go. The first three signs they performed before the Pharaoh were as follows:

1. Moses cast down his staff and it turned into a serpent (7:10).
2. Moses struck the water in the Nile River with his staff and the water turned into blood (7:20).
3. Aaron stretched his hand over the waters and caused frogs to swarm out (8:6).

After each miracle, Pharaoh called for the magicians of Egypt to see if they could reproduce the wonders. The Bible tells us the magicians and sorcerers of Egypt were able to replicate the feats by using their "secret arts." The clear, literal reading of Exodus 7 and 8 would have us believe the magicians were able to turn their staffs into snakes, convert water into blood, and summon frogs by a power that was supernatural yet opposed to the true God of Israel.

While some argue that the magicians' signs were accomplished through sleight of hand, illusions, and trickery, the Bible tells us they "did the same by their secret arts" (v. 22). The text reads "did the same," not "appeared to do the same," and it says they "did the same" "by their secret arts," not "by optical illusion."

The magicians accomplished what Moses did by the use of a different power. Eventually, the magicians' power failed them, and they were not able to reproduce the upcoming seven miracles that plagued Egypt, causing them to conclude that this was happening by the "finger of God" (8:19). This is not the only instance when magic is described as being possible with the aid of demons. Interestingly, Scripture is full of references to signs and wonders being caused by satanic agency:

- The Antichrist will be energized by the power and capability of Satan producing false signs and wonders (2 Thessalonians 2:9).
- The Pharisees believed Beelzebub, the prince of demons, was operating through Jesus giving him power over spirits (Matthew 12:24). Jesus did this by the power of God, but this at least indicates the Jews believed it was possible to perform miracles by the power of demons.
- False Christs and false prophets will produce great signs and wonders (Matthew 24:24, Mark 13:22).
- The Beast of Revelation worked miraculous signs, calling down fire from Heaven to earth (Revelation 13:11–14).

- Demonic spirits proceed from the mouth of a dragon performing signs (Revelation 16:14).

So, when it comes to magik (spelled with a "k" to differentiate it from sleight-of-hand/illusionist magic), witchcraft, and sorcery, the Bible says these practices are real and function through the agency of demons. This does not mean that every New Ager who attempts to dabble in sorcery or divination actually makes contact with demonic power. It does, however, mean that, when practiced to its full extent, it is accomplished is through cooperation with demons. God's Word affirms that these practices produce real effects in reality with the assistance of satanic power.

Pagan Prayer, Sacrifice, and Worship

While blood sacrifice is not pervasive in the New Age movement, sacrificial altars of sorts are prevalent. It is common for an altar to be set up decorated with crystals, runes (symbols used for magik and divination), tarot cards, incense, symbols, candles, and pictures of favorite Ascended Masters, angels, or alien races. At these altars, prayers and chants are said to these foreign beings (or their spirit guides, guardian angels, or the universe at large) in hopes of receiving information, guidance, and blessings.

Ceremony, celebration, song, prayer, chanting, and incense-burning are regularly used to honor dead ancestors, the spirits of nature, nature itself, or interdimensional beings of some kind. This, of course, is a textbook example of idolatry. But interestingly, when it comes to the sin of idolatry, the Bible tells us that there is a spiritual reality behind the idol. The idol itself has no power or agency in and of itself, and the Bible is very clear about this, but the object refers to demonic principalities in the spirit realm over this powerless object. The object is nothing but rearranged matter, but it points back to demons who engage with mankind through the activity of idol worship.

In Leviticus 17:7, we are told that the Israelites who went apostate in the wilderness and participated in pagan idol worship made "their sacrifices to goat demons." The psalmist spoke to this same moment in history, saying, "They sacrificed their sons and their daughters to the demons" (Psalm 106:37) to describe the time when the Israelites had begun to worship pagan idols. Deuteronomy 32 tells us that when Israel began to make sacrifices to the false gods of the surrounding nations (who, by the way, are often revered in the New-Age movement as legitimate gods), they were really making sacrifices to "demons that were no gods" (v. 17), which stirred God to jealousy (v. 16).

The Apostle Paul reiterates this in 1 Corinthians 10:19–22:

> What do I imply then? That food offered to idols is anything, or that an idol is anything? No, I imply that what pagans sacrifice they offer to demons and not to God. I do not want you to be participants with demons. You cannot drink the cup of the Lord and the cup of demons. You cannot partake of the table of the Lord and the table of demons. Shall we provoke the Lord to jealousy? Are we stronger than he?

Pagan worship, prayer, and sacrifice of any kind are ultimately offered to demonic principalities, whether or not the practitioner is aware this is happening. The Lord likens involvement with idols to drinking the cup of demons because the idolaters are partaking of the substance of the demonic, feeding off of the spiritual meat they offer. Biblically speaking, the idol is powerless in itself, but refers to a principality in the spirit realm whom we interact with in the practice of idolatry.

Astral Projection

A wildly popular practice in the New Age movement is "astral projection," the name given to the experience of having one's "astral body" separate from the physical body. The astral body (also called the "etheric body" or "spirit body") is believed to be, essentially, the human soul; the part that animates the body, thinks, and feels is not material but metaphysical by nature. This metaphysical component that animates one's physical vehicle is believed to be an energetic imprint of the physical body—almost like a phantom or a ghost.

In layman's terms, we understand this as the soul disconnecting from the body and floating around in a parallel spirit realm. This is why the result of this practice is also called an OBE, or out-of-body experience, because it involves the separation of consciousness from the body. Described as being a natural extension of the "awakening" process, it is thought to be a sign that one has truly mastered his or her own body. This remains a fundamental practice in the New Age movement and is considered evidence of a person's spiritual development.

The Bible does not condone astral projection by any stretch of the imagination, but it may confirm that it is at least theoretically possible. However, in the Bible, astral projection is an experience God initiates and controls, while in New Age practice, it is initiated and (attempted to be controlled) by the person. In 2 Corinthians 12, the Apostle Paul describes a vision of being "caught up" to the third heaven (v. 2). The Greek word used here for "caught up" is harpazo, the same word Paul uses in 1 Thessalonians 4:17, where he describes those who will be caught up in the Rapture:

> Then we who are alive, who are left, will be caught up together with them in the clouds to meet the Lord in the air, and so we will always be with the Lord.

Harpazo is also used in Revelation 12:5 regarding the child who was "caught up" to the throne of God. This indicates that Paul was translated to the third heaven mentally at the very least, and perhaps even spiritually (in terms of his soul actually leaving his body) or physically. The third heaven, of course, refers to a supernatural realm. Psalm 148:4

and 1 Kings 8:27 speak of the "highest heavens," and Deuteronomy 10:14 speaks of the "heaven of heavens," indicating that there may be multiple layers to the realm of Heaven. In Ephesians 6:12, we are told that demons operate within the "heavenly places"—in the plural— indicating not only multiple strata to God's kingdom but to the demonic realms as well.

Paul emphasizes twice that he may have been outside of his body while having this divine revelation from the Lord: "whether [I had this vision] in the body or out of the body I do not know" (v. 2, 3). He was convinced it was possible in principle to have an experience outside of one's actual body. He knew the soul could leave the body, have an experience in another realm, and then return to the body. This may be reiterated in Revelation, where the Apostle John reports his apocalyptic visions that were "in the Spirit" (1:10, 4:2).

As body-soul composites, our bodies are nothing more than temporary dwelling places for the soul and spirit. In the same letter to the Corinthians quoted from earlier (2 Corinthians), Paul had just finished writing in chapter 5 that the body is a "tent" with which we have been "clothed," one that we will one day remove to be with the Lord. The New Testament is full of verses indicating that we are ultimately non-physical beings inhabiting flesh for a limited period, so what we see from Paul is a possible reference to a separation of soul from body prior to physical death. Biblically speaking, a theoretical framework for out-of-body experiences is at least possible.

Astral Projection in Satanism

Astral projection is an essential practice of any satanic magician, including Aleister Crowley. We will delve more into his work later, but for our purposes here, he was a famous occultist and Satanist from the 1900s who referred to himself as "The Beast 666" and once said "I was not content to just believe in Satan, I wanted to be his chief of staff."

Crowley, who wrote extensively about astral projection, describes the beginning stages of it in his book, *Magick in Theory and Practice.*[20] He also gives instruction on astral projection in *Magick without Tears.*[21] In the spiritual organization Crowley started called A∴A∴, mastering the astral plane was one of the requirements for graduating.[22] He taught and encouraged astral projection as essential to the ascension process. According to Crowley, a person could even create his or her own satanic temples for magical purposes in the astral plane.

One Satanist describes the astral temples:

A satanic astral temple is a place where you can follow magick rituals in any form you want, even when physical conditions are not ritual friendly. There is a main hall with a huge Baphomet figure on the altar and glowing pentagram on the floor, black and red candles around and pillars. It's a place where I summon demons, do celebration rituals for Satan and shape energy as I want. Pentagram is some sort of universal portal to demonic dimensions. If I need a tool I can materialize it in my hands or before me. In a different room I can make potions and more witchy stuff so it's a place full of odd things that I use as ingredients. In another area I can do healing techniques both on me or on astral body of others. An astral temple can be used as an alternative method of summoning demons. If you are not doing well with standard rituals and you have no results, research demon, imagine him/her in your astral temple.[23]

Demonic Attacks in the Astral Planes

Anyone in the New Age who has a lot of experience with astral projection is well aware that it is not all fun and games to be outside of one's body. While it's often advertised as a free, floaty experience, it's also common knowledge that the astral realm is filled with demons. These entities are called "trickster entities" or "negative astral entities" instead of demons, but they bear the same traits and behaviors.

Books, articles, and videos on astral projection usually provide a list of ways we can to protect ourselves against attacks, such as visualizing white light around us, loving the demons until they leave us alone, and speaking positive affirmations over ourselves before bedtime, etc. A big hint often offered is to make sure we aren't operating from a place of fear, since fear attracts demons. The demons aren't the cause of our fear; they are a response to our fear. These sources also coach us into thinking that the demons can only do to us what we allow them to do.

None of this is true. The Internet is filled with testimonies of those who have been tormented by demons on a regular basis while outside of their body.[24] Both authors of this book have had astral projection experiences against our will, even though I (Steve) was taking the suggested protective measures. Some examples of what might occur to people while "out of body" are:

- Demons posing as "spirit guides"
- Torment and violation
- Demons mocking God by having them read the Bible while being tormented
- Demons disguising themselves as romantic partners and as other significant people
- Demons paralyzing them against their will
- Astral parasites: Demons attaching themselves to some level of their soul and entering the body as the person returns to the natural realm.

The shape-shifting of astral entities begs the question: How do we know the original form they appear to us in isn't already a shape-shifted form? How do we know their first appearance to us isn't already a disguise? According to the Bible, Satan is able to transform into an angel of light (2 Corinthians 11:14). His ministry is one of smoke and mirrors.

Just because a being manifests one way to us in the astral doesn't mean that is the being's actual form.

Aren't There Good Astral Planes?

From a Christian perspective, we say a spiritual realm exists. We typically do not call it the "astral" realm, but that's merely a matter of labeling. To most Christians, it's probable that demonic activity goes on in the so-called astral planes. People involved in New Age may say, "Well that's just because they were in the LOWER astral realms, perhaps because of their fear. There are a whole bunch of different astral realms, and they just had bad experiences in the lower realms." It is said that most experiences can be pleasant and that all bad experiences are a result of the person doing something wrong, not an indicator that the entire realm or practice is spiritually dangerous.

However, that is simply false. The idea that demonic activity only happens on some lower astral plane is a textbook ad hoc fallacy. An ad hoc explanation is one adopted purely for the purpose of trying to save a theory without any independent reason or rational motivation. If someone is abused by a demon in the astral (which many, including the authors of this book, have reported), we can save the illusion that the astral planes comprise a beautiful realm of peace by postulating an infinite number of astral realms and lumping all of the demonic activity into the lower realms. But this is just intellectually dishonest when we look at the testimonies of people with negative experiences, which can be found frequently in online forums concerning astral projection in New Age, witchcraft, satanism, and more.

Typically, no accounts of astral attacks mention the person being in a different astral plane. Nobody ever says after a bad experience: "I found myself in a different astral plane than the one I usually travel in." For those who have astral experiences on a regular basis, it is clear that nobody ever finds himself or herself in a different astral plane depending on whether the experiences are good, neutral, or demonic. Also, nobody participating in astral projection looks around and realizes he or she is in a totally different astral plane. Demons inhabit the astral realm regardless of whether they reveal themselves.

Jesus Christ Stops Demonic Astral Attacks

Hundreds of people have claimed to be able to stop night terrors, astral attacks, alien abductions, and sleep paralysis immediately by doing nothing more than calling out for Jesus.[25] Beings appear in their room during an astral-projection experience, and those beings retreat when the person uses the name of Jesus. One former ufologist discovered that UFO research organizations were covering up testimonies of abductions and spiritual attacks being stopped when they used the name of Jesus and created a website exposing the hidden agenda of these beings.[26]

Often, people who call out to Jesus and receive supernatural help with astral attacks don't actually believe in Jesus. Atheists themselves testify to the effectiveness of calling on the Lord when under attack. It's not as though people have faith and bring a certain thought-form into existence in the spirit world using the power of their mind, they lack all faith and cry out in desperation and still receive breakthrough. If true, this seem to imply the spirits fear the name of Jesus regardless of the mind of the person.

If you are ever in a scary situation in the spirit, these testimonies are proof that these beings fear and are under the authority of the name of Jesus Christ. If they were just "negative trickster entities," "thought forms," or "astral aliens," why would they be subject to people saying His name? This tells us a lot about both the nature of these beings in the spirit realm and the nature of Jesus Christ. Even astral demons know Jesus is Lord. His name is poison to them.

The Truth about Astral Projection

The testimonial evidence makes it clear that the astral plane is not realm of sunshine and gumdrops. Nor is it a magical place where we can sail endlessly through the universe experiencing infinite mystery and wonder. Instead, it is inhabited by demons disguised as beings of light who seek to confuse, deceive, and destroy. They want to make us comfortable with the false ideas about the astral realm so they can lead us down a rabbit trail of false theology and absurd theories about the afterlife to further pervert our ideas of spirituality. Some people have been led to believe that when we die, we get to float around in the astral realm until we decide to reincarnate again. Some believe that we experience a good or bad astral realm temporarily, depending on whether we were a "good" or "bad" person, and that the bad astral experience only lasts until we forgive ourselves.

The astral plane serves as leverage for demonic beings who inhabit it to infuse participants with a false sense of godhood and spiritual power. They feel like the captain of their own ship, and everyone around them in the community sees their new ability as evidence of their spiritual development. But they are actually being groomed to take deeper steps into the occult world before they are so far into it that nothing except New Age thought makes sense anymore. This is accomplished through deceptive spirits initiating astral experiences and interacting with people in the astral realm.

"Astral entities" are demons acting out the role they believe will most likely lead people as far away from the cross of Christ as possible. The astral plane is a like a movie set. If you were to walk through a set of a movie and didn't see any of the cameras or directors, you might think your surroundings were reflective of a real state of affairs in that part of the town. Just like people act out roles in movies, demons act out roles in the astral realm. If participants are unaware that they are in a spiritual movie set orchestrated by the same shape-shifting demons that torment people in the astral realm, they may fall for the charades.

If narcissists, sociopaths, and even ordinary people tell elaborate lies to produce a certain result, why would we assume any less from inter-dimensional beings? Just because they exist in a realm beyond nature doesn't mean they are morally infallible. Even the words of the Apostle Paul imply that the astral realm is the wrong neck of the woods to be in, which is why he called Satan the "ruler of the kingdom of the air" (Ephesians 2:2) and why he says that we fight "not against flesh but against the powers of this dark world and against the spiritual forces of evil in the heavenly realms" (Ephesians 6:12).

Demons work from the spirit realm. The Bible tells us this. It may be possible to project our consciousness outside of our body, but that doesn't mean it's safe or wise to do so. For all we know, astral projections may exclusively be travels through a demonic air kingdom that dark forces oversee and operate from. Even supposedly benevolent beings that exist in the astral planes, such as the Ascended Masters (more on them later) are nothing more than demons in disguise.

Demons wish to facilitate the experience of astral projection so they can make us think we are our own god. They wish to instill false doctrines of ascension into us to make us think we can become like the gods through knowing hidden, transcendental knowledge. This is the same lie Satan fed to Eve in the Garden of Eden, which we will explore further a bit later. It's the same deceptive and false promises that led to the Fall of Man.

This can be tested, as it has been in scores of written testimonies. While I (Steve) maintain that this is never a good idea to try to initiate and would immediately and vehemently discourage anyone from taking part in it, if you ever find yourself in the astral realm (whether voluntarily or involuntarily), assume for the sake of experiment that this chapter is true and that you are in the devil's playground. Tell the first astral being you see, "I rebuke you in Jesus' name. In the name of Jesus, I command you to leave me alone." The being will either transform before your eyes into the demon it is, or it will run for the hills as hundreds of personal testimonies have revealed. For the people who have given these testimonies, the veil of delusion has been lifted from their eyes and they see the astral realm and the beings that inhabit it for what they truly are: deceptive demons who are subject to the name of Jesus Christ. For an understanding of where Josh and I are coming from on a personal basis, we have detailed our experiences for this book.

Josh Peck's Personal Experiences

Born in 1984 and raised in the Church, I had a strong Baptist upbringing with a heavy focus on not just knowing biblical principles, but on living them also. My falling-away from the Church into New Age then back to Jesus is certainly a strange story. It began with unwanted spiritual encounters when I was a child.

I don't remember much from my childhood prior to the age of 12. The little I do remember, however, about being a child during the '80s included being afraid, especially at night. On the surface, this may seem typical. Most children at one time or another are afraid of the dark or of monsters in their closet. However, for me, it wasn't the dark I was afraid of; rather, it was disembodied whispers I feared—and my monster wasn't in the closet, but in the backyard.

My mother had to fill in the blanks for me when I became an adult, because much of this I had long ago forgotten. My mom said that when I was a young child, I was afraid of voices in my room and of an indescribable monster in the backyard. She was never able to get more information from me but, at the time, she believed—as I imagine most mothers would—that I was experiencing nothing more than a combination of bad dreams and an overactive imagination. However, one morning, the monster made itself known to my family and neighbors.

This is one incident my mom did not have to recall for me. I vividly remember waking up and hearing my mom, dad, and a couple of neighbors talking in the backyard. Upon opening the back door and heading outside to see what they were talking about, I saw an incredibly strange sight: All the grass in our backyard was completely flattened, as smooth as a tight sheet on a freshly made bed. My family and neighbors, clearly shocked at this discovery, were discussing what could have done something like that. This was an occurrence no one had seen before, and our half-acre backyard was the only place in the neighborhood where it had happened. No one had witnessed the cause; the adults assumed it had happened the night before while everyone was sleeping. After some discussion, they decided the most natural explanation was that a herd of deer had come into our backyard, laid down in such a way as to perfectly flatten every blade of grass, then left without leaving any tracks, without being seen, and without being hit by any cars that might have been driving by at the time. We lived in Flint, Michigan, at the time, and while deer were not uncommon, a herd big enough to fill every inch of our backyard and behaving that way would have been unimaginable. Yet, without a better explanation, my family and neighbors left it at that, and, as far as I know, the incident was never discussed again.

Later, my mom admitted that she believed there was something spiritually demonic about the house we had been living in. She detailed other experiences she had as well as others I claimed to have had, yet to this day still cannot remember. While it would certainly be interesting to delve into all of those forgotten experiences, it is a bit outside the direction of what led me to New Age and will likely be something I will explore another time in another project. For our purposes here, however, I admit I believe my mother was correct in believing that there were demonic influences over that house.

After I had turned 12, my mom and I moved out of the house in Flint and moved to Holly, Michigan with my stepdad. From then and into adulthood, I suffered from frequent sleep paralysis (about three times a month). For those not familiar with that term, sleep paralysis is a condition in which a person tries to fall asleep, but instead finds himself fully awake, yet unable to move. This is commonly a horrific experience involving auditory and visual hallucinations, according to medical professionals. Personally, I do not know how much of these experiences are hallucinations and how many of them are real, spiritual encounters.

When I would tell my mom about what I was going through at night, she would say they were only dreams and nothing to worry about. I found out years later that she had been having similar experiences, but hadn't wanted to tell me about them at the time. She worried that would only scare me more—and she didn't know what to do about it, anyway. Though, like I, my mom was raised as a Baptist, neither she nor I was well-versed in the subjects of demonic entities and spiritual warfare.

The problem I had believing these experiences were just dreams or hallucinations was that the physical environment was sometimes altered. For example, one time I saw a shadowy, hooded figure open my bedroom door (I always slept with my door closed) and attempt to initiate an attack on me. Not knowing what else to do, I instinctively cried out to Jesus in my mind and the hooded figure left the room. The next morning, however, my door was still open.

Some might say I probably opened the door while sleepwalking, or that someone else in the house had opened it for some reason. That is certainly within the realm of possibility; however, I have never sleepwalked before. Further, I asked my mom and stepdad if they had opened my door and they said they hadn't. There are absolutely many possible natural explanations, but I can only detail what happened and how I felt about it, though admittedly my feelings are subjective by nature. While the experience was occurring, I had no doubt in my mind the hooded figure was pure evil.

When I turned 18, I moved out and spent some time living in one place and then another with various friends, but the sleep paralysis never stopped. It even got to the point that I felt obligated to tell people before moving in with them about my sleep paralysis problem. Only one time were further questions asked and a possible solution was presented. This conversation was what hurled me into the New Age movement.

I was invited to stay at an engaged couple's apartment for a while until I could save enough money to live on my own. For sake of this book and to protect their privacy, I will just refer to them as "Rachel" and "Bob." I had known Rachel from high school and had become friends with Bob while working with him at a fast-food restaurant. Shortly after I moved in, I told Rachel about my sleep paralysis. She was incredibly interested, which was a first to me. She quizzed me with many questions and ended up asking if I thought there was anything spiritual behind what I was going through. I told her I believed the occurrences were demonic, but due to my lack of knowledge on the subject despite being raised in the Church, I wasn't able to articulate anything further.

At this point, Rachel expressed she believed it was probably demonic, too. Before this, I had not known if she believed in anything spiritual at all, let alone in actual demons. She asked if I had ever heard of something called "astral projection." I had not. She explained that some people believe that, through training and meditation, a person can train his or her consciousness to leave the physical body and enter the astral plane. She told me the astral plane looks just like our physical reality, and in fact *is* our reality; it's just the part of it we cannot see or experience while we are in our physical bodies. She suggested that, if I could learn this skill, maybe I could escape or defend myself when the demons attacked again. She then gave me a book that detailed exactly how to astral project.

Before this, no one had taken me seriously when I tried to talk about my strange experiences. Most times, people would say it was all in my head or dreams or hallucinations. A couple of people even went as far as to suggest I might have had schizophrenia. Because of these responses, I had finally stopped talking about the possible spiritual aspects of my sleep paralysis. But there, for the first time, a friend was taking me seriously, believing me, and offering a solution. Not even my own family or church had done that. Therefore, it was incredibly easy for me to fall into the New Age deception.

To be clear, I do not believe Rachel was trying to deceive me in any way. In fact, I fully believe she was deceived herself. She was only trying to help a friend. Unfortunately, the help she was offering would only make my spiritual problems far worse than I could have ever imagined.

The book Rachel gave was my introduction to New Age theology. I studied that book in far more depth than any book I had read before, including the Bible, and I followed every instruction it contained. I participated in daily breathing exercises and meditation practices, and even became a vegetarian because the book said doing so would help me be able to astral project. Six months and a complete worldview change later, I had my first breakthrough into the astral plane.

What I am going to explain here I have no way of proving. I have no doubt it was real, but I also have zero evidence to support or prove that to anyone. That is one of the maddening aspects of New Age: the possession of a supernatural ability without any way of proving it to anyone else. Since I came out of New Age and into Christianity, realizing the real truth of Jesus Christ, the fact that I can't prove my New Age experiences does not bother me at all. In fact, I would be totally at peace even if it was proved someday that I really had just imagined or hallucinated all of my astral projection experiences. What I see now but couldn't see then is that New Age is nothing more than spiritual bondage. The truth sets you free, and Jesus is the Truth, Way, and Life.

The first time I experienced something like leaving my body started like any ordinary night. I was living with a different group of friends at this time. I had gone upstairs to my bedroom, where I was doing my meditation practices. While going through the process of trying to leave my body, I felt myself become lighter as I began to rise through the air. I opened my eyes and realized I was standing upright, but was hovering about a foot off of the ground. Though I did not turn back to see my physical body, I had the feeling that I was outside of it. I began to uncontrollably float down through the floor and walls into the first-floor living room, where two of my friends were talking. I recognized that their conversation was too quiet and too far away from my room for me to be able to hear with my physical ears from the other side of the house. That realization was so shocking that I instantly found myself back in my physical body.

The next day, having remembered a piece of the conversation my friends were having, I wanted to investigate whether it had been real. It had *felt* completely real to me, but I wanted confirmation. I asked my friends if they had been up talking the night before and if so, what they had been talking about. I was careful to not ask any leading questions; I wanted to hear it from them and them alone. After a few moments, they told me the part of the conversation I had heard the night before while I had been outside of my body. I did not tell them why I was asking or tell them about my experience, but this convinced me that the New Age was a movement worth pursuing.

A few months passed before I had another experience. In the meantime, I had become completely engrossed in the New Age, reading everything I could get my hands on. I didn't want to completely let go of my Christian upbringing, so I attempted to blend the two beliefs. After all, the authors of many of the books I was reading quoted Bible verses to support their positions, and I was just biblically ignorant enough to believe all of it. However, instead of chasing knowledge and wisdom, I was chasing an experience.

My next successful attempt at astral projection occurred when I lived by myself in my own apartment. At that time, I had an elderly neighbor who was fond of coming to my apartment in the middle of the afternoon to tell me to turn my television or music down. He always kept his blinds drawn and door closed, so I never saw the inside of his apartment—but I imagined it was a perfectly clean and immaculate apartment. Turns out, I was wrong, and I found out in a very unusual way.

One night, I was lying on my couch in the living room meditating. Similar to the first time, I felt myself lift up into the air. I opened my eyes and saw I was facing the shared wall between my apartment and my neighbor's. I decided to test whether this was a real experience or something I was imagining or hallucinating, even though like the first time, it felt completely real. I noticed this time I had a bit more control over where I was going, so I travelled through the shared wall into my neighbor's apartment. What I saw was not what I expected. I only saw the living room and the kitchen, but they were a complete mess, with pizza boxes and newspapers strewn across the floor of the living room and with opened and spilled boxes of sugary cereals on the countertops and floor. Unwashed dishes were piled up in the sink and all over the apartment. I didn't see my neighbor in the apartment so assumed he was in bed. I was about to turn around to head back to my apartment, but once again, I found myself instantly back in my body. After that, confused, I decided to go to sleep for the night.

The next day, I was starting to believe that I had hallucinated or dreamed the entire experience. I wanted to be sure, however, so I found an excuse to go to my neighbor's apartment that afternoon. When I knocked on his door, he opened it a crack and asked what I wanted. I told him I was missing some mail and asked if any had been accidentally delivered to his apartment. He told me to wait there while he went inside to check through his already-delivered mail. While he was doing that, I was able to take a look inside his apartment. It was the same mess I had seen the night before: From the pizza boxes to cereal to dirty dishes, everything was precisely as I had seen the night before. After a moment, my neighbor came back to say he didn't have any of my mail, then closed the door.

For years after that, I continued my New Age study and experiences. I had many travels to the astral plane, but was far removed from the original intention of learning this skill. Originally, I wanted to use astral projection to help during sleep paralysis. However, I had long since realized too much precise concentration was required to be able to achieve astral projection during a demonic attack. I had also noticed, but attempted to conveniently ignore, that the more I astral projected, the worse and more frequent my sleep paralysis became. I was now having sleep paralysis two or three times a week rather than a couple times a month. Spiritually, things were getting worse, but I was already hooked, so I continued on.

Looking back, astral projection (and really all New Age theology) was like a drug to me. After one taste of the experience, I became addicted. I couldn't be reasoned with (though, to be honest, no one tried). No one would have been able to talk me out of what I was doing. I kept my activities secret from my family and only told a few close friends, none of whom told me it was a bad idea. While I was searching for personal enlightenment, outwardly I became more selfish, self-centered, and untrustworthy. My personality was degrading and real, physical life became increasingly dull. I believed I had a whole reality in the astral plane to discover, so the real world had lost its appeal to me. I didn't care about friends, family, work, or anything else that wasn't rooted in New Age. Also, much like a drug, I began wanting more than the initial experience of astral travel. I wanted to meet a being from the astral plane.

The books I was reading mostly called them "spirit guides," but because my Christian upbringing was still influencing me, I thought of the beings as angels. This worked out well, because some of the books I was reading would also call them "angels." As I said before, those in the New Age movement have gone to great lengths to try to make their beliefs palatable for Christians. I believed I was using an ability that was available for all humans, it was acceptable to God, Adam himself was probably able to astral travel, and what I was doing was well within biblical teachings. Of course, this was easy for me to believe because I didn't bother to take the time to read the Bible or to understand the original meaning of any of its passages. The only Bible verses I read were the ones laid out in my New Age books, and I foolishly took their interpretation as pure truth.

Ironically enough, the first book I ever tried to write was about Christianity from a New Age perspective—which is basically the exact opposite of this book. I wanted to write about how Christians could engage in New Age practices without forsaking their beliefs. I began writing the book and made it about halfway through, when one day my computer mysteriously completely shut down on its own. There was no power outage and no problems with the computer; nothing would logically explain what had happened. Even stranger, when I turned the computer back on, all of my files for the book were gone. I had no backup copies.

Nothing like that had ever happened to me before or since. I look back now and see that, whether by natural or supernatural means, this was an intervention by God. After losing so much I had worked so hard on, there was no way I was going to go back and start over. I immediately gave up my dream of writing a pro-New Age book for Christians, and I honestly thank God for that.

A while after that, I was still continuing my astral projection pursuits and learning as much as I could about New Age when I decided the next step would be to meet and converse with an astral entity. I still wasn't sure if I was comfortable with the term "spirit guide" or even "guardian angel." In fact, I thought of them "over there" as similar to us here, just from a different place. I was wrong.

I began reading as much as I could about spirit guides, guardian angels, and astral beings. I even began using binaural beats (special audio frequencies said to have been designed to assist in meditation and achieving astral projection). Then came the time when I would have my final venture into the astral plane.

At this time, I had been married to my wife, Christina, for about a year, and we had just had our first child, Jaklynn. We lived in a tiny, single-wide trailer with a roommate, a friend of ours from work (for the purposes of this book, I will refer to her as "Amy"). Amy claimed to be an atheist, yet she had an interest in Wiccanism and also denied the existence of anything spiritual. She did not know about my New Age practices.

One day, I was alone in the trailer and decided to meditate with my recording of binaural beats. This led to astral projection, and I found myself outside facing the street. This was the first time I had ever seen any other entity in the astral plane, and the environment around me was full of them. To my left, in the distance, I saw a large, bright opening in the middle of the street. It looked like someone had sliced and pulled apart reality itself and there was nothing but light on the other side. Innumerable entities, of all different sizes and shapes for as far as I could see, were heading toward this light. Some were walking, some were floating, some were in groups, some were alone, some were in the street, and some were on the rooftops of the neighboring trailers; these beings were everywhere. I decided to talk to the members of a group that was nearest to me, about thirty feet away. This group consisted of about five or six beings; some looked human and others looked monstrous, though I felt no fear. As I approached, I felt as normal as if I were in a supermarket and went up to a group of shoppers to ask if they knew where the oranges were located. I asked what they were doing and what that glowing opening was, but instead of answering my questions, they became extremely interested in me. In a very friendly and nonthreatening way, they asked questions of their own. One of the human-looking entities wanted the group to continue and ignore me, but the rest did not comply. The other members asked me if I came from their world. I told them no, that I was from the physical world and was astral projecting outside of my body. They seemed pleased with that answer. One of the entities then kindly and gently told me that if I ever wanted help leaving my body, I could ask them to help and they would. Even though the demeanor of the entities seemed pleasant, something about that encounter did not sit well with me. I thanked them and said I had to go back home. They said goodbye, and I found myself back in my body again.

A couple of days later, I tried to astral project again, but was unsuccessful. I felt like something external was blocking my attempts. I remembered the group's offer to help but I still felt uncomfortable about that. I was tempted, but ultimately it felt too much like praying to something that wasn't God. I decided not to ask the astral beings for help and not to even astral project that day.

That was when all hell broke loose.

Not long after that, everyone living in our trailer began experiencing horrifying manifestations of things otherworldly. We all began having sleep paralysis every night. My daughter, who was a little over a year old at the time, was having night terrors constantly. Even our atheist roommate Amy, who didn't know about anything I was involved in spiritually, began telling me she was seeing glowing orbs shoot into the bedroom

I shared with Christina. Christina and I would have sleep paralysis at the same time and see the same entities—only these were not peaceful and benevolent. They were gnarled, twisted, dark, hate-filled, and evil, yet somehow I knew they were the same beings I had met before. They began manifesting even during the day as black, shadow creatures or as angry, whispering voices outside in the yard. We would all hear loud, explosion-like crashes in the bathroom at night only to find nothing unusual or out of place when we investigated. The disturbances drove us to the point that we all began sleeping on the living room floor at night for fear of being alone. At this time, I explained to Amy and Christina what I believed was happening: I had inadvertently infuriated and offended those beings when I had not accepted their offer to help, and now they were demanding attention and seeking revenge. We were now seeing their true forms. They were not benevolent astral beings. They were malevolent demons.

Out of pure desperation and hopelessness, I did something I had not done honestly or genuinely in years. I called out and begged Jesus for help. I didn't know what else to do. My family was being terrorized by an enemy I could not see, understand, or defend ourselves against. I couldn't tell anyone about what was going on, because, of course, the entire story sounded completely crazy. I had no options left, and realized I was responsible for this turn of events; I had invited these things into my life. They might have been following me since I was a child, but this was the first time I had actively sought them out. Only, I didn't know what I was doing. I didn't know whom I was seeking. I didn't know that the "angels" I wished to talk to were in fact the same evil spirits terrorizing me since childhood. Most frightening, now that I had invited them in by looking for them in the first place, I didn't know how to make them leave. Therefore, out of desperation, I called out to the only One I thought might be able to help: Jesus Christ.

No more than a day or two after that prayer, I received an answer. I turned on the television and was flipping through the channel when I came across a program that featured a guest who was talking about

aliens and the mark of the Beast from the biblical book of Revelation. I
had a long-time interest in aliens and, since I was a child, had wondered
how, if at all, they might fit in the Bible. As a child, I had always been
told "aliens aren't real, they're demonic," but had never seen a Bible verse
to support that; I was expected to believe it without having any biblical
support whatsoever. I had long since believed the Bible did not contain answers about aliens. However, the person talking on the program
was providing answers to my questions straight from the Bible itself. I
recorded the program on my DVR and continued to listen to the guest's
testimony, which included a past in New Age, conversion to Christianity, and learning skills in spiritual warfare.

At the end of the show, the host gave out the name and web address
of the guest, L. A. Marzulli. I wrote down his information and waited
for my wife to come home. I told her she must watch the show, so
we watched it together. She was just as amazed at what she was learning as I had been. We had never heard terms like "spiritual warfare" or
"nephilim," before, nor had we heard about the connection between
the sixth chapter of Genesis and the modern UFO and alien abduction
phenomena. I felt this information would lead to us finding the ultimate
answer to our spiritual problem.

After that, I decided to rededicate my life to Jesus. I went through
the salvation prayer (telling Jesus I believe He exists, I believe He died
on the cross for my sins, I accept His gift of salvation, and I believe He
rose from the dead to show He conquered death, and, if I believe and
follow Him, I can be in eternity with Him as well after I die). I had done
this as a very young child, but this was the first time I offered this prayer
while understanding exactly what I was doing and accepting what it all
meant. I repented of my sins and completely renounced New Age theology. I vowed to never astral project again. I threw out all of my books,
CDs, and other New Age literature. Christina and I began doing Bible
studies together and watching more Christian TV programs, including
more interviews and presentations from L. A. Marzulli, which led us to
other researchers such as Tom Horn, Gary Stearman, and Derek Gilbert.

However, Christina and I were still dealing with the demonic manifestation problem in our trailer.

I decided to take a chance and reach out to L. A. Marzulli, so I sent him an email through his website describing our problems and asking for his advice on how to make it stop. L. A.'s wife, Peggy, responded to my email with her husband's phone number, telling me that he would like me to call him. When I did so the next day, he personally gave me a crash course in spiritual warfare. From that call, I learned about using the authority of the name of Jesus to cast out demonic entities, but also to close any spiritual portals I may have opened. Since I had now dedicated myself to Jesus, these demonic beings had no legal hold over me, so all I had to do was command them to leave in His name. L. A. explained that evil spirits had been defeated at the cross. He gave me some Bible verses and prayed with me, then we concluded the call. That day I went through every room of the trailer, commanding any and all evil spirits to leave and every demonic portal to be closed in the name of Jesus.

After that, there was peace in the trailer.

The manifestations, constant sleep paralysis, whispers, noises—all of it stopped. Even more, a spiritual peace was within me that I had never known before.

Shortly after, I felt called by the Lord to write a book and get involved in ministry. I completed my first self-published book, *Disclosure: Unveiling Our Role in the Secret War of the Ancients,* and, after only a few short years of a lot of hard work and study, began working side by side with the very people who had originally helped me get out of New Age through their television appearances, radio interviews, and Internet presentations. I now work at SkyWatchTV with Tom Horn and Derek Gilbert (both of whom I have coauthored books with) and frequently speak at conferences alongside L. A. Marzulli—all of whom have become close, personal friends to me and my family.

Since the time I rededicated my life to Christ, I had known there would be a time when He would call me to write about my experience with New Age deception. That time is now. As stated in the introduction, I do not tell these things to berate or insult anyone involved in the New Age movement. I would be the biggest hypocrite in the world if that were the point of this book. Rather, I've written this as a dire warning to all those involved with New Age, spirit guides, and astral travel. My experience is not unique. Just because it hasn't happened to you yet doesn't mean it won't. The enemy is smart. The entities will bide their time and come across as the most loving, peaceful, and benevolent beings you could ever imagine. Eventually, though, they will tip their hand. Maybe it will be when they ask you to do something and you don't do it. Maybe they will offer a favor you don't take. Maybe they never ask anything of you, but simply decide to turn on you one day. Maybe they will keep deceiving you until the day of your death, when it will be too late. At that time, your choice will be sealed in eternity. I beg you to consider the objective evidence and subjective experiences throughout this book before deciding to reject Jesus in favor of these astral beings. Learn from my mistake so you don't have to learn from your own. You owe it to yourself to at least hear what Jesus through His Word has to say about the modern New Age movement. It might seem surprising, but He has extremely strong feelings about it.

Steven Bancarz's Experience Out of Body

I was deeply entrenched in a practice called "lucid dreaming." This is a dream wherein you become consciously aware that you are in a dream. Lucidity sets in, and you have full consciousness as you operate in a dream world. While I was involved in the New Age movement in a season of studying material on how to astral project, I had a very lucid dream one night in which I became consciously aware that I was in a dream state. When I first became lucid, it seemed no different than the dozens and dozens of dreams I had before. I was driving my car down to a local coffee shop within my dream, and when I dented my front bumper as I pulled into the parking lot, the people who were riding with me began to inform me I had badly damaged my car. I told them not to worry, because it was a lucid dream; by the time we were done in the coffee shop, the dent would fix itself. Surely enough, when I walked back to my car after exiting the coffee shop, I checked my front bumper and it was back to normal.

I hopped back into my car and started to reflect on my own state of consciousness. I started to feel like the lucid dream was becoming more real, almost as if I was crossing over from a lucid dream to some ultra-vivid, intermediary state between lucid dreaming and waking consciousness. I remember thinking within the lucid dream, I can't tell if this is a lucid dream or real life anymore. This seems so real. If I can't tell if this is real life or a dream, how can I be so sure that real life isn't just one big dream? After what seemed like a minute later, the car I was driving in the lucid dream started glitching out and jerking down the street. My dream was interrupted, and I lost all fundamental control of my vehicle and myself.

I started to get pulled out of the roof of my car and found myself hovering over my neighborhood about a hundred feet above the house-tops. Twenty feet in front of me appeared a lizard-looking humanoid being with red skin and black markings on his face. He was dressed in a red cloak, stood maybe six feet tall, and had an eerie, sinister smile on his face. As unbelievable as this may seem, a third eye then appeared on his forehead and began to open at me as his other two eyes shut.

I began to feel myself (my awareness, my mind) get sucked into his third eye. I was getting pulled closer to his third eye as if it were a vortex, and I began to feel more and more disoriented the closer I got. After I had appeared to have my awareness fully pulled into his third eye, about three seconds of darkness passed before I opened my eyes. When I opened them, I found myself "lying down" in the air four feet over my bed. I sat up and looked around the room from this new, elevated position, noticing that the room was dimly lit from my "astral body" or "light body," as I understood it. Terrified of how unfamiliar it felt to be in this new state, I frantically tried to reenter my body by forcing myself back down to the bed.

I noticed that my astral leg was going in and out of my physical leg that was lying on the bed, and my consciousness began to flicker almost like a light bulb as I began to get closer to settling back into my physical body. Frightened, I began to pinch the leg of my astral body in the hopes that I would wake up—but I was unable to feel anything. When I finally reentered my body, I found myself in a state of sleep paralysis; I was unable to move. A loud, buzzing sound was taking place in the middle of my forehead, which I had learned from my research was a precursor to out-of-body experiences. Knowing I was about to be pulled out of my body a second time, I opened my eyes and was once again a foot over the top of my body. I fought to go back in, finally settling into my body and waking up. This is one of two primary experiences I had with astral projection, and to this day I am convinced through my own experience in all different states of consciousness (lucid dreaming, sleep paralysis, false awakenings, out-of-body experiences) that it is indeed possible alongside the aid of demonic power to disconnect our spirit-man from our physical body as an occult practice.

An important takeaway here is that I did not ask to encounter the being with the red skin. I did not ask him to pull me out of my body. I did not ask to get pulled out of my body a second time once I had already settled in. All of this was independent of my will and actively against my will. All I did was consent in a general sense—through research, verbal affirmation, and guided meditations—to the idea of being out of body. People think demons can only harm them if they allow them to, or if they attract them into their reality through fear. Demons, in actuality, can harm you the minute you sign up as a participant in one of their offices. I gave them legal rights to step into my life through my research and practices, and as a result, I became a pawn on their chessboard. I played by their rules when I didn't want to. They didn't play by mine when I wanted them to. Thankfully, Jesus pulled me out of their game entirely.

Warnings of Spiritual Danger

We could continue to explore at length the full spectrum of practices within the New Age movement, but we need only to establish that there is something more going on here (biblically and evidently) than smoke and mirrors. Mass hallucination and collective delusion are not appropriate classifications of the subject for the primary reason that they do not sufficiently describe what is going on. Anecdotal testimony and circumstantial evidence of those within and outside the movement testify against this, and so does the perfect witness of the Word of God. These authors are personally aware of many—including previous spiritual Satanists, mediums, channelers, astral travelers, yoga instructors, etc.— who were deeply entrenched in the things of the occult and came to Christ. Interestingly, when they come to Christ, they always affirm that what they experienced apart from Christ was legitimate and not illusory. They say they were deceived about the meaning of the experience, but they did not dream the experiences up. The things they saw and did are always classified as being both real and demonic, just as the Word of God describes.

New Age: Not Just a Different Worldview, a Supernatural Playing Field

In addition to being a new religious system of faith and practice, New Age is a demonic playing field that Scripture forces us to acknowledge as being veridical. It's not just a false set of propositions about God and the human soul, it's an entirely separate spiritual arena that offers exceedingly rich encounters to its practitioners. In an honest discussion about this movement, it's crucial to lay down this interpretive framework as the lens through which we understand New Age thought and practice. New Agers are genuinely convinced they have had real encounters with "energy" or "entities" that extend beyond the natural realm, and the

Bible not only leaves this possibility open, it often specifically confirms the supernatural reality behind the pagan practices. This is one of many reasons this conversation needs to be taken seriously, especially as the movement continues to gain traction in our culture.

2

NEW AGE IS NOTHING NEW

THE MODERN NEW AGE MOVEMENT can be traced possibly as far back through history as the beginning of mankind. It speaks to the flawed human condition Christians call "sin nature," our perpetual desire to rebel against God, usurp the divine authority of God, and seat ourselves in His place. To properly understand New Age today, it is important to see how this thinking has grown throughout history.

Back to Gnosticism

Author Dan Brown's *The Da Vinci Code* brought the ancient beliefs and practices of gnosticism back into pop culture. However, this was not the introduction of gnosticism into modern times. The New Age movement and occultism were far ahead of Dan Brown, as we will see in the next chapter. First, we can look at gnosticism as a whole: what was taught, what was believed, and what has been borrowed by the New Age movement. On the surface, New Age seems very friendly to gnosticism. There are principles within gnosticism, however, that even those who follow New Age would likely disavow if they knew about them. This is an example of the "picking and choosing" method New Age theology adherents take in deciding what to teach. Let's explore some of the basics of gnosticism along with the more controversial and atrocious issues associated with it.

Gnosticism (meaning "having knowledge") originated as heretical groups within Jewish/Christian circles in the first and second century AD. It combined many different ancient religious ideas into one (much like the New Age movement does today). The basic teaching of gnosticism was that the physical world was created by an emanation of the highest god/force that instilled a "divine spark" within humanity. This divine spark is taught to be realized by gnosis (a type of knowledge or insight into humanity's nature as being divine itself). This was seen as heretical within Christian circles for many reasons, one of the most important being it teaches finding salvation in one's self instead of submitting to Jesus Christ and His sacrifice on the cross. Another reason is that it implies that God and man are ontologically equivalent, meaning they both share the same fundamental nature as one another. This, too, is explicitly refuted by Scripture, as we will see in a later chapter.

The Monad

In many gnostic teachings, the overall highest spiritual power and supreme being is known as the Monad (from the Greek *monas* meaning "one unit").[27] The Monad goes by other names as well, such as "the One," "the Absolute," *Aion Teleos* (the "Perfect Aeon"), *Bythos* ("Beoth of Prufundity"), *Proarche* ("Before the Beginning"), *He Arche* ("The Beginning"), "the Ineffable Parent," and "the Primal Father." It was taught that the Monad is the source of the Pleroma, a light that makes up "the fullness of the godhead." Various divine entities and spiritual realms are said to have emerged from the Monad, which are arranged as a hierarchy based on their closeness to the Monad. The divine entities are known as *Aeons*. Among them are Christ, who exists close to the Monad (but is also very different from the Christian understanding of Jesus Christ).

The lowest Aeon is Sophia, whose rebellion is blamed for the creation of the physical world.

This view was likely inspired by the Pythagoreans, according to Hippolytus.[28] To the Pythagoreans, the first existing thing was the Monad, from which came the dyad, then the numbers, points, lines, and so on.[29] However, Pythagorean and Platonic philosophers such as Plontinus ad Porphyry, were critical of, to the point of condemning, gnosis and gnostic circles for their characterization of the Monad.[30]

The Monad is described in the Apocryphon of John, a second-century Sethian gnostic text containing "secret teachings." It describes Jesus appearing to John the Apostle and teaching him gnosis and other secret knowledge. It describes the Monad as a "monarchy with nothing above it." The Monad is described as being indescribable and inconceivable. Human beings have no way to explain, let alone have any kind of personal relationship with, the Monad. Therefore, the Monad can be described as a sort of impersonal force out of which everything else was brought into existence.

A feminine divine entity called Barbelo, described as "the first thought" and the "image" of the Monad, is produced from the Monad. While Barbelo is always referred to as "she," she is also said to be both the primordial mother and father, to the extent of being regarded as "the first man" as well as other terms of androgyny. She is the first of the Aeons and an exchange between herself and the Monad produces the other Aeons. Also, the Light and Mind are born from the Monad's reflection on Barbelo. The Light, Mind, Barbelo, and the Monad create more Aeons and powers together.

Sophia and Yaltabaoth

Sophia (meaning "wisdom"), according to the Apocryphon of John, is the lowest of the Aeons. She decides to engage in creation without including or informing the Monad and without her male consort (the

Christ). She creates an entity named Yaltabaoth, who is the first of new creations of incomplete, deeply flawed entities called Archons. Yaltabaoth is described as malevolent, evil, and arrogant, and possesses a grotesque form of a serpentine body with the head of a lion. Realizing the deformed and imperfect nature of her creation, Sophia tries to hide it where the other Aeons cannot find it. Because of this, Yaltabaoth believes he is alone with no other beings above him.

Yaltabaoth, despite being malformed and imperfect, still has the power to create. He creates the Archons, each of whom is evil like Yaltabaoth himself. Yaltabaoth also creates a world for the Archons to inhabit. This world is completely inferior to what the Monad and Aeons have created above. It is made from darkness but animated by a light stolen from Sophia. Therefore, the world is described as neither light nor dark, but instead dim. Yaltabaoth declares himself as the only god of this realm; he is also incredibly jealous.

After seeing all of this, Sophia eventually repents for her creative actions. The spirit of the Monad forgives her by assisting the other Aeons and powers in attempting to redeem Sophia and her creation. During this process, Yaltabaoth and the lesser spirits hear the voice of the Monad, which leaves a type of imprint of the Monad's spirit on the waters that form the roof of Yaltabaoth's realm. Yaltabaoth and the Archons then try to harness that power for themselves and end up creating the first human man, Adam. Sophia and the pleroma then trick Yaltabaoth into breathing his own spiritual essence into Adam, thereby animating Adam and emptying Yaltabaoth of the portion of his being which came from Sophia.

After seeing the obvious superiority of the living Adam, Yaltabaoth and the Archons try to imprison or kill him. After failing to do so, they try to limit Adam by putting him in the Garden of Eden. This garden is far different from the one described in the Bible, however. In the Apocryphon of John, the Garden of Eden is described as a false paradise where the fruit of the trees is sin, lust, ignorance, confinement, and death. Adam is given access to the Tree of Life, but the Tree of the

Knowledge of Good and Evil is hidden from him. In the Apocryphon of John, the tree of the Knowledge of Good and Evil represents the influence of the higher forces into Yaltabaoth's realm.

In the story, this is where Christ tells John that it was actually He who caused Adam to eat the fruit from the Tree of the Knowledge of Good and Evil. It is also revealed that Eve was a helper sent by the higher Aeons to help liberate the light imprisoned in Yaltabaoth's creation, including in Adam himself. When Adam sees Eve, he sees a reflection of his own essence and is freed from the holding power of Yaltabaoth.

After this, Yaltabaoth tries to regain control over the light by initiating within humanity the activity of sex in the hope of creating new human bodies that can be inhabited by a counterfeit spirit. It is by this spirit that Yaltabaoth and the Archons can keep the human race ignorant of their true nature through deception. This is the source of all human evil and causes people to die without knowing the truth.

After this, the story concludes with John the Apostle asking Christ a series of questions, including who is truly able to be saved. Contrary to biblical teaching, the Apocryphon of John states that those who come into contact with the true Spirit will be saved while those who are dominated by the counterfeit spirit will be damned. This salvation doesn't come through Jesus Christ's sacrificial death on the cross, but instead comes through self-realization (gnosis).

The Yaltabaoth and Sexism Problem in Gnosticism

If it hasn't become obvious now, Yaltabaoth is what the ancient gnostics thought of YHWH, the God of the Bible. They considered the God of the Bible as stupid and evil, and even blamed Him as being the serpent in the Garden of Eden who tempted humanity into sin. They taught, much like New Age theology today, that salvation is found subjectively in one's own self rather than objectively in the literal, sacrificial atoning death of Jesus Christ on the cross.

The other problem with this has to do with the gnostic view men have of women. Gnosticism teaches that the female Sophia introduced error into the lower world. Also, Adam, not Eve, received the divine spark. The gnostic text, *The Gospel of Thomas,* states that "women are not worthy of life" and "every female who makes herself male will enter heaven's kingdom." Anti-female portrayals within gnosticism are found in external sources as well. Clement of Alexandria wrote, "They say that the Saviour himself said 'I come to destroy the works of the female,' meaning by 'female' desire, and by 'works' birth and corruption."[31] Other examples have been clearly outlined by researchers including Dr. Michael Heiser and others.[32, 33]

Many times, New Age theology is conflated with various political movements such as feminism and liberalism. Within these movements, a female's worth, power, identity, and role are seen as at least equal to, if not higher than, a male's. Therefore, in order to adopt the teachings of gnosticism, New Age theology is forced to pick and choose which parts are acceptable and which are not, thereby distorting it away from its primary meaning to something that suits the philosophy of New Age practitioners. Adopting gnosticism as it *really* is would jeopardize the socio-cultural objectives of the New Age by causing disunity and hierarchy within genders.

Eastern Mysticism Influences in New Age Theology

To say the New Age movement is influenced by Eastern mysticism would be an understatement. According to certain understandings within Eastern mysticism, specifically Vedanic Hinduism, Brahman is considered the ultimate, absolute, formless source of reality.[34] Brahman is the source of everything, yet it is impersonal. It is a metaphysical force from which everything in the universe comes.[35] Yet, therein lies the fallacy. How can an impersonal force be responsible for the personhood of human beings?

How can something lacking personal consciousness bring forth personal consciousness? How can something that has no personal mind, free will, or volition design and fine tune a universe for intelligent human persons to live within? The notion of Brahman fails to explain how a universe as marvelously complex as ours could emerge from something that lacks personal intelligence, and how something as miraculous as personal agents could emerge from something that has no personhood.

In the Upanishads (a series of Hindu sacred treatises written in Sanskrit c. 800–200 BC), a variety of themes with multiple possible interpretations is offered.[36] Gavin Flood summarizes the concept of Brahman in the Upanishads to be the "essence, the smallest particle of the cosmos and the infinite universe," the "essence of all things which cannot be seen, though it can be experienced," and describes it as the "self, soul within each person, each being," the "truth," the "reality," the "absolute," and the "bliss" (ananda).[37] According to some interpretations, the Upanishads teach that Brahman cannot be seen or heard, but this ultimate essence of material reality can be known through one's own development of self-knowledge.[38]

In Hindu philosophy, the Atman is the true self of a person or the essence of individuality.[39] The Atman is also considered identical with the "transcendent self," Brahman. As Richard King in Early Advaita Vedanta and Buddhism puts it, "Atman as the innermost essence or soul of man, and Brahman as the innermost essence and support of the universe.... Thus we can see in the Upanishads, a tendency towards a convergence of microcosm and macrocosm, culminating in the equating of atman with Brahman."[40] An individual attains moksha (liberation) by acquiring atma jnana (self-knowledge), which is to realize that his own Atman (true self) is the same as the Brahman. As David Lorenzen in The Hindu World explains, "Advaita and nirguni movements...stress an interior mysticism in which the devotee seeks to discover the identity of individual soul (atma) with the universal ground of being (brahman) or to find god within himself."[41] This also allows the individual to enter moksha (state of enlightenment), where he can now escape the cycle of samsara (cycle of reincarnation) by transcending the need for further reincarnation.[42]

In essence, much like modern New Age theology, Eastern mysticism, and many other ancient and modern belief systems around the world teach, this is another example of the belief in self-godhood. It is an ancient belief that states the goal for an individual's life is to find salvation (or "liberation") by realizing that he or she is God itself. Everything from self-divinity to pantheism to yoga to reincarnation has its origin in Hindu philosophy, a viewpoint that Jesus diametrically opposed in His earthly ministry. New Age theology today is nothing more than rehashed Eastern mysticism, but this deception goes much deeper and much farther back in time than that.

The Ancient Root of Modern Self-Godhood

As we have seen, the pursuit of being one's own god is nothing new. Whether this means pushing God to the side through self-exaltation over one's life, working one's way up to a state of self-deification through special knowledge, or coming to a realization that God and man are ontologically equivalent by nature, the issue ultimately boils down to man being deceived into believing that godhood is intrinsically contained within. In fact, according to the first book of the Bible, this is the oldest deception since human beings came into existence:

> Now the serpent was more crafty than any other beast of the field that the Lord God had made. He said to the woman, "Did God actually say, 'You shall not eat of any tree in the garden'?" And the woman said to the serpent, "We may eat of the fruit of the trees in the garden, but God said, 'You shall not eat of the fruit of the tree that is in the midst of the garden, neither shall you touch it, lest you die.'" But the serpent said to the woman, "You will not surely die. For God knows that when you eat of

it your eyes will be opened, and you will be like God, knowing good and evil." (Genesis 3:1–5, ESV)

Being God or Godlike is, literally, a Luciferian pursuit that originates from the Garden of Eden where the enemy of God tricks man into desiring deification. In the New Age movement, we see echoed the same lie that caused mankind to fall from fellowship with God into the curse of sin. It is being offered to us as the solution to our suffering, yet the Bible attributes it to the actual cause of our suffering. To believe one can be like God or can become God-realized through special knowledge is to believe the first lie Satan ever told mankind.

Furthermore, we can trace this desire of human beings to be gods in the story of Nimrod and the tower of Babel:

Cush fathered Nimrod; he was the first on earth to be a mighty man. He was a mighty hunter before the Lord. Therefore it is said, "Like Nimrod a mighty hunter before the Lord." The beginning of his kingdom was Babel, Erech, Accad, and Calneh, in the land of Shinar. (Genesis 10:8–10, ESV)

Now the whole earth had one language and the same words. And as people migrated from the east, they found a plain in the land of Shinar and settled there. And they said to one another, "Come, let us make bricks, and burn them thoroughly." And they had brick for stone, and bitumen for mortar. Then they said, "Come, let us build ourselves a city and a tower with its top in the heavens, and let us make a name for ourselves, lest we be dispersed over the face of the whole earth." And the Lord came down to see the city and the tower, which the children of man had built. And the Lord said, "Behold, they are one people, and they have all one language, and this is only the beginning of what they will do. And nothing that they propose to do will now

be impossible for them. Come, let us go down and there confuse
their language, so that they may not understand one another's
speech." So the Lord dispersed them from there over the face
of all the earth, and they left off building the city. Therefore its
name was called Babel, because there the Lord confused the language of all the earth. And from there the Lord dispersed them
over the face of all the earth. (Genesis 11:1–9, ESV)

The non-canonical Book of Jasher gives us some more interesting
details of the Tower of Babel story and discloses the author's beliefs about
the true motivation:

And king Nimrod reigned securely, and all the earth was under
his control, and all the earth was of one tongue and words of
union. And all the princes of Nimrod and his great men took
counsel together; Phut, Mitzraim, Cush and Canaan with their
families, and they said to each other, Come let us build ourselves
a city and in it a strong tower, and its top reaching heaven, and
we will make ourselves famed, so that we may reign upon the
whole world, in order that the evil of our enemies may cease
from us, that we may reign mightily over them, and that we may
not become scattered over the earth on account of their wars.
And they all went before the king, and they told the king these
words, and the king agreed with them in this affair, and he did
so. And all the families assembled consisting of about six hundred thousand men, and they went to seek an extensive piece of
ground to build the city and the tower, and they sought in the
whole earth and they found none like one valley at the east of the
land of Shinar, about two days' walk, and they journeyed there
and they dwelt there. And they began to make bricks and burn
fires to build the city and the tower that they had imagined to
complete. And the building of the tower was unto them a trans-
gression and a sin, and they began to build it, and whilst they

were building against the Lord God of heaven, they imagined in their hearts to war against him and to ascend into heaven. And all these people and all the families divided themselves in three parts; the first said We will ascend into heaven and fight against him; the second said, We will ascend to heaven and place our own gods there and serve them; and the third part said, We will ascend to heaven and smite him with bows and spears; and God knew all their works and all their evil thoughts, and he saw the city and the tower which they were building. (Jasher 9:20–26)[43]

This account shows the desire within mankind to ascend above the rest of humanity, achieve godhood, and reign over the unenlightened. While maintaining a belief in the historically literal accounts of the Bible, we could even think of the story of Nimrod and the Tower of Babel in a metaphorical sense to learn something about the human condition. Nimrod, the individual, seeks to ascend past humanity. Even more, he wishes to rise above and vanquish the view of God held by the rest of the world in order to establish himself as god. The remaining human beings in the world, being of one language and the same words (meaning they not only spoke the same physical language, but even expressed the same ideas and were in agreement about everything), were completely unenlightened. Yet, Nimrod was able to use them to initiate his own ascension. At the end of the story, however, God Himself completely ruins the plan, teaching that there is no one higher than the God of the Bible.

The desire of Nimrod is a similar promise made within the New Age movement, only instead of ruling politically, the individual has the benefit of feeling more enlightened than non-New Age friends and family who, metaphorically, share "one speech and one language," completely inferior from the individual New Age believer's inner "Nimrod" who desires to move past such things. In a sense, the "enlightened" individual has the option of enjoying a sense of spiritual superiority over others. This is how a New Age believer can use the unenlightened, much like Nimrod if thought of metaphorically, to aid in his own ascension: by consistently and increasingly thinking of himself as more enlightened than them and feeding off his own sense of superiority. However, much like in the Nimrod account, this cannot be maintained forever. There will come a point when the whole process will be destroyed and the individual will be busted down to Earth with the rest of us.

This goes back to that ancient deceptive promise of personal godhood Satan made in the garden. Instead of inspiring benevolence, it can be used as an excuse to indulge in pride, arrogance, and a sense of superiority. Rather than being freeing and enlightening, New Age and gnosticism promote the ancient ideas of being in bondage to one's own self-glorification, of striving to become God-realized, and of one day escaping the limitations of humanity and the physical world by achieving a heightened state of consciousness. These ideas are not "new" and in fact belong to the very cultures, leaders, and spiritual forces Yahweh constantly opposed throughout Scripture.

3

NEW AGE AND THE OCCULT

MODERN NEW AGE AS WE know it today came into being not only by borrowing from ancient gnosticism and the Luciferian philosophy pushed by the enemies of God in Scripture, but also from nineteenth- and twentieth-century, Western occultism. Surprisingly, in terms of their doctrine of man, ancient gnosticism, Western occultism, and the modern New Age teach similar principles. The main takeaways from these three belief systems are: 1) the God of the Bible is the enemy of human enlightenment; 2) Christianity is an outdated system that keeps man in a lower state of consciousness; and 3) people should do whatever they want regardless of the consequences.

These three ideas are fundamental to occult teachings and were first introduced by the serpent in the Garden, who, as we will see, is actually praised by New Age teachers as being the first intelligence to free man from being enslaved to Yahweh. Satan, ancient gnosticism, and Western occultism all chalk up Yahweh as the obstacle in the pursuit of man's self-divinity and revere Lucifer as the great bringer of light. Surprisingly, the entire New Age movement owes its origins to teachers who hold Satan in a higher regard than Jesus.

Helena Blavatsky

Helena Petrovna
Blavatsky (1831–1891),
founder of modern
theosophy

Helena Petrovna Blavatsky was a Russian occultist, author, and the cofounder of the Theosophical Society, whose purpose was to promote the esoteric religion of theosophy. She claimed to have traveled the world in 1849, when she met a group of interdimensional spiritual leaders called the "Masters of the Ancient Wisdom," who then sent her to Tibet. She claimed that while in Tibet, she was trained to develop a deeper understanding of the connections between religion, philosophy, and science. However, critics and biographers have by and large argued that some or all of these world travels and experiences were fictitious.

By the early 1870s, Blavatsky had become involved in the Spiritualist movement (which taught that the spirits of the dead exist and are able to communicate with the living), though she disagreed and even argued against the idea that the contacted entities were actually spirits of the dead. She moved to America and gained public fame as a spirit medium, which also earned her accusations of lying to the public about her abilities.

In 1875, Blavatsky, along with Henry Steel Olcott and William Quan Judge, founded the Theosophical Society, which introduced Eastern mysticism, gnosticism, and occultism into the mainstream. Following that, in 1877, Blavatsky published *Isis Unveiled*, which taught her theosophical belief system. She asserted that theosophy was a reviving of a universal ancient wisdom that is at the root of all of humanity's religions. In 1880, Blavatsky moved to India and became one of the first Westerners to officially convert to Buddhism. In 1885, she moved back to Europe, where she published three more books: *The Secret Doctrine, The Key to Theosophy,* and *The Voice of the Silence.* Shortly later, she died of influenza. Her theosophical doctrines spurred the spread of Hinduism/Buddhism in the West, which led to Western esoteric movements such as Ariosophy, Anthroposophy, and of course, the New Age movement. Blavatsky was remembered as an enlightened guru by some and as a fraudulent liar by others.

While she was writing the book she would most be remembered for, her first book, *Isis Unveiled*, Blavatsky claimed that a second consciousness inspired her ideas, which she referred to as "the lodger who is in me."[44] The book connected Western esotericism of Hermeticism and Neoplatonism to ancient wisdom and Spiritualism.[45] In *Isis Unveiled*, Blavatsky spoke out against Darwinian evolution by saying it only dealt with the physical world and not with anything spiritual.[46] The book became a huge success, though it received a large amount of negative press. It was stated the book extensively quoted about one hundred other books, yet provided no acknowledgment.[47] Despite the negative reviews, the initial print of a thousand copies sold out in a week.[48] Though *Isis Unveiled* was a large success, the Theosophical Society had basically faded to nothing at this time, despite new lodges throughout the United States and London being established and prominent figures like Thomas Edison and Abner Doubleday joining.[49]

Though Blavatsky seemed to be a spiritually enlightened person to some in her own day and to many today, she actually held some rather evil views concerning race and religion. Scholar of religion, Olav Hammer, noted that some of Blavatsky's writings were "overtly racist."[50] He said her anti-Semitism "derives from the unfortunate position of Judaism as the origin of Christianity" and refers to "the intense dislike she felt for Christianity."[51] Blavatsky wrote, "Judaism, built solely on Phallic worship, has become one of the latest creeds in Asia, and theologically a religion of hate and malice toward everyone and everything outside themselves."[52] She wrote that Jews were "degenerate in spirituality"[53] and that aboriginal Australians were "half-animal."[54] It is only a wonder how much of her philosophy contributed to the Holocaust, as it has been reported that *The Secret Doctrine* was a favorite work of Adolf Hitler.

Despite Blavatsky's overt racism and intolerance to religion, her development of theosophy has been cited as a major influence of the New Age movement.[55] Even the *New Age Encyclopedia* recognized this, stating: "No single organization or movement has contributed so many components to the New Age Movement as the Theosophical Society.... It has been the major force in the dissemination of occult literature in the West in the twentieth century."[56] In fact, the "Chronology of the New Age Movement" section in *New Age Encyclopedia* begins with the formation of the Theosophical Society in 1875.[57] However, as mentioned earlier, the New Age movement itself is designed to pick the things about spiritual teachings it likes and ignore the rest, a responsibility that lies with the individual student rather than a group of like-minded believers or educated theologians.

For example, something about Blavatsky that gets overlooked was her open commendation of Satan and the wonderful work he did in delivering free will to man in the Garden of Eden. Given that she is the "mother of the New Age movement," the following quotes should concern us:

> God created Satan, the fairest and wisest of all his creatures in this part of His Universe, and made him Prince of the World, and of the Power of the Air.... Thus, Satan being perfect in wisdom, and beauty, His vast empire is our earth, if not the whole solar system.... Certainly no other angelic power of greater or even equal dignity has been revealed to us.[58]

> It is "Satan who is the god of our planet and the only god," and this without any allusive metaphor to its wickedness and depravity. For he is one with the Logos, "the first son, eldest of the gods."[59]

> In this case it is but natural—even from the dead letter standpoint—to view Satan, the Serpent of Genesis, as the real creator and benefactor, the Father of Spiritual mankind. For it is he

who was the "Harbinger of Light," bright radiant Lucifer, who opened the eyes of the automaton created by Jehovah, as alleged; and he who was the first to whisper: "in the day ye eat thereof ye shall be as Elohim, knowing good and evil"—can only be regarded in the light of a Saviour.[60]

Satan, the enemy of God, is in reality, the highest divine Spirit.[61]

Lucifer is divine and terrestrial light, the "Holy Ghost" and "Satan," at one and the same time.[62]

The New Age was founded upon the teachings of someone who openly praised Lucifer/Satan for his influence on mankind. It is common knowledge in the history of religions that nobody has contributed more to the development of New Age spirituality in the West, and she did so as a proud Luciferian who demonized the God of the Bible and praised His enemy. Blavatsky, however, is not the only "founder" of the New Age movement with dark, occult ties.

Alice Bailey

Alice Ann Bailey (June 16, 1880– December 15, 1949)

Following Helena Blavatsky, Alice Bailey wrote more than twenty-four books on theosophy. She was one of the first writers to use the term "New Age" in reference to her belief in a coming "Age of Aquarius," which would be a time of spiritual enlightenment within humanity. Bailey wrote on a wide variety of topics, including meditation, healing, spiritual psychology, and telepathy. She claimed most of her work had been telepathically dictated to her by "Djwal Khul," whom she described as a "Master of Wisdom."[63] Bailey's writings differed in some ways to Blavatsky's teachings of theosophy, but they also had very much in common. Bailey was heavily influenced by Blavatsky and became involved in the Theosophical Society in 1917.[64]

In 1921, Alice and Foster Bailey were married and, the following year, founded the Lucis Trust, which set up the Arcane School that gave instruction on meditation.[65] Alice and Foster Bailey also founded Lucifer Publishing Company, which later was changed to Lucis Publishing Co.[66] If any doubts about the Satanic origins of New Age could be questioned, one can still see early copies of the "Lucifer" online pushing an explicitly anti-Christian worldview. Bailey continued her work until her death in 1949, and like Blavatsky, also received criticism for the racist themes in her material.

While New Age and Satanism are generally seen as two different things in our modern culture, they actually have nearly identical roots and teachings. From their doctrine of man, to their theology, to their doctrine of the afterlife, to the practices they both endorse, they mirror Luciferianism and spiritual Satanism to a tee. This may seem like a highly controversial claim according to New Age believers; however, it can be clearly demonstrated by comparative analysis. As we will see, even famed occultists and Satanists understood this as fact.

Aleister Crowley

(October 12, 1875–
December 1, 1947)

Aleister Crowley

Aleister Crowley was an English occultist and ceremonial magician who founded the religion of Thelema. Crowley wrote *The Book of the Law*, the central text of Thelema, which he (similar to Blavatsky and Bailey) claimed to have received from a spiritual entity named Aiwass. He announced what he called "The Aeon of Horus" and, in *The Book of the Law,* taught his followers to "do what thou wilt." The Aeon of Horus, Crowley believed, was marked in the twentieth century. He saw it as a new era in which humans would take control over their own destiny (similar to Bailey's Age of Aquarius).

The A∴A∴ (Argentium Astrum) is a spiritual organization he founded in 1907. Students would enter the order and then master certain occultic tasks and study esoteric knowledge in order to graduate to the next level. If you were to be initiated into the order of A∴A∴, here are some of the things you would learn about:

- Astral projection
- Hinduism
- Qabala
- Yoga
- Magick
- Non-duality
- Ascended Masters (Secret Chiefs)
- Tree of Life
- Transcendental meditation
- Higher selves
- Buddhism
- Mysticism
- Gnosticism
- Sorcery
- Rituals of the pentagram and hexagram
- Tarot cards
- The Zodiac
- Many other topics taught under the umbrella of the New Age movement

Crowley's "do as thou wilt" teaching has made a significant impression not only in occult and esoteric movements, but also in the modern American culture itself. However, like many teaching within these movements, "do as thou wilt" is only self-serving and ultimately fails on a personal and social level. It doesn't require the individual to think about others when making choices, which causes destruction and suffering. It lifts the individual to godhood while ignoring the rest of humanity. This slogan is still held in modern Satanism today and is a basic moral principle in the Satanic Bible. It is also heralded by New Agers.

Throughout his life and afterward, Crowley was described as a Satanist, though he himself stated that he did not consider himself a Satanist because he did not accept the Christian interpretation of spiritual existence in which Satan exists.[67] However, Crowley used Satanic imagery, described himself as "the Beast 666," and referred to the "Whore of Babylon" in his work.[68] In fact, he even identified Aiwass as Satan and called him "Our Lord God the Devil."[69] Despite Crowley not being fond of the term "Satanist" to describe himself, he seemed to be very comfortable with the idea of following Satanic teachings, beliefs, and practices. Though once called the most evil man in the world, he is now praised as one of the founding fathers of the New Age movement in our culture. Legend has it that his final words were "I am perplexed… Satan, get out."

Anton Szandor LaVey was the founder of the Church of Satan and the religion of LaVeyan Satanism

Anton LaVey

While Crowley may have been uncomfortable with the term "Satanist," Anton LaVey (1930–1997) certainly was not. Anton LaVey wrote several books, including *The Satanic Bible, The Satanic Rituals, The Satanic Witch,* and *The Devil's Notebook*. He also founded the Church of Satan.[70] Academic scholars of Satanism Per Faxneld and Jesper Aa. Petersen described LaVey as "the most iconic figure in the Satanic milieu."[71] LaVey is heralded as being the "Father of Satanism."[72]

Anton LaVey criticized New Age as being nothing more than thinly veiled Satanism. It was actually his interest in the occult that caused him to form the mystery school called the Order of the Trapezoid in the 1960s, which became a functioning arm of the Church of Satan. He knew the occult and the mystery school teachings as well as the next, and he is quoted as saying, "But in truth, all 'New Age' labeling is, again, trying to play the Devil's game without using His Infernal name."[73] He also expressed his desire to see New Age practices reclaimed by Satanists and dedicated to their rightful owner, Satan himself.[74]

Why did the Mother of the New Age (Blavatsky) say that Satan is the spiritual father of mankind? Why is the most famous occultist in history a borderline Satanist who practiced blood sacrifice to demons? Is it possible that Anton LaVey was right and that New Age ideas and themes really belong attached to Satanic or Luciferian philosophy?

This may seem far-fetched to the friendly neighborhood New Ager, but the truth is that theistic Satanism engages in every New Age practice under the sun in their dedications to Satan and Satanic philosophy. For example, a popular spiritual Satanism ministry offers teachings on astrology, auras, magick, self-hypnosis, incense, pendulums, runes, telekinesis, brain waves, clairvoyance, past lives, chanting, the pineal gland and the third eye, the chakras, bioelectric technology, the astral plane, spells, the Kundalini serpent, and trance.[75, 76, 77]

If New Age teachings and practices are the highest will of God for our life, why do Satanists teach and practice the exact same things, and why is the father of Satanism accusing the New Age of stealing from Satanism? In addition to these topics, you can also learn about how Satan is the one true God and is the one who brought spiritual knowledge to man, just like Helena Blavatsky taught.

A brief skim through the Satanic Bible reveals similarities to New Age thought such as the Age of Aquarius, the five elements and the pentagram, Lucifer as the personification of enlightenment, Thoth, God as man and man as God, spirit guides, pantheism, sensual indulgence, spiritual rebirth through studying the "mysteries," the All-Seeing Eye, and being your own redeemer and savior through "enlightenment." These practices are all inconsistent with the Bible but perfectly consistent with Satanism, which speaks volumes about the spiritual nature of the movement itself.

Gerald Gardner

Gerald Garner (1884–1964) was an author, anthropologist, archaeologist, and most infamously, an English Wiccan known by the craft name of "Scire." In his younger years, Gardner traveled the world, met new people, and learned about various cultures.[78] Due to poor health, he never gained any formal education but instead taught himself to read.[79] He developed a belief in the afterlife from the book that influenced him the most, *There Is No Death* (1891), by Florence Marryat.[80]

Gerald Gardner, regarded by many as the father of Wicca and modern witchcraft

Later in life, Gardner became personally close with a part of his family known as the Surgenesons, who regularly talked with him about the paranormal, the belief in fairies, and a rumor about an ancestor named Grissell Gairdner who had been burned as a witch in Newburgh in 1610.[81] In 1910, Gardner was initiated as an Apprentice Freemason into the Sphinx Lodge No. 107 (affiliated with the Irish Grand Lodge). He had risen to the 3rd Degree of Freemasonry before his resignation the following year.[82] He then moved to Borneo, where he became fascinated with the local Dyak and Dusun peoples' weapons, tattoos, and religious beliefs.[83] He attended Dusun seances and healing rituals before leaving Borneo and moving to Singapore.[84]

In 1939, while Gardner was living in England, he joined the Rosicrucian Order Crotona Fellowship, an organization that blended Rosicrucianism, theosophy, and Freemasonry.[85] In 1946, he was ordained as a priest in the Ancient British Church, which was open to anyone who believed in monotheism. He also joined the Ancient Druid Order (ADO) and attended annual Midsummer rituals at Stonehenge.[86]

In 1947, a mutual friend introduced Gardner to Aleister Crowley. Before his death, Crowley initiated Gardner to the 4th Degrees of Ordo Templi Orientis (OTO) and decreed that Gardner could admit people into its Minerval degree.[87] The father of witchcraft was in agreement with the doctrines and teachings of someone who practiced blood sacrifice rituals to demons, and was actually a colleague working alongside him. In 1954, he published his nonfiction book, *Witchcraft Today*, which espoused the survival of the witch-cult, his belief that faeries in Europe were actually a secret, pygmy race living alongside humans, and that the Knights Templar had been initiates of the Craft.[88] In 1960, Gardner's official biography, *Gerald Gardner: Witch,* was published by the Sufi mystic Idries Shah, who went by the name of Jack L. Bracelin for fear of being associated with witchcraft.[89] In 1964, at the age of 79, Gardner died of a heart attack and was buried in Tunisia.[90] Years later, Wiccan High Priestess Eleanor Bone discovered that the cemetery where Gardner was buried was going to be redeveloped, so she arranged to have his body moved to Tunis, where it remains today.[91] In 2007, a plaque was attached to his grave that described him as "Father of Modern Wicca. Beloved of the Great Goddess."[92]

Jiddu Krishnamurti
(1895-1986)

Jiddu Krishnamurti

Jiddu Krishnamurti was groomed early in life by the theosophy movement to be the new World Teacher, also known as the Maitreya or Lord Maitreya, which is described in theosophy as an advanced spiritual entity and high-ranking member of a hidden spiritual hierarchy called the Masters of the Ancient Wisdom. According to theosophy, the Masters oversee the evolution of humankind. The Maitreya is said to hold the office of the World Teacher in accordance with the Masters. Theosophy says the purpose of this office is to facilitate the transfer of knowledge about the true constitution and workings of existence to humankind. One way the knowledge transfer is accomplished is by Maitreya occasionally manifesting or incarnating in the physical realm. The manifested entity then assumes the role of World Teacher of Humankind.[93]

At the age of 14, Krishnamurti was discovered by the Theosophical Society, who quickly began grooming him to become the new World Teacher.[94] A new organization called the Order of the Star in the East was formed in 1911 to support the effort to make Krishnamurti the coming Maitreya, also known as the World Teacher Project. The effort gained widespread publicity and cultivated a worldwide following, mainly among other Theosophists. The effort completely imploded, however, when in 1929, Krishnamurti rejected the role he was expected to fulfill. He removed himself from the World Teacher Project and severed ties with the Theosophical Society, which damaged theosophical organizations and theosophy as a whole.[95]

Krishnamurti attracted attention to the religious establishment in India. He interacted with several Hindu and Buddhist leaders, including the Dalai Lama,[96] who regarded Krishnamurti as a "great soul." Krishanmurti put forth his ideas in the fields of religion, education, psychology, physics, and consciousness studies. He began melding his philosophical and spiritual views into physics, even to the point of meeting and discussing with physicists David Bohm, Fritjof Capra, and E. C. George Sudarshan.[97]

Despite having an interest in science, which would seem to be a pursuit of objective truth, Krishnamurti said "truth is a pathless land," which was the core of his teachings.[98] He believed and taught that human beings cannot come to truth by any organization, creed, dogma, priest, ritual, philosophy, or psychology. Instead, he believed truth could only be found through the understanding of one's own mind through personal observation and subjective experience. He believed that man has built images of religion, politics, and individuality within himself as a fence of false security.

The idea that "truth is a pathless land" flies right in the face of the teachings of Jesus Christ, who taught He alone was the path:

> Jesus saith unto him, I am the way, the truth, and the life: no man cometh unto the Father, but by me. (John 14:6, KJV)

To deny there is no path is to directly deny Jesus Himself, for He revealed Himself as truth embodied. Unfortunately, many people take the pathless land to nowhere rather because of armchair talking points like these, rather than the path to truth itself. According to Jesus, this ensures destruction:

> So whatever you wish that others would do to you, do also to them, for this is the Law and the Prophets. Enter by the narrow gate. For the gate is wide and the way is easy that leads to destruction, and those who enter by it are many. For the gate is narrow and the way is hard that leads to life, and those who find it are few. (Matthew 7:12–14, ESV)

While generally regarded as a great thinker and respected philosopher by most people who have heard of him, Krishnamurti was nothing more than a teacher of "anything goes and there is no path." If there is no path to truth, truth is not real. If truth is not real, everything is hopeless and nothing has any meaning. This is completely antithetical to the teachings of Jesus Christ and the Bible as a whole, and his ties to theosophy can only make us wonder who so many influencers of the New Age movement had a hand of theirs in Luciferian philosophy.

Edgar Cayce

Edgar Cayce (1877–1945) was an American clairvoyant who claimed to have answers to questions regarding healing, reincarnation, wars, Atlantis, and future events. He came up with these answers while in a trance, which earned him the nickname "The Sleeping Prophet." He is a prominent figure and the source of many characteristic beliefs within the New Age movement.[99]

Edgar Cayce circa 1911

During my (Josh's) days in the New Age movement, I was enthralled with Cayce. Stories of him falling asleep on a Bible as a child and waking up with full recall of Scripture fascinated me. Even the depiction of the self-sacrifice with which he continued to use his gifts for the benefit of others until it eventually killed him really spoke to me. At the time, I was thinking, *"Now here is a good man and an example of what the world needs more of."* It was easy for me to justify Cayce's New Age theology by believing he was truly a Christian and that everything else he taught was just an extension of that. Of course, this was during a time when I wasn't taking the Bible very seriously and was going out of my way to ignore all of the inconsistencies between Edgar Cayce's teachings and the truth of the Bible.

Rededicating my life to Christ caused me to look at New Age theology through a truthful lens. Suddenly I felt awake and could not believe the types of things I had been involved in. Looking at Edgar Cayce through a biblical lens was especially eye-opening. Once I realized what a Christian actually is, any belief I had that Edgar Cayce was a true follower of Christ was dispelled. To be clear, I am not saying Edgar Cayce wasn't saved. Besides God, no one can know that. For all anyone knows, Cayce could have repented at any point in his life. He could have accepted Jesus just before he died. No one knows. However, being saved and being a follower of Christ is a different matter. Accepting Jesus as your Savior is the first step toward a relationship with God. Actively cultivating that relationship, however, is what it means to be a follower of Christ.

We do have the information available to deduce, based on biblical principles, whether he was a true follower of Christ.

One of the biggest indicators we can look at are his prophecies. First, Cayce did not have a 100 percent accuracy rate in his prophecies. Also, of the prophecies he gave that his followers claim came true, nothing in them could not have been told to him by some other demonic force or entity. True prophecy does not necessitate benevolent origin. An evil spirit is able to make predictions about the future based on the data available, just as we saw in Acts 16 with the spirit of python. Nothing in his prophecies was truly unknowable to any given spiritual or physical being.

Despite the fact that coincidentally true prophecy does not mean you follow Jesus (as even demon-possessed people made true prophecy), many today still assume that Cayce was somehow a true Christian. Let us examine that claim and see if it holds up biblically.

Jesus' own words, recorded in Matthew 7:15–20, read:

Beware of false prophets, which come to you in sheep's clothing, but inwardly they are ravening wolves.

Ye shall know them by their fruits. Do men gather grapes of thorns, or figs of thistles?

Even so every good tree bringeth forth good fruit; but a corrupt tree bringeth forth evil fruit.

A good tree cannot bring forth evil fruit, neither can a corrupt tree bring forth good fruit.

Every tree that bringeth not forth good fruit is hewn down, and cast into the fire.

Wherefore by their fruits ye shall know them.

Jesus tells us we can know people, specifically false prophets, by their fruits. What have they produced? What is the cause or motivation of their actions? Do they win people to the Lord or lead them astray from salvation through faith in Him?

Edgar Cayce is certainly not known for bringing people to salvation through Jesus Christ. He is most known for his large number of prophecies. Numbers vary on just how many prophecies and other writings Cayce produced, but they are usually counted as somewhere around twenty thousand. He also had a vast array of teachings on subjects including astral travel, the Akashic records, and reincarnation. Here is one source of interpretation of Cayce's teachings:

> Cayce predicted that the so-called "Battle of Armageddon" described symbolically in the Bible would begin in 1999. Cayce foresaw that this "battle" will not be a war fought on Earth. Rather, it will be a spiritual struggle between the "higher forces of light" and "lower forces of darkness" for 1000 years of Earth time. The reason for this struggle is to prevent souls from lower afterlife realms from reincarnating to Earth. By preventing souls from the lower afterlife realms from reincarnating to Earth, only enlightened souls will be permitted to reincarnate. The result will be 1000 years of building a world of peace and enlightenment. After 1000 years, souls from lower afterlife realms will be permitted once again to reincarnate to Earth. By this time, the so-called "kingdom of heaven" will have been established on Earth.[100]

This type of teaching is common in New Age theology; I (Josh) remember it quite well. However, we can see that New Age theology and Edgar Cayce's teachings are incompatible with those of the Bible. In this example, the first thing to point out is that the Battle of Armageddon did not begin in 1999. Also, nothing in the Scriptures signifies that this is meant to be understood as symbolic. The specific text, Revelation 16:16–21, reads:

And he gathered them together into a place called in the Hebrew tongue Armageddon.

And the seventh angel poured out his vial into the air; and there came a great voice out of the temple of heaven, from the throne, saying, It is done.

And there were voices, and thunders, and lightnings; and there was a great earthquake, such as was not since men were upon the earth, so mighty an earthquake, and so great.

And the great city was divided into three parts, and the cities of the nations fell: and great Babylon came in remembrance before God, to give unto her the cup of the wine of the fierceness of his wrath.

And every island fled away, and the mountains were not found.

And there fell upon men a great hail out of heaven, every stone about the weight of a talent: and men blasphemed God because of the plague of the hail; for the plague thereof was exceeding great.

Very literal language is used here. There is talk of angels, of course, but this is not an event happening in Heaven or in another spiritual location. We read about an earthly place called "Armageddon" in the Hebrew language, a physical earthquake, an earthly city, earthly islands, earthly mountains, earthly men, and hail falling on the Earth. These are all physical and literal things and events mentioned throughout the text. Therefore, if Cayce taught that the battle would not be on Earth, we have a choice: Believe Edgar Cayce or the Bible? Either the Bible contains the truth or it does not. Biblical teachings compared to Cayce's teachings offer no middle ground or compromise. We cannot believe Cayce got his prophecies from God or was a follower of Jesus if he is in fundamental disagreement with what the Bible is communicating.

Reincarnation plays a big role in the belief system taught by Cayce and other more modern New Age sources. However, Hebrews 9:27 states:

And as it is appointed unto men once to die, but after this the judgment.

Again, we have a choice: Are we going to believe Cayce or the Bible? The Bible teaches that once we die, our eternal choice is sealed. Either we have accepted Jesus or rejected Him. We have either followed God or we haven't. Cayce taught reincarnation. These beliefs cannot go hand in hand.

Then the question inevitably comes up: Did Edgar Cayce have prophesies that turned out to be true? Yes. In fact, he is regarded as one of the greatest worldly prophets because, based on certain estimations, he has a more than 80 percent accuracy rating. Does this mean he was a Christian or received wisdom from God? Quite simply, no. First, many of the prophecies were not anything that a computer couldn't predict based on the sociopolitical climate at the time he made these predictions.

Second, the Bible teaches that anything less than 100 percent accuracy in the realm of prophecy is unacceptable. In fact, in the ancient days of Israel, one false prophecy was enough to earn a "prophet" a death sentence. This is because any prophecy of God comes to pass exactly as it was stated. However, a prophecy from any other source never has that kind of accuracy. This is how we can tell whether a prophet is representing God. YHWH, the God of the Bible, takes prophecy very seriously. Jesus consistently warned against false prophets, and the Old Testament gives a method of determining whether a prophet is true or false. Deuteronomy 18:19–22 states:

And it shall come to pass, that whosoever will not hearken unto my words which he shall speak in my name, I will require it of him.

But the prophet, which shall presume to speak a word in my name, which I have not commanded him to speak, or that shall speak in the name of other gods, even that prophet shall die.

And if thou say in thine heart, How shall we know the word which the Lord hath not spoken?

When a prophet speaketh in the name of the Lord, if the thing follow not, nor come to pass, that is the thing which the Lord hath not spoken, but the prophet hath spoken it presumptuously: thou shalt not be afraid of him.

We have another contradiction between the Bible and Edgar Cayce's teachings. If Edgar Cayce is correct, why did he get some prophecies wrong and how do we explain his endorsement of, yet failure to follow, the teachings of the Bible? What we have is a major influencer on the New Age movement who was possessed by a spirit of divination, and while under the influence of this spirit, got some prophecies correct while simultaneously leading people to fundamentally reject Christ. True prophecies do not mean someone's worldview is correct, nor do they make someone a follower of Jesus (even if he or she professes His name).

Spirit Science, Lucifer, and Thoth

Spirit Science is arguably the largest New Age organization in the world, with 12 million Facebook likes, 1.1 million Instagram followers, and 720,000 YouTube subscribers. I (Steve) used to write for its website while I was involved in the New Age movement, and I was close friends with the founder for a season. Even though the organization revolves around an innocent-looking cartoon character named Patchman, Lucifer still makes an appearance by name in the *Human History Movie*, a video that has been viewed more than 3.5 million times. Here is an excerpted transcript from the video:

According to Thoth, Mars looked like earth a little less than a million years ago. It was beautiful, it had oceans and water and trees that were just fantastic. But something happened to them and it has to do with something called The Lucifer Experiment.... If Spirit decides to cut itself off from the rest of consciousness and create a separate reality on it's own, it can do that too. This is called The Lucifer Experiment. Because Spirit is God, it can do this. There is nothing wrong with that. We have kind of been led to believe that Lucifer is evil and the devil, this just isn't true. Lucifer is just another means of perceiving the reality.[101]

Additionally, an article from the website (which has since been deleted but was included in an exposé I did on the Satanic underpinnings of the New Age movement) further entertains Lucifer's fall from Heaven:

"The Lucifer Experiment," if you recall from the Human History Movie, was about a particular consciousness connected to the All who didn't want to play the same boring song. He wanted to be his own rockstar, and so he split himself off from the God-Source-Consciousness-Field and did his own thing, creating chaos and destruction in his wake.[102]

Lucifer shows up in the largest New Age organization in the world because the material of Spirit Science comes primarily from the work of a teacher named Drunvalo Melchizedek, who wrote *The Ancient Secret of the Flower of Life*, Volumes 1 and 2. The inspiration for the largest New Age website in the world is a publication that openly endorses Lucifer, just as the popularizers of New Age thought have done throughout history:

About a year ago, at the beginning of 1999, two new angels appeared together to me while I was about to give an Earth/

Sky workshop. It was none other than archangels Michael and Lucifer. They were holding hands.[103]

Lucifer did not create free will, but it was through his actions and decisions that free will became a reality. It was God who created Lucifer so that free will would exist.[104]

So, evidently with God's blessing (since He created him), Lucifer started on a great experiment to see what could be learned by creating in a different way from how God/Spirit had made the original creation.[105]

Lucifer told the angelic worlds that we needed to do this experiment because the universe had missing information, and the only way to get the information was to live it.[106]

A relief carving of the Egyptian god Thoth from the Temple of Ramesses II (1279–1213 BCE), Abydos

Drunvalo credits the ancient Egyptian and Greco-Roman deity named "Thoth," god of science, religion, philosophy, astrology, alchemy, and magic, and judge of souls in the afterlife, for giving him a great deal of the information he included in Volume 1.[107] He refers to Thoth well over a hundred times.

The trouble is, Thoth is well known within Satanism to be a demon-god. According to the Joy of Satan Ministries, "Thoth is one of the most active demons and is a crowned prince in Hell. … He is the busiest of all of the Demons and it can be difficult to get him to appear in a summoning unless one is of importance to him."[108]

Thoth makes appearances in the Necronomicon, a dangerous, pseudo-fictional magic textbook known for making its readers go literally insane.[109] Aleister Crowley wrote *The Book of Thoth*, which contains the magik of Thoth and ancient Egypt. It also outlines the philosophy of the Thoth tarot card deck he created for divination. Even the Satanic Bible lists Thoth as a demon and has a special invocation by which Satanists may conjure him for their purposes.[110]

Blavatsky also makes a link between Thoth and Satan in ancient Egypt: "Hermes, the god of wisdom, called also Thoth, Tat, Set, and Sat-an; and that he was, furthermore, when viewed under his bad aspect, Typhon, the Egyptian Satan, who was also Set."[111]

It's interesting that Thoth, the deity responsible for inspiring the most pervasive New Age ministry in the world, has been thought to be a demon for a very long time by high-ranking occultists. Yet in the *Spirit Science* cartoons, he has his own character made out to be cute and charismatic. What makes matters worse is what the New Age teachers themselves have to say about Thoth.

According to legend coming from channeled materials, Thoth started a colony in ancient Egypt at the beginning of Egyptian civilization after Atlantis sank following the fall of Atlantis roughly ten thousand years ago. He established himself as a high priest there. New Age anthropologist Dr. Sasha Lessin tells us that Thoth (under the name Ningishzidda) oversaw ancient Egypt starting in 8670 BCE and remained there until around 4350 BCE–3450 BCE before leaving Egypt.[112, 113] History tells us that first-dynasty Egypt practiced human sacrifice in the form of "retainers," in which servants were buried with their masters so they could serve them in the afterlife. But some evidence may suggest this practice carried over from predynastic Egypt as the Naqada II culture dwelt there in 3500 BC.[114] Thoth, as the god of religion and rituals and as the high priest of Egypt, would have been overseeing this religious practice, according to New Age mythology.

Other legends taught by Dr. Lessin indicate that Thoth brought civilization to the Mayans and appeared to them in the form of Quetzalcoatl, a feathered serpent to which the Mayans made human sacrifices.[115] The method of offering a sacrifice to Quetzalcoatl was to cut someone open while they were alive, pull out their heart, and offer it up as a sacrifice. This was arguably the most brutal culture in history in terms of human sacrifice, and New Age teachers tell us it was founded by the same deity who taught Drunvalo his material (which inspired Spirit Science).

Thoth also apparently helped start the Sumerian culture and was known to them as Ningishzida, a serpentine god of the underworld whom the Simon Necronomicon reveres as "the horned serpent, the lady of the magick wand" and "the serpent of the deep."[116, 117] Sir Leonard Woolley was a excavator of the famous ancient Mesopotamian city of Ur in Sumeria.[118] There, among more than 1,800 tombs, he found sixteen elaborate, "royal" tombs, one of which contained the remains of more than seventy human sacrificial victims piled on top of each other.[119] This site later became known as the Great Death Pit, inspired by Thoth's handiwork as overseer and author of the Sumerian culture, according to New Age material.

New Age legends seem to place Thoth in time periods when, as the god of religious ritual, he would have been literally implementing the practice of human sacrifice. Remember, this false deity known as a demon in modern Satanism inspired the material that sparked the most popular New Age teaching series and website in the world. The Bible warns that people will be led astray in the final days by the teachings of demons (1 Timothy 4:1), and it appears that we may have a perfect example of that with the Thoth-Spirit Science connection.

Occultism, Satanism, and New Age Connected

As we have seen, the most popular influencers in the history of the New Age movement are practitioners in Theosophy (Luciferianism) or some form of Satanism. The ideas and themes of the New Age are the same ideas taught in spiritual Satanism, which are the same ones that Helena

Blavatsky and Aleister Crowley advocated alongside a Satanic philosophy, and are the very concepts that Anton Levay accused the New Age of stealing from the devil.

There have been longtime efforts to introduce Satanism into Christianity through New Age, and as we will see later on, some of these efforts have been somewhat successful. As Anton LaVey helped point out, New Age was nothing more than a more culturally acceptable Satanism repackaged with a bow of post-modernism for a twenty-first-century audience.

The fact is, however, occultism, Satanism, and New Age leaders and adherents do not have any way to prove their claims. Yes, these beliefs are overtly dangerous because of their origin (and persistence) in Luciferianism, and they are dangerous because of the demonic spiritual reality that lies behind them when put into practice, but they are also dangerous because they simply do not correspond with reality. Satan's method to cause man to fall wasn't just to teach something different, it was to teach something false. A Satanic idea that deviates from the truth is the most dangerous one there is.

As with anything in life, there are consequences to being wrong. If I don't think that I have a physical disease that is slowly eating away at my body because someone convinced me there is no such thing as disease, my false belief would be contributing to my destruction. Believing the truth matters in the immediate and even more so in light of eternity. We have already clearly established spiritual dangers of the movement and will continue to throughout the book, but another category of danger is that the New Age makes claims that can easily be proven false in light of science, reason, history, and Scripture.

We can easily prove the claims it makes range anywhere from wrong to self-defeating to impossible. Some claims are so far removed from reality that the only way to make them tolerable is to revise what it means for something to be "true" in the first place. In the last few decades in particular, there has been a massive attack on the "truth" as a concept, and this resuls in an anti-truth attitude with no concern for the accuracy of ideas. This, along with the previous aforementioned dangers, has caused incalculable harm to New Age practitioners and our society as a whole.

4

SCIENCE FALSELY SO CALLED

"For this purpose I was born and for this purpose I have come into the world—to bear witness to the truth. Everyone who is of the truth listens to my voice." Pilate said to him, "What is truth?"

JOHN 18:37–38

"Truth...What Is Truth?"

What is truth? Truth, as Jesus reveals in this verse, is what He came into the world to bear witness to. This may not seem to reveal much about the nature of "truth" itself, but if we look closely, we learn a few things about the epistemology of Christ. Epistemology is the study of knowledge and truth, so when Pilate asks "What is truth?" he is asking an epistemic question. First, in order for Jesus to "bear witness" to the truth, the truth must exist in a meaningful way that can be discussed. Jesus would be unable to bear witness to something with no existence, for that which has no existence cannot be evidenced or spoken of. Jesus believed that truth exists. This is basic enough.

Now, does this truth exist subjectively in a personal sense relative to the individual or objectively in a way that stands wholly apart from personal feeling and opinion? This truth must exist in a way that is objective, according to Jesus. By "objective," we mean that the truth exists in a concrete manner independent of anybody's opinion.

To say that 2 + 2 = 4 is an objective truth is to say that 2 + 2 = 4 even if you and everyone you know is convinced that 2 + 2 = 5. We know that Jesus believed in an objective notion of truth because truth was what He came to bear witness to. To "bear witness" means "to show that something exists or is true."[120] It means to "testify" or "provide evidence" that something is the case.

In this verse, Jesus is not in the business of encouraging each person to find his or her version of the truth, but He seeks to testify about something that is in fact the truth. You can't "bear witness" to something you believe depends on the opinion of the person you're speaking to. You can't bear witness to a subjective preference that can vary from person to person.

You can't provide proof that vanilla ice cream is tastier than chocolate ice cream. You may have the personal *opinion* that vanilla tastes better, but it's not anchored to reality as a concrete truth about the world that someone discovers. It's a personal preference—unless, of course, you wanted to show that your preferences *reflect* objective truth about something, in which case you would graduate from relativity to the realm of objectivity because you are now trying to bear witness about the way things truly are.

Anything that follows the words "bear witness" in a sentence implies, by definition, that the speaker believes what he or she is saying corresponds to reality. Jesus makes it clear that He is not interested in sharing His personal feelings about the truth; He is interested in "bearing witness" to a state of affairs in the world, something that cannot be done if "truth" is in the eye of the beholder. The objective opinion/independent nature of truth is the second takeaway point from this passage.

Third, there are those who are "of the truth" and those who are not. Those who listen to the voice of Jesus are on the side of truth, and those who reject His voice are in opposition to the truth. Jesus tells us that the truth is dichotomous. A person can't be in the truth and out of the truth at the same time. To agree with the witness Jesus bears about the truth is to be "of" the truth, and to disagree with Him is to be in untruth. This further supports the idea that Jesus believed truth was objective. Jesus says that some things are truth and some are not. Some people believe the truth and some people believe falsehoods. Not every person believes correctly.

Fourth, Jesus believed that He held divine authority from another world to deliver the truth to us. "His voice" is the standard and revelation of truth itself. If Pilate had analyzed the words of Jesus a little more, he would have found out that the truth is the objective revelation of Jesus about the way things are that we have the ability to come into agreement with and so be in the truth. This is called the "correspondence theory of truth," which is the view "that truth is correspondence to, or with, a fact."[121] Simply put, there is an external world with a real "state of affairs" consisting of facts and events. Apart from the human mind, there is a real world. A true proposition is one that expresses an accurate reflection of the real world. Not only did Jesus believe this, but the Bible as a whole teaches that to believe the "truth" is to believe accurately about the way things are.

- "I did not speak in secret, in a land of darkness; I did not say to the offspring of Jacob, 'Seek me in vain.' **I the LORD speak the truth; I declare what is right**" (Isaiah 45:19, emphasis added).
- "**For my mouth will utter truth;** wickedness is an abomination to my lips" (Proverbs 8:7, emphasis added).
- "A truthful witness saves lives, but one who breathes out lies is deceitful" (Proverbs 14:25).
- "**Everyone deceives his neighbor And does not speak the truth,** They have taught their tongue to speak lies; They weary themselves committing iniquity" (Jeremiah 9:5, emphasis added).
- "Sanctify them in the truth; **your word is truth**" (John 17:17, emphasis added).

To speak the truth is to declare what is right. "The Grand Canyon exists" is a true claim because it corresponds to a fact about reality, whereas the claim that "dogs can fly" does not correspond to reality and is therefore false. "Mammals have body hair" is a true claim, whereas "the moon is made of cheese" is not. If someone were to say that the moon is made of cheese, that person would be saying something that is demonstrably false, because it does not correspond with the state of affairs of the moon being made of rock.

For a claim to be true, it must reflect the way things actually are in the world. To be in the truth is to believe accurately about the way things really are, and to be in untruth is to believe incorrectly about the way things really are. Truth is something we align ourselves with, not something we create for ourselves. It's something we discover, not something we fashion. Your research is premised upon the idea that some things really are true and some things really are false. You hope that by reading this book, you will come to believe more true things and less false things about God, spirituality, and the New Age movement. Even the *Oxford Dictionary* defines something to be "true" if it is "in accordance with fact or reality."[122] So why is it necessary to define truth?

We must define truth because this blatantly obvious view of truth is virtually universally rejected within the New Age movement. I (Steve) had never heard the correspondence theory of truth defended in interacting with tens of thousands of people online. Taken to the literal extreme, there are theories of truth held in the New Age movement that allow the claim "the moon is made of cheese" to be "true for them," despite the fact that those saying that could be holding a piece of moon rock in their hands and be able to see it's not *actually* cheese.

In the New Age movement, truth is in the eye of the beholder. What is "true" for one person may not be "true" for the next, because "truth" is up to each individual to define and create. The sky is the limit. How you define "truth" is up to you. What justifies or warrants a belief is up to you. There is no real sense in which truth can be spoken of, and nobody can step into another person's world and tell that person what he or she believes is false. That person might believe a "different truth," but the belief isn't incorrect. It's an epistemic free-for-all.

This means that everything Jesus came to reveal to us has been rendered void right out of the gate because the very foundation of His mission (truth) has been undermined by false theories of truth so as to make all of His claims vacuous and immaterial. If truth is up to each person to define and fashion individually, the words of Jesus are no more significant than the words of your atheistic grandmother. Why should we value the words of Jesus over the words of Buddha if truth is determined by the subjectivity of the hearer?

If there is no set of facts about the world to which Christ's teachings ultimately correspond, then we have no reason to value anything He says. If following Christ over Buddha, Gandhi, or Oprah won't bring us any closer to the truth but only serve to help us construct a worldview that suits our preferences, then what makes Jesus' teachings so special? We are free to cherry pick from all the teachings we like and disregard those we don't, since both sets of teachings are neither true nor false. They simply exist as subjective points of view able to be adopted or rejected according to each person's liking.

This is also dangerous, because it removes Jesus' attribute of omniscience (ability to be all-knowing). Knowledge has been classically defined as being a "justified true belief." For Jesus to have all knowledge, He would have to be justified in believing every true proposition that exists. It would not make sense for Jesus (or the Father) to possess all knowledge if knowledge is a "justified true belief" and "truth" doesn't exist. Sure, there might be a general set of claims that Jesus holds in particular and believes to be His own truth, but these beliefs of His aren't *actually* true. They are justified by virtue of the fact that He is convinced in His own mind of them, but they don't *really* correspond to the world.

Jesus might be able to create a system of knowledge in His own mind that works for Him, but He wouldn't be able to possess the truth in any real sense if it doesn't exist apart from His own psychology. Jesus would, at most, be justified in believing in one of many different versions of reality that we are free to agree or disagree with without any epistemic concern for accuracy. The truth that exists in the mind of Jesus is no more valuable or correct than the "truth" in the mind of Judas or of Lucifer.

All of the Bible verses about the character of God, the function of the cross, the necessity of faith in Jesus for salvation, the reality of Heaven and Hell, and all other claims made in Scripture lose significance the minute we determine that "truth" is something other than correspondence with reality. If "truth" is something we construct inside our consciousness instead of something outside of us that we discover, then the words of Jesus lose all authority and significance. Jesus had His opinion and you have yours. Correspondence with reality doesn't matter; what matters is how this belief serves you and feels when you decide to subscribe to it.

The Devil's Plan from the Beginning

It should not surprise us that the New Age movement all but removes truth from the equation of spirituality, as the devil's plan from the beginning has always been to attack the standard of truth. The first move Satan ever pulled on mankind was to try to persuade Eve to reject something she knew was legitimately true because it had been spoken by God.

If Satan could get Eve to doubt the objective standard of truth (God's Word), call into question the idea that the Word of God corresponds with reality, and convince her to pursue knowledge elsewhere, he could get her to act against the truth and reap the consequences. God had just said if Adam and Eve ate the fruit from the Tree of Knowledge of Good and Evil, they would die. Satan's question to Eve shortly afterward, recorded in Genesis 3, was: "Did God actually say you can't eat of any tree:... You will not surely die" (vv. 2, 5).

Satan asks Eve to question something about which she already knows the answer, and then tries to tell her that God does not want her and Adam to eat the fruit from the tree, because if they do so, they will become like Him, knowing good and evil (v. 5). Satan undermined Eve's confidence in the Word of God, which implied a correspondence theory of truth, and encouraged her to pursue truth in a subjective experience of eating fruit from a tree.

Satan's bait to lure Adam and Eve away from an objective standard was to promise that their experience in eating fruit from the tree would become the new objective standard. The standard of truth shifted from God's mind to man's mind, from transcendent objectivity to personal subjectivity. And Satan's whole means of doing this was to get the couple to consider that eating from the tree would be pragmatic. It would serve them well and bear utility in their lives, as if to imply that the highest pursuit should be the practical application of something and not its correspondence with reality. You can almost hear Satan saying, "Are you really sure God meant that? Even if He did, God's Word is not the objective standard of truth. In fact, there is no objective standard of truth apart from the experience you can have by doing what God said not to. If you look for your *own* truth in your own experience, you can become like God, and He doesn't want you to be like Him. You can become the standard of truth for yourself, if only you eat from the tree. Your own mind will expand through acquired knowledge, and when it expands, you will no longer need the Word of God because you can equip yourself with everything you need through direct spiritual experience."

Satan's method was as follows:

1. Cause Adam and Eve to doubt their confidence in something God had just said.
2. Overthrow the Word of God as correspondence with reality.
3. Encourage Eve to seek truth and knowledge in subjectivity, apart from an objective standard, as if personal revelation held more authority than divine revelation.
4. Urge them to desire what may serve them rather than what is true.

5. Lie about what the consequences would be of deviating from correspondence with reality.

This is the same kind of epistemic perversion we see in the New Age movement. The ground of truth (correspondence to reality) is being undermined, and people are being encouraged to find their own version of the truth through experience and judge such "truth" in terms of its apparent usefulness. Satan was the first to teach that man could be God, but he was also the first to teach that God was wrong and people should search for the truth in whatever expands their consciousness. If it broadens the landscape of your paradigm, it must be held in higher regard than the actual truth.

There are three different theories of truth advocated in the New Age movement that are helpful to become familiar with and learn how to refute. After all, if any of these notions of truth are correct, then the words of Jesus are relative and inconsequential, and nothing the Bible says holds any weight.

The Pragmatic Theory of Truth

The pragmatic theory of truth says truth is that which is useful and beneficial (pragmatic) for any given individual. The truth is that which serves you. We can determine whether a statement is true by considering its practical consequences. Pragmatist William James framed "truth" in the following way:

> Ideas…become true just in so far as they help us to get into satisfactory relations with other parts of our experience.… Any idea upon which we can ride…; any idea that will carry us prosperously from any one part of our experience to any other part, linking things satisfactorily, working securely, saving labor; is true for just so much, true in so far forth, true instrumentally.[123]

According to the *Stanford Encyclopedia of Philosophy*, the pragmatic theory of truth can take the form of defining truth as that which enhances our quality of life. "If religious belief makes me feel better, then that can contribute to the pragmatic clarification of 'God exists....' This suggests that a belief can be made true by the fact that holding it contributes to our happiness and fulfillment."[124]

In other words, a belief can be said to be true based on how practical it is for us to hold that belief. For example, Alcoholics Anonymous believes it is psychologically advantageous to believe in a version of God that fits whatever definition and characteristics the alcoholics want. They are told to pray to God as "they understand him" for the purpose of psycho-emotional recovery, even if everyone in the room holds contradictory views of who this God is. If believing in a supernatural therapy partner named "Big Dipper" is soothing to one's sense of welfare and adds value to his or her life, it can be said that this version of God is "true" for that individual.

Or perhaps someone in the New Age movement believes that he or she existed prior to birth and specifically chose in advance all the abuse he or she was going to suffer in this life for the development of that person's own soul. Many people believe this and experience a great sense of release by imagining all their suffering was chosen by them for a definite purpose. If this belief offered considerable pragmatic benefit (such as freedom from depression, anxiety, or trauma), it would all of a sudden acquire a new truth-value independent of whether it corresponds to anything on the other side of the veil.

A claim's truth-value is generated by the psychological impact and pragmatic value a belief has on a subject. As philosopher Bertrand Russell put it, "It is only after we have decided that the effects of a belief are good that we have a right to call it 'true.'"[125]

This is a demonstrably false theory of truth. People hold pragmatically helpful beliefs that seem to be "true" given the initial effects of the belief, but that turn out to be dangerously false. For example, the belief used to be that smoking cigarettes was actually healthy, with doctor-recommended brands being the smoke of choice.

The following ad claims that smoking a certain brand of cigarettes has absolutely no negative health impacts according to a recent study. Other ads attributed cigarettes with aiding digestion, speeding up weight loss, and curing colds.

Misleading cigarette advertisement

Remember, truth is not defined in this model by what is actually true, but by what is believed beneficial to the individual. For one to believe smoking was healthy was to open doors of pleasure and benefit beyond previous experience.

By believing smoking was healthy, smokers had no guilt, shame, or anxiety about their habit. In fact, their psychological and emotional health was greatly elevated, because they believed smoking was healthy. This belief enhanced their social lives as well: Families could smoke together and bond over a pack of Camels without any fear of what they were doing to their bodies. "Smoking is good for you" was a pragmatic belief for smokers.

Did the emotional pleasure and psychological satisfaction that came from believing smoking was healthy mean that the belief that smoking was healthy was true? Did the enhanced attitude of the smokers somehow cause the toxicity of cigarettes to vanish? Did peace of con-science coming from believing smoking is harmless mean that smoking is indeed harmless?

Of course not. Believing smoking was healthy served smokers greatly in a pragmatic sense given the knowledge available at the time. Accord-ing to this theory of truth, smoking greatly enhanced their lives and could therefore be said to be healthy. Of course, we have since learned that smoking is one of the deadliest habits in the world, killing around six million people each year.[126] One problem with the pragmatic theory of truth is that we often don't know what the utility of a belief is ahead of time. We don't always have perfect access to the full consequences of a belief in the moment. It may be serving us to the best of our knowledge while slowly killing us in ways that are hidden.

For example, it might be immediately beneficial to one's existen-tial welfare to believe that 100 percent of people spend an eternity in Heaven regardless of how they choose to believe and behave. It's not psychologically advantageous to believe that loved ones who reject the Gospel face the eternal judgment of God. People in the New Age move-ment often reject the notion of Hell on the grounds that it makes them feel afraid and gives them a sense of doom. They often don't inquire about how a belief in Hell corresponds to the state of affairs in the world and immediately reject the belief on the grounds that it impedes on their psycho-emotional well-being.

The desire for existential relief may cause people to reject the Gos-pel, and in exchange receive a certain level of peace and security pertain-ing to their future and the future of those they love. But by rejecting the Gospel for existential relief, they condemn themselves to an eternity of destruction where the apparent and initial utility of their rejection of Hell will prove to be falsely calculated. The consequences of the belief do not appear in their fullness until after it is too late to reassess the practi-cal consequences of that belief. They choose to judge the idea of Hell in terms of the effect that their belief about Hell has on their lives, rather than on whether there is good reason to believe in Hell. But the problem is they aren't *really* able to judge the effects this belief has on their life as a whole.

Our limitations in time and space in the natural realm can cause us to view utility through a very narrow lens and cause us to misjudge the pragmatic implications of a particular belief. A seemingly pragmatic belief may turn out to be eternally destructive. Our cognitive limitations in calculating the full implications of a belief make such judgments of pragmatism near impossible in some instances. There are some things we simply cannot know ahead of time. Yet, the New Age movement tells us to find what "works for us," even though what "works for us" right this second might have eternal consequences in the next second. This is why we need to define truth in terms of what conforms to reality, not according to what serves us.

Likewise, many true facts about the world serve no pragmatic benefit. Not everything that is true is useful or helpful to believe, which is proof that we cannot judge truth based on its usefulness. Pragmatism and truth are not necessarily identical, for many true things are useless to believe. Consider the following beliefs that are true but are void of all utility.

1. Donald Trump has (x) number of hairs on his left arm right now.
2. There is a speck of dust fifty feet below the surface of the ninety-five thousandth crater on the moon.
3. Somewhere in the world today, an ant was born and died before it had lived for one full day.

These beliefs are true despite serving absolutely no benefit to those who hold them. If beliefs are true despite offering no pragmatic value, then pragmatic value is not what gives something its truth value. We can think of many such beliefs that lack practical utility but still maintain their truth, which shows that pragmatic benefit is not identical to truth. The pragmatic theory puts an unjustified confidence in our ability to determine the utility of a belief from our limited cognitive /

spatio-temporal constraints and fails to account for a vast number of true propositions that lack pragmatic significance.

Clearly, something is not true just because it "works" for you and adds value to your life. Something may happen to be true that adds value to your life, but it doesn't *become* true simply because it adds value. It's true first and adds value second (if at all). The New Age movement operates from this principle in reverse, wherein a belief adds value first and hence becomes true secondarily to its effects. This is the first false theory of knowledge that pervades New Age circles.

The Coherence Theory of Truth

In the New Age movement, truth is generally defined as that which "resonates" with you. I (Steve) would be unable to count the number of times I have heard this phrase used in the community. "I understand where you are coming from, but that idea just doesn't resonate with me." By "resonate," they mean something that seems palatable and intuitive and that meshes well with their current path in life or paradigm. Even if your belief does not correspond with reality, it can be "true for you" if it fits well within your current set of beliefs and attitudes about the world.

One New Age blogger defines "resonance" as meaning "to be aligned with, at the same frequency of, sharing a vibration, and is a term that has defines our new ways of connecting with each other."[127] This is the essence of New Age epistemology. Something "resonates" if it is aligned with your life and seems as though it is on the same wavelength as you, which is a layman's way of saying that something is true if it coheres well with the beliefs and attitudes you already hold. In philosophy, this is called the "coherence theory of truth." A statement becomes true if it is appropriate to hold in light of the other beliefs in your paradigm, even if it doesn't correspond to reality.

Philosophers William Lane Craig and J. P. Moreland define "coherence theory of truth" the following way:

According to the coherence theory, a belief (statement, proposition, etc.) is true if and only if it coheres well with the entire set of one's beliefs, assuming that the set is itself a strongly coherent one. Thus the truth or falsity of a belief is not a matter of its match with a real, external world. Rather, it is a function of the belief's relationship with other beliefs within one's web of beliefs.... Since truth is an adequate coherence of a belief with an appropriate set of beliefs, when a belief is justified by way of a coherence account, it is automatically true. Truth is a matter of a belief's internal relations with one's other beliefs, not its external relations with reality outside the system of beliefs itself.[128]

If you have a current set of beliefs, you are justified in believing (x) is true by virtue of the fact that (x) blends well into what you already believe to be true. If Jimmy Smith believed he was a coffee table, that coffee tables were conscious, that his bones were made of wood, and that there was a conspiracy against all coffee tables to convince them that they are really not coffee tables and everyone around him was systematically lying, Jimmy's beliefs about himself could be said to be true by virtue of its overall coherence and consistency.

If Sarah Jones wanted to believe that she was an alien hybrid, that some species of aliens visited her in UFOs for the purpose of evolving the consciousness of the planet, and that she had aliens appearing to her in dreams as a child telling her that she was one of them, then her belief that she will be transported back to her original planet in a spaceship when she dies fits well with her other beliefs and can therefore be said to be true, even if it's not true in actuality.

This theory of truth is usually blended with the pragmatic theory of truth to give a system of beliefs that both serve you and "resonate" well with your current convictions. As New Age teacher Teal Swan has stated:

Your life should be a unique cocktail of what resonates with you. It should not contain any ingredients that do not resonate with you. Sometimes those very same ingredients that work for you, will work for other people too, but the ingredients aren't what matters as much as the mixture of ingredients which adds up to your specific and unique recipe of well being.[129]

The New Age movement by and large determines truth on the basis of the effects and coherence of a belief with the other beliefs the person holds. We have already seen why pragmatism is a false theory of knowledge: Beliefs that "add to your specific and unique recipe of well being" are not necessarily true, and true beliefs are not necessary pragmatic, demonstrating that truth and pragmatism are not identical. But what about the coherence model?

This view is obviously false for a few reasons. For one, there are some propositions that we know are false and nobody actually believes, despite the fact that they cohere well with other propositions. The statement "the moon is made of blue cheese" could be true for an individual who had been raised believing that Dr. Seuss books were accounts of history. If some people were terribly brainwashed into believing that all the planets were made up of different foods because they had been read children's books their whole lives by people who legitimately convinced them this was so, then their belief that the moon is made of blue cheese would be a true belief due to its coherence with their other beliefs.

There is a set of propositions out there that would cohere well with the belief that "the moon is made of cheese," but there is also a set of beliefs that corresponds with the belief that "the moon is made of rock." Virtually everyone believes the latter, and nobody would believe the former despite the existence of an obscure set of propositions that could deem this belief coherent and therefore true. Some statements cohere well with others and are demonstrably false, indicating that coherence is not identical to truth.

We can clearly see that this model doesn't take into account how far removed someone's beliefs are from the external world. It does not consider what exists in the world and relies solely on the relationship between beliefs in a person mind. There doesn't need to be an actual relationship between a belief and the world, only a relationship between a belief and other beliefs. If your theory of truth forces you to disregard the world right in front of you as having any bearing on your beliefs, it's time to go back to the drawing board.

But the biggest problem with this theory of truth as exhibited in the New Age movement is that it allows for two sets of contradictory beliefs to be held simultaneously "true." "Jesus was the Son of God" can be believed by one person, and this can be true for him because of how it coheres with his other beliefs gathered from the New Testament. The belief that "Jesus was not the Son of God" can be said to be true for the Muslim, because this belief coheres well with the witness of the Quran.

"Jesus was a Buddhist" coheres well with another set of beliefs, "Jesus was a gnostic" coheres well with another, and "Jesus never existed" coheres with another. Since correspondence to fact is not what determines whether something is true, all these beliefs can be held as true if the person holding them subscribes to a paradigm in which this belief meshes well.

Five people can hold five mutually exclusive beliefs about Jesus, and all can congratulate one another on finding the truth at the same time, even though each belief explicitly negates the other four. This is obviously a serious problem and defies logic itself. Two contradictory sentences cannot be true at the same time, let alone five of them. "Jesus is (x)" can be both true and false at the same time in this model, which is enough to render this model useless. If a sentence can be said to be both true and false simultaneously, we are worse off than where we started.

So far, we have seen that something is not true just because it appears to be useful, and something is not true just because it "resonates well" with other beliefs. So we now approach a third theory of knowledge that is so far removed from reality that it doesn't even believe there is a reality.

Postmodernism

Postmodernism is a philosophy that underpins the very heart of New Age thought and practice that is known for rejecting the following ideas:

1. Objective truth
2. Objective reasoning
3. Objective morality
4. Objective reality
5. Accurate definitions / meanings of words
6. Authoritative texts

There is no one way the world *really* is because we cannot separate reality from the language we use to describe it. Everything we think about, everything we value, and everything we talk about is socially constructed ideas that are impossible to consider as they actually exist. We can't speak of "God" as He actually is since our only frame of reference is a collection of ideas and theories that have been shaped by our culture and language. Because of this, the Gospel of John, for example, cannot be said to be a Christian text. There is a Christian Gospel of John, a kabbalist Gospel of John, a Marxist Gospel of John, a gnostic Gospel of John, and a Buddhist Gospel of John, etc.

Culture and language make it so that there is no "God's-eye view of things" for any text or claim. There are relative ways of understanding, and no person's understanding is more valid than the next. Even if one perspective is more valid than the next, there is no way to know which one is more valid because postmodernists believe that there is no legitimate way by which we can judge between competing worldviews.

The claims of Jesus, the claims of Buddha, and the claims of Krishna are up in the air for each person to pick and choose from for his or her own liking. There is no one way of interpreting words that is any more valid than the next, and there is no way to objectively discern which prophet has the actual truth.

There is no actual truth, and if there was, there is no way to get there. Everything is relative to the individual. No single worldview is true for everyone. There are just worldviews shaped by language and culture, and even the worldview that we do we believe in cannot be believed in with certainty.

"There is no truth" is the motto, and therefore "do as thou wilt," as Aleister Crowley famously said, becomes inevitable moral code. One problem with Postmodernism renders it absolutely false before it can even get off the ground: It is self-refuting.

"There is no truth" is a self-contradiction. If there is no truth, then the statement "there is no truth" is false. If the statement is false, then truth exists. In order for the statement "there is no truth" to be true, "truth" must in fact exist in the first place, which means the statement itself is self-refuting because it says that there is no truth. The principle of postmodernism cannot conform to its own standard and is therefore unworthy of intellectual assent.

"There is no truth" implies objective truth, objective reasoning used to discover this objective truth, an objective reality this truth corresponds to, and accurate / objective meanings to words. Postmodernism defeats itself. Everything cannot be relative, for the claim that everything is relative defeats itself.

Inference to the Best Explanation

The New Age movement has overthrown what it means for something to be "true," so much so as to make the words of Jesus inconsequential. It doesn't matter what Jesus said if He wasn't speaking the truth. If He was just speaking *a* truth among many others, there is no justification for saying He is the only way to God.

Touching on the issue of "justification," the New Age movement has also done away with every method we normally use to assess truth claims. Every practice, every principle, and every system we have used to verify statements over the course of human history gets virtually thrown out, especially at a popular level.

There is something called "inference to the best explanation," which is a reasoning process we use every single day in our lives. If we live in a full house and see that a light has been left on in the garage, we infer that someone from the house must have been in the garage and left the light on. We don't infer that the light is broken and turned on by itself, or that a burglar broke in to turn the light on and then leave, or that a spirit from another realm turned it on as a practical joke. We infer the best explanation available out of the options we have currently available and that act in accordance with that explanation.

The New Age movement attempts to explain the phenomenon of *deja vu*. When an experience or a personal encounter feels strikingly familiar, New Agers are quick to assume this is the smoking gun indicating a past-life connection. It *must* be the case that they experienced something similar to this in a past life or that they knew this soul from their "soul group" they studied with before incarnating to Earth.

Why would an experience of familiarity with someone or something warrant us to believe this is evidence of an experience we had in a past life? Well, it doesn't. There are far better, simpler explanations that account for the same data that don't require us to bring in so many new unsubstantiated beliefs into the equation. There are seven criteria accepted by philosophers as contributing to something being the best explanation for a body of data. Few (if any) are upheld in the New Age movement:

1. *Explanatory scope.* The best explanation will explain the most amount of data compared to other explanations.
2. *Explanatory power.* The best explanation will explain the data effectively.
3. *Simplicity.* The best explanation will not multiply causes beyond what is necessary.

4. *Plausibility.* The best hypothesis is implied by truths we already accept. It's implied by what we already know.

5. *Degree of ad hocness.* The best explanation will involve fewer new suppositions about the world and will fit well into beliefs already accepted.

6. *Accord with accepted beliefs.* When we combine the best explanation with what we accept to already be true, it will result in few falsehoods.

7. *Comparative superiority.* The best explanation will meet criteria 1–6 better than rival explanations.

The Bigfoot phenomenon, for example, is thought-provoking to some and humorous to others, but to be intellectually responsible, we ought to infer the best explanation that complies with the following criteria. We have to look at incidents on a case-by-case basis. Certainly there could be biblically defined supernatural manifestations (demons) behind some sightings, but generally speaking, the evidence seems sufficient on the grounds of Bigfoot sightings as hoaxes, as being certain species of apes or other animals, or as being an unknown/lost species of giant sloths.

The New Age movement puts forth that Bigfoot creatures inhabited by the interdimensional spirits of a highly developed intelligent race once lived on a planet Maldek almost a million years ago. They incarnated here in apelike, Bigfoot bodies a half million years ago to alleviate karma from their previous lives. They are inhabited by the spirits of dead extraterrestrials, and this is held to be true because a self-identified alien explained this through a woman while she was in a trance.[130]

This explanation fails on the grounds of simplicity, because it attributes the sightings to an unnecessary number of causes and a complex back story. We can simply say it's an ape, not an ex-alien spirit inside the ape. Everything is explained just as powerfully but more simply if we leave out the latter part of the equation. We don't need additional causes to explain the effect.

Occam's Razor is a principle that says the best explanation is the simplest with the most explanatory scope and power, so any unnecessary causes can be shaved off if they aren't needed. It fails on the grounds of plausibility because this belief is not implied by anything we know to be true about the world. No belief would imply so strongly that it's an alien spirit in an ape body that we need not investigate it further.

It also fails on the grounds of being too ad hoc because it smuggles in a host of new suppositions that we don't know to be true (such as the existence of other life-permitting planets and other species of intelligent life, reincarnation, certain spiritual laws, etc.). This explanation, if true, implies a ton of falsehoods in science and history and therefore does not accord well with accepted beliefs. And it certainly doesn't outperform other explanations (such as the sightings possibly being a hoax or a different species of primate) in categories 1–6.

We are therefore unjustified in believing such an explanation when other, better explanations are available. This is what differentiates a valid inference from an invalid one. Truth is that which corresponds to reality, but when it comes to trying to *discern* the truth, we have to infer the best explanation from the evidence available. The best explanation is one that is simplest and explains the most amount of data most powerfully without smuggling in a new suppositions about reality that go against what we currently know and accept to be true.

If the New Age movement consented to the correspondence theory of truth and valued the process of inferring to the best explanation, many of the beliefs and explanations would not only be overturned, but would have no epistemic legs to stand on in the first place. This is because many New Age beliefs and practices lack evidence or oppose evidence. The best explanation is one that best explains the evidence, not the one that is void of evidence.

For example, the multimillion dollar crystal industry is built upon the claim that crystals either have intrinsic healing abilities or can act as healing wands to channel energy. Those who participate in crystal healing derive this idea primarily from the "feelings" they get when crystals are used on them, which they describe as being a vibrating, energetic pulse emanating from the crystal outward. An entire pseudo-science is based around the mechanisms of crystal healing, with programs, classes, and books sold to promote crystal healing despite that there is not a shred of evidence to suggest that crystals work in this way. One New Age book describes the process in the following terms:

> When we bring the crystal into our electromagnetic field, two things occur. The electromagnetic frequencies carried by the stone will vibrate with related frequencies in our own energy field through the physical law of resonance, creating a third larger vibration field. The nervous system is attuned to these shifts in energy and transmits this information to the brain. Here the frequencies stimulate biochemical shifts that affect the physical body and shift brain function.[131]

Psychologist Dr. Christopher French and colleagues from the University of London conducted a study to determine if crystal healing was legitimate. The researchers asked eighty participants to fill out a questionnaire to indicate how open they were to the supernatural, and then asked them to meditate with a crystal in their hand. Some of these crystals were real and others were fake. Before meditating, the participants were asked to observe any tingling or energy running through their hand when they were holding the crystal.

After they finished meditating, those being surveyed answered another questionnaire in which they recorded any effects they had felt from holding the crystal. Those who held real crystals experienced no greater effects than those who held the fake ones. There was no difference in the reactions generated by the two types of crystal. This suggests that what participants feel in their hand is the general atomic energy of the object, or is completely generated in the mind of the subject.

Additionally, those who were more open to supernatural phenomena experienced more sensation in their hand, as did those who were primed and encouraged more by the person conducting the study. "We found that lots of people claimed that they could feel odd sensations while holding the crystals, such as tingling, heat and vibrations, if we'd told them in advance that this is what might happen," remarked Dr. French. "In other words, the effects reported were a result of the power of suggestion, not the power of the crystals."[132]

"There is no evidence that crystal healing works over and above a placebo effect," said Dr. French to Live Science. "That is the appropriate standard to judge any form of treatment. But whether or not you judge crystal healing, or any other form of [complementary and alternative medicine], to be totally worthless depends upon your attitude to placebo effects."[133]

So what is the explanation for the "crystal healing" phenomenon that best meets the criteria we've already looked at? What explanation has the most power and scope while being the most plausible and simple, without implying a whole host of new suppositions? The best explanation is that the power of the mind to impact the body is what gave rise to the sensation and degree of sensation in the subjects' hands, and that "crystal healing" can be boiled down to a classic case of the placebo effect. The New Age movement neglects inference by putting preference above correspondence with reality, and so has rightfully been dubbed as being "woo-woo" and "snake oil" in some of its beliefs in practices such as crystal healing.

Open-Minded, Not Mindless

Shouldn't we be open to new ways of thinking and of looking at the world? We should strive to be open-minded, but this doesn't mean we should be so open-minded that our brains fall out. It does not mean that we should be open to self-defeating philosophies or scientifically and historically unverifiable claims. Being open-minded means to be willing to follow the evidence where it leads, regardless of how it makes us feel. That's all it means. It means being willing to follow the evidence.

To believe a scientific claim that has been proven false is not "open-minded," it is unjustified. There is a scientific method in place in place to test the claim in a demonstrable way using instruments and experimentation, and if a hypothesis fails the test, it is to be disregarded (or at least shelved until further testing can verify it). The results are to be peer-reviewed by experts to check for correct procedure and to help eliminate confirmation bias from the results. Scientific claims require scientific evidence and proper methodology.

To believe that Jesus was a Buddhist monk despite there being no legitimate historical evidence for this claim is not "open-minded," it is deviant from the historical documents available. There is a historical method in place by which we can determine whether historical claims are authentic. When it comes to a claim made about a figure of the ancient past in the form of written accounts, historians look at a few things to assess credibility:

1. *Early attestation.* Sources that date back to an appropriate span of time from the figure / event.
2. *Multiple attestation.* Multiple, independent sources attesting to the same figure/event (with added historical weight if one or more of these sources comes from an enemy of the person or the wrong side of the camp).
3. *Embarrassment.* The information is counterproductive, embarrassing, or awkward to those who are sharing the information.
4. *Congruence.* The information is consistent with the historical facts known to exist in the time and place the person or event was said to live or take place.

These are called the Criteria of Authenticity. If twenty-seven historical documents were written independently of one another (the New Testament), tell us Jesus was a monotheistic Jew who claimed to be the Messiah, and were written by the apostles or companions of the apostles during their lifetimes, and if this is in agreement with what the disciples of the apostles wrote down during the period of the early Church (the early Church fathers), there is no justification for piecing together obscure, isolated sentences that contradict every reliable source from books like the Gospel of Judas written almost two hundred years after all eyewitnesses had died off. Historical claims require historical evidence.

Philosophical claims (about God, for example) must be justifiable in the form of philosophical argument. Ideally, we want a logically valid argument with premises that are more probably true than false leading to our conclusion. We want our conclusion to follow reasoning that can be broken into a step-by-step argument known as a "syllogism," wherein we can look at the structure of the argument and see whether it is "sound." A "sound" argument consists of premises that are truth and that logically necessitate the conclusion. We want to make sure our argument agrees with the rules of logical inference. The following is an example of a sound philosophical argument.

Premise 1: Socrates was a man.

Premise 2: All men are mortal.

Conclusion 1: Therefore, Socrates was mortal.

If Premises 1 and 2 are true, the conclusion is inescapable. Premises 1 and 2 are indeed both true, making this the holy grail of philosophical argumentation: a sound argument. Philosophical claims require philosophical argument. As atheist thinker Christopher Hitchens famously stated, "What can be asserted without evidence can also be dismissed without evidence."[134] He was right in saying this, but wrong in assuming there is no evidence for God or the Christian worldview. The point is that evidence matters. We need to be responsible about how we arrive at our beliefs about the world with the aim that our beliefs correspond to the way the world really is.

There would be no greater shame than to miss out on eternal life because we refused to examine Jesus' teachings with a clear set of eyes because we bought into a false theory of truth that says His words can't be considered truth in the first place, or if we did not look at the evidence for the reliability of the New Testament or the resurrection of Jesus because our epistemology says that evidence is meaningless. Truth is not that which serves us, truth is not that which resonates with us, and truth is not relative. Truth is objective, and it corresponds to the way things are.

It's up to us to discover how things really are in scientific, historical, and philosophical integrity as we make an honest attempt correspond our beliefs to the actual world and infer the best explanations available. The New Age movement loses its grip on our culture the moment we hold it up to the light of reason. The fuel in its intellectual engine consists of false theories of truth, a self-defeating philosophy, and an irresponsible neglect of reason and right procedure.

"Come now, let us reason together" (Isaiah 1:18).

Observation and Interpretation

When it comes to science, the scientist follows a process when conducting an experiment or making a discovery. First comes observation, next comes interpretation. Observation, which is easy and should be something everyone can agree on, is simply acknowledging an objective truth. In the realm of quantum physics, this could be seeing a previously unknown subatomic particle coming from the aftermath of a particle collision. The new particle can be measured and observed. No one seeing the particle can logically deny its existence; it is an observable fact. This is observation.

Science gets tricky during the second step of the process: interpretation. This is when the temptation to leave science and enter subjective belief comes into play. Once something is observed, the observer now must decide what it means. Interpretation is not scientific. Not everyone agrees on any given interpretation. Yet, far too often, scientists include their interpretations while explaining their observation and call the entire thing science.

For example, some time ago, I (Josh) was watching a physics lecture about Quantum Field Theory (QFT). The basic theory states that particles aren't really particles in the way we normally think of them, but are instead fluctuations within quantum fields. QFT today is actually the most accurate science ever developed and is able to make astonishingly accurate mathematical predictions. There is no logical reason to believe QFT is incorrect.

But then, however, the physicist giving the lecture included some of his interpretation without labeling it as such. He said something along the lines of, "This is how we know there is no afterlife, because there is no quantum field to take the information of the deceased anywhere." While he is surely entitled to his opinion, this was not a scientific statement. This is not a provable, observable, and undeniable fact. The truth is, quantum physics has not yet been able to identify all of the quantum fields in existence or their complete functions. Also, the idea of an afterlife and spiritual reality is so incredibly unknown to us by a scientific standard, we would not have any way of knowing whether quantum fields would even be involved in the process of a deceased person moving on to an afterlife. There is too much we don't know to be able to make a statement like that and have it be anything more than merely opinion. QFT has observable science within it, yet the physicist's opinion about the afterlife was only his subjective interpretation of the observable science; it was not science itself.

The Scientific Method

The scientific method has been a great tool to help decide what is objective observation and what is subjective interpretation. Yet, the scientific method still has limits. It can only describe what is physically and observably true. It is not the be-all, end-all of truth. It is limited in its scope to empirical claims about the natural world. You can't access things like morality, aesthetics, theology, mathematics, the reality of the past, or even some aspects of nature (such as human consciousness). For example, you cannot prove or disprove God with the scientific method since God is outside of the physical, observable parameters required by the scientific method

The scientific method includes five to seven steps, depending upon how it is explained. The main five steps generally agreed upon are:

- Question
- Hypothesis
- Prediction
- Test
- Analysis

As an example of this process in action, we can use the scientific method on DNA. The question could be, "How is genetic information stored in DNA?" In the past, when that question was asked, Linus Pauling, Francis Crick, and James D. Watson hypothesized that genetic information was stored in DNA through the then-unknown double helix structure of DNA strands.[135] The prediction was that if DNA was structured like a double helix, the X-ray refraction should be shaped like the letter X.[136] Next came the experiment in which Rosalind Franklin crystalized pure DNA and performed X-ray diffraction, which in turn produced an X shape on the photo, later named "Photograph 51."[137] Last came the analysis. When Watson saw the diffraction pattern, he recognized the shape; thus, the hypothesis was proven correct.

This is how science is supposed to work. Any interpretation that was put on DNA in the future would exist in the realm of opinion and speculation. The true science, discovered through the scientific method, was in. Scientists now knew how DNA stored genetic information.

New Age Borrowing from Science without the Scientific Method

New Age theology has a bad habit of borrowing from science, especially quantum physics, to push its beliefs. This, of course, is done without using the scientific method. New Age teachers take the observable science and put their own spin on it. Or even worse, they label something as "observable science" even though it is rejected by the majority or entirety of the scientific community. We even see this in occultism (as we will see a bit later). The issue is, instead of admitting that the interpretations are subjective opinions and that there are other ways to look at the data, many New Age teachers and followers say their beliefs are *proven* by the scientific observation itself. They say, for example, that the spooky relationship between human consciousness and quantum mechanics proves that both arise out of a field of universal consciousness. This implies nothing even close. This is why it is so important to understand the difference between observation and interpretation.

Quantum Physics and the New Age

Because quantum physics is strange and difficult to understand, New Age teachers have used it to promote their beliefs for quite some time. It is difficult to disprove something based on a science that is not well understood in today's culture. Most people don't know much about quantum physics, which makes it easy for New Age teachers to take advantage of people. For example, consider these claims made on a popular "quantum healing" website:

> What has been proven but not understood by physics or modern medicine is that we do have a communication with the quantum field which was proven to exist back in the 1960s. This field

has been mentioned for thousands of years. The Chinese called it Chi. The Indians called it Prana. Christians call it the Holy Spirit. It is a field of infinite energy and infinite knowledge. Carl Jung described the field as the collective unconscious. If a physician can access this field, and or teach his patients to influence this field for health and healing it would be quantum healing.[138]

Everything stated in that passage is false. It has not been proven that we have a communication with "the quantum field." In fact, there is no "the quantum field." There are many quantum "fields" in the plural. Also, we do not communicate with them. One could say we interact with them, though more precisely, QFT states that, on a subatomic level, our bodies are comprised of them. A particle is a fluctuation, or ripple, in a quantum field. We are made of particles. We, at least our physical bodies, are made of fluctuations in quantum fields. It is interesting and exciting for sure, but it is not as esoteric, mysterious, and spiritual as the excerpt above would have us believe. It has literally no supernatural implication.

Also, no quantum field is full of infinite anything, because infinity within the parameters of physical existence is impossible. Mathematician Carl Gauss said about infinity, "I protest against the use of infinite magnitude...which is never permissible in mathematics." The "potential infinite" is used in mathematics for the purpose of calculation, but an "actual infinite" amount of time or objects is known to be a mathematical impossibility and philosophical absurdity. Finally, since we are made of quantum fields, quantum fields cannot be used to heal ourselves. If we have the flu, the quantum fields that make up that flu virus are the same ones that make up our body as well. It would be like adding ketchup to more ketchup in the hope of producing mustard.

Sadly, however, this is a perfect example of how New Age teachers use quantum physics to take advantage of people's ignorance. If one is not intimately familiar with quantum physics, the excerpt above would probably sound correct. The language sounds scientific, it makes confident claims, and it seems to tie religion and science together in order to heal people. What could be wrong with that?

It's wrong because it's a lie. These are completely unfounded and untested claims rejected by the scientific community. The science is incorrect. There is no medical data showing the results of clinical trials to prove any of this stuff works. We can't run any of it through the scientific method. What we have here is a spiritual belief based on twisting and lying about scientific facts. It's not medicine, it's not science, and it's not factual. Unfortunately, the world is full of New Age teachers pushing this stuff on the unsuspecting public.

"What the Bleep Do We Know?"

Possibly one of the best modern examples of the misguided merging of quantum physics and New Age teachings comes from the documentary film *What the Bleep Do We Know?* released in 2004. The plot of the movie follows a fictional story of a photographer who experiences certain obstacles in her life, causing her to consider the possibility that individual and group consciousness can influence the physical world. Her experiences are used in the film to present the idea that quantum physics and consciousness are connected.

The film was directed by William Arntz, Betsy Chasse, and Mark Vicente, all of whom were students at Ramtha's School of Enlightenment, established in 1988 by J. Z. Knight, who claims to channel a thirty-five-thousand-year-old being named Ramtha the Enlightened One. The school, whose teachings are based on these channeling sessions, was first called the American Gnostic School.[139]

The film was picked up by a major distributer and grossed over $10 million.[140] It was later criticized for both misrepresenting science and containing pseudoscience. Several of the scientists interviewed in the film went on record to say their quotes had been taken out of context.[141] Some of the ideas put forth in the film include:

- The universe is constructed from thoughts and ideas rather than matter.
- Personal beliefs about who one is and what is real are a direct cause of one's own subjective interpretation of reality.
- We each have the ability to create our own reality.
- Objective reality is an illusion.
- Meditation can reduce violent crime rates.
- Consciousness is the ground of all being.
- People can travel backward in time.
- Water molecules can be influenced by thought.

The film was highly accepted and praised in the New Age movement. It has been described as "a kind of New Age answer of *The Passion of the Christ* and other films that adhere to traditional religious teachings."[142] It is also regarded as offering spiritual alternatives characteristic of New Age theology, which include critiques of traditional religions, such as Judaism and Christianity, in favor of what are considered universally recognized and accepted moral values by New Age believers.[143]

Quantum Physics in the Real World

However, back in the real world, scientists have been highly critical of *What the Bleep Do We Know?* In her book *Knocking on Heaven's Door*, physicist Lisa Randall refers to the film as "the bane of scientists."[144] In a letter published in *Physics Today*, the authors write, "The movie illustrates the uncertainty principle with a bouncing basketball being in several places at once. There's nothing wrong with that. It's recognized as pedagogical exaggeration. But the movie gradually moves to quantum 'insights' that lead a woman to toss away her antidepressant medication, to the quantum channeling of Ramtha, the 35,000-year-old Lemurian warrior, and on to even greater nonsense."

The letter went on to say that "most laypeople cannot tell where the quantum physics ends and the quantum nonsense begins, and many are susceptible to being misguided." Further, "a physics student may be unable to convincingly confront unjustified extrapolations of quantum mechanics," a shortcoming the authors attribute to the current teaching of quantum mechanics, in which "we tacitly deny the mysteries physics has encountered."[145]

Regarding the film, Richard Dawkins is quoted as saying, "The authors seem undecided whether their theme is quantum theory or consciousness. Both are indeed mysterious, and their genuine mystery needs none of the hype with which this film relentlessly and noisily belabours us." He concluded that the film is "tosh." Professor Clive Treated wrote, "Thinking on neurology and addiction are covered in some detail but, unfortunately, early references in the film to quantum physics are not followed through, leading to a confused message."

Simon Singh called the film's contents "pseudoscience" and said the idea that "if observing water changes its molecular structure, and if we are 90 percent water, then by observing ourselves, we can change at a fundamental level via the laws of quantum physics" was "ridiculous balderdash." Even the American Chemical Society's review states the film is a "pseudoscientific docudrama."[146] Professor of theoretical physics at Imperial College, Joao Magueijo, said the film deliberately misquotes science.[147]

Why all the scientific backlash? Because, as Professor Magueijo said, it is a deliberate misrepresentation of science. This is done in order to promote a belief system science does not support. Those who make such claims in New Age circles (minus a few theoretical physicists whose ideas are opposed by almost all of academia) lack the necessary training to even know in a thorough way what is being talked about. And the ones who have the training lack the philosophical skill to make interpretations. New Age practitioners lack both.

If the New Age theological arguments were logical enough on their own, a twisting of science such as this would never need to take place. However, this exposes how weak and flimsy New Age theology is. New

Age does not have science on its side. It only has strange twistings and subjective interpretation of scientific facts. Of course, the effort to distort mainstream science into a belief system in order to fool the unknowing public is nothing new.

Blavatsky Interpreting Evolution into Eastern Avatars from Isis Unveiled

Regardless of whether individual Christians accept any version of evolution as a truth or deception, mainstream scientific circles generally regard it as true and have for quite some time. It seems that whenever science has deemed something as true, there is a temptation by teachers of various spiritual beliefs to incorporate it into their own already-held beliefs. The idea is that if the science is true, and if the beliefs are attached to the science, the beliefs must be true, too. This is why New Age latches so tightly on to quantum physics.

Helena Blavatsky, in her book Isis Unveiled, did something similar to what New Age is doing to quantum physics. She attempted to tie Darwinian evolution to Hinduism. Vishnu is a Hindu deity of preservation who is said to exist in a progression of various avatars. The ten avatars, called the dashavatara, are described in an ancient text called the Puranabharati. Hinduism teaches that nine of these avatars have occurred in the past. The final avatar is expected to occur in the future as an entity known as Kalki. This happens at the end of Kali Yuga, which is the last stage of four in a cycle the world goes through. It is taught that Vishnu will descend in the form of the avatar Kalki in order to restore cosmic order. This is foretold in the Bhagavata Purana:

> At that time, the Supreme Personality of Godhead will appear on the earth. Acting with the power of pure spiritual goodness, He will rescue eternal religion. Lord Vi u—the Supreme Personality of Godhead, the spiritual master of all moving and non-

moving living beings, and the Supreme Soul of all—takes birth to protect the principles of religion and to relieve His saintly devotees from the reactions of material work.[148]

The list of avatars varies depending on region and sect, but the standard list is as follows:

1. Matsya: The fish – Vishnu took the form of a fish to warn Vaivasvata of a great flood. Vaivasvata then built a boat to save his family and seven sages. This account is reminiscent of the story of Noah in the Book of Genesis.
2. Kurma: The tortoise – The devas and asuras tried to obtain the nectar of immortality by using Mount Mandara to churn the Ocean of Milk. This put the mountain in jeopardy of being destroyed, so Vishnu took the form of a tortoise to support its weight.
3. Vahara: The boar – A demon named Hiranyaksha took the Earth to the bottom of the cosmic ocean. Vishnu took the form of a boar to place the Earth in its original place by carrying it in his tusks after defeating Hiranyaksha.
4. Narasimha: The half man/half lion – The older brother of Hiranyaksha was given a boon from Brahma which made it so he could not be killed by man or animal, inside or out, day or night, on earth or in the stars, with a weapon either living or inanimate. Finding loopholes to all conditions, Vishnu took the form of a human with the head and paws of a lion to kill the evil older brother at the courtyard threshold of his house, at dusk, with his claws, while he lay on his thighs.
5. Vamana: The dwarf – Vishnu descended in the form of a dwarf to petition Bali for three strides of land, only to later turn into a giant, thereby making the strides much larger.
6. Parashurama: The warrior with an axe – Parashurama is the first warrior-saint in Hinduism. He was born of earthly parents and

was given an axe by Shiva. He was immortal and is believed to still be alive today in the Mehendra Mountains.

7. Rama: The prince and king of Ayodhya – Sita, the wife of Rama, was taken by the demon king of Lanka, Ravana. Rama defeated the demon king and saved Sita.

8. Krishna: The eighth son of Devaki and Vasudev – Descriptions of Krishna vary; sometimes he is a young child playing a flute or a prince offering guidance. Sometimes he is portrayed as a hero, god-child, or Supreme Being. Krishna is said to ride a chariot pulled by four horses.

9. Buddha: The founder of Buddhism – Descriptions of Buddha vary as well. At times he is seen as leading heretics and demons away from the teaching of the Vedas. Other times he is seen as a teacher of non-violence.

10. Kalki: The final incarnation – Kalki is understood as the final incarnation of Vishnu. It is said he will ride a white horse with a sword that blazes like a comet.

In 1877, when Helena Blavatsky published her first major work, *Isis Unveiled*, in which she interpreted the Dashavataras as representing the progression of biological evolution, she interpreted the avatar list as follows:[149]

1. Matsya – fish, the first class of vertebrates; evolved in water
2. Kurma – amphibious (living in both water and land; but not to confuse with the vertebrate class amphibians)
3. Varaha – wild land animal
4. Narasimha – beings that are half-animal and half-human (indicative of emergence of human thoughts and intelligence in powerful wild nature)
5. Vamana – short, premature human beings
6. Parasurama – early humans living in forests and using weapons
7. Rama – humans living in community, beginning of civil society

8. Krishna – humans practicing animal husbandry, politically advanced societies

9. Buddha – humans finding enlightenment

10. Kalki – advanced humans with great powers of destruction

It is convenient to be able to coincidentally "discover" new things about spirituality at the same time science begins to shift in that direction. All of a sudden, the "wisdom of the ancients" just so happens to be about the very thing science has discovered. As discoveries about quantum mechanics continue to be made, we will continue to see New Age teachers read them into their worldview and twist them to support their presuppositions, despite their interpretations being rejected by the scientific community.

Objective Science vs. Subjective Beliefs

When it comes to objective science and subjective beliefs, it is not that one is right and the other is wrong. There is a time and place for both, yet each is very different. As human beings, we exist in an objective, physical reality. We should be able to agree on the parameters of this reality; however, we don't. The reason is that we all have our own, individual, subjective beliefs about our objective, physical reality.

This is why it is so important to know the difference between these two things. To combine them into one thing ends up undermining each one and rendering everything into confusion. This is why materialistic and objective science will never agree with subject of New Age teachings, and New Age will never agree with objective, scientific truth. The minute you look at a scientific discovery as supporting New Age theology, you have went from the realm of science to the realm of religion. It's not that science can't make discoveries with theologically rich implications, it's that we need to be know when the implications are warranted and when they aren't, and the difference between observation and interpretation.

When it comes to Christianity, there is an understanding of one's human limits. There is an objective world out there, yet reality is filtered through our limited perception facilitated by the five senses. Therefore, the only One who can have perfect clarity of physical reality, as well as spiritual reality, is the One who created it all in the first place: the God of the Bible. We are too cognitively limited to make such claims objectively unless we have access to the thoughts of the One with all knowledge. In the revealed Word of God, we not only have perfect knowledge of what lies beyond the grave, we have been provided everything we need to get there. Since we have access to God's perspective on everything, Christianity is the only worldview that gives you an objective interpretation on things that, when left to our own subjectivity, would otherwise be impossible to know or decipher. We can proceed with both humility and confidence knowing that the beliefs we hold aren't contrived from compiling from obscure bits of data, but are rooted in the very mind of God Himself.

5

PERSONAL GOD VS. IMPERSONAL FORCE

IT IS POPULAR IN THE modern world, especially within New Age, to think of God as an impersonal force rather than as a personal Father. This gets fleshed out in a variety of ways as we will shortly see, but how often have we heard people, sometimes even Christians, lament that their prayers are not being answered? Many times, when people feel this way, they see the prayers of their friends being answered, yet not their own. "Why didn't it work for me?" they might be inclined to ask. In the secular world, this plays out when people notice that others seem to be accomplishing and achieving more in life. They notice good things happening to less-deserving, or even bad, people, and bad things happening to themselves. It is almost as if there is an subconscious belief in the principles fairness, justice, and equality. Yet, these principles are generally believed to be abstract forces at work in the universe somehow, rather than the properties of a divine being

In New Age, spirit guides, Ascended Masters, and angels are regarded as having personalities, but the overall governing force of the universe is generally seen as lacking personhood. During meditation, the goal is more to tap into a universal energy field at the heart of nature rather than to communicate personally with a transcendent creator. If there is any communication, it is generally with a spirit being lower in the hierarchical rankings than the all-pervading impersonal force of the universe. Ironically, a personal relationship with this force is impossible because it is not a person, meaning it has no awareness, free will, rationality, etc. It cannot reciprocate or interact with you and your intentions. It is like turning on a microwave and trying to have a relationship with the frequencies it emits.

Christianity is different. It offers something richer and deeper than trying to tap into an impersonal force or energy field. The Bible describes a God who is a person, not a force, and who loves His children. Of course, because we are all subject to our modern culture at times, Christians can fall into the trap of inadvertently treating God as a force rather than a person. If God is a force and if a prayer is answered favorably for one person, then that same prayer, if said in the same way, should be answered the same, no matter who utters it. Yet, this is not the case. While New Age (along with Satanism and witchcraft) relies on practices to achieve desired results, Christianity understands God as a person whom the individual must speak with. If there is a desire, the Christian is expected to ask God. At that time, God, through His wisdom, may decide to answer the prayer favorably or unfavorably. In short, prayer is not a spell or incantation. Prayer is speaking with God. If a question is asked, it is up to God how He will answer it.

This is similar to how a good father interacts with his children. At the time of this writing, I (Josh) have three kids, and while I love them all equally, I interact with them in different ways because they are individuals. Each child has his or her own strengths, weaknesses, and ways of communicating with me. My youngest son, Adam, is still under 2 years old, so verbal communication with him is limited. However, I show him he is loved in different ways—for example, by playing with him and chasing him through the house. My oldest daughter, Jaklynn, is 7, so she can understand a lot more than Adam or my other son, Nathan (who is 4). Nathan is learning things now that Jaklynn has already learned. Also, because each has different interests and ways of looking at the world, communication and interaction are a bit different. For example, Jaklynn communicates more verbally while Nathan would rather be doing something to interact with me, such as building with blocks.

There are situations in which Jaklynn and Nathan could both ask me for the same thing, and I might say yes to one but no to the other. For example, Jaklynn might ask to stay up an hour past her bedtime. Because I've let her do this before and she has proved that she can get up without issue the next morning for school, I will tell her yes. If Nathan were to ask, however, I would likely say no, because of his age and his attitude when he doesn't get enough sleep. It doesn't mean he did anything wrong. It doesn't mean I love Jaklynn more. It only means they are individuals with their own strengths and weaknesses.

According to Christianity, our relationship with our children can serve as an example of how God interacts with us. We all have a personal relationship with Him. We are all individuals. God Himself is an individual with likes and dislikes. He has His own set of attributes and preferences. He also knows us better than we know ourselves. Therefore, when we pray and talk with Him, He communicates with us according to what He knows is best. He might say yes to some of our requests; other times, He might say no. At times, it might not even seem like He is saying anything at all. But, to the Christian, God is always there, always taking care of us and always listening when we speak to Him. The theology of New Age spirituality cannot lead people to the Father who made them because it presents a notion of God that is no more personal a microwave.

The Chaos Dragon Leviathan Compared Against the New Age Force

Strangely enough, the writers of the Bible did believe and describe a type of "force" in reality, but it was seen completely different from what New Age teaches today. In the ancient Near East, there was an understood personification of the impersonal force of chaos.[150] The ancients called it Leviathan.[151] This entity was seen as a type of sea dragon even though it personified something that was impersonal. In ancient times, the seas were associated with chaos because they were dangerous and deadly. There were land-beast personifications of this as well, since chaos is not limited to the sea.

There were other names for this force and similar entities to Leviathan, depending on the region and ancient text, including Litanu, Lotan, Behemoth, Tiamat, Mot, Seth-Horus, and Cerberus, etc. The Enuma Elish is the Babylonian epic of creation describing the birth of the gods, the universe, and human beings.[152] In the beginning, according to the story, nothing existed except chaotic water everywhere. Out of the movement of the waters, they divided into fresh water and saltwater. The fresh water is personified as the god Apsu while the salt water is personified as the goddess Tiamat. Through these two entities came the birth of younger gods.

The younger gods were noisy and were troubling Apsu, so he decided to kill the younger gods. Tiamat heard of this and warned her eldest son, Enki (sometimes Ea), who then killed Apsu. Tiamat became angry over Apsu's death, summoned the forces of chaos, and created eleven monsters to destroy the younger gods. Ea/Enki and the other younger gods fought against Tiamat but were unable to win the battle until Marduk emerged as a champion among them. Marduk killed Tiamat by shooting her with an arrow, splitting her in two. Marduk created the heavens and the earth from Tiamat's corpse (half to make the heavens, half to make the earth). He then appointed jobs to the younger gods and bound Tiamat's eleven monsters to his feet as trophies.

Marduk then talked with Ea, recognized as the god of wisdom, and decided to create human beings. Ea created Lullu, the first man. Lullu's job was to help the gods in their task of maintaining order and restraining chaos. The story ends with a long praise of Marduk for everything he did. The entire story is about chaos being subdued by the destruction of a great sea beast. In other words, the sea beast is a symbol for chaos.

A similar story can be found in the Ugaritic Baal Cycle. Ugarit was an ancient city located at what is now Ras Shamra in northern Syria. The Baal Cycle isn't as much about creation as it is about a competition between gods for a position of rulership with the supreme god El. It describes a battle between Baal ("lord") and Yam ("sea") and another battle between Baal and Mot ("death"). Yam is also called Nahar ("river") and is also described as a sea monster with seven heads named Litanu (the Canaanite word for 'Leviathan"). In the Baal Cycle, Yam is a symbol for the sea and the forces of chaos, comparable to Tiamat in the Enuma Elish. Baal defeated Yam and was declared king of the other gods, yet he was still under El. He was given the titles "the Rider on the Clouds," "Most High," and was described as having everlasting dominion.

As we can see, the cultures in the Ancient Near East personified chaos as a sea beast, sometimes with a land beast counterpart. They understood that the universe itself was pervaded with a non-living, yet very real, chaotic force, one that we needed divine protection against. The basic idea behind this was to answer the questions: Why do bad things happen in the world? What is chaos and why does it exist? As stated in the Bible, especially in the Book of Job, the answer is that, while chaos/Leviathan is subdued, it is not yet vanquished, but will be when God deems it time to restore all of creation to Edenic conditions. Chaos entered the world when sin did. The main point is that, yes, the world is chaotic and yes, bad things happen to good people, but God ultimately is in control and does not allow chaos to have full reign over the planet.

The Book of Job is a great source of information to help answer this type of question. When Job questioned God and essentially suggested He should be running things differently, God challenged Job with a series of questions. This is where we are introduced to Behemoth, the personification of chaos on land:

Behold, Behemoth, which I made as I made you; he eats grass like an ox. Behold, his strength in his loins, and his power in the muscles of his belly. He makes his tail stiff like a cedar; the sinews of his thighs are knit together. His bones are tubes of bronze, his limbs like bars of iron. He is the first of the works of God; let him who made him bring near his sword! For the mountains yield food for him where all the wild beasts play. Under the lotus plants he lies, in the shelter of the reeds and in the marsh. For his shade the lotus trees cover him; the willows of the brook surround him. Behold, if the river is turbulent he is not frightened; he is confident though Jordan rushes against his mouth. Can one take him by his eyes, or pierce his nose with a snare? (Job 40:15–24, ESV)

Next, we are introduced to Leviathan, the personified sea beast of chaos:

Can you draw out Leviathan with a fishhook or press down his tongue with a cord? Can you put a rope in his nose or pierce his jaw with a hook? Will he make many pleas to you? Will he speak to you soft words? Will he make a covenant with you to take him for your servant forever? Will you play with him as with a bird, or will you put him on a leash for your girls? Will traders bargain over him? Will they divide him up among the merchants? Can you fill his skin with harpoons or his head with fishing spears? Lay your hands on him; remember the battle— you will not do it again!

Behold, the hope of a man is false; he is laid low even at the sight of him. No one is so fierce that he dares to stir him up. Who then is he who can stand before me? Who has first given to me, that I should repay him? Whatever is under the whole heaven is mine. I will not keep silence concerning his limbs, or his mighty strength, or his goodly frame. Who can strip off his outer garment? Who would come near him with a bridle? Who can open the doors of his face? Around his teeth is terror.

His back is made of rows of shields, shut up closely as with a seal. One is so near to another that no air can come between them. They are joined one to another; they clasp each other and cannot be separated. His sneezings flash forth light, and his eyes are like the eyelids of the dawn. Out of his mouth go flaming torches; sparks of fire leap forth. Out of his nostrils comes forth smoke, as from a boiling pot and burning rushes. His breath kindles coals, and a flame comes forth from his mouth.

In his neck abides strength, and terror dances before him. The folds of his flesh stick together, firmly cast on him and immovable. His heart is hard as a stone, hard as the lower millstone. When he raises himself up, the mighty are afraid; at the crashing they are beside themselves. Though the sword reaches him, it does not avail, nor the spear, the dart, or the javelin. He counts iron as straw, and bronze as rotten wood. The arrow cannot make him flee; for him, sling stones are turned to stubble. Clubs are counted as stubble; he laughs at the rattle of javelins. His underparts are like sharp potsherds; he spreads himself like a threshing sledge on the mire. He makes the deep boil like a pot; he makes the sea like a pot of ointment. Behind him he leaves a shining wake; one would think the deep to be white-haired. On earth there is not his like, a creature without fear. He sees everything that is high; he is king over all the sons of pride. (Job 41, ESV)

God makes the point that Job is unable to even face Leviathan and Behemoth. Job, who is mortal and not eternal, does not know enough about spiritual and physical reality to question God's reasonings. Instead of questioning, therefore, Job should trust that God knows what He's doing and understand there is information he doesn't have about the nature of chaos within creation. It is the same for us today.

When tragedy occurs, such as mass shootings, hurricanes, and other such things, they are expressions of chaos (sometimes including intelligent evil, such as in the cases of mass shootings). However, while the chaos itself is antagonistic and hostile to humanity, God is ultimately sovereign over the chaos. We don't have to fear it because God subdues chaos. Even more, Scripture tells us what we can do in light of these tragedies, such as praying and loving one another, and this does not include giving all our attention to the terror of Leviathan while disregarding the power of the Almighty.

While ancient cultures understood the universe to be permeated with an impersonal force of chaos that threatened our existence, the New Age takes a different approach and sees this impersonal force as something to be incorporated into one's spirituality. They assume, naively, that the background force radiating into the created world must be benevolent and life-giving, even though the universe is a chaotic, death-filled place. Instead, New Agers fully embrace the "energy of the universe" without a second thought to what kind of energy they might be embracing. However, the danger, if the biblical description is correct, is that New Age believers might inadvertently be tapping into the energy or force of chaos that entered creation at the Fall, perhaps even the same one modern science says responsible for the gradual decline and disorder of all things in the universe (entropy).

What if the energy force we are connecting with is the same one the ancients were terrified of, and the same one causing death, decay, and degradation in the natural world? A simple practice such as meditation can open a door for chaos to enter one's life. This is exactly what happened to me (Josh). While my experience was more a spiritual manifestation of chaos, it might not always come about that way. Chaos could come in unrecognizable form to humans living in a fallen world. If we get hurt, a loved one gets sick, we lose our job, or we go through divorce, we don't typically see these things as anything more than what life usually has to offer. What if that's not the end of the story? What if there is a reason these events occur to some people at certain times rather than others? What if there is something we humans are doing to invite the old chaos dragon into our lives?

The New Age movement is in the business of bringing people into contact with the impersonal energy force of the universe, not consider-ing that the universe is a chaos-driven and has been understood to be such by the same cultures its adherents so highly revere. The Apostle Paul understood that all forces of destruction have their origin in the god of this world (2 Corinthians 4:4), whom he calls the prince of the power of the air (Ephesians 2:2). "It could be that the "air" indicates the lower reaches of [the spirit] realm and therefore emphasizes the proximity of this evil power and his influence over the world. In later Judaism the air is in fact thought of as the region under the firmament as in 2 Enoch 29.4, 5, 'And I threw him out from the height with his angels, and he was flying in the air continuously above the abyss.'"[153]

Leviathan and the chaos it represents belong to the dominion of Satan, who brought death and chaos into the world through sin. We should not assume that, just because we are in touch with an imper-sonal force in the universe, this force is benevolent or from a benevolent source. The Bible tells us that at least one impersonal universal force is destructive (Leviathan) and comes from a malevolent source (Satan). It also tells us to avoid practices that bring us into contact force (such as mediation, trance, chanting, and drugs, etc.), as these practices bring us not only into contact with the force itself (which opens the door for chaos to enter our lives), but also with the personal spiritual forces over-seeing such practices (Ephesians 6:12)—making it doubly dangerous.

Those in the New Age movement are obsessed with trying to con-nect with the impersonal forces of nature, not realizing that the imper-sonal forces of nature were understood by the ancients to be so chaotic as to be personified in the form of sea monsters and dragons that threat-ened the survival of the human race. If science, the Bible, and the Medi-terranean world reveal that chaos is the universal force fueling cosmic goings on, perhaps the New Age practice of tapping into the impersonal forces of the universe is an invitation to destruction.

Strangely enough, while many New Agers recognize an impersonal force that drives the entire universe, there is still a belief in other spiri-tual beings. These spiritual beings are not malevolent like the dragon of chaos, of course. They are understood as benevolent. Many times, these beings are seen as making up a hierarchy with a pantheon of powerful beings at the top. This pantheon consists of personal beings rather than impersonal forces; however, the overall impersonal force still drives everything at a fundamental level.

Pantheism: The Theology of the New Age Movement

Pantheism is "a doctrine that equates God with the forces and laws of the universe."[154] "At its most general, pantheism may be understood positively as the view that God is identical with the cosmos, the view that there exists nothing which is outside of God, or else negatively as the rejection of any view that considers God as distinct from the universe."[155] Pantheism is a type of theology that believes there is nothing beyond the nature world that we could call "God," because "God" is just a word used to describe the laws of nature, the material world, and all of space-time reality.

Etymologically, pantheism literally means "all is God." God is thought to be the universe and all things in the universe. There is no transcendent, personal deity outside of time and space. There is no moment in which a divine agent decided to create the world. The universe, in a variety of different contexts, is simply equated with God so as to attribute nature itself with divinity. There are three primary ways pantheism is expressed within the New Age movement.

- God is the substance and innermost essence of each individual thing in the universe.
- God is Being itself as opposed to an individuated being, and is therefore inseparable from all things that participate in Being.
- The universe emanated from God as an extension of God, meaning that all things in the universe can be said to be identical to their source of origin.

Most pervasive in the New Age movement is the angle that all things in the universe are reducable to a single substance, and that substance is consciousness. This philosophy is called "monism," which means that reality is ultimately reducible to a single substance or part. Consciousness, New Agers say, is a fundamental property of the universe just like time, space, matter, and energy existing as a universal field. Consciousness is not a byproduct of brain activity, but is the building block of the universe itself. It's the "stuff" that matter is made of and the glue that holds reality in place.

Dr. Dean Radin, who explores mind-science at the Noetic Institute, summarizes this point in the following way: "The idea of field consciousness suggests a continuum of nonlocal intelligence, permeating space and time. This is in contrast with the neuroscience-inspired, Newtonian view of a perceptive tissue locked inside the skull."[156]

New Agers believe consciousness is a building block in the context of there being a field of universal consciousness at the most fundamental level of nature. Beneath molecules, atoms, subatomic particles, and quarks lies a subterranean field of pure intelligence. Catchphrases for this field of consciousness include "Source Field," "Universal Consciousness," "All-One," "Brahman," or "Intelligent Infinity."

Usually, a loose understanding of quantum physics is dragged into the equation as justification for believing that God is the universe. The superstring field in theoretical physics is believed to be a unified field anchoring all the forces, particles, and laws of nature. Physicists and philosophers who have mystical leanings often attribute this field with the property of consciousness or intelligence.

Former theoretical physics professor at the university of Oregon, Dr. Amit Goswami, frames it this way:

The new paradigm posits instead a monism based on the primacy of consciousness— that consciousness (variously called spirit, god, godhead, ain sof, tao, brahman, etc., in popular and spiritual traditions), not matter, is the ground of all being; it is a monism based on a consciousness that is unitive and transcendent but one that becomes many in sentient beings such as us. We are that consciousness. All the world of experience, including matter, is the material manifestation of transcendent forms of consciousness.[157]

The pantheist, simply put, is committed to the belief that all things in the universe fall into the being of God, which is ontologically sourced in a field in consciousness at the most fundamental level of nature. This is the primary substance out of which all things in creation emerge from and are sustained by. Some additionally say that God is also a current of life-force energy flowing through the universe (called Prana), or the background energy of the cosmos, or the place of silence in between thoughts, or a combination of some of the above. However one wishes to splice it, New Age theology explicitly denies the idea of a transcendent, personal Creator and posits an identification between God and the natural world.

Robinson Jeffers, a famous monistic poet, said:

I believe that the Universe is one being, all its parts are different expressions of the same energy, and they are all in communication with each other, therefore parts of one organic whole.... This whole is in all its parts so beautiful, and is felt by me to be so intensely in earnest, that I am compelled to love it and to think of it as divine.[158]

Pantheism as the Crutch of New Age Practice

This position is central to New Age thought and practice. Meditation and yoga, for example, are both predicated on the assumption that there is a fundamental field of consciousness (God) that lies at the foundation of the natural world. The word "yoga" literally means "union" and refers to the unification of the personal self (Atman) with the universal

Self (Brahman). Yoga cannot properly exist definitionally or in practice without its commitments to pantheism, and mediation loses spiritual context if there is no ultimate reality available in nature that one can access. The originator of the infamous practice of transcendental meditation, Maharishi Mahesh Yogi, predicates his philosophy and practice upon the idea that all is God because all is consciousness:

> The Transcendental Meditation technique is an effortless procedure for allowing the excitations of the mind to settle down until the least excited state of mind is reached. This is a state of inner wakefulness with no object of thought or perception, just pure consciousness aware of its own unbounded nature It is wholeness, aware of itself, devoid of differences, beyond the division of subject and object–transcendental consciousness. It is a field of all possibilities, where all creative potentialities exist together, infinitely correlated yet unexpressed. It is a state of perfect order, the matrix from where all the laws of nature emerge.[159]

The New Age's commitment to the divinity of man also hinges upon pantheism. Man, as a bearer of the substance and essence of God's being, is believed to be intrinsically divine. If everything is God, then man, too, must be God. One form of "awakening" and "enlightenment" described in the New Age movement is to reach a state of consciousness wherein one is aware of being this unified field temporarily expressed as a human being. Dr. John Hagelin, a theoretical physicist at the Maharishi Institute, summarizes it in the following way:

> The unified field, experienced as the most fundamental state of human awareness, is considered to be a level of reality at which such a separation cannot be inferred. The experience of the unified field of consciousness, in which the observer, the process of observation and the observed are unified, is considered to be a means of realizing the ultimate inseparability of the observer and

the observed, leading to a completely unified view of self and the environment traditionally known as "enlightenment" or "unity consciousness."[160]

If there is a distinction between creator and creation, man cannot be seen as inherently sharing identity with God. We will explore the doctrine of man in the New Age movement more thoroughly in an upcoming chapter, but the very bedrock of "spiritual enlightenment" in the New Age movement is a theology that equates God with the universe and all its contents.

The deification of the sun, moon, and earth also necessitates pantheistic thought. If everything can be said to be divine, every celestial body should be revered as such without reservation. If the planets participate in God as God, they are worthy of worship as God. Pagan worship and ceremony is the logical extension of pantheism. If the objects of the heavens are distinct from God, then worshipping them would clearly be idolatry and futile.

If pantheism is false, the New Age movement and everything it strives to achieve becomes empty and without substance. The essential pillars of the movement fall immediately the minute we this theology is negated, such as the spiritual aspirations of toward a state of "God-consciousness," the practices of yoga and meditation, the doctrine of man, the affinity with and deification of nature, and many others.

Before we begin to explore what Jesus and the Bible have to say about God and His relationship to the created world, let us first examine pantheism under the light of philosophical scrutiny and see if it can stand on its own.

The Beginning of the Universe Refutes Pantheism

Whatever begins to exist has a cause. This is a basic philosophical principle. If something begins to exist, something must have brought the thing into being. Horses, babies, vehicles, and trees don't blink into existence, uncaused out of nothing, for out of nothing, nothing comes. A series of events leads up to the Ford Model T participating in being. The vision of Henry Ford, the materials used to build the vehicle, the construction of the vehicle by members of the assembly line, and other types of causes were at play to produce the Model T. It did not magically appear out of nowhere in someone's garage. If someone tried telling you that was how the Model T came into being, you would think he was either crazy or joking.

Why is it important to know that everything that begins to exist has a cause? An astonishing fact that experts almost universally agree upon is that the universe, more likely than not, began to exist a finite time ago. The idea of an eternal universe is philosophically and scientifically problematic. The gradual expansion of the universe, for example, is arguably one of the most significant scientific discoveries of all time indicating a cosmic beginning. In 1929, Edwin Hubble discovered that the universe (including space itself) is in a constant state of cosmic expansion. Simply put, everything is moving away from everything else. Surrounding galaxies are moving farther away from our galaxy, and they are moving farther away from each other.

Essentially, if the universe is in a state of expansion, we can trace this expansion back to a certain point at which all things in the universe become collapsed into a singularity. If it is expanding, there must be a starting point at which it began to expand outward from.

The Second Law of Thermodynamics expresses that everything in the universe is in a process of breaking down and is headed toward chaos. A certain amount of "thermodynamic free energy" is required to sustain stellar activity, and in a relatively short cosmic time, the universe will simply run out of usable energy. There will be no more gas left in the tank. The universe is headed for an inevitable heat death in which the sun and all other stars will burn out, and there will be no atomic energy left for any natural process to extract from. The eschatology of cosmology predicts a universe in utter ruin, in which nothing will remain but lifeless, galactic corpses expanding forever into pitch-black darkness. Here is the question: If the universe had existed for an infinite amount of time into the past, why hasn't it reached this state of heat death already?

If an infinite amount of time has passed, we should have already reached the point at which stars burn out and the universe has run out of energy. If a limited amount of usable energy is within the contained system of the universe, and if a certain amount of this energy is used up every second, and if an infinite amount of seconds have already passed, then we should expect to find ourselves in a state in which all the limited amount of energy has already been used. The fact that we have not yet run out of energy is evidence that we have not yet crossed an infinite amount of time, but only a finite amount of time.

Further scientific evidence and philosophical arguments against an infinite amount of time give us confidence that the universe is not eternal into the past, but came into being a finite time ago. According to modern estimates, all of space-time reality popped into existence in a single instant in an event known as the Big Bang roughly fourteen billion years ago. Whether we adopt young Earth or old Earth leanings in our theology, a conservative scientific fact found in any textbook on cosmology is that the universe began to exist.

According to Stephen Hawking, "Almost everyone now believes that the universe, and time itself, had a beginning at the big bang."[161] Physics professor and director of the Institute of Cosmology at Tufts University, Alexander Vilenkin, explains that scientists "can no longer hide behind a past-eternal universe. there is no escape, they have to face the problem of a cosmic beginning."[162]

Now, if the universe began to exist, then it must have a transcendent cause. This means the universe must have been caused by something outside the universe, for the universe did not exist yet for a cause to exist within. The universe did not create the universe. The universe was brought into being by something beyond itself. Whatever caused all of space-time reality must have, itself, existed outside of space-time reality.

Whatever caused nature to come into being must have been operating outside of nature. When we unpack what it would mean for something to cause space, matter, energy, and time itself to come into being and take a look at what kind of properties such a transcendent cause must have, we arrive at the following list: spaceless, timeless, formless, immaterial, beginningless, changeless, and incredibly powerful. These are the attributes normally ascribed to God. In fact, this is how the Bible describes the Father—as an immaterial, invisible, unchanging Spirit. The scientific evidence for the beginning of the universe yields rich theological significance, indicating that God and the universe are not identical, because the universe needs something outside of itself to explain its origin. God existed outside the universe at a time when nothing existed. The beginning of the universe is the smoking gun indicating that we are dealing with a transcendent being that exists outside of the universe.

The argument, broken down, is as follows:

Premise 1: Whatever begins to exist has a cause.

Premise 2: If the universe began to exist, the universe has a transcendent cause.

Premise 3: The universe began to exist.

Conclusion: Therefore, the universe has a transcendent cause.

If the premises of this argument are true, then the conclusion is inescapable. We are directed to a supernatural cause of the universe the minute we agree that the universe had a beginning. If there was a time at which the universe did not exist but its cause died (i.e., God), then this means God and the universe are not identical to one another. God existed without the universe prior to creating it, meaning God is not the universe. God existed outside the universe and then brought it into being.

And let us remember: The cause of the universe must be beyond space and time, and therefore immaterial, spaceless, formless, unchanging, and immensely powerful.

Only two different types of entities we can think of fit these descriptions: Abstract objects (such as numbers) or unembodied minds. No other type of entity possesses these types of characteristics. Since numbers lack causal powers and can't bring anything into reality, the only entity that could fit such a description is an unembodied mind. Therefore, we are well within our rational rights to believe the cause of the universe is an unembodied personal mind.

By "personal," we don't mean that God is a human being. What we mean is that God is an individual center of consciousness that is self-aware, rational, and endowed with His own freedom of choice. These are typically seen to be the sufficient conditions for "personhood." Angels are persons. Demons are persons. The Holy Spirit is a person. The only kind of being that could classify as being a spaceless, beginningless, timeless, unchanging, formless, powerful First Cause of the universe is a supernatural, personal mind.

Let's contrast that with an impersonal force such as the force of gravity, a microwave, or a beam of light. These forces are not self-aware or rational in nature. They do not have freedom of will and therefore cannot bring a new effect into being out of nothing. The beginning of the universe is evidence of a transcendent cause that extends beyond the universe that existed without the universe. This argument singlehandedly defeats Pantheism by showing the necessity of having a supernatural cause beyond the universe that existed prior to the universe. The cause of the universe existed timelessly from eternity past before the first moment of space-time reality, meaning that the universe and its cause are not identical to one another.

The Fine Tuning of the Universe
Refutes Pantheism

A fascinating scientific fact is that our universe is delicately tuned for intelligent life with constants and quantities so precise that it boggles human imagination. When we express physical laws and conditions of the universe in mathematical numbers, we get "constants" and "quantities." The cosmological constant, for example, is the value of the energy density of the vacuum of space. It's the term given to the pressure and energy present within empty space that prevents the universe from collapsing in on itself. If the value of this constant were increased by just one part in 1,000,000,000,000,000,000,000,000,000,000 with another 90 zeros on the end (10^{120}), the universe would not be able to sustain life.

By contrast, the number of seconds that have passed in 13.4 billion years is only 10^{20}. Roger Penrose, a mathematical physicist of Oxford University, has calculated that the low-entropy state's odds of existing by chance alone are one part in $10^{10^{123}}$, a number so incalculably small that this value fell into place by sheer chance must be seen as worse than magic.[163] We could write a "0" on every single particle in the universe and still wouldn't have enough zeros to amount to this figure. Penrose goes on to say, "I cannot even recall seeing anything else in physics whose accuracy is known to approach, even remotely, a figure like one part in $10^{10^{123}}$."[164]

Obviously, the constants do not have to be balanced this way. We can easily imagine a universe in which the cosmological constant is different and the only universe that exists is one with only helium, or where the mass of the electron is different. Other constants include Plank's constant; Plank mass-energy; the mass of the electron, proton, and neutron; the ratio of electron to proton mass; the gravitational constant; the Hubble constant; Higg's vacuum expectation value, etc. The fact that all of these fell within a life-permitting range at the same time cries out for an explanation. As professor of mathematics and leading cosmological theorist Dr. George Ellis has said, "amazing fine tuning occurs in the laws that make this [complexity] possible. Realization of the complexity of what is accomplished makes it very difficult not to use the word 'miraculous' without taking a stand as to the ontological status of the word."[165]

Agnostic cosmologist Dr. Paul Davies has said: "There is for me powerful evidence that there is something going on behind it all…. It seems as though somebody has fine-tuned nature's numbers to make the Universe…. The impression of design is overwhelming."[166]

Famous astronomer Sir Fred Hoyle framed it this way: "A common sense interpretation of the facts suggests that a superintellect has monkeyed with physics...and that there are no blind forces in nature.[167]

If there was a drum filled with tens of billions lottery balls, and all were white with black numbers written on them except for one solid, life-permitting black lottery ball in the mix, you would think somebody rigged the game if you pulled that black lottery ball out and missed all the billions of non-life-permitting lottery balls.

If you pulled this single life-permitting ball out over a dozen times in a row when there are tens of billions of other non-life-permitting balls in there, you would be more justified in believing the game is somehow rigged than you would be to chalk it up to pure chance. In fact, your intellect may demand that you conclude it was designed to turn out that way.

As philosopher William Lane Craig has said: "To get a handle on how many tiny points on the dial this is, compare it to the number of cells in your body (10^{14}) or the number of seconds that have ticked by since time began (10^{20}). If the gravitational constant had been out of tune by just one of these infinitesimally small increments, the universe would either have expanded and thinned out so rapidly that no stars could form and life couldn't exist, or it would have collapsed back on itself with the same result: no stars, no planets, no life."[168]

Premise 1: The fine-tuning of the universe is due to either physical necessity, chance, or design.

Premise 2: The fine-tuning of the universe is not due to physical necessity or chance.

Conclusion 1: Therefore, the fine-tuning of the universe is due to design.

The best explanation is that these improbable features are a result of design. But design implies a plan—s thought, intention, and a purposed, willful action. An impersonal force cannot "plan" anything. A non-rational cosmic energy field cannot draw up a blueprint for an apartment complex, get all the materials together, construct it from the ground up, and erect it perfectly in the middle of New York City. A light beam cannot formulate the laws of combustion and then build a fully functional transport truck. Only self-aware, rational agents have the ability to plan something, design something, and bring that thing into being.

Computers and robots can design objects, but only after they have been programmed by a person to do so. There must be an intelligent to plug in the data so that the computer (which has no intelligence of its own) can function. In the creation of the universe, we are looking for the initial Programmer who existed outside the universe and plugged the values of the constants and quantities into the very first moment of space-time itself so that life would be permitted to exist. It is most plausible to conclude that design implies a designer, and a designer must be a personal agent by definition. Let us look briefly at two separate reasons for why the cause of the universe must be a personal agent and not an impersonal force.

1. There are only two potential types of causes: scientific or personal, and the universe doesn't have a scientific cause.

For any given effect (such as the universe), only two possible kinds of causes can explain the effect. For example, one could ask you the question: "Why is the television on?" One response would be, "Because the television is plugged into the outlet in the wall providing an electrical current through the wires to the motherboard, and the power button was pushed, causing a wireless signal to the motherboard to turn on and receive the current coming from the electrical outlet." This would be a scientific explanation in terms of the physical conditions that came together to produce the effect of the television being on.

Or you could answer, "Because I wanted to watch the game tonight." This would be an explanation at the level of a personal agent simply explaining the effect by referring to the free will of a person. Both of these are perfectly valid, yet different, explanations. Now when it comes to the beginning of the universe, there was no scientific explanation available, because matter, space, time, energy, and the corresponding laws of nature did not yet exist. A scientific explanation requires a prior physical state, but there was no physical state prior to the universe by which we can infer a scientific explanation. Physics, matter, and space did not exist yet. The only kind of explanation that remains is one at the level of a personal agent who chose to bring the universe into being.

2. A personal creator is the only way we can explain the origin of the universe from necessary and sufficient conditions that are permanently and timelessly present.

Necessary and sufficient conditions refer to the conditions that are required and adequate in order to produce an effect. Since we know that the cause of the universe must be timeless and eternally existing (since time itself began to exist at the moment of creation), we know that the cause contained all of the conditions permanently and timelessly that are required to produce the universe.

This means that all of the necessary and sufficient conditions needed to produce the universe were permanently present within the cause before the universe existed. But if all the conditions required to cause the universe were timelessly and permanently present, we should expect to see the effect also existing eternally. If every condition needed to create the universe has always been contained within the cause, we should see an eternally existing universe that has always been its effect. If everything needed to produce the effect was always present, why hasn't the effect always been present?

The beginning of the universe is the origin of a new effect with an absolute beginning from a cause that has eternally contained all the conditions necessary to produce the universe. The only way we can explain the creation of the universe with an absolute beginning from a set of permanently present necessary and sufficient conditions is to infer what is called agent causation.

A personal agent with free will chose to spontaneously create a new effect without any prior determining conditions, which is the only we can explain how the universe had an absolute beginning from a permanently and timelessly present set of necessary and sufficient conditions.

If everything needed to produce the universe always existed, we would see a universe that has always existed. Since we don't see a universe that has always existed, there needs to be an explanation for how a new temporal effect can be brought about out of permanently present sufficient conditions. The answer is agent causation. God is a free being with His own will, rationality, and consciousness who made a choice to bring the universe into being.

Pantheism is a philosophically illegitimate worldview that cannot stand on its own two feet. The best evidence we have pertaining to origin and design of the universe points us to a transcendent personal agent that existed without the universe. Ironically, the vast majority of New Age thought and practice rests upon a theology that is negated by the very universe it seeks to deify.

Is Consciousness a Fundamental Field?

One hotly contended question in the physics community is: What is consciousness? Coming up with a working theory of consciousness has proven incredibly difficult, if not impossible. Earlier theories that continue to be developed today, such as CEMI Field Theory, included the idea that perhaps consciousness is an interaction in the electromagnetic field.[169] However, that theory was dismissed because when an electromagnetic field is increased, such as inside an MRI machine, a person's consciousness is not affected.[170]

Another theory, called Quantum Brain Dynamics (QBD), suggests that there might exist an as of yet undiscovered quantum field behind consciousness. QBD suggests that a "consciousness" field, hypothetically called the "cortical field," produces particles called "corticons."[171] The theory basically states that consciousness is the interaction between our brains and the cortical field. If ever proven true, this would of course be fascinating, but it would not mean souls and spirits within people don't exist. QBD, CEMI, or any other quantum theory of consciousness would not speak to the spiritual reality of anything; it would only speak to the biological and quantum processes involved in consciousness in our physical reality.

Furthermore, even *if* there is a field of consciousness at the lowest, most fundamental levels of nature, there is a major problem: The universe (and all its properties) began to exist. If consciousness was inseparable from the universe as a sort of substrata to ground reality, the issue here is that the universe and its properties all began to exist.

Space, time, matter, energy, and universal consciousness may be fundamental to our universe. Let's grant that they are. All these properties, including this fundamental field at the lowest level of nature, began to exist as a part of space-time reality. Whether consciousness is somehow woven into the fabric of reality at a fundamental level or not is irrelevant to the question of God, because "reality" itself had a beginning and we therefore need to look beyond the universe and all its properties (including universal consciousness) to an external cause.

This field is an attribute and fundamental property of the universe. It's the primary substance of the universe. The universe, and all its properties and substances, began to exist. Therefore, this field began to exist. If consciousness is the substance of the universe, that doesn't solve our problem. We still need a transcendent first cause to explain the origin of the universe and all its substances/properties, including this field of universal consciousness.

The problem is, even if we grant the existence of a sort of universal field of consciousness that unifies all things at a fundamental level, we are still only describing our space-time universe. This doesn't lead us to God as a supernatural being. In fact, it doesn't lead us to anything beyond the natural world. It, at most, leads us to a better understanding of how God, as a supernatural transcendent being, chose to structure the physical universe.

John Hagelin, PhD, a major proponent and developer of this theory of consciousness, said in an interview that this field is "the very core of nature" and "unites gravity with electromagnetism, with radioactivity, with the nuclear force" as "the most concentrated field of intelligence in nature."[172]

This theory of universal consciousness was never intended to describe anything beyond nature. It is not a theory of the supernatural. It does not point us to anything outside the universe, it only *describes* the universe. At most, it's a deeper way of understanding the design of the universe, not the Designer.

The Bible Refutes Pantheism

The Bible tells us that the universe itself serves as a refutation of pantheism because we can learn about the characteristic of God through studying the creation, just as we have done. In Romans 1:19–20, we are told that God has shown mankind His "eternal power" and "divine nature" in the things that have been created so that man is without excuse. We don't just derive a loose idea of God in some vague sense upon studying the created world. We are confronted with a beginningless, spaceless, immaterial, formless, timeless, personal, unembodied mind. Simply put, we have an idea of what kind of God is responsible for the sunsets, waterfalls, and star systems that we take pleasure in. Their design cries out for an explanation at the level of a personal, transcendent Creator.

God did not leave Himself without witness (Acts 14:17). The heavens declare the glory of God, and the sky testifies of His handiwork: "Night to night reveals knowledge" (Psalm 19:1–2). The Bible affirms that we have an in-built awareness of there being a single, personal, transcendent God who has revealed general characteristics about Himself in the created world.

In the following verses in Romans 1 (vv. 21–23), the Apostle Paul gives an illustration of how people are turned over to a morally debased mind through the worship of created things rather than the Creator. The infamously controversial passage in Romans tells us that mankind has a general revelation of God, but suppresses this knowledge (v. 18) because they would rather serve their flesh and the pleasures of sin. In other words, pantheism is not just a false theology, it's a symptom of moral rebellion against a holy God. It's evidence of spiritual corruption, run-off from a preexisting desire to suppress the God who has revealed Himself in nature.

The creation narrative in Genesis 1 is the most explicit refutation of pantheism we find in Scripture. We see that God, prior to the creation of the universe, existed outside the universe in "the beginning" (v. 1). This simply means that the act of creation was initiated by a God who had prior existence to the things He created. God began to speak things into creation, starting with "Let there be light," and then He saw that it was good (v. 3).

We see a Creator/creation distinction where God brings the creation into existence ex nihilo (out of nothing) through His spoken word, and then uses His awareness to reflect upon this creation that is now before Him. Such behavior is only possible if God is personal and if He is not identical to the creation. It does not say "He saw that He was good," but that "He saw that it was good." "It" can only be understood as a thing distinct from the God who created it.

In Genesis 1:26, there is a conversation between Father, Son, and Spirit wherein they say, "Let us make man in our image." The creation of the first human being proceeded from a divine dialog that included a plural verb in the original Hebrew. How could the universe speak itself into existence before it existed, see itself as being good, and then converse with itself in the plural? The Bible is clear: God existed without the universe, made the universe through spoken word out of no pre-existing substance, and has revealed Himself as personal designer in the things that have been created.

The Theology of Jesus Refutes Pantheism

Contrary to the radical claims made about Jesus in the New Age movement (which we will address shortly), one of the most certain facts of history is that Jesus was a Jewish man who identified with the monotheistic deity of the Old Testament, Yahweh. The Hebrew Bible was the Bible of Jesus. Yahweh is someone whom Jesus claimed was His Father.

The things Jesus has to say about God are confrontational, precise, and exclusive, automatically ruling out every other Pantheistic, polytheistic, or monotheistic religion in the world. If we put any weight into the words of Jesus Christ, the only option we have to choose from is a form of radical monotheism that maintains a Creator/creation distinction. The following is a brief list of attributes and properties of God as outlined by the words of Jesus in the Gospels.

God has a will:

- "Your kingdom come, your will be done" (Matthew 6:10).
- "For whoever does the will of my Father in heaven is my brother and sister and mother" (Matthew 12:50).
- "For this is the will of my Father, that everyone who looks on the Son and believes in him should have eternal life, and I will raise him up on the last day" (John 6:40).

God can act on His will:

- "If you then, who are evil, know how to give good gifts to your children, how much more will your Father who is in heaven give good things to those who ask him!" (Matthew 7:11).
- "Again I say to you, if two of you agree on earth about anything they ask, it will be done for them by my Father in heaven" (Matthew 18:19).

- "For God so loved the world, that he gave his only Son, that whoever believes in him should not perish but have eternal life" (John 3:16).

God has knowledge:

- "But concerning that day and hour no one knows, not even the angels of heaven, nor the Son, but the Father only" (Matthew 12:36).
- "For all the nations of the world seek after these things, and your Father knows that you need them" (Luke 12:30).
- "Just as the Father knows me and I know the Father; and I lay down my life for the sheep" (John 10:15).

God verbally speaks:

- "And behold, a voice from heaven said, 'This is my beloved Son, with whom I am well pleased'" (Matthew 3:17).
- "He was still speaking when, behold, a bright cloud overshadowed them, and a voice from the cloud said, 'This is my beloved Son, with whom I am well pleased; listen to him'" (Matthew 17:5).
- "Father, glorify your name." Then a voice came from heaven: "I have glorified it, and I will glorify it again" (John 12:28).

God transcends nature in Heaven:

- "Our Father in heaven, hallowed be your name" (Matthew 6:9).
- "But whoever denies me before men, I also will deny before my Father who is in heaven" (Matthew 10:33).
- "For whoever does the will of my Father in heaven is my brother and sister and mother" (Matthew 12:50).
- "So it is not the will of my Father who is in heaven that one of these little ones should perish" (Matthew 18:14).

God is called a person by Jesus:

- "Yet even if I do judge, my judgment is true, for it is not I alone who judge, but I and the Father who sent me. In your Law it is written that the testimony of two people is true. I am the one who bears witness about myself, and the Father who sent me bears witness about me" (John 8:16–18).

This last passage cited is arguably the most revealing Scripture on the nature of God in the Gospels. The Pharisees (a Jewish sect) had just accused Jesus of having an invalid testimony of Himself since He lacked multiple witnesses. In Old Testament law, the witness of two or three people was necessary to establish a charge against someone (Deuteronomy 17:6; Numbers 35:30). The Pharisees were telling Jesus, "If you want to be compliant with the standard of truth God laid out in the Old Covenant, you cannot be your own witness."

Jesus responded by saying the Father who sent Him bears witness to His testimony and confirms that He is speaking the truth. In order for the Father to qualify as a witness to the testimony Jesus gave of Himself, he must be a "person," since two or three people must be in agreement in order for a testimony to be true. He also must be able to intellectually assent to what Jesus was saying, a function that is only possible by a personal mind with the ability to agree upon a set of propositions. If God wasn't a person, the witness Jesus bore about Himself would not be compliant with Old Testament law.

Jesus, as the resurrected miracle worker, knew a thing or two about God, and Jesus was a monotheistic Jew who affirmed the transcendent deity of the Old Testament. Even if one rejects the divine inspiration of Scripture, it is historically unviable to accredit Jesus with the worldview of pantheism. He denied pantheism, the Old Testament that He continuously affirmed as truth denied pantheism, and the disciples/apostles who wrote letters to the early churches denied pantheism.

Pantheism cannot account for the scientific evidence for design we see in the universe. It is refuted by the beginning of the universe and the fine tuning of the universe, not to mention other arguments from logic, morality, and consciousness that would serve as additional nails in the coffin of pantheism. Ironically, the universe itself serves as the best evidence against pantheism by bearing witness to transcendence. Most importantly, it is radically opposed to the version of God taught throughout Scripture and by Jesus Himself. As we have now undermined the worldview that acts as the unifying adhesive that holds almost all New Age, Eastern, and pagan philosophies together, we make room for the true witness that Jesus Christ bore about Himself in relation to the Father and we will see how the Christology taught in the New Age movement contradicts everything we know to be true about the theology of Jesus.

6

FALSE CHRIST, FALSE GOSPEL

IF SOMEONE ASKED YOU IF you knew who Michael Jordan is, you would know exactly who they are talking about: the ex-NBA basketball player with six championship rings and his own successful clothing brand who is famous for his professional career as number 23 with the Chicago Bulls. If they told you, "Actually, Michael Jordan never played basketball. He has been a father living in Toledo for the last thirty years as a mineworker," you would know that they are referring to a *different* Michael Jordan. The Michael Jordan they are talking about has different attributes and properties than the Michael Jordan you are referring to, meaning that you cannot be referencing the same person.

A sufficient condition to say that two different names are referring to the same person is if they have identical properties. If they have different properties, then there are two different people. We have all had many instances in ordinary conversations in which we *think* we are talking about the same person as someone else, but upon further inquiry, we realize the descriptions are too far off to be the same person.

Imagine, however, if the person who asked you about Michael Jordan kept pressing you, saying that the two of you *are* referring to the same person; the Michael Jordan you are referring to never played basketball before. You and everyone who knows him is mistaken. All the videos of and stories about him are fraudulent, and the real Michael Jordan has worked in a coal mine for the last three decades.

How strange would it be if that person said you ought to believe this about Michael Jordan because that person had gone into a trance and an alien-like being had come through the veil and said MJ was a mine-worker and all the other stories about him are all part of a conspiracy. Or what if that person told you this "revelation" had come during a deep state of meditation in the mountains of Tibet? Or perhaps the person tried to take snippets out of context from the media about how Michael works as hard a miner and how Michael once said that he got a piece of coal for Christmas. If someone told you any of these things, you would answer that it doesn't matter what that alien being said, that those quotes of MJ need to be understood in the context of the actual life he lived, and then you would present overwhelming evidence that MJ was actually a basketball player.

In the New Age movement, lots of extravagant claims are made about Jesus of Nazareth, but none refer to the Jesus who existed in history. The attributes and properties given to the person of Jesus are so far removed from our historical records of Jesus that they cannot refer to Jesus. Just like your friend did with Michael Jordan, they are referring to an idea of Jesus that is diametrically opposed to everything we know about Him, a version of Him that has absolutely no record of having existed in the world. And just like your friend did during the MJ conversation, New Agers often justify their assertions about Jesus on the basis of private spiritual revelation and by isolating a small handful of words out of context.

Nobody in the New Age movement goes around saying that Buddha was an Old Testament Jew, that Muhammad was a gnostic, or that Gandhi was an atheist. We know what they taught because we have historical records of their teachings. Yet, Jesus is accused of believing in things that 100 percent of the historical records available tell us He full-on rejected. As someone who started the largest spiritual movement in history, we should have an intellectually honest answer as to who Jesus is, what His teachings mean in their proper context, and why His followers simultaneously came to believe He had risen from the dead and appeared to them.

The New Age movement teaches a variety of concepts about the person of Jesus.

Jesus Mythicism

A percentage of the adherents of New Age insist that Jesus never existed as a historical figure and that His story is ancient mythology fashioned by the early Christians for the purposes of power and control—or even by accident. Some say Jesus was a conspiracy created by the world elite to keep mankind spiritually enslaved and stuck in a lower state of consciousness.

For one reason or another, the legend of Jesus Christ was fabricated in first-century Jerusalem out of thin air, resulting in a new religious system rooted entirely in mythology. This position is called "mythicism," and while it's not typically the go-to position for New Agers, it does occupy a portion of the Christological landscape. It's important to know that this idea is not taken seriously by any expert in any relevant field of study. Dr. Bart Ehrman is the James A. Gray Distinguished Professor of Religious Studies at the University of North Carolina. He is an atheist historian who said the following at a conference on the historical evidence for the existence of Jesus:

> This is not an issue for scholars of antiquity. There is no scholar in any college or university who teaches classics, ancient history, new testament, early christianity, who doubts that Jesus existed. He is abundantly attested in early sources. Early and independent

sources indicate that Jesus certainly existed. Paul is an eyewitness to both Jesus' disciple Peter and the brother of Jesus. Like, I'm sorry. Atheists have done themselves a disservice by jumping on the bandwagon of mythicism because it makes you look foolish to the outside world.[173]

He goes on to say in an article, "There is not a single mythicist who teaches New Testament or Early Christianity or even Classics at any accredited institution of higher learning in the Western world.... Whether we like it or not, Jesus certainly existed."[174]

Atheist historian Dr. R. Joseph Hoffman is even less sympathetic to Jesus mythicists who often scoff at those who are confident of a historical Jesus: "Only in the age of instant misinformation and net-attack is this kind of idiocy possible. Only in the atheist universe where the major premise—"religion is a lie so the study of religion is a study of lying"—infects everything is this kind of lunacy possible."[175]

Professor Graeme Clarke of the Australian National University echoes this rhetoric by saying, "Frankly, I know of no ancient historian or biblical historian who would have a twinge of doubt about the existence of a Jesus Christ—the documentary evidence is simply overwhelming."[176]

Bart Ehrman testifies in an interview elsewhere that he knows "thousands of scholars of the ancient world.... These are people who have devoted their entire lives to this," and no legitimate historian (whether atheist, Jewish, agnostic, etc.) doubts that a man named Jesus Christ existed in first-century Jerusalem.[177] The reason for this is that we have too many early independent sources that attest to a historical Jesus of Nazareth. Some ancient figures are established in history based on only a few sources, but for Jesus we have literally dozens, all of which are considerably early.

Historians Dr. Gary Habermas and Dr. Mike Licona outline forty-two historical sources attesting to the existence of Jesus within 150 years after His death.[178] They list the sources as follows:

Traditional New Testament authors:

Matthew, Mark, Luke, John, Paul, author of Hebrews, James, Peter, and Jude

Early Christian writers outside the New Testament:

Clement of Rome, Ignatius of Antioch, Polycarp, Martyrdom of Polycarp, Didache, Barnabas, Shepherd of Hermas, Fragments of Papias, Justin Martyr, Aristides, Athenagoras, Theophilus of Antioch, Quadratus, Aristo of Pella, Melito of Sardis, Diognetus, Gospel of Peter, Apocalypse of Peter, and Epistula Apostolorum

Heretical writings:

Gospel of Thomas, Gospel of Truth, Apocryphon of John, and Treatise on Resurrection

Secular Sources:

Josephus (Jewish historian), Tacitus (Roman historian), Pliny the Younger (Roman politician), Phlegon (freed slave who wrote histories), Lucian (Greek satirist), Celsus (Roman philosopher), Mara Bar Serapion (prisoner awaiting execution), Suetonius (Roman historian), and Thallus (Roman historian)

When looking at this list, we have to keep in mind that biblical sources are still historical sources. Galatians, for example, is a letter Paul wrote to a church in Galatia in the mid 50s AD. Hundreds of years later, this letter was assembled with a group of other documents and put under a cover called the New Testament. Paul's letter to Galatia doesn't lose its status as a source about Jesus just because the Christian Church decided to include it in the canon centuries later. It existed as a separate document and still stands as its own separate document. There is no justification for thinking that a source is no longer historical just because someone puts it into a collection of texts later on.

Our best secular source about Jesus is the reliable Roman historian and senator Tacitus (c. AD 55–c. AD 117), who mentions Jesus and the persecutions of Christians under the orders of Roman emperor Nero in *Annals, Book XV*:

> Consequently, to get rid of the report, Nero fastened the guilt and inflicted the most exquisite tortures on a class hated for their abominations, called Christians by the populace. Christus, from whom the name had its origin, suffered the extreme penalty during the reign of Tiberius at the hands of one of our procurators, Pontius Pilatus.

When Roman Emperor Claudius ruled in Rome from AD 41–54, he ordered that all Jews must leave Rome because of their religious influence over the local Gentiles. This is recorded in Acts 18:2, and by the historian Seutonius in Claudius 25: "Since the Jews constantly made disturbances at the instigation of Chrestus, he expelled them from Rome."

We could go on and on listing extrabiblical sources about Jesus. We not only have more extrabiblical sources about Jesus than we do for other historical figures of the ancient world, but the ones we have also date exceedingly early in comparison. The earliest writings we have about Jesus is Paul's first letter to the Thessalonians, which dates to about AD 51. Jesus is believed to have died in AD 30. This means that within about twenty years of Jesus' death, we have written accounts of Jesus written by Paul, someone whom scholars agree was an eyewitness to Jesus' brother James and disciple Peter.[179]

We have written records produced very near the time of Jesus's life by someone who not only claimed to have seen Him arise, but who was friends with those who knew Jesus intimately. To give perspective on how significant this is, the earliest recorded mention of Siddhārtha

Gautama Buddha doesn't come until some four hundred years after his death, long after all eyewitnesses had deceased.[180] The entire New Testament, including four biographies of Jesus, was completed around sixty to sixty-five years after his death, as dated by all historians. The first biography written about Buddha was Buddhacarita, a poem written by Aśvaghoṣa dating to the beginning of the second century over five hundred years after Buddha had died.[181]

There is a four-hundred-year gap between the time when Buddha lived and the first historical text mentioning him, and there is a twenty-one-year period between Jesus' lifespan and the writings of Paul. There is a five-hundred-year gap between Buddha's lifetime and the first biography written about him, yet the first biography written about Jesus (Mark's Gospel) dates to no more than forty years after His death. We simply have too many early independent sources to doubt a historical Jesus, so much so that if we doubt the existence of Jesus, we would have to doubt almost every figure of the ancient world, including Buddha, whom nobody in the New Age movement doubts existed.

Professor of history Dr. Paul Maier claims boldly that "there is more evidence that Jesus of Nazareth certainly lived than for most famous figures of the ancient past.... Skeptics should focus instead on whether or not Jesus was more than a man. That, at least, could evoke a reasonable debate among reasonable inquirers, rather than a pointless discussion with sensationalists who struggle to reject the obvious."[182]

Professor of religion at Butler University, Dr. James McGrath, says "to suggest that these various authors and sources independently invented a historical Jesus, or that despite their divergent views they conspired together to do so, is (to put it charitably) less plausible than the explanation of this state of affairs accepted by all scholars and historians teaching at accredited institutions."[183]

This goes back to what it means to be "open-minded," because if we are truly open and willing to follow the evidence where it leads regardless of how it makes us feel, we will see that there is no legitimate reason to doubt that Jesus existed. To be blunt, Jesus mythicism is often fueled by a desire to run from the moral implications that may arise in the conscience of a sinner. There is a preexisting bias the person erects against Jesus or the Church at large, and the denial of a historical Jesus keeps that person a safe distance away from having to deal with whatever the truth of the Gospel may present.

A desire to "suppress the truth in unrighteousness" leads to the rejection of someone whom no expert rejects to avoid the consequences of a historical Jesus. The New Age movement reconciles historical scholarship with the desire to suppress the truth by creating distorted versions of Jesus that suit their own philosophical and theological preferences, and the versions that are postulated are just as far removed from actual history as Jesus mythicism.

Master Jesus of the Great White Brotherhood

Ascended Masters, or the Great White Brotherhood, are believed to be spiritually enlightened teachers who in past incarnations were ordinary humans, but have gone through spiritual transformation to the point of reaching ascension. Also called "mahatmas," "Ascended Masters" does not refer to any spiritual teacher, but only to those who have moved up the scale of deification to a sixth-level initiation such that they have fully embodied the "I Am Presence" and transcended an individual sense of self.

The Theosophical Society, out of which this idea was first popularized, believes there are nine levels of "initiation" people work through as they conform their minds to theosophical wisdom and occult practice.

Initiation, or the process of undergoing an expansion of consciousness, is part of the normal process of evolutionary development, viewed on a large scale, and not from the standpoint of the individual.... Each initiation marks the passing of the pupil in the Hall of Wisdom into a higher class, marks the clearer shining forth of the inner fire and the transition from one point of polarisation to another, entails the realisation of an increasing unity with all that lives and the essential oneness of the self with all selves. It results in a horizon that continuously enlarges until it includes the sphere of creation; it is a growing capacity to see and hear on all the planes.[184]

The whole purpose of initiation is for a person to be aware that he or she is fundamentally one with all things in and outside of creation. "First: With himself, and those in incarnation with him. Second: With his higher Self, and thus with all selves. Third: With his Spirit, or 'Father in Heaven,' and thus with all Monads. Fourth: With the Logos, the Three in One and the One in Three."[185]

Most of humanity is not even at the first rung of initiation (birth), which consists of a person having full control of his or her body. The second level (baptism) has to do with being in control of one's astral body, and the third level (transfiguration) has to do with clairvoyance and psychic ability.

The fourth level of initiation (crucifixion) is where people remember all their past lives, have supernatural abilities, and no longer need to continue reincarnating here over and over for spiritual development. Since they are no longer required to reincarnate, they are presented with seven different options for what they can do next, such as staying with humanity in a higher dimension as a member of the "Hierarchy" (the office that Jesus chose for Himself) for service to humanity, or join the staff corps of the Solar Logos and exist inside the sun as a solar spirit.

At the fifth level (the resurrection), participants begin to levitate and teleport, and at the sixth level of initiation (ascension) they have fully ascended to unity with the Most High, the True God Self that is the Source of All. Their individualized sense of self becomes replaced with the Universal Self, and they, along with Jesus, who is currently a sixth-level initiate, can bear the title of Ascended Master. All of these stages were successfully accomplished by Jesus when He walked this earth two thousand years ago. As a side note, it is hard to understand how Jesus could be virtually superhuman, touching His own humanity when the Bible tells us that He was made to be exactly like us in His humanity, in every respect: "Therefore he had to be made like his brothers in every respect, so that he might become a merciful and faithful high priest in the service of God, to make propitiation for the sins of the people" (Hebrews 2:17).

He did this to "make propitiation," meaning that at the time of His crucifixion, He was still exactly like us in His humanity. He couldn't have been a fourth-level initiate at the time He died for mankind; otherwise, He wouldn't be able to make propitiation. How could Jesus be made like His brothers in every respect to die for them if Jesus was a fourth-level initiate in His humanity when He died, and they were mostly at level zero?

This scale posits three higher levels of initiation that are occupied by beings more advanced than Jesus, putting Him on a lower spiritual development than at least six other beings. At the seventh level is Lord Matraiya, who is given the title the "Christ," and was the active teacher of Jesus during His incarnation. According to theosophy, Jesus is an Ascended Master but is not the Christ. The "Christ" is a different higher-level initiate being properly named Lord Matraiya who operated through the physical body of Jesus once He laid it down as an offering during His incarnation here during three years of His ministry. Jesus was a highly advanced human being who received His insight through the influence of his superior Matraiya who was a sort of interactive "spirit guide" for Jesus of Nazareth.[186]

According to a theosophical foundation called *Share International*:

The method he used is called spiritual overshadowing, that is, his consciousness informed and guided the actions and teachings of his disciple Jesus. It was, therefore, the consciousness of the Christ, Maitreya, which was seen and experienced by those around Jesus.... Thus the seemingly paradoxical claim that Jesus and the Christ are not the same person, in the literal sense of the word, is more reasonable than it would appear.[187]

So Jesus was only able to do what He did because of Lord Matraiya operating through Him. Matriaya came over Him in His baptism and was with Him until resurrection, giving Him the means by which to carry out the life He lived. Jesus is not unique, however, as Matraiya has also overshadowed Hercules, Hermes, Rama, Mithra, Vyasa, Confucius, Zoroaster, Krishna, Shankaracharya, Gautama, and Mohammed. As theosophical kingpin Benjamin Creme puts it, "Just as the Buddha worked through the Prince Gautama, so in Palestine Maitreya worked through Jesus of Nazareth."[188]

So we have a version of Jesus who did things by the power of another Ascended Master who is not the Father, yet Jesus tells us, "I do nothing on my own authority, but speak just as the Father taught me" (John 8:28), and that He "only what he sees the Father doing. For whatever the Father does, that the Son does likewise" (John 5:19). According to theosophists, his supernatural abilities were derived from the influence of the "actual" Christ, Lord Maitreya, who to this day occupies a higher level of initiation than "Master Jesus." This blatantly contradicts what Jesus says about His source of inspiration.

It also contradicts what the Bible says about the authority of Jesus, who is Creator of all beings in existence: "For by him all things were created, in heaven and on earth, visible and invisible, whether thrones or dominions or rulers or authorities—all things were created through him and for him" (Colossians 1:16). This is in specific reference to Jesus (v. 13), and under Jesus that all things in Heaven and Earth have been placed (Ephesians 1:22; 1 Corinthians 15:27) "'putting everything in subjection under his feet.' Now in putting everything in subjection to him, he left nothing outside his control. At present, we do not yet see everything in subjection to him" (Hebrews 2:8).

This means Jesus is above every being and authority. There is none above Him. Because Jesus is truly divine (Colossians 2:9), Creator (Hebrews 1:10), and is the highest authority in Heaven and on Earth, He can properly be called "God over all" (Romans 9:5). Jesus can't be called "God over all" if He is spiritually inferior to Lord Matraiya, who himself is spiritually inferior to other beings.

Both Jesus and Matraiya are inferior to the leader of the Masters, the founder of the Great White Brotherhood who goes by the name "Sanat Kumara." Sanat Kumara is usually depicted as having the appearance of a 16-year-old boy. Believers claim he descended to Venus from a higher spiritual plane with a group of followers called "Lords of the Flame." Benjamin Creme defines him as "the Lord of the World; the etheric physical expression of our Planetary Logos who dwells on Shamballa. A great Being, originally from Venus, Who sacrificed Himself to become the personality vehicle for the ensouling deity of our planet 18.5 million years ago. The nearest aspect of God that we can know."[189]

According to Alice Bailey, Sanat Kumara is the one to whom Jesus referred when He said "I and my Father are one."[190] Interestingly, Sanat Kumara primarily goes by the name "Lord of the World" in theosophy, a title never given to the Father in the Bible. This sounds eerily similar to the title the Bible gives Satan, however. Paul calls Satan "the god of this world" (2 Corinthians 4:4), and Jesus refers to Satan as being the "ruler of this world" three times (John12:31, 14:30, and 16:11). Even the Satanic Bible refers to Satan as the "Lord of the earth."[191]

Some theosophists themselves concede that the one the Bible refers to as Satan is actually Sanat Kumara. Famous theosophist Dan Rudyar wrote: "Satan is an anagram for Sanat Kumara, who in the esoteric philosophy of India is the promethean being who gave mankind the fire of self-conscious and independent, individual self-hood."[192]

This goes back to the gnostic principle that Yahweh was evil, and those who chose to rebel against Yahweh are those who sought to release mankind with the gift of free will. The *New Encyclopedia of the Occult* says, "Satan has a possible echo in Theosophical lore, where the Lord of the World, the ruler of the earth, and the head of the Great White Lodge, is Sanat Kumara."[193]

"The one whom Jesus serves" is given a title that both the Bible and the Satanic Bible give only to Satan, and some theosophists concede that Sanat Kumara is actually Satan, though some would dispute this correlation. At worst, Jesus serves Satan. At best, Jesus serves a fallen angel who fell with Lucifer:

> Not all of the beings who belonged to Lucifer's group rebelled against God. However, some of them volunteered to descend into the material universe in an attempt to help those who fell with Lucifer find their way back to God. Sanat Kumara was one of the beings who descended to the material realm on such a rescue mission. The reason planet earth descended to such a low state was in large part due to the corrupting influence of Lucifer and his group of fallen beings. Because Sanat Kumara was originally part of the same group as Lucifer, he volunteered to hold the spiritual balance for earth in an attempt to raise the evolutions of earth out of the influence of Lucifer.[194]

So here we have teaching coming from channeled material given by interdimensional beings telling us that Jesus is not the Christ and that He serves either Satan or a highly developed fallen angel. This is a textbook example of the "teachings of demons" in 1 Timothy 4:1. Additionally, Ascended Masters teachings from a variety of sources maintain that Jesus Himself has incarnated here nearly a dozen times through His soul's existence going under different names:

• Emperor of Atlantis in 33,050 BC
• Emperor of Atlantis in 15000 BC
• Joseph, Son of Jacob

- Joshua, son of Nun, whom Moses appointed
- Jeshua, high priest in the time of Ezra
- David, king of Israel
- Joshua in Zechariah
- Jesus of Nazareth
- Elisha, prophet
- Apollonius of Tyana
- Ramanuja, Indian guru

From time to time, Jesus decides to occupy bodies and walk around without revealing His true nature as an Ascended Master. At the time Alice Bailey channeled *Initiations, Human and Solar* in 1922, He occupied a Syrian body in Israel.[195] As of right now, He is believed to occupy a body in Rome.[196] Theoretically, Jesus could have taken a flight from Rome to America this morning and was riding in front of you on the road today in an Uber car on his way to get a Fillet-o-Fish sandwich at McDonald's. This proposition is not only comical, it's impossible in light of Scripture. The Bible tells us that Jesus died once for all (Romans 6:10), and since His death, He has been in Heaven—where He will remain forever making intercession for us (Hebrews 7:25). The Master Jesus (who is not even Christ, remember), cannot have died once and eleven times at the same time, and cannot be in Rome while making intercession for us beside the Father at the same time.

It goes without saying that, according to the Ascended Masters teachings, it is not Jesus who is coming to Earth a second time. Jesus has already come back to Earth multiple times and is on Earth right now! The Second Coming everyone is waiting for is the return of Lord Matraiya, who will make a grand appearance to the world announcing himself as being the Christ, fulling the biblical prophecies about the "son of perdition" who proclaims himself to be God (2 Thessalonians 2:3).

Eastern Jesus of Christ Consciousness

In Eastern philosophical systems there's an established idea of a path through personal consciousness to a collective conscience to a universal conscience, which people call the divine. I concluded that Jesus must have experienced this consciousness.
——Deepak Chopra[197]

Christ Consciousness is by far the most prevalent idea of Jesus taught in the New Age movement. This idea looks at "Christ" as being an inward state of consciousness and a state of divine awareness that can be accessed by each person. "Christ Consciousness" is a state wherein people realize that they are indwelt with the I Am Presence, the pseudo-divine, impersonal force of Life itself. In this model, mankind is inherently divine by virtue of the fact that all things in the universe are God. As a beam of light hits a prism and splits off into the colors of the rainbow, so the being of God fractals into individualized portions of divine energy that comprise all things in existence. Whether or not we are aware of this, we are all expressions of the impersonal God. To tap into our true identity, we are told to shift our consciousness from thinking to pure awareness or "presence," for when take our attention away from the thought-stream in our mind, we are met with the river of pure impersonal consciousness that underflows our personal minds and also all things in creation.

Christ, like God, is also impersonal. Jesus is a person, but "Christ" is a reference to a divine state of consciousness. Christ is not someone outside of us, He is something that we become through awakening to our true nature. Since our true nature is constant union with God, our true potential is to become a Christ. Christ Consciousness is believed to be the state of realizing that one is as Christ was: unified with God. To be truly self-conscious (aware of oneself) is to be truly Christ-Conscious (aware of oneself as inseparable from God).

Popular New Age teacher Eckhart Tolle writes about this in the following ways:

Jesus speaks of the innermost I Am, the essence of identity of every man and woman, every life-form in fact. He speaks of the life that you are. Some Christian mystics have called it the Christ within; Buddhists call it your Buddha nature; for Hindus, it is Atman, the in-dwelling God.[198]

Christ is your God essence or the Self, as it is sometimes called in the East.... Christ refers to your indwelling divinity regardless of whether you are conscious of it or not.... Thus, the man Jesus became Christ, a vehicle for pure consciousness.[199]

So Jesus is someone who *became* Christ by realizing that He and all things in creation are deity. Since deity is all that exists, we are all unrealized Christs blinded by the individuality of the ego. Because of a pantheistic theology that equates God with everything in existence, even the Pharisees and Judas (enemies of Jesus) can be said to be God as well. They were simply acting in their egos from a place of self-ignorance, but they have the same potential for Christhood as Jesus of Nazareth did if only they had achieved a state of Christ Consciousness through self-knowledge, divine contemplation, walking in the teachings of Jesus, and Eastern practices of meditation and mindfulness.

The *Course in Miracles* teacher's manual tells us that every individual is Christ. "Is he (Jesus) the Christ? O yes, along with you."[200] In *Conversations with God*, Neale Donald Walsch is apparently having a conversation with God, who tells us that we can all become as Jesus was: "And many have achieved such consciousness. Many have been Christed, not just Jesus of Nazareth. You can be Christed, too.... Now—I tell you this: You want to be 'Christed'? Act like Christ, every minute of every day."[201]

"Christ Consciousness" (sometimes called "God-Consciousness," "Krishna Consciousness," or "Unity Consciousness"), is the spiritual agenda of the New Age movement on an individual level. To say that you have "Christ Consciousness" is the highest claim you can make about your own spiritual development. It's the goal each person is working toward, but the goal is an inward journey into deeper, more fundamental levels of consciousness where the individual sense of self is replaced by complete identification with the presence of God that already lies within.

So in one sense, the New Age movement wants to affirm that we are striving toward Christ Consciousness, but that the "striving" itself conflicts with being and therefore we shouldn't use the word "strive," "goal," or "work." We realize and discover our divine nature and thus become Christ Consciousness; we don't work for it as something outside of us that we don't have access to yet.

Jesus did what many other people have done before Him (Such as Buddha or Krishna), and what many other people have done after Him. He, like all spiritual teachers, brought salvation to the world in the form of enlightenment. Rather than saving people from the penalty of their sins before a holy God, Jesus came to save people from a state of self-ignorance and the suffering it produces in their lives: "The salvation Jesus offered was the same as Buddha's: release from suffering and a path to spiritual freedom, joy, and closeness to God."[202] This view is so pervasive and has become so common that even Oprah Winfrey publicly advocates both Chopra, Tolle, and this view of Christ Consciousness. Before a live audience, Oprah answers a question a guest has about the person and mission of Jesus. This was her response:

> I mentioned this also in this book called *Discover the Power within You* by Eric Butterworth, where he talks about the Christ Consciousness, and up until then, I was like you. I thought Jesus came, died on the cross, that Jesus's being here was about his death when it really was about him coming to show us how to do it, how to be. To show us the Christ Consciousness that He had, and that that consciousness abides with all of us.[203]

This is advocated by one of the most influential people in the world, but is it true? Does it correspond with the historical teachings of Jesus? This version of Christ may be more socially palatable than the esoteric Jesus of theosophy, but it is equally as fanciful. The primary way we know that Jesus Christ did not come to earth to teach us "Christ Consciousness" is that the Bible explicitly states that man is not divine. Christ Consciousness implies, as we have seen, that man holds divinity within himself. The Bible, however, tell us that man is not only ontologically distinct from God (meaning he is of a separate nature), but is severed relationally from God through sin.

Ontological distinction:

Put them in fear, O Lord! Let the nations know that they are but men! Selah (Psalm 9:20)

The Egyptians are man, and not God, and their horses are flesh, and not spirit." (Isaiah 31:3)

Son of man, say to the prince of Tyre, Thus says the Lord God: "Because your heart is proud, and you have said, 'I am a god, I sit in the seat of the gods, in the heart of the seas,' yet you are but a man, and no god, though you make your heart like the heart of a god.... Because you make your heart like the heart of a god, therefore, behold, I will bring foreigners upon you, the most ruthless of the nations;... Will you still say, 'I am a god,' in the presence of those who kill you, though you are but a man, and no god, in the hands of those who slay you?" (Ezekiel 28:2, 7, 9)

On an appointed day Herod put on his royal robes, took his seat upon the throne, and delivered an oration to them. And the people were shouting, "The voice of a god, and not of a man!"

Immediately an angel of the Lord struck him down, because he did not give God the glory, and he was eaten by worms and breathed his last. (Acts 12:21–23).

The king of Babylon in Isaiah 14 tried to ascend to the height of God, and God brought him down to the "far reaches of the pit" (v. 15). The Antichrist of 2 Thessalonians 2:3–4 will sit in the seat of God "proclaiming himself to be God" (v. 4), and we are told in Revelation 19:20 and 20:10 that his sentence will be an eternity in the Lake of Fire. Not only does the Bible teach a fundamental distinction between God and man, the only biblical precedent we have for divinity-claimers is capital punishment and eternal judgment carried out by the Lord Himself.

Why would the Father of Jesus Christ want us to see ourselves as God and then strike down King Herod for seeing himself as God? Why would the Father of Jesus send people to kill the king of Tyre for making his heart like the heart of a god if "god-consciousness" was the God's will for mankind? Biblically speaking, human beings are so far distinct from God and so far removed from the divine nature that to claim divinity for oneself is considered a capital crime of blasphemy.

Relational separation via sin:

But your iniquities have made a separation between you and your God, and your sins have hidden his face from you so that he does not hear. (Isaiah 59:2)

And I will surely hide my face in that day because of all the evil that they have done, because they have turned to other gods. (Deuteronomy 31:18)

And you were dead in the trespasses and sins in which you once walked, following the course of this world, following the prince of the power of the air, the spirit that is now at work in the sons of disobedience—among whom we all once lived in the passions of our flesh, carrying out the desires of the body and the mind, and were by nature children of wrath, like the rest of mankind...remember that you were at that time separate from Christ, excluded from the commonwealth of Israel, and strangers to the covenants of promise, having no hope and without God in the world. (Ephesians 2:1–3, 12)

Once you were alienated from God and were enemies in your minds because of your evil behavior. (Colossians 1:21, NIV)

God is morally perfect and therefore cannot be in relationship with people who are still in their sin. We are made of a different substance than God and have been cut off from vertical relationship with Him through wicked works. The doctrine of Christ Consciousness teaches that people and God are inherently connected ontologically (which we have seen is false), and that relationship with God can be had instantaneously upon a shift of consciousness from ego to "presence." This overlooks the function of the cross, the Old Testament sacrificial system, and the entire New Covenant God has made with mankind. The theme of the Bible from cover to cover is God's plan to redeem mankind from the penalty and power of sin through the atoning death of Jesus Christ. If Christ Consciousness is true, the Bible cannot be true, because the Bible teaches that we are alienated sinners, not identity-sharers with God. If the Bible is true, then the doctrine of Christ Consciousness is false, because Christ Consciousness teaches that man is unified with God which the Bible denies. The Bible and Christ Consciousness hold two mutually exclusive doctrines.

Another point against this idea of Christ Consciousness is the fact that John the Baptist, whom Jesus said was the greatest among any man who has ever lived in all of history, denied being Christ. If Christ is something we all can become, why did the greatest man ever deny being Christ? Jesus said, "Truly, I say to you, among those born of women there has arisen no one greater than John the Baptist" (Matthew 11:11).

Now let's at what John says about himself:

And this is the testimony of John, when the Jews sent priests and Levites from Jerusalem to ask him, "Who are you?" He confessed, and did not deny, but confessed, "I am not the Christ."... "Then why are you baptizing, if you are neither the Christ, nor Elijah, nor the Prophet?" John answered them, "I baptize with water, but among you stands one you do not know, even he who comes after me, the strap of whose sandal I am not worthy to untie." (John 1:19–20, 26–27)

This is speaking of someone who was led by the Spirit of God into the wilderness to live off of bugs and honey, someone whose birth was predicted in the Old Testament a thousand years before he was born, someone who baptized Jesus Himself, and someone whom Jesus said was the greatest who ever lived. Yet this man denies being Christ. If the greatest man ever to have lived isn't Christ, how can we be Christ? If being second best to Jesus doesn't warrant the title of "Christ," at one point could one wear this title? If the greatest man who ever lived wasn't Christ, then nobody is.

John the Baptist, as the greatest ever, knew a thing or two about the truth, and the first thing he said when he saw Jesus was, "Behold, the Lamb of God, who takes away the sin of the world!" (John 1:29). The man whose spiritual life was more refined than any other person denied being Christ and said that Jesus was here to die a sacrificial death for human sin. This is vastly different from the witness the New Age movement bears about Jesus. Shall we believe the testimony of the one whom Jesus personally confirmed, or of those who never met Him and lived two thousand years later?

Another problem with this Eastern concept of Christ Consciousness echoes the lie told in the Garden of Eden, where Satan promises Eve that she and Adam they shall "be as gods" because of the increased knowledge they would gain by eating the forbidden fruit. Satan is the first to come up with the idea that through some kind of inner wisdom or knowledge you can become like God, and we are hearing this repeated by New Age teachers who say we can all become Christ by raising our consciousness to a higher level of self-divinity. Jesus came to destroy the works of the devil (1 John 3:8), and the first and most significant work of the devil was to tell Eve she could be like God.

This is the lie that led to mankind's separation from God and infected humanity with sin, which Jesus came to abolish in His death and resurrection. The lie that we can be God or be like God ultimately brought sin into the world in the first place and eventually led to the death of Jesus on the cross. It's ironic to think that the version of Christ taught by the New Age movement actually caused the sin that Jesus said He came to die for in the first place.

More ironic is that Jesus warns in the Gospel of Matthew prohibiting people from believing themselves to be Christ. To say "I am Christ" (which New Agers have said before) is not only false, but actually fulfills prophecy about the end times in which "many" shall come declaring themselves to be Christ:

> And as he sat upon the mount of Olives, the disciples came unto him privately, saying, Tell us, when shall these things be? and what shall be the sign of thy coming, and of the end of the world? And Jesus answered and said unto them, Take heed that no man deceive you. For many shall come in my name, saying, I am Christ; and shall deceive many. (Matthew 24: 3–5)

To call yourself Christ is to be deceived and to deceive others, and is also a sign of the spiritual corruption that Jesus told us to beware of in times close to His return. This warning of may refer to the dozens of individuals who have claimed to be Jesus Christ incarnate since His death and resurrection, or it may refer to the hundreds of New Age teachers who have spread this doctrine to hundreds of millions of people, convincing an entire spiritual movement that they can be or are Christ.

We are not made of God; we are separated from a relationship with God; the greatest man ever denied being Christ; this view echoes the lie Satan told Eve; and it fulfills Jesus' prophetic warning of those who will say "I am Christ." This doctrine stands wholly opposed to Scripture.

The Kingdom of God Is Within You?

A handful of verses are taken out of context of the rest of Scripture to push New Age versions of Jesus. These same few passages are recycled, in book after book, lecture after lecture, attempting to read Eastern philosophy into the ministry of Jesus.

> And when he was demanded of the Pharisees, when the kingdom of God should come, he answered them and said, The kingdom of God cometh not with observation: Neither shall they say, Lo here! or, lo there! for, behold, the kingdom of God is within you. (Luke 17:20–21, KJV)

This is a popular proof-text in the New Age movement used to serve the idea that divinity is intrinsic to each person and that the *real* message of Christ was that of enlightenment through raising one's consciousness. Isolated from the rest of the Bible, it appears that Jesus may telling us of an internal Kingdom that is to be found within each person. Chopra elaborates:

> No matter what version of Jesus you accept, the goal of a Christian life is to reach the Kingdom of God. Millions of believers hold that this means going to Heaven after you die. But Jesus is much more ambiguous than that. There is just as much evidence in the gospels that reaching the Kingdom of God means arriving at a higher level of consciousness.[204]

Eastern mystic Osho adds his own commentary:

If the Kingdom of God is within you then you need not go anywhere, a single step outside and you will be going away from the kingdom. You will not be coming closer to the kingdom.[205]

Was Jesus really saying that God's Kingdom is already within each person? This verse cannot possibly mean git is within everyone, because Jesus told those whom He was addressing (the Pharisees) that they belonged to another kingdom. He called them blind guides (Matthew 23:16), fools (Matthew 23:17), full of dead man's bones and all uncleanness (Matthew 23:27), serpents, a generation of vipers (Matthew 22:33), hypocrites (Luke 11:44), damned to Hell (Matthew 22:33), and spiritual children of Satan who belonged to their father the devil (John 8:44).

Jesus told the Pharisees specifically that they "are not of God" (John 8:47), so He clearly is not saying that the Kingdom of God is within the same people who are of Satan. How could the Kingdom of God dwell in a spiritual child of Satan? Interpreting this verse to mean the Kingdom of God is already within each person doesn't compute, because Jesus made it clear that the Kingdom of God was absent from the Pharisees. When we combine this with what the Bible says about man being ontologically and relationally separate from God, we see that the Bible tells us that the Kingdom of God is not inherent within man.

This proof-text used by New Age teachers also relies on a minority translation of the Greek text. In Koine Greek, the original language of the New Testament, the word used for "within" is *entos*, which doesn't just mean "within"; it can also mean "among"[206] or "in the direction of."[207] Some of the best English translations we have today don't translate this verse as saying the Kingdom of God is within you. The English Standard Version, New American Standard Bible, New International Version, New Revised Standard Version, New Living Translation, Holman Christian Standard Bible, International Standard Version, Lexham English Bible, New English Translation, and the majority of other translations do not render *entos* as "within." The New Age interpretation of this verse relies on cherry-picking from the minority of Bible translations, and even then, takes this verse out of context from the rest of Scripture.

The Christian is at liberty to choose any translation, for even if Christ intended to speak of an indwelling Kingdom, this is perfectly compatible with rest of Scripture, which tells us we receive the indwelling of the Holy Spirit (1 Corinthians 3:16, 6:19; 2 Timothy 1:4) upon putting our faith in Jesus Christ and His finished work on the cross (Ephesians 1:13; Galatians 3:2). God's living Spirit bears Himself in those who believe the Gospel, and therefore the Kingdom of God, two-fold. It is a reference to a literal coming kingdom under the messianic reign of Jesus Christ, but it equally is true that the Kingdom of God is already present on earth because "the kingdom of God is not a matter of eating and drinking but of righteousness and peace and joy in the Holy Spirit" (Romans 14:17).

The kingdom is manifest right now in the indwelling Holy Spirit, whom not everyone has (Romans 8:9; Jude 19), but whom everyone *can* have. Jesus may have been referring to Himself as the arrival of God's Kingdom on Earth ("in the midst of you"), or the coming of the Holy Spirit whom He said has not yet come but will soon be in His disciples (John 14:17). Both interpretations are compatible with Scripture. The New Age interpretation ignores what Jesus says about those to whom He was talking; it depends upon a single rendering of *entos* used in the minority of translations, ignores the Biblically consistent interpretation of the indwelling of the Holy Spirit, and ignores what the rest of the text has to say about man's separation from God.

Did Jesus Say We Are All "Gods"?

The second proof-text used regularly in the New Age movement to justify the doctrine of Christ Consciousness comes from John chapter 10:

"I have shown you many good works from the Father; for which of them are you going to stone me?" The Jews answered him, "It is not for a good work that we are going to stone you but for blasphemy, because you, being a man, make yourself God." Jesus answered them, "Is it not written in your Law, 'I said, you are gods'? If he called them gods to whom the word of God came—and Scripture cannot be broken—do you say of him whom the Father consecrated and sent into the world, 'You are blaspheming,' because I said, 'I am the Son of God'?" (John 10:31–36)

Jesus is referring to a verse in Psalm 82 verse 6: "I said, 'You are gods, sons of the Most High, all of you.'" This verse is often flouted proudly by New Age teachers as the final nail in the coffin of fundamentalism. It's often interpreted gnostically to mean that we are little gods ascending up a ladder of deification, or mystically to mean that God is within all things and is therefore within us. As Deepak Chopra says about this verse, "I interpreted this as "those who have knowledge of God are God."[208] Eastern yogi Paramahansa Yogananda says that "when Jesus quotes the scripture that "ye are gods," he signifies that all souls are made in the pure image of God, the Father.... Persons identified with their human egoity lack that realization; even though they are potential gods, they have no actual perception of the presence of God within themselves."[209]

A popular New Age website attempts to use this verse to push a mystical version of Jesus:

I am not sure how this is explained away in the major religions that use the bible, but Jesus is clearly telling each and every one of us, resounding to the world from two thousand years ago, that we are indeed God; that you are God. He knew and he discovered within himself that he was not only connected to the creative force of the universe, the unified field, or the matrix of all matter as physicist Max Planck called it, but he realized that he was that creative force, and that all of creation was in a literal sense God.... If everything in the universe is formless energy, and we are all connected by that energy, and if we are made up of that energy, and if that energy is the force we call God...how could we be anything but God?[210]

At least four major interpretations of this verse have dominated Church history and modern scholarship, two of which seem to be more plausible than the others. The first, the popular interpretation, is that we are seeing a mytho-poetic reference to the quasi-divine role of divinely appointed human judge in the nation of Israel acting as a representatives of God. Let's look at this in the context of the surrounding verses:

God has taken his place in the divine council; in the midst of the gods he holds judgment: "How long will you judge unjustly and show partiality to the wicked? Selah. Give justice to the weak and the fatherless; maintain the right of the afflicted and the destitute. Rescue the weak and the needy; deliver them from the hand of the wicked." They have neither knowledge nor understanding, they walk about in darkness; all the foundations of the earth are shaken. I said, "You are gods, sons of the Most High, all of you; nevertheless, like men you shall die, and fall like any prince." Arise, O God, judge the earth; for you shall inherit all the nations! (Psalm 82:1–8)

Notice that in verses 2, 3, and 4, God is telling the divine council to do a better job of restoring justice on the earth: "Judge justly," "give justice to the weak," "maintain the right of the afflicted and destitute." For someone who wants to say this verse refers to all of mankind, the average person does not have the authority to maintain another person's rights. That is a legal and judicial function, which is the job of legal authorities such as judges, kings, and magistrates. It appears that these "gods" are limited to beings (whether human or spirit) who are in a position of judgment over mankind.

There is a rich history of judges and kings in the Old Testament, starting Exodus 18:25–26 when Moses elected people as God's representatives to settle disputes among the people of Israel:

> Moses chose able men out of all Israel and made them heads over the people, chiefs of thousands, of hundreds, of fifties, and of tens. And they judged the people at all times. Any hard case they brought to Moses, but any small matter they decided themselves.

This verse is significant and will be revisited in a moment, but this is how legal and moral disputes were resolved. God rebukes such judges in a very similar manner in Isaiah 3:13–15, Isaiah 3:24–26, Micah 3:9–12, and in Psalm 58:1–3, which says:

> Do you indeed decree what is right, you gods? Do you judge the children of man uprightly? No, in your hearts you devise wrongs; your hands deal out violence on earth. The wicked are estranged from the womb; they go astray from birth, speaking lies.

Once again, the average person does not have the authority to "judge the children of man uprightly." Those who are called "gods" are those who have tremendous legal authority over an entire nation. The object of the Lord's admonishment, the ones He is calling "gods," are in a position to enforce the law of God in criminal matters.

If this is in fact a reference to mankind, it does not refer to all of mankind but to judges—and not to judges of all nations, but to judges of Israel in particular. These are the "sons of the most high," the chosen people "to whom the word of God came," as Jesus says. We often forget that Jesus tells us this verse refers to a specific group of beings. Jesus called them gods "to whom the word of God came." Only those "to whom the word of God came" were referred to as gods, and the word of God did not come to everyone in the world, but, according to the most popular interpretation, to God's chosen people on Mt. Sinai.

This makes an exclusive reference that excludes 99.9999 percent of people who have ever lived, including everyone who is reading this right now. Unless you are an Old Testament judge in Israel three or four thousand years ago, this verse does not apply to you. The Hebrew word used here is *elohim*, which is used more than 2,500 times in Scripture—with more than 2,000 of those instances referring to God and 259 pointing to any kind of spiritual being in general. The word is also used to refer to human judges put in God's place to carry out His will. The elected judges of Exodus 18 are called *elohim* in Exodus 21:6: "But if the slave plainly says, 'I love my master, my wife, and my children; I will not go out free,' then his master shall bring him to God [lit. *elohim*], and he shall bring him to the door or the doorpost."

The KJV, NKJV, CSB, GNV, NET, ISV, NIV, and MEV translate *elohim* to "judges" because these verses may refer to human judges acting in God's place. They bore the title *elohim* not because they held deity within themselves, but because the One who holds the fullness of deity decreed that they were to stand before man as a direct extension of His will.

As sixteenth-century reformer John Calvin said in his commentary on this verse:

> Scripture gives the name of gods to those on whom God has conferred an honourable office.... The passage which Christ quotes is in Psalm 82:6, I have said, You are gods, and all of you are children of the Most High; where God expostulates with the kings and judges of the earth, who tyrannically abuse their authority and power for their own sinful passions, for oppressing the poor, and for every evil action.[211]

According to the traditional interpretation of the text, Jesus is making an argument from lesser to greater. He had just finished saying He is one with the Father. In John chapter 5:22, He says: "For the Father judges no one, but has given all judgment to the Son." In John 8:16, He says, "Yet even if I do judge, my judgment is true, for it is not I alone who judge, but I and the Father who sent me." He claimed He was given the position of judge by the Father, and that when He judges, both He and the Father are judging.

The "human judges" interpretation of this passage would render Jesus as saying, "If even human judges can be called 'gods' in the sense that they are representatives of God's justice, how much more appropriate is it for me to call myself the Son of God if He has given me all authority in Heaven and in Earth? If mere mortals they were called *elohim* for representing His law in Israel, how much more can I claim deity for myself when I represent Him in all things? Why do you say I blaspheme when I have more power, authority, and deity than the ones called gods in the Old Testament?"

This would be to deflect the charges of blasphemy against Him and demonstrate that He was well within His rights and authority to claim deity. Jesus is not making a universal statement that all of mankind is divine; He is making a particular reference to those whom God appointed as judges. It's mytho-poetic rhetoric. Also, let us not forget that the gods mentioned in Psalm 82 are said to "have neither knowledge nor understanding" (v. 5). This debunks Deepak Chopra's interpretation that through knowledge of God we become gods, since the ones who were called gods have "no knowledge or understanding." They were called "gods" despite having no knowledge or understanding. This whole psalm is a rebuke of their ignorance, which means He must be calling them "gods" for a reason other than enlightenment or special knowledge. If an enlightened person is acting ignorantly, then he or she isn't enlightened and hence cannot be called a god.

This also debunks Yogananda's interpretation that all men are "potential gods" through awareness of God's presence within us, since the judges lacked all knowledge (meaning they had unfulfilled potential) and yet still wore the title "gods." If those who are ignorant can be called "gods," then this is not a title for the enlightened. It's a title for something else. The "gods" to whom Jesus referred meet none of the conditions laid out by New Age teachers.

Elohim, the Divine Council, and the Sons of God

Another possible interpretation of this passage in Psalm 82 has been popularized by Hebrew scholar Dr. Michael Heiser, who puts forward the idea that *elohim* refers to the heavenly council of Yahweh, not to human judges in Israel. In the original Hebrew, this term shows up a fair amount in reference to nonhuman entities. Within the New Age movement, the term *elohim* has a variety of meanings, most of which involve humans living on earth.

Some say the *elohim* are a species of human that originate from another planet, even going as far as to *say* the term means "those who came from the sky."[212] It doesn't. Others refer to them as beings of love that are expressed as twelve rays of light and life.[213] They aren't. Still others, such as Helena Blavatsky in *Isis Unveiled*, believe the *elohim* are a race of humans that originated on Earth preceding our current human race.[214] They didn't. Or they will say, as we have already seen, that it refers to those who have knowledge of God or who have the potential to self-realize as God. It doesn't.

The first time we see the Hebrew word *elohim* in the Bible is in the very first book, chapter, and verse: "In the beginning, God created the heaven and the earth" (Genesis 1:1, KJV).

Here, the English word "God" was translated from *elohim*. However, *elohim* is not limited to referring only to God. According to *Strong's* Concordance, it can have a number of meanings, depending on the context, including: God, lesser divine beings, judges, rulers, and angels.[215]

This doesn't mean God (*elohim*) is equal in nature or status to angels (*elohim*). It's just a general Hebrew word that apply to both types of spiritual beings. As Dr. Heiser has said:

> Yahweh is an elohim, but no other elohim are Yahweh…. But why refer to spiritual beings as elohim? The association is not difficult to understand, actually. Since God is a spirit, and in fact the supreme spirit, and he is "father of all spirits" (Heb. 12:9), then the realm of the spirits is "where God lives." The beings who belong to the spirit realm are therefore "divine." The best word to capture that conception is elohim. An elohim is a divine being, in that an elohim is an inhabitant of the spiritual plane of reality.[216]

In Scripture, at least six different spiritual beings are referenced as *elohim*:[217]

- Yahweh, the monotheistic God of Israel
- The *elohim* of Yahweh's heavenly/divine council (Psalm 82 and a 89; cf. Deuteronomy 32:8–9, 43; Psalm 58:11)
- The gods of foreign nations (1 Kings 11:33)
- Demons (Deuteronomy 32:17)
- The disembodied human dead (1 Samuel 28:13)
- Angels (Genesis 35:7; cf. the context of the plural predicator with אלהים [*elohim*] subject)

Notice that *elohim* is not used to refer to all of humanity, or even to a group of spiritually advanced people. This is another example of how New Age theology borrows concepts from other religions, twists their original meaning, and forces them to fit in a place where they were never meant to be. According to ancient Hebrews, *elohim* were residents of a spiritual reality described throughout the Bible.

The *elohim* were not aliens from another planet, a race of humans, mankind at large, or a group of enlightened teachers. The only possibly exception to this in all of Scripture is when Yahweh (*Elohim)* breathed His word into the hand of Moses. Then, the ones whom Moses appointed to enforce that word could be called *elohim* in a special circumstance since they held a God-ordained office enforcing God-breathed revelation in His place for a season.

Wise people were not called *elohim*. Prophets of the Bible were not called *elohim*. People indwelt with the Spirit of God were not called *elohim*. Miracle workers, military leaders, teachers, oracles, diviners, spiritists, sorcerers, and practicers of magic arts were not called *elohim*. We cannot apply this word to whomever we wish to look at in a pseudo-divine context. We need to let the texts of history define these terms without inventing meanings that have never been adopted. When we compare Scripture with Scripture, we find an important parallel passage to compare "ye are gods" with in Psalm 89. The *elohim* of Yahweh's "council" in Psalm 89:5–7 are said to be a council in "in the clouds," which means this cannot refer to enlightened people walking the Earth:

> Let the heavens praise your wonders, O Lord, your faithfulness in the assembly (קהל) of the holy ones! For who in the clouds (בשחק) can be compared to the Lord? Who among the sons of God/the gods (בני אלים) is like the Lord, a God greatly to be feared in the council (סוד) of the holy ones, and awesome above all who are around him?

Who is this council of the holy ones who are in the clouds? It certainly isn't the Pharisees, and it certainly isn't yogis and bodhisattvas in riverside caves in India.

> The term divine council is used by Hebrew and Semitics scholars to refer to the heavenly host, the pantheon of divine beings who administer the affairs of the cosmos. All ancient Mediterranean cultures had some conception of a divine council.[218]

The OT exhibits a three-tiered council (the craftsman tier is absent). In Israelite religion, Yahweh, at the top tier, was the supreme authority over the divine council, which included a second tier of lesser elohim ("gods"), also called the "sons of God" or "sons of the Most High." The third tier comprised the mal'akhim ("angels").[219]

In this view, Jesus was quoting from Psalm 82:6 to prove He was more than human by refreshing His listeners' (Jewish) minds with the plurality of usages for *elohim* in the Hebrew Scriptures, in particular the "divine council" of Yahweh. Jesus was not trying to get on His audience's level by saying He could be called "gods" just like all mortals. His critics would have no reason to respond by wanting to stone Him if the extent of His claim limited Him to their level of divinity. He was communicating that He is a spiritual being above those in the heavenly council of Yahweh spoken of in the Psalms, implyings supernatural preexistence and lordship.[220]

Dr. Heiser concludes that "because [Jesus] calls himself the son of God and has in fact just claimed to be one with Yahweh, he not only puts himself in the class of the sons of the Most High of Psalm 82:6— divine אלהים—but implies that he is Lord of the council."[221]

The Pharisees wanted to stone Jesus for claiming He was an *elohim* who is one with Yahweh. Academics debate which interpretation exhibits more biblical and historical accuracy, but what doesn't have support is the pantheistic interpretation that Jesus was speaking to man's ontology. This is not even on the map of contemporary scholarship and is a perfect example of the intellectually flippant business of "eisegesis," reading into the text one's own biases and preferences to make it say what one wants apart from context. This is contrasted with exegesis, allowing the text to interpret itself and stand on its own—independent of human bias. No interpretive method would permit the conclusion that this text in Psalm 82 is a Hindu reference to enlightened human beings, aliens on another planet, or a lost race from the ancient past.

The New Age interpretation of this verse does not account for the role these "gods" had as judicial enforcers; it attributes the property of enlightenment to those who had no knowledge or understanding; and it misuses the Hebrew word *elohim* by giving it a translation and application that are found nowhere in the ancient world.

The Second Coming of Christ Consciousness

In the New Age movement, the Second Coming of Jesus is believed to be a metaphor for the arrival of "Christ Consciousness" within each person who awakens to his or her identity as God. Christ will incarnate, in a sense, in all people who exhibit a divine level of consciousness as they move from being identified with their self-concept to being identified with the consciousness in them that is deity itself. The Second Coming is not the coming of a person but an emergence of man's own self-divinity by embodying God-Consciousness, which means that the "Second Coming" is not a historical event to take place in the future but is instead a shift in consciousness that has been happening before and since Jesus was born.

According to Eckhart Tolle:

> The "second coming" of Christ is a transformation of human consciousness, a shift from time to presence, from thinking to pure consciousness, not the arrival of some man or woman. If "Christ" were to return tomorrow in some externalized form, what could he or she possibly say to you other than this: "I am the Truth. I am divine presence. I am eternal life. I am within you. I am here. I am Now."[222]

Deepak Chopra teaches that "the Second Coming will be a shift in consciousness that renews human nature by raising it to the level of the divine."[223] Jesus isn't coming back physically; "Christ" is coming back psycho-spiritually. We are to be looking for a collective shift in human consciousness, not for a literal person coming back in a cataclysmic event.

Paramahansa Yogananda wrote an entire book dedicated to putting an Eastern spin on the ministry of Jesus, His resurrection, and His Second Coming:

> In titling this work "The Second Coming of Christ," I am not referring to a literal return of Jesus to earth. He came two thousand years ago and, after imparting a universal path to God's kingdom, was crucified and resurrected; his reappearance to the masses now is not necessary for the fulfillment of his teachings. What "is" necessary is for the cosmic wisdom and divine perception of Jesus to speak again through each one's own experience and understanding of the infinite Christ Consciousness that was incarnate in Jesus. That will be his true Second Coming.... In his little human body called Jesus was born the vast Christ Consciousness, the omniscient Intelligence of God omnipresent in every part and particle of creation. This Consciousness is the "only begotten Son of God," so designated because it is the sole perfect reflection in creation of the Transcendental Absolute, Spirit or God the Father.[224]

This simply is not what Jesus tells us about His own Second Coming, which He describes as being a literal and apocalyptic event. See, for example, Matthew 24:30–31:

> Then will appear in heaven the sign of the Son of Man, and then all the tribes of the earth will mourn, and they will see the Son of Man coming on the clouds of heaven with power and great glory. And he will send out his angels with a loud trumpet call, and they will gather his elect from the four winds, from one end of heaven to the other.

We know from Scripture that the Second Coming of Jesus is described in the following terms:

- He will descend from Heaven (1 Thessalonians 4:16–17).
- He will come with great glory (Matthew 24:30–31; Mark 8:38).
- He will come with His angels (Matthew 24:30–31; Mark 8:38).
- We will see Him in the clouds/sky (Matthew 24:30–31; 1 Thessalonians 4:16–17; Revelation 1:7).
- That ALL the nations of the earth will mourn and wail when they see Him (Matthew 24:30–31; Revelation 1:7).

As we can see, the Second Coming metaphor does not meet a single one of these descriptions of what Jesus said the event will be like. If one were to watch a presentation on Christ Consciousness by Hindu guru Mooji, ET channel Bashar, or transcendentalist speaker Alan Watts, the New Age will tell us that the Second Coming is happening in people all over the room in the audience, despite that not a single biblical criteria has been met. There is no Jesus or angels in the clouds when this Second Coming is apparently happening all over the room. There are no trumpets, there is no mourning, and there is no wailing. It's just a bunch of people sitting on the floor in silence in front of another human being, yet Jesus clearly describes His Second Coming as a literal, supernatural, and apocalyptic event that interrupts the entire world in a single instant.

Of the sixty to seventy verses that speak about the Second Coming, each says specifically that Jesus Himself is returning as a person. Since they speak of "Jesus" or "the Lord" coming back—for example, "and to grant relief to you who are afflicted as well as to us, when the Lord Jesus is revealed from heaven with his mighty angels" (2 Thessalonians 1:7)—we know it's not a reference to a state of consciousness but to the person of Jesus.

1 Peter 4:13, Colossians 3:4, and Hebrews 9:28 speak of the Second Coming as "Christ" coming back, and these verses offer the only theoretical hope for the Second Coming metaphor, because if it says "Christ," then the word "Christ" can be redefined to mean a state of

consciousness. This is why the word "Christ" is in quotation marks in the Eckhart Tolle quote we looked at, because he slips in a new definition of this word and turns *Christos* in Greek from a "he," a person, to an "it," an abstract, psycho-spiritual state of self-awareness. The author of 1 Peter and Colossians (Paul) speaks about the Second Coming of Jesus by name in other writings in the New Testament (1 Peter 5:4; 2 Thessalonians 1:7), and the verse in Hebrews speaks of Christ later on as a "him" in the same verse as the one offered up for the sins of the people: "So Christ, having been offered once to bear the sins of many, will appear a second time, not to deal with sin but to save those who are eagerly waiting for him" (Hebrews 9:28).

Christ is identified as "him" who died for our sins and who will come back a second time. Every verse about the Second Coming in the New Testament is a reference to Jesus coming back as a person. If the Second Coming of Jesus is about an awakening to a state of Christ Consciousness, why don't we find a verse speaking of the event as being anything other than the return of Jesus Himself? Not only are there zero verses that speak about a metaphorical Second Coming, there are not even any verses that could be twisted to *mean* a metaphorical Second Coming. Not a single verse in the Bible supports this position.

Another reason the Second Coming can't be the oncoming of a higher state of consciousness is that Jesus said nobody—not even He, Himself—knows when it will happen: "But concerning that day or that hour, no one knows, not even the angels in heaven, nor the Son, but only the Father" (Mark 13:32, also see Matthew 24:36). Yet, the New Age proponents say it's already happening, and has been for the last two thousand years.

If even Jesus says He doesn't know when He will return, how does Eckhart Tolle know? To say it's happening now is to say that you know the day and hour that it's happening—namely, when a shift is made from thought to presence or from ordinary consciousness to Christ Consciousness. But, again, Jesus Himself said He even doesn't know the timing. If one's definition of the "Second Coming" involves pinning down an actual moment when it will occur), then it's not really the Second Coming.

Zeitgeist and Pagan Mythology

Some in the New Age movement are less extravagant about how they twist Scripture out of context. They concede that Jesus existed as a historical figure but claim that the *story* of Jesus was plagiarized or adopted from pagan deities. They assert that the ideas of His virgin birth, baptism, gathering of disciples, miracle working, title as the Son of God, death, and resurrection were taken from pre-Christ pagan myths and mishmashed to produce the unoriginal and recycled story of another dying and rising savior-figure: Jesus Christ.

We are told that Jesus is just one of many dying and rising gods present in history, and that every culture has its own savior figure with the same stories as the story of Jesus in every way. Mithra, Dionysus, Attis, Adonis, Osiris, Krishna, Horus, and others are said to be the original dying-and-rising figures with virgin births who inspired the early Christians to turn the account of an ordinary Jewish man into their own mythology. Since we apparently have narratives of gods that predate Jesus who have the same outline and ministry as He did, it's suggested that the story of Jesus is an amalgamation of stories that came before Him.

Misconceptions about other gods

Many "gods" were born of a virgin, buried, and resurrected after the third day, which is supposed to imply that the details of Jesus' life (even if He was real) were mythologized by first-century Jews desperate to have their own version of a savior. *Zeitgeist: The Movie* and *Religulous* are the two most prevalent popular films that teach this material, though its pervasiveness is predominantly observed in online forums, the blogosphere, and social media threads.

This "one of many similar stories" thinking was one of the most popular objections I (Steve) received from people in the New Age movement when I tried sharing Christ with them. After all, why believe in Jesus if He is a copycat savior figure fashioned after the likeness of Krishna? Why not just believe in Krishna and have a higher likelihood of believing in the original savior—or why not reject all of such stories as clearly devised myths and pursue Christ Consciousness instead?

Something interesting happens when we look into the historical accounts of the ancient world to see what the primary texts of these religions say. We find that the parallels are almost entirely made up, and where they do correlate to the story of Jesus, they are radically spurious. Let's briefly examine Mithra, Dionysus, and Horus, the three pagan gods most often credited with inspiring the story of Jesus.

According to well-known ancient mythology, Mithra had no virgin birth. In fact, Mithra was not even born in a literal sense; he emerged from a rock, so was only "born" metaphorically. We find many artifacts in the ancient world of Mithra's petra genetrixes, carvings indicating his birth from a rock. Mithra even emerged from this rock as an adult, not as a baby. Mithra has no real mother, no virgin birth, and no manger.[225, 226] Further, Mithra was never even killed, let alone crucified. As Mithraic scholar Gordon Richard says, there "is no death of Mithras."[227] If he didn't die, he could not have been crucified, buried, or resurrected from the dead. Despite this, Christians are accused of believing in someone who borrowed from the life story of Mithra.

Dionysus is another biography said to parallel that of Jesus, but Greek mythology tells us that Dionysus was born after Zeus had intercourse with Semele. Hesiod's ancient Greek poem "Theogony" is one of many sources that informs us the Greco-Roman world never believed Dionysus was conceived of a virgin:

> And Semele, daughter of Kadmos was joined with him [Zeus] in love and bare him a splendid son, joyous (polygethes) Dionysos,—a mortal woman an immortal son. And now they both are gods.

While some other stories site Persephone as the mother of Dionysus, none indicate a virgin birth.[228]

Here's how Dionysus is said to have died (not on a cross): Titans tore him up into a bunch of pieces, boiled him in a pot, and ate him. There are at least six different accounts of what happens to his remains after that, depending on which source we refer to. While most restoration accounts of Dionysus are too ambiguous to even mention, one story that reads that "Dionysus was deceived by the Titans, and expelled from the throne of Jupiter, and torn in pieces by them, and his remains being afterwards put together again, he returned as it were once more to life, and ascended to heaven." This somewhat mirrors what we find in Scripture. The problem is that this quote comes from a work called *Contra Celsum* written by the early Church father Origen in AD 248, more than two hundred years after the accounts of Jesus' life, death, resurrection, and ascension had already been established and circulating. This is a post-Christ resurrection story. If anything, the Dionysus cults may have adopted this idea from Christianity.

As historian Dr. Gary Habermas said, "I don't know anybody who thinks that Dionysus is pre-Christian, not the resurrection portion."[229] So when it comes to Dionysus, we find no virgin birth, no crucifixion, and no pre-Christ, bodily resurrection from any historical sources.

As for Horus, he had no virgin birth either. Isis had sex with Osiris after reassembling his body parts that were torn apart and scattered over Egypt. As Egyptologist and professor at the University of Arizona, Dr.

Richard Wilkinson, wrote: "Through her magic Isis revivified the sexual member of Osiris and became pregnant by him, eventually giving birth to their child, Horus."[230] Historian and professor Françoise Dunand said: "After having sexual intercourse, in the form of a bird, with the dead god she restored to life, she gave birth to a posthumous son, Horus."[231]

This theory ignores what we *do* know about the historical Jesus. Just as sure as historians are that Jesus existed, they are equally as certain about specific events in His life, such as the crucifixion. If Jesus did live as a man and was crucified as a man, it doesn't matter that pagan mythology has stories of dying gods, since this portion of Jesus' life is rooted in an actual event that took place. Historical evidence reveals a dozen or more sources that provide accounts of the crucifixion of Jesus of Nazareth:

1. Pre-Mark Passion Narrative
2. Hypothetical Gospel Q
3. John
4. Paul
5. Hebrews
6. 1 Peter 2:24
7. Clement of Rome
8. Ignatius
9. Justin Martyr
10. Josephus Flavius
11. Cornelius Tacitus
12. Lucian
13. Mesa Bar Serapion
14. Thallus
15. Talmud

Skeptic and professor of New Testament History at the University of Gottinggen, Gerd Lüdemann, says that "Jesus' death as a consequence of crucifixion is indisputable."[232] Critical non-Christian scholar John Dominic Crossan has said "that he was crucified is as sure as anything historical can ever be."[233] Atheist historian Bart Ehrman agrees that "one of the most certain facts of history is that Jesus was crucified on orders of the Roman prefect of Judea, Pontius Pilate."[234]

So even *if* we have pre-Christ myths of gods who died in some way, they are simply irrelevant, since Jewish Roman and Christian history confirm that Jesus was killed on a cross. And if it happened in history, that means it wasn't plagiarized. Because this portion of Jesus' story (and others) is rooted in actual history, pagan myths have no bearing or relevance to the origin of these beliefs about Jesus. Jesus' followers believed He was crucified because He was crucified, not because they heard a story through the grapevine about Osiris being cut up and scattered across Egypt.

We don't even know whether the disciples knew the details of these stories at a time when the literacy rate was so low, and when mystery schools were the ones that typically housed such knowledge. Jesus' disciples were Jewish. Any knowledge they had of such gods would have been dismissed as idolatry, just as we see frequently throughout the Old Testament. As Dr. Ehrman comments in his book refuting Jesus mythicism, "anyone who thinks that Jesus was modeled on such deities needs to cite some evidence—any evidence at all—that Jews in Palestine at the alleged time of Jesus's life were influenced by anyone who held such views."[235]

It's not enough to say that Jesus' resurrection story sounds a little like the story of Mithra. We must prove historically that the disciples knew these stories and were influenced by them to such an extent that they made up the story of Jesus, which is too heavy a burden of proof for any historian or skeptic to bear. There is no evidence that this happened. Here are many other reasons scholars reject the idea that Jesus is a knock-off of pagan gods:

- Jesus' death was unlike pagan myths because He died voluntarily a single time for humankind as an atonement for sin.
- Christian doctrine is entirely original (trinitarianism, penal substitution, salvation by faith, etc.).

- Paul rebukes pagans and their "false" gods in Acts 14 (penned in AD 62 or 80s).
- The Christians were executed for their refusal to worship Greco-Roman gods (The Great Persecution).
- Paul's creed in 1 Corinthians 15 dates to within three years of Jesus' death, too short a time for legend to develop.
- The Jewish concept of a bodily resurrection is different than pagan beliefs.
- Jesus claimed to be God incarnate, something never seen in pagan myths.
- Most sources of "dying and rising" gods come after Jesus (Attis, Adonis, Apollonius, etc.).
- The existence of Jesus is confirmed by non-Christian historical sources (Tacitus, Suetonius, etc.)
- The details of mystery religion gods were not well known to the public.
- The Old Testament of the Jews strictly warns against participating in pagan religions.
- Most pagan stories were meant to be metaphors for the crops dying and regrowing each winter/spring.
- No historical evidence from any source suggests that the early Christians were influenced by pagan gods.
- The pagans did not accuse the Christians of stealing their story.
- The story of Jesus was of a historical man, not of a mythological god.
- Some early apostles (including Paul) were martyred for their belief that Jesus had appeared to them.
- Christianity arose from a Jewish culture and context (Hebrew Scriptures, monotheism, etc.).
- Jesus is not the kind of figure we would expect to be mythicized from pagan stories (because of His meek personality, voluntary death, selflessness, etc.).

- The Gospels were written in the literary genre of historical biographies, not as myths.
- We have good reason to believe the Gospels contain early, eyewitness testimony of Jesus.
- Paul was an eyewitness to the brother of Jesus and His disciple Peter.
- Jesus was believed to be divine in nature, not merely a divinized human.

Atheist historian Bart Ehrman, professor of religious studies at the University of North Carolina, comments on the pagan copycat theory:

The alleged parallels between Jesus and the "pagan" savior-gods in most instances reside in the modern imagination: We do not have accounts of others who were born to virgin mothers and who died as an atonement for sin and then were raised from the dead (despite what the sensationalists claim ad nauseum in their propagandized versions).[236]

Historian Jonathan Z. Smith famously said in his essay in the *Encyclopedia of Religion*:

The category of dying and rising Gods, once a major topic of scholarly investigation, must now be understood to have been largely a misnomer based on imaginative reconstructions and exceedingly late or highly ambiguous texts.... There is no unambiguous instance in the history of religions of a dying and rising deity.[237]

Tryggve Mettinger, a Swedish scholar and former professor at Lund University, has authored one of the most comprehensive works ever written in the field of dying and rising gods and its relationship to Christianity. He concludes his book by saying the following:

There is, as far as I am aware, no prima facie evidence that the
death and resurrection of Jesus is a mythological construct, drawing on myths and rites of the dying and rising gods of the
surrounding world. While studied with profit against the background of Jewish resurrection belief, the faith in the death and
resurrection of Jesus retains its unique character in the history of
religions.[238]

The Gospels Reveal the Real Historical Jesus

We know all of the above perspectives on Jesus are false because Matthew, Mark, Luke, and John are historical books that give us an unal-
tered perspective of the life and teachings of Jesus Christ. If we want to
know what Jesus *really* believed regarding theology, man, and his own
self-concept, all we have to do is refer to the Bible. When we do this,
we allow the historical Jesus to define Himself. A variety of claims get
thrown around the New Age movement pertaining to the Gospels that
have been included in the New Testament:

First, many in the New Age movement claim the Church altered
the Gospels from the original texts so dramatically that nothing reliable can be extracted from them. They say we have no idea of what the
original translations say. Second, many New Agers believe the Gospels
were made up by men who later became early Church fathers for the
purpose of geopolitical control. Third, New Age thinking asserts that
the Gospels were written so long after the life of Jesus that they are not
reliable sources for what He did and said. I (Steven) had a difficult time
sharing the Gospel of Jesus with people I encountered in the New Age
movement because the Internet is so widely polluted by pseudo scholarship and disinformation pertaining to the Gospels.

In reality, the Gospels are arguably the most authentic, pure, and
reliable works in all of antiquity. As historian John T. A. Robinson has
said:

The wealth of manuscripts, and above all the narrow interval of time between the writing and the earliest extant copies, make it by far the best attested text of any ancient writing in the world.[239]

Bart Ehrman agrees that historians (and the general public) ought to rely upon the Gospels as historical sources:

If historians want to know what Jesus said and did they are more or less constrained to use the New Testament Gospels as their principal sources. Let me emphasize that this is not for religious or theological reasons—for instance, that these and these alone can be trusted. It is for historical reasons, pure and simple.[240]

Professor of philosophy William Lane Craig has said:

No modern scholar thinks of the gospels as bald-faced lies, the result of a massive conspiracy. The only place you find such conspiracy theories of history is in sensationalist, popular literature or former propaganda from behind the Iron Curtain.[241]

We must understand that the Gospels were written to be biographies of the life of Jesus—not fictions, legends, or mythologies. They don't reflect the style and literary flare of fictional works. As biographies, they were intended to be literal historical accounts of His life and ministry. British New Testament scholar James Dunn says that "it has become clearer that the Gospels are in fact very similar in type to ancient biographies."[242] Scholar Graham Stanton agrees that, "the gospels are now widely considered to be a sub-set of the broad ancient literary genre of biographies."[243] In an interview, professor Craig Keener reveals how historians generally view the Gospel materials: "Most Gospel scholars today—not all, but most—see the Gospels as biographies."[244]

As biographies, the Gospels are intended to represent the life of Jesus as witnessed by those who knew Him.[245] The accounts were either written by eyewitnesses themselves (Matthew and John) or by companions of eyewitnesses (Mark and Luke) during their lifetimes. The primary reason we know that the documents haven't been altered over time is the sheer volume of ancient manuscripts we have, all of which corroborate one another. The number of copies we have at our disposal is quite impressive; for example, we have more than 5,800 manuscripts in the original Greek, with more than 2.5 million pages of text copied in different decades and different centuries by different people, with some twenty thousand other copies in Syriac, Latin, and Coptic.[246] If one (or a group) of manuscripts was altered, we could compare that manuscript or those documents with the others to weed out the errors through a process of elimination. We know what the Gospels are intended to contain by comparing manuscripts. If one manuscript states that "Jesus was the Sun of Gog," yet a thousand manuscripts dating before and after that one say in the same verse that "Jesus was the Son of God," we can have confidence in knowing what the author originally wrote.

Let's compare these numbers with the number of copies we have for a few other ancient works to see just how reliable the Gospels really are. For *Caesar's Gallic War* (written sometime between 50 and 58 BC), only ten decent manuscripts exist, the earliest of which was written some eight hundred years after Caesar lived. The *History of Thucydides* (fifth century BC) only comes down to us in the form of eight manuscripts, the earliest copy of which came in around AD 900 (although a few small fragments date to the Christian era), about 1,300 years later.[247] Arguably the next best-preserved work besides the Bible is that of Homer's *Iliad*, which boasts around 650 copies with the earliest coming a thousand years after the original.[248]

Our earliest extant fragments for Matthew's Gospel (general consensus puts Matthew at AD 70–80) date between AD 150 and 250, a large fragment from Mark (consensus is AD 60–70) is dated to around AD 250, and several large fragments from Luke (consensus is AD 80) date to between AD 175 and 250. The earliest fragment of John's Gospel (consensus: AD 90–95) is called P52, which is dated to AD 125 and is our earliest fragment of any New Testament text, dating to within thirty years after the original was written. And the text of this fragment corresponds to other fragments of John copied in different places in different time periods, indicating that the content of the original has not been corrupted over time. Further, our first complete books of the New Testament date to around AD 200, while the first complete copy of the entire New Testament, Codex Sinaiticus, dates to the AD 300s. Bearing in mind that our entire New Testament was completed no later than AD 95, this leaves a gap of over two hundred years before our entire first copy.

Remember, many individual fragments date earlier than that. Scholar Gary Habermas explains:

What is usually meant is that the New Testament has far more manuscript evidence from a far earlier period than other classical works. There are just under 6000 NT manuscripts, with copies of most of the NT dating from just 100 years or so after its writing. Classical sources almost always have less than 20 copies each and usually date from 700–1400 years after the composition of the work. In this regard, the classics are not as well attested. While this doesn't guarantee truthfulness, it means that it is much easier to reconstruct the New Testament text. Regarding genre, the Gospels are usually taken today to be examples of Roman biographies.[249]

We know what the disciples wrote. We know what they intended to say because we have thousands upon thousands of manuscripts transmitted by scribes from the original texts, and these documents themselves date very early to the time of Jesus. If Jesus died in AD 30 and Mark's Gospel was written in AD 65, we have a maximum of thirty-five years for the apostles to butcher and forget the very accounts of the person they were willing to give their lives for. The material scholars believe Mark used to write his Gospel has been dated to as early as AD 37, just seven years after the death of Jesus.[250] Do we really think that, in a Jewish culture where oral tradition was prized and practiced, a full-blown legend developed in *all* the minds of those who lived with Jesus within just seven years? This position is untenable.

Scholar Frederick Bruce claims:

> The evidence for our New Testament writings is ever so much greater than the evidence for many writings of classical authors, the authenticity of which no one dreams of questioning.... It is a curious fact that historians have often been much readier to trust the New Testament records than have many theologians.[251]

Reflecting on the early dates of the Gospels to the time of Jesus, we must consider that they were written when many eyewitnesses were still alive and could have protested or corrected those who were spreading lies about their Jewish teacher. The absence of their rebuttal serves as evidence that the witness the Gospels bore about Jesus was true, along with eleven other reasons outlined by English philosopher William Paley:

- The Gospels were cited by contemporary and soon-after Christian sources (Epistle of Barnabas, Epistle of Clement, etc).
- The Gospels were quoted from as authoritative soon after they were written (Theophilus, Hippolitus, Origen, etc.).
- The Gospels were collected into volumes by early Christians (Ignatius, Eusebius, and Irenaeus refer to early collections involving the Gospels).
- Disciples of disciples and other early Christians referred to the Gospels as Scripture (Polycarp, Justin Martyr, Dionysius, etc).
- Early Christians (Justin Martyr, Turtullian, Cyprian, etc.) publicly read and taught from these writings .
- Early Christians wrote commentaries on these books.
- Even heretics (Valentinians, Carpocratians, etc.) accepted these books as legitimate sources of information about Jesus.

- The Gospels' authenticity was not doubted by those in the Church who doubted the authenticity of other books in our New Testament. The early Christians received the Gospels without dispute.
- The enemies of Christianity (Celcus, Porphyry, Julian, etc.) agreed that the Gospels contained the accounts Jesus' followers based their faith on.
- The published catalogs of Scripture always contained the four Gospels.
- None of the apocryphal books of the New Testament were treated this way.

Philosopher and apologist Dr. William Lane Craig summarizes:

No apocryphal gospel is ever even quoted by any known author during the first three hundred years after Christ. In fact, there is no evidence that any inauthentic gospel whatever existed in the first century, in which all four Gospels and Acts were written.... The external evidence strongly confirms the authenticity of the Gospels. Even if it should be the case that the names of the authors traditionally ascribed to the authors are mistaken, it still could not be denied that the Gospels do contain the story that the original apostles proclaimed and for which they laboured and suffered.[252]

These facts provide strong evidence that the manuscripts of the Gospels (again, of which we have numerous and early copies) represent eyewitness testimony corresponding to the life and ministry of Jesus. For these reasons and others, as historian Gary Habermas has said, "The predominant view today in New Testament studies is that the Gospels are basically Roman biographies. Scholars think, at the very least, that the Gospels are good enough sources that we may answer the key questions about Jesus' life."[253]

The historical evidence for the reliability of the Gospels is sufficient. The material in the Gospels was accepted by the disciples themselves and the disciples of the disciples, something that cannot be said for any of the material coming from New Age teachers about the life and teachings of Jesus. Why are no Buddhist or Hindu texts adopted by the disciples of Jesus if Jesus was really a mystic? Why weren't the gnostic Gospels quoted from as Scripture by the same Christians who held the four Gospels in divine authority? Why do we see the books of the New Testament revered by those who sat under the apostles, and those revered by the New Age movement totally absent of their consideration? The answer is obvious. The Gospels represent reliable eyewitness testimony and are historically accurate regarding the ministry of Jesus, whereas the other sources often quoted from by New Age teachers (such as the Gospels of Thomas or Peter) do not.

Jesus, the Jewish Monotheist

If we want to know the "real" teachings of Jesus, we can have confidence in the manuscripts that have been collected under the cover of the New Testament. It does not require any high-level scholarship, special insight, or elevated state of consciousness to understand the teachings of Jesus. All we have to do is look what His followers said about Him. As we have explored in a previous chapter on pantheism, Jesus believed in a personal (John 8:16–18), transcendent (Matthew 6:9) being who exists outside of time and space.

More specifically, Jesus believed that this transcendent person/creator was the God of the Old Testament. In fact, Jesus tells us that the most important of all commandments is to love Yahweh, the God of Israel:

The most important is, "Hear, O Israel: The Lord our God, the Lord is one. And you shall love the Lord your God with all your heart and with all your soul and with all your mind and with all your strength." (Mark 12:29–30)

This, according to Jesus, is the apex of spiritual pursuit: not to expand our consciousness or move up a scale of deification, but to love the God of the Hebrew Bible. This commandment alone debunks the entire New Age perspective of Jesus, for Jesus tells us specifically that God is the One who revealed Himself to the nation of Israel. Jesus confirms regularly that the Father He was referring to is the monotheistic God of the Israelites: But that the dead are raised, even Moses showed, in the passage about the bush, where he calls the Lord the God of Abraham and the God of Isaac and the God of Jacob. (Luke 20:37)

In that place there will be weeping and gnashing of teeth, when you see Abraham and Isaac and Jacob and all the prophets in the kingdom of God but you yourselves cast out. (Luke 13:28)

The one the prophets and figures of the Old Testament called God is the one Jesus identified as God. The most important verse touching the theological worldview of Jesus comes from a conversation He had with the Pharisees. In John 8:54, Jesus said to them, "If I glorify myself, my glory is nothing. It is my Father who glorifies me, of whom you say, 'He is our God.'"

The Father, according to the words of Jesus, is the onewhom the Pharisees called "God." They believed in Yahweh and Yahweh alone. Jesus said His Father is the one the Pharisees proclaimed to be their God (Yahweh). This verse is a knock-down argument to all New Age interpretations, because we know that the Pharisees weren't Hindus, gnostics, or theosophists. They weren't pantheists, religious pluralists, or transcendentalists. They were monotheistic Jews. Jesus believed in their God; therefore, Jesus was a Jewish monotheist.

Jesus believed in the authority and divine inspiration of the Torah and the Scriptures of the Jewish prophets (Matthew 5:18, John 10:35, Matthew 15:3, etc.). He constantly referred to them in His teachings and went as far as to call the words of the Old Testament the Word of God: "You leave the commandment of God and hold to the tradition of men."

He also said:

You have a fine way of rejecting the commandment of God in order to establish your tradition! For Moses said, "Honor your father and your mother"; and, "Whoever reviles father or mother must surely die." But you say, "If a man tells his father or his mother, 'Whatever you would have gained from me is Corban' (that is, given to God) then you no longer permit him to do anything for his father or mother, thus making void the word of God by your tradition that you have handed down. And many such things you do. (Mark 10:9–13)

What kind of mystic would believe the commandments Moses gave in the Old Testament are the literal Word of God? Is this something we would expect someone who is teaching "Christ Consciousness" to say? If one were to believe the Torah is God's inspired Word, he or she would be either Jewish or Christian, since the Torah testifies to One True God. The Scriptures of the Old Testament "cannot be broke[n]" (John 10:35) in the eyes of Jesus, meaning they were perfect and accurate. Jesus also said the Old Testament predicted His coming, and He claimed to be a fulfillment of the messianic prophecies (John 5:46, Luke 24:44, Luke 24:27, etc.).

Further, Jesus kept all the Jewish high feast days such as Passover (Luke 2:41–42), the Feast of Tabernacles (John 7:2–14), and the Feast of Dedication (John 10:22). He also claimed to be the Lord of the Sabbath (Matthew 12:28), which He also kept as a commandment from God. Jesus' Jewish disciples called him Rabbi (a Jewish teacher) more than a dozen times in Scripture (see, for example, John 1:49, 3:26, 4:31, 6:25, 9:2, and 11:8; Mark 9:5, etc.)

The *Lexham Bible Dictionary* states:

The New Testament's account of the life, death, and resurrection of Jesus Christ and the establishment of His church by His followers is inextricably united with Judaism. The historical setting of the birth of Christianity was Jewish. Jesus was a Jew, and most of His earliest followers were Jews. Even Paul, the apostle to the Gentiles (Rom[ans] 11:13), was a Jew (Phil[ippians] 3:5). Thus, the ideas, symbols, structures, and patterns that they were familiar with was in and of itself Jewish.[254]

Professor of Judaic Studies and of Religious Studies at Brown University, Shaye Cohen, answers the question of Jesus' religious orientation rather bluntly:

Of course, Jesus was a Jew. He was born of a Jewish mother, in Galilee, a Jewish part of the world. All of his friends, associates, colleagues, disciples, all of them were Jews. He regularly worshipped in Jewish communal worship, what we call synagogues. He preached from Jewish text, from the Bible. He celebrated the Jewish festivals. He went on pilgrimage to the Jewish Temple in Jerusalem where he was under the authority of priests.... He lived, was born, lived, died, taught as a Jew. This is obvious to any casual reader of the gospel text. What's striking is not so much that he was a Jew but that the gospels make no pretense that he wasn't. The gospels have no sense yet that Jesus was anything other than a Jew.[255]

Non-Christian New Testament historian Dr. Marcus Borg claims that the majority of historians agree about the following points about Jesus:[256]

- Jesus was born sometime just before 4 BC. He grew up in Nazareth, a small village in Galilee, as part of the peasant class.

Jesus' father was a carpenter and He became one, too, meaning that his family had likely lost their agricultural land at some point.

- Jesus was raised Jewish and remained deeply Jewish all His life. His intention was not to create a new religion. Rather, He saw Himself as doing something within Judaism.

- He left Nazareth as an adult, met the prophet John, and was baptized by John. During His baptism, Jesus likely experienced some sort of divine vision.

- Shortly afterwards, Jesus began His public preaching with the message that the world could be transformed into a "Kingdom of God."

- He became a noted healer, teacher, and prophet. More healing stories are told about Jesus than about any other figure in the Jewish tradition.

- He was executed by Roman imperial authority.

- His followers encountered Him after His death. It is clear that they had visions of Jesus as they had known Him during His historical life.

The contents of the Gospels need to be understood in light of first-century Judaism, not of Eastern mysticism. The former was the world-view of Jesus and all those who followed Him; the latter was a worldview Jesus implicitly and explicitly rejected. He was a Jew who claimed to pre-exist alongside the Father from eternity past (John 17:5), sharing unity with Yahweh (John 8:58, John 1:1–3), the God of Israel. He claimed to be sent by God (John 3:16) to give His life and die on the cross as a ransom (Mark 10:45) for the forgiveness of human sin (Matthew 26:28). He claimed that salvation could be found in faith and faith alone in Him as a person (John 5:24, John 6:47), and that those who do not believe will die in sin (Mark 16:16, John 3:36, John 8:24), which would result in eternal judgment (Matthew 13:42, 25:46).

All this comes from the mouth of Christ Himself. When we allow Jesus to define Himself, we see a man of Jewish faith claiming to be fully unified with God who had a radical self-concept of being the fulfillment of Old Testament prophecy of a coming Messiah. Jesus told people their eternal destiny depended upon whether they believed in Him for the forgiveness of sins. There is nothing New Age, gnostic, or mystical about Jesus and His ministry.

Jesus as Risen Lord

Surprisingly, the New Age movement generally wants to affirm the basic outline of Jesus' life as revealed in the Gospels. Those who do believe in a historical Jesus generally don't have a problem with His bodily resurrection. They typically understand it as being "ascension" of one form or another. We must, however, combine what we know about the resurrection narratives with the teachings of Jesus. Jesus was raised from the dead by God as Jewish Messiah who claimed He was the only path to the Father (John 14:6). He was raised claiming to be the sacrifice for human sin (John 10:11). If Jesus was raised from the dead by God, this would be His stamp of approval on the ministry and self-revelation of Jesus. Unless we want to say that God raised Jesus from the dead as a liar or a lunatic, the resurrection story understood in the context of Jesus' Jewishness leads us not to an Ascended Master but to our risen Lord and Savior.

The tomb of Jesus was found empty; the Gospels are clear about this. Matthew 28:11–15 and reports by Justin Martyr and Tertullian tell us that the Pharisees tried to *explain away* the missing body, not *deny* that there was a missing body. All they had to do was point to the tomb where they had buried Him and the entire Christian faith would have never developed, but rather than debunk the claim, they tried to explain *how* the body had gone missing. This suggests that it really was missing. Furthermore, the first reports of the empty tomb were given by women—a culturally unlikely choice of messengers for reliable testimony if they were trying to develop a legend of a savior-god.

For these reasons and many others, historian Gary Habermas states:

An intriguing development in recent theological research is that
a strong majority of contemporary critical scholars seems to support, at least to some extent, the view that Jesus was buried in a
tomb that was subsequently discovered to be empty.[257]

The empty tomb is reported in at least three, if not four, of these
Gospel sources. This helps to understand why these items are
taken so seriously by contemporary critical scholars.[258]

Shortly after the tomb was found empty, the disciples saw appearances of the risen Jesus. We have record of this in Mark, Matthew, and
John. We also have a record of His appearing to the women in Matthew and John. In 1 Corinthians 15:1–11, Paul tells of information
he "received" during a meeting with the apostles; we learn that Jesus
appeared to more than five hundred people at one time as well as to
James, Peter, the disciples, and Paul himself.

At the very least, most scholars concede that they have had experiences that caused them to believe that Jesus arose. They attribute these
experiences to mass vision, hallucination, or some kind of illusion created out of trauma. New Testament scholar Dale Allison reminds us that
"typical encounters with the recently deceased do not issue in claims
about an empty tomb, nor do they lead to the founding of a new religion. And they certainly do not typically eat and drink, and they are not
seen by crowds of up to five hundred people."[259]

Because of the empty tomb, the historical records we have of the
appearances of Jesus, the willingness of the disciples to die for their belief
that they saw Jesus, and the conversion of skeptics like Thomas, James,
and Paul, the majority of historians (including atheists) agree that the
disciples came to believe Jesus had risen because they had real experiences that lent credence to these beliefs.

Skeptical historian Gerd Ludemann says that "it may be taken as historically certain that Peter and the disciples had experiences after Jesus's death in which Jesus appeared to them as the risen christ."[260]

Another historian and professor at Duke University, Ed Parish Sanders, has said:

> Finally we know that after his death his followers experienced what they described as the "resurrection" the appearance of a living but transformed person who had actually died. They believed this, they lived it, and they died for it... That Jesus' followers (and later Paul) had resurrection experiences is, in my judgment, a fact. What the reality was that gave rise to the experiences I do not know.[261]

The best explanation is, of course, the one adopted by all of Jesus' followers. God raised Jesus from the dead, leaving an empty tomb. If what Jesus says is true, we cannot save ourselves from the penalty of our own sin. If what Jesus says is true, we cannot have a relationship with God unless we come to Christ with a repentant faith (Luke 13:3). If what Jesus says is true, the entire New Age worldview is rendered illegitimate. We must choose to allow the words of Jesus and the evidence of his lordship to speak for themselves, and when we do, we're left with only two intellectually honest options:

- We accept the testimony Jesus and His followers bore about Him.
- We reject the testimony Jesus and His followers bore about Him.

What is not an option is to change the testimony Jesus and His followers bore about Him to make Jesus into someone who looks more like us, which is precisely what the best-selling authors of the New Age movement do in publication after publication, selling millions of copies of books that unapologetically pervert the simplicity of the gospel of Jesus Christ. The New Age movement literally makes its money selling a false version of Jesus to those who are simply unfamiliar with modern scholarship and who are unaware of what the historical man-God taught during His life here—and it's all motivated by the desire to turn Jesus into someone He wasn't.

His message was simple and understood with perfect clarity by all the disciples and their disciples. As much as it may offend our self-dependence, a radically Jewish Jesus tells us that He alone is Lord, and we need His atoning work on the cross applied to us through faith to enter a relationship with the God of Israel. We cannot save ourselves, but we have perfect access to someone who can, someone who made us and loves us. This is good news.

7

RELIGIOUS PLURALISM, TOLERANCE, AND POSTMODERN RHETORIC

A POPULAR OBJECTION SURFACED WHEN I (Steve) tried sharing my newfound faith with people. This was that all religions somehow point toward the same set of universal principles. A higher truth undergirds all religions and unites them in such a way that none can be said to be the only way. They all contain the way. Each religion is just a different way of understanding God. My new way might be different from my old way, but both are valid human attempts to understand the Infinite. This position is called "oneism," "all-theism," or "religious pluralism," and asserts that all spiritual paths are equal in validity.

The objection was not motivated by the searing similarities between each faith, but by the desire to affirm each person in the path he or she has chosen in life. Someone once told me, "I can't understand how it can be right to walk out my door each morning and feel in my soul that everyone around me is wrong. How can there be thousands of world religions, yet only one is true? It's not very highvibe to insinuate that everyone who disagrees with your opinion is objectively wrong. Isn't it just absurd, bigoted, judgmental, and even arrogant to claim that you have the one true path to God and the majority of the world is lost? Isn't it ignorant to believe that everyone who disagrees with Christianity is not only false but in danger of hellfire?"

First, it's important to know that if we want to show that a position is false, we can't do so by pointing to the qualities of the person holding that position. In someone's eyes, it may be arrogant to claim that another person's path to God is a deception, but that doesn't mean the claim itself is wrong. Religious fundamentalists may seem bigoted, but that doesn't mean their worldview is incorrect. They may seem judgmental, but their attitude has no bearing on the accuracy of their beliefs.

To prove a claim is false, we need to argue against that claim instead of labeling the person presenting it as "arrogant" or "intolerant." Otherwise, we are attacking the speaker instead of the validity of his or her beliefs, and this makes us guilty of committing a patented *ad hominem* logical fallacy. A logical fallacy is an error in reasoning. We are making an argument "against the man" (literal), not against the proposition itself.

We also can't invalidate a belief by pointing to its social consequence (whether this be division, offense, exclusion, etc), for this is to commit the logical fallacy of *ad consequentium*. The fact that a proposition, if true, may result in undesirable consequences does not mean the belief is incorrect. Sure, it might be hurtful or divisive to believe everyone who disagrees with you is wrong. But that is simply irrelevant. We must assess ideas on their own merits and hold them up to the light of reason and evidence, regardless of the possible consequences.

Pluralism: More Extreme than One True Religion

Since, we are told, all religions contain the same true principles at their core, it ultimately doesn't matter which avenue you choose for yourself. Whether you are a Buddhist, a Catholic, or a Hindu, you are on the right path, for there is no such thing as a wrong path. All religions are different ways man attempts to explain the Divine, and the Divine can be understood in a variety of ways depending on a person's nature and nurture.

The New Age movement takes the attitude of a religion (ironically) known as Bahai. According to the Bahai faith:

Throughout history, God has sent to humanity a series of divine Educators—known as Manifestations of God—whose teachings have provided the basis for the advancement of civilization. These Manifestations have included Abraham, Krishna, Zoroaster, Moses, Buddha, Jesus, and Muhammad. Bahá'u'lláh, the latest of these Messengers, explained that the religions of the world come from the same Source and are in essence successive chapters of one religion from God.[262]

As mystical poet Rumi once said, "How many paths are there to God? There are as many paths to God as there are souls on the Earth." Eckhart Tolle says:

If we look more deeply into humanity's ancient religions and spiritual traditions, we will find that underneath the many surface differences there are two core insights that most of them agree on. The words they use to describe those insights differ, yet they all point to a twofold fundamental truth.... All religions are equally false and equally true, depending on how you use them.[263]

This common "truth" is usually identified as one of the following:

- The belief that love is the prime virtue
- The practice of service and charity to other people
- The belief that you are more than your body
- The belief that the Higher Power loves and wants the best for people
- The belief that there is a higher state of consciousness by which we can live
- The belief that there is something beyond this world

As long as we believe one of these things, we can walk out the door each morning and believe in our soul that 100 percent of people are aligned with the path of God in a general sense. This seems far more socially tolerable than Christian fundamentalism, but here is why the New Age idea of religious pluralism is far more intolerant: The person who believes there is no single path that leads to the truth must believe that every religion in the history of the world that claims exclusivity is fundamentally false, regardless of whether it is supported by evidence.

The New Age movement rejects the idea that Jesus is the only way and that Allah is the one true God. The gods of Hinduism are not the only true gods. Judaism is not a result of the one true God revealing Himself to one specific people. If someone says, "I have found the truth; it's called Islam," and you reply, "There is no one true path; Islam is not the only way to God," then you are calling Islam fundamentally false because it teaches that it is the only path to God. Religious pluralism itself is a claim that fundamentalist religions and their main beliefs cannot possibly be true as a matter of principle. Statistically, this is equivalent to saying that almost every religious person in the world is wrong.

According to a new comprehensive demographic study of more than 230 countries and territories conducted in 2010 by the Pew Research Center's Forum on Religion and Public Life, 84 percent of people identify under a specific religion. "There are 5.8 billion religiously affiliated adults and children around the globe, representing 84 percent of the 2010 world population of 6.9 billion," the report states.[264] Here are the stats based on an analysis of more than 2,500 censuses, surveys, and population registers:

- 2.2 billion Christians (32 percent of the world's population)
- 1.6 billion Muslims (23 percent)
- 1 billion Hindus (15 percent)
- 500 million Buddhists (7 percent)

- 400 million people (6 percent) practicing various folk or traditional religions, including African traditional religions, Chinese folk religions, American Indian religions, and Australian aboriginal religions

There are 14 million Jews, and an estimated 58 million people—slightly fewer than 1 percent of the global population—belong to other religions, including the Baha'i faith, Jainism, Sikhism, Shintoism, Taoism, Tenrikyo, Wicca, and Zoroastrianism, "to mention just a few," the study says.

The religions in the category of "other" are the only ones that are even partially compatible with this pluralistic philosophy, and it is safe to assume based on the list that even some of those may been too exclusive, dogmatic, idealistic, or narrow. Less than 1 percent of self-identified religious people hold beliefs that are compatible with pluralism. So, the religious pluralist has to defend the claim that 99.5 percent of the world's religious people have beliefs that are fundamentally false, and the claims to exclusivity they make are in grave error. Furthermore, they are obliged to believe this prior to examining the evidence of support of such claims because their philosophy, by definition, requires that they reject every exclusive claim pertaining to religious truth.

Christianity, Islam, Hinduism, and Judaism may all contain aspects of truth, but they claim to be exclusively true and are therefore fundamentally false. The New Ager who seeks to be all inclusive is, ironically, making the most divisive claims out of every other spiritual category in the world. You would have to say that 84 percent of the world's population (almost all religious people) are wrong, except .5 percent of those in the "other" category. The Christian can quite comfortably say that 32 percent of the world's religious population have it right compared to the New Agers' "extreme" statement that only .5 percent have it right. Which position is more extreme, divisive, or narrow? Which position is more intolerant?

This doesn't mean Christianity is true or religious pluralism is false by any stretch of the imagination, but the point is it's not extreme or arrogant to claim that one out of every three religious people identifies with the correct worldview. The religious pluralist occupies less than .5 percent of the religious population and needs to provide justification for the extreme claim that all fundamentalist religions are necessarily false prior to even looking at the evidence. This is not only more divisive, it is more dogmatic. Division and dogma increase by adopting pluralism. The New Age movement ends up creating more division than any other spiritual movement in the world by opposing all beliefs that create division. This idea creates more of the problem it seeks to solve.

Pluralism: Premised on a False Idea of Tolerance

> Do you think that I have come to give peace on earth? No, I tell you, but rather division. For from now on in one house there will be five divided, three against two and two against three. They will be divided, father against son and son against father, mother against daughter and daughter against mother, mother-in-law against her daughter-in-law and daughter-in-law against mother-in-law. (Luke 12:51–53)

Jesus clearly thinks division is fine if it is a result of siding with the truth. Those in the New Age movement feel separated from those who believe Jesus is the only way to God. Since these two worldviews conflict, this is only natural. Division is a consequence of choosing sides. The remedy is to unify on the side of truth, not systematically reject every school of thought that results in disunity. Pretending there is no right or wrong side is not the solution.

Unity has become the god of the New Age movement by exalting the absence of conflict over the presence of truth. A false peace is enforced by eliminating every idea that may cause some level of separation between us and our fellow man, even if these ideas correspond to reality. Disagreement is the enemy because it breeds negativity, so to avoid disagreement, "tolerance" is redefined to mean "complacency"— even in the presence of error.

It's thought unloving or disrespectful if we imply that someone is wrong. Tolerance, however, doesn't mean that we have a compliant atti- tude toward untruth. To be tolerant means to love and accept a person even if we vehemently disagree with their worldview or life choices. It means we respect that everyone has a right to his or her opinion as an image-bearer of God, so much so that we will fight to the death for the preservation of that right. Their belief system does not give us permis- sion to overlook others' God-given worth and rights.

Every person has a right to believe whatever he or she wants, but that doesn't mean what every person believes is right. Also, it doesn't mean that every person is exempt from hearing that what he or she believes is wrong. Tolerance does not mean that we should remain uncritical of false and dangerous beliefs. We can be tolerantly loving of a child who is lost in the New Age movement, but that doesn't mean we have to bend our belief system and begin to accept what the child believes. It doesn't mean we can't disagree with the child in conver- sation. We can tolerate a boss at a personal level while passionately rejecting his or her atheism at an intellectual level. We can love the person and hate the belief.

Two different types of tolerance are at play here. The first we could call "social tolerance," and it obligates us to love and accept all people of all religions and lifestyles. Jesus, remember, often associated with the guiltiest of sinners, including Judas, whom Jesus called "friend" even after he betrayed Him. He tolerated and loved people He told were in error and danger of Hell's fire (the Pharisees), because love obligates us to speak honestly and give the correction necessary to enhance the well- being of those around us. All of this is to be done by being tolerant of people, wholly apart from their worldview and lifestyle. Jesus died to save the people He told were wrong. In fact, it's precisely because we have thought and acted incorrectly that Jesus died for us.

The second kind of tolerance at play here could be called "epistemo-logical tolerance," the idea that we should be tolerant of false/dangerous beliefs and worldviews. If people voice their opinion that Jesus did not exist as a historical figure, I am told by the New Age movement (and post-modernism in general) that I am to "respect their beliefs." Social tolerance is confused with epistemological tolerance such that world-views, not people, are entitled to respect. The religious pluralism of the New Age movement is largely built upon the false idea that ideas have the same "rights" as humans to be tolerated and respected. In a post-modern world, worldviews should be exempt from criticism as abstract entities.

Something to remember about the nature of thought is that beliefs don't "deserve" respect, even if they are true. People deserve respect because they have moral worth, but beliefs have no moral worth. Beliefs are mental commitments to propositions. If we were to write the content of our beliefs on a piece of paper, we would see a collection of sentences. These sentences are either true or false and worthy of assent or rejection, but a collection of sentences doesn't "deserve" "respect." How could a sentence even be "respected" in the first place? What would it look like to treat a sentence with "respect"? Ideas are not moral agents, they aren't alive, they don't have rights, and they don't have feelings. They exist as abstract objects in the thought world of people.

The language of needing to "respect" a belief makes people morally obligated to a sentence of conjoined words. We can't have a moral obli-gation to a sentence, just like we can't have a moral obligation to a set of numbers. What the sentence is referring to may be worthy of respect (such as a person or an event), but the sentence itself has no moral value. The subject of a sentence may be worthy of our life's worship, but the sentence itself is just an idea. Ideas are mental objects. A sentence may be "respectable" in the sense of being intellectually considerable, but a segment of words is not worthy of respect, honor, and tolerance in the way that people are.

Tolerance and respect should be extended to the person with the ideas, not to the ideas in the mind of the person. Nobody has a moral obligation from God to respect, honor, or tolerate an idea in someone else's mind. I will tolerate you as you consent to this idea, but I will not respect or condone the idea you consent to. False concepts deserve to be exposed for the well-being of human persons, especially in matters of human salvation in which life and death hinges upon the words of Jesus. The Bible is filled with verses about confronting false worldviews:

- "We destroy arguments and every lofty opinion raised against the knowledge of God" (2 Corinthians 10:5).
- "Take no part in the unfruitful works of darkness, but instead expose them" (Ephesians 5:11).
- "But even if we or an angel from heaven should preach to you a gospel contrary to the one we preached to you, let him be accursed. As we have said before, so now I say again: If anyone is preaching to you a gospel contrary to the one you received, let him be accursed" (Galatians 1:8–10).
- "Preach the word; be ready in season and out of season; reprove, rebuke, and exhort, with complete patience and teaching" (2 Timothy 4:2).
- "And the Lord's servant must not be quarrelsome but kind to everyone, able to teach, patiently enduring evil, correcting his opponents with gentleness. God may perhaps grant them repentance leading to a knowledge of the truth" (2 Timothy 2:25).

We are actively commanded to be intellectually opposed to untruth while being perfectly accepting of the person. Being intolerant of untruth, however, does not mean throwing all discernment and charity out the window when we confront false ideas. We are to correct in gentleness without being quarrelsome.

The truth is, some false beliefs have negative consequences and deserve to be exposed and renounced even if it creates social disharmony. Racism, sexism, and all other types of discrimination are worthy of confutation. Our entire lives require that false ideas about government, economics, nutrition, mental health, and medicine have no room to dominate our society. False ideas about morality and ethics can destroy nations overnight—and have done so throughout history. For the well-being of humanity, we must actively protest destructive ideas. We have done this collectively as a society for thousands of years.

And what could be more destructive than eternal destruction away from the presence of the Lord? If the Christian worldview is correct (which it is), Christians are charged with a moral obligation to actively share their faith in love in the hopes that others who don't know Christ as Savior may be saved. Atheist Penn Jillette summarizes the urgency of evangelism accurately:

> I've always said that I don't respect people who don't proselytize. I don't respect that at all. If you believe that there's a heaven and a hell, and people could be going to hell or not getting eternal life, and you think that it's not really worth telling them this because it would make it socially awkward—and atheists who think people shouldn't proselytize and who say just leave me alone and keep your religion to yourself—how much do you have to hate somebody to not proselytize? How much do you have to hate somebody to believe everlasting life is possible and not tell them that? I mean, if I believed, beyond the shadow of a doubt, that a truck was coming at you, and you didn't believe that truck was bearing down on you, there is a certain point where I tackle you. And this is more important than that.[265]

The New Age movement ought recognize the necessity of esteeming truth above everything else in our thought lives. The Church must recognize this as well. It's important that we, as believers, aren't pressured by a postmodern world into thinking that we are "intolerant" because we tell other people their worldview is wrong. We must stand up for the truth and share it with people in the Spirit of Christ, just like we stand up for truth as a society in every other facet of life. Yes, there is a way to communicate these beliefs without being verbally alienating. We need to start conversations in love and keep them grounded in love. But we mustn't think the pinnacle of human enlightenment lies in adopting a postmodern idea of "tolerance" wherein we are silenced from sharing the truth with people who need it.

People are to be tolerated; false ideas are to be refuted. This has been the pattern throughout history until the last sixty years or so. One could only imagine if Plato and Socrates were having a dialogue about the true nature of the phenomenal world, and Plato accused Socrates of being intolerant because social unity had been violated by their disagreement. This attitude does not appear on the historical map of philosophical discussions anywhere in the ancient world, and it has nothing to do with the ministry of Jesus.

Also, this postmodern idea of epistemic tolerance is self-defeating. To think it is intolerant to passionately disagree with someone's beliefs is to make one guilty of intolerance—namely, the person has to be intolerant of what "tolerance" means in order to uphold that we shouldn't be intolerant. The New Age movement is intolerant of every idea that it perceives as intolerant. More intolerance is created by being intolerant to those who are intolerant (Christian fundamentalists). The sociological glue that holds pluralism in place is a self-defeating notion of unity that cannot live up to its own standard.

We need to get back to the way things used to be in the world so that we can have open discussion about ideas and worldviews, regardless of their implications on social "unity." Now that we understand that the motivating ethic of pluralism is not as congruent as it may seem, let's take a brief look at its claims.

Pluralism: Impossible Because
Religions Contradict Each Other

Not only is pluralism more statistically extreme than particularism, and not only does pluralism rest upon a false, self-defeating idea of tolerance, it is impossible for it to be true when we examine the structural pillars in each faith. Prevalent in the New Age movement is the idea that Buddha and Jesus taught the same basic doctrine and lived with the same moral code. The comparison between these two teachers is the most frequently used defense for an underlying Truth that exists universally across all religions. We can identify, we are told, with either Christianity or Buddhism because there is no tangible difference between the two. One popular New Age teacher says we must consider the possibility that "Jesus was actually a Buddhist monk...two different men living two different time periods with the exact same state of mind."[266]

Another argument claims that "although not identifying himself as a Buddhist for good reasons, Jesus spoke like a Buddhist. The similarities are so striking that, even if no historical evidence existed, we can suspect that Jesus studied Buddhist teachings and that the prophecy and legend of Jesus was derived from Buddhist stories."[267]

This is the most common comparison used in the New Age movement to establish a common link among all faiths because each one—Jesus and Buddha—promotes love, compassion, forgiveness, and kindness. The problem is, the Buddha and Jesus Christ have next to nothing in common.

Jesus taught that the single most important thing to do is to believe in Him for the forgiveness of sins. In fact, He said to believe in Him is the ultimate will of God (John 6:29). The reason for this is that Jesus was the sacrifice for human sin (Mark 10:45), and only He can reconcile us back to God (John 14:6). Without faith, we will die in our sins (John 8:24). Jesus taught about a literal kingdom of Heaven and a place of eternal torment called Hell, where the wicked will be punished (Matthew 13:41–42). We need to be supernaturally born again through Him in order to see God (John 3:3). Faith in Him is the condition of eternal life (John 5:24), and we will be rewarded in the afterlife according to our works for His Kingdom on Judgment Day (Matthew 16:27).

These ideas are fundamental to Christian theology and don't even appear on the map of Buddhist philosophy. The World Buddhist Directory outlines clear distinctions between Buddhism and Christianity:[268]

- There is no almighty God in Buddhism. There is no one to hand out rewards or punishments on a supposed Judgement Day.
- Buddhism is strictly not a religion in the context of being a faith and worship owing allegiance to a supernatural being.
- No saviour concept in Buddhism. A Buddha is not a saviour who saves others by his personal salvation. Although a Buddhist seeks refuge in the Buddha as his incomparable guide who indicates the path of purity, he makes no servile surrender. A Buddhist does not think that he can gain purity merely by seeking refuge in the Buddha or by mere faith in Him. It is not within the power of a Buddha to wash away the impurities of others
- A Buddha is not an incarnation of a god/God (as claimed by some Hindu followers). The relationship between a Buddha and his disciples and followers is that of a teacher and student.
- The liberation of self is the responsibility of one's own self. Buddhism does not call for an unquestionable blind faith by all Buddhist followers. It places heavy emphasis on self-reliance, self discipline and individual striving.
- Taking refuge in The Triple Gems i.e. the Buddha, the Dharma and the Sangha; does not mean self-surrender or total reliance on an external force or third party for help or salvation.
- Dharma (the teachings in Buddhism) exists regardless whether there is a Buddha. Sakyamuni Buddha (as the historical Buddha) discovered and shared the teachings/ universal truths with all sentient beings. He is neither the creator of such teachings nor the prophet of an almighty God to transmit such teachings to others.

- In Buddhism, the ultimate objective of followers/practitioners is enlightenment and/or liberation from Samsara; rather than to go to a Heaven (or a deva realm in the context of Buddhist cosmology).
- The idea of sin or original sin has no place in Buddhism. Also, sin should not be equated to suffering.
- The concept of Hell(s) in Buddhism is very different from that of other religions. It is not a place for eternal damnation as viewed by 'almighty creator' religions. In Buddhism, it is just one of the six realms in Samsara [i.e. the worst of three undesirable realms]. Also, there are virtually unlimited number of hells in the Buddhist cosmology as there are infinite number of Buddha worlds.

The beliefs of Buddhism are logically incompatible with the beliefs of Christianity. Every essential tenet of the Christian faith is the opposite of the teachings of Buddhism, which makes at least one set of teachings false. We could say that Christianity is false, Buddhism is false, or both are false, but to say both are true is a logical impossibility. Two opposing views can't be true at the same time.

The differences between Islam and Hinduism, Judaism and Chinese religions, and African religions and Wicca are just as radical. All of these religions have radically opposing views on sin, the afterlife, the nature of God, the moral will of God, God's plan for human history, the purpose and meaning of life, ethics and self-conduct, salvation/liberation, and the nature of the soul. All religions cannot be valid paths to God if they contradict one another in telling us how to get there.

The most important doctrine in the Christian faith is that Jesus Christ died and rose for the sins of humanity:

For I delivered to you as of first importance what I also received: that Christ died for our sins in accordance with the Scriptures. (1 Corinthians 15:3)

However, Islam explicitly denies that Jesus died on the cross:

And [for] their saying, "Indeed, we have killed the Messiah, Jesus, the son of Mary, the messenger of Allah." And they did not kill him, nor did they crucify him; but [another] was made to resemble him to them. And indeed, those who differ over it are in doubt about it. They have no knowledge of it except the following of assumption. And they did not kill him, for certain. (Quran 4:156–158)

How can Jesus and Muhammad be prophets of the same God if the Bible tells us that Jesus died on the cross for our sins (Mark 10:45, Colossians 2:14, 1 Peter 2:24, etc.), and Islam tells us that Jesus never died on a cross in the first place? If He didn't die on the cross, He sure didn't die on the cross for our sins. If He didn't die on the cross for our sins, Christianity is false. If he did, Christianity is true. But both ideas can't be affirmed as true like the "oneism" of the New Age movements wants to do. Religious pluralism is rendered invalid when we examine the teachings of each religion.

But Don't All Religions Teach Love?

The main defense of the position that all paths lead to God is that all teachings are based on a similar morality: "Well, they all teach forgiveness, kindness, and love, and this is ultimately the path to God." Deepak Chopra tells us that the teachings of Buddha and Jesus "are similar in relation to the Golden Rule; do unto others as you would have them do unto you; and in the total embodiment of nonviolence; you must turn the other cheek and love your enemies…. So the teachings are similar even if they are enclosed in different languages, which reflect the cultures they came from."[269]

Aside from the fact that social morality makes up a very small percentage of the teachings in fundamentalist religions, the main problem with this is that the doctrines of love vary from religion to religion as well. "Love" in each religion is contextualized by a very specific theological and philosophical backdrop. We can't isolate commands from their religious context in an attempt to prove universalism because they are woven into a particular theological framework. For example, Jesus says to love our neighbors as ourselves in Matthew 22: 34–39:

> Hearing that Jesus had silenced the Sadducees, the Pharisees got together. One of them, an expert in the law, tested him with this question: "Teacher, which is the greatest commandment in the Law?" Jesus replied: "Love the Lord your God with all your heart and with all your soul and with all your mind. This is the first and greatest commandment. And the second is like it: Love your neighbor as yourself. All the Law and the Prophets hang on these two commandments."

Jesus' commandment is be properly understood in these verses in the context of monotheistic Judaism, for Jesus taught love as a requirement of fulfilling the highest moral will of Yahweh and the commands laid out in the Torah. All the commandments in the Old Testament Law given by the God of Israel can be fulfilled through love. Love, in this context, is a means to the end of fulfilling God's moral will.

In Matthew 5:16, we see Jesus teach that we are to do good works as a means by which the Father will receive glory:

> In the same way, let your light shine before others, so that they may see your good works and give glory to your Father who is in heaven.

> Jesus also teaches that our love is evidence that we are His disciples: By this all people will know that you are my disciples, if you have love for one another. (John 13:35)

Jesus teaches that we are to forgive others in order to be forgiven by the Father:

> For if you forgive others their trespasses, your heavenly Father will also forgive you, but if you do not forgive others their trespasses, neither will your Father forgive your trespasses. (Matthew 6:14–15)

He says that when we give, we should do so secretly so that we will receive our reward from the Father and not from man:

> But when you give to the needy, do not let your left hand know what your right hand is doing, so that your giving may be in secret. And your Father who sees in secret will reward you. (Matthew 6:3–4)

Even the Golden Rule was given by Jesus in a religious context:

> So whatever you wish that others would do to you, do also to them, for this is the Law and the Prophets. (Matthew 7:12)

All religions don't simply teach love, they teach it as a part of their theological model and in reference to their own religious ideologies. It's always contextualized with a religious end in mind. Jesus didn't teach us to forgive because it creates good karma for the next life or helps us leave the cycle Samsara. He taught us to forgive so that we may be forgiven by our Father in Heaven for our sins. Every moral virtue for each religion is woven into a specific theological model.

Everyone in the New Age movement affirms the teachings Christ gave on "love," but not everyone acknowledges that He used the word "love" more in reference to the love owed Him and the Father than He did in reference to people. Moral virtues make up a small percent of the teachings of world religions, and they are contextualized by a religious framework. Separating the moral commandments of Jesus from their Jewish context to pass them off as Buddhist philosophy is nothing short of hijacking.

Comparing Jesus with Buddha is tantamount to comparing Hitler with Kennedy. To say that that Christianity and Buddhism are essentially the same because they both teach love as a moral virtue is like saying Adolf Hitler and John F. Kennedy endorsed the same political model because they both believed citizens should pay taxes. Taxation makes up a very small percentage of each leader's political ideology, and even their tax models differ from each other. They both believe people should pay taxes. So what? That doesn't mean Hitler and Kennedy had the same political philosophy. Jesus and Buddha both taught love (in different contexts). So what? That doesn't mean they had the same spiritual philosophy.

The vast differences between religions cannot be remedied by simply isolating a few moral qualities from their theological context. Going up to the leading defenders of each world religion and saying they are all true because they all teach morality in some degree is like going to the top chefs in each country and saying the recipes for their national dishes are all the same because they all contain salt in some degree. It takes more than one ingredient to make a dish.

Being "Spiritual" Doesn't Make Us Experts in World Religion

This view of pluralism tends to dawn on people via transpersonal mystical experiences. It just "feels" as though there must be an all-encompassing answer to world religions when one relaxes his or her mental faculties and meditates on the question from an expanded state of consciousness. Something we must understand is that there is nothing about the pursuit of psycho-emotional health or spiritual experience that allows us to step into the field of religious studies and make the historically inaccurate claim that all religions teach the same thing. People in the New Age movement, as we once did, make the mistake of thinking that their own psycho-spiritual pursuits equip them to step into the field of religious studies and make the assumption that every religion in the world is fundamentally about the experience they just had.

If we want to know what these religions teach, we should study comparative religion—or better yet, read the religions' primary texts. We cannot infer from the experiences we have in silence that all religions are fundamentally false or that they all teach the same thing. Nothing about adopting love and compassion as core virtues or meditation and mindfulness as core practices allows us to conclude that all religious beliefs are somehow about these subjective personal experiences we are having, or that the truth or falsity of religious beliefs can be discerned from said experience.

There is no personal experience you can have in the boundlessness of your heart, the stillness of your mind, in the solitude of your spirit, the alteration of your consciousness, the homeostasis of your nervous system, or the spaciousness of your energy field that will allow you to conclude that God did not raise Jesus from the dead in first-century Jerusalem. Likewise, there is no dose of DMT (dimethyltryptamine) you could take that would warrant you to think that Jesus didn't believe in the Old Testament, or that Jesus and Buddha taught the same doctrine.

Private revelation offers no insight on questions about the historic teachings of historical figures, only historical sources do. So many teachings of the New Age movement would be dismissed if New Agers would recognize the error in thinking we can download private knowledge about world religions through spiritual experience, wholly apart from referring to historical sources.

Religious pluralism is statistically the most divisive spiritual philosophy on the planet, it is driven by a self-defeating idea of "tolerance," and it is impossible because it maintains that mutually exclusive sentences can be affirmed as truth at the same time. Religious particularism is the only other option. Now it's just a matter of being honest with the evidence and following it where it leads, even if it means our lives must yield and conform to the truth.

8

DEATH AND BEYOND

And just as it is appointed for man to die once, and after that
comes judgment.

HEBREWS 9:27

THIS IS ONE OF THE most useful verses in response to New Age thought
because it solidifies the orthodox biblical account of the afterlife. It needs
to become the official standard of assessing all claims pertaining to the
afterlife, the measuring stick by which we compare the eschatology of
the Bible with other worldviews. We die physically a single time, and
after physical death comes a final, eternal judgment. This verse serves as
the knockout punch against deception. The apologetic neatness of this
verse is exceptional and proves very effective in dialogue with those who
have New Age leanings, for virtually all schools of thought in the movement affirm the doctrine of reincarnation.

The word "reincarnation" comes from Latin roots meaning "entering the flesh again, and is the view that the human soul/spirit disconnects from the physical body at death and goes into the spirit world,
which Christians affirm. Then, say proponents of reincarnation, the
soul is either magnetized into a newly conceived pregnancy within frac-
tions of a second apart from the person's will, or the soul goes through a
series of events in the spirit world, eventually willing its next incarnation
(which we will examine in a moment).[270]

If Hebrews 9:27 is true, all New Age and Eastern accounts of the afterlife become void. I (Steve) was unaware of this verse while I was involved in the New Age movement, and a good portion of Christians appear to be unaware of it as well, considering that a recent survey from the Pew Research Foundation found that 22 percent of professing Christians believe in reincarnation:[271] "Roughly one-in-ten white evangelicals believes in reincarnation, compared with 24% among mainline Protestants, 25% among both white Catholics and those unaffiliated with any religion, and 29% among black Protestants."[272]

These statistics cause concern, to say the least, because reincarnation contradicts the gospel. We don't have sin we need to be saved from if we can save ourselves from it with good deeds in the next life. If we can work our negative karma off in a future incarnation, then Jesus died for nothing. We can pay for our own sins. But if we have a moral debt to God that only Jesus can pay, then reincarnation serves no hypothetical purpose. Jesus' death is absolutely necessary if, after we die once, we face judgment with no atonement for our sins available apart from the blood of Jesus.

The Bible says Jesus died as the atonement for our sins (1 John 2:2; Romans 3:25). If we atone for our own sins in a future incarnation, then Christ died unnecessarily. But if we only have one life (Hebrews 9:27) and good deeds can't erase our sins (Romans 3:20), a ransom must be made on our behalf to pay our debt of justice to God (Mark 10:45). It's important for the Church to reawaken to the urgency of the gospel in light of a single life lived. If we live once and good deeds don't justify us, we need the sacrifice of Jesus.

The Journey and Destiny of Souls in the New Age

The popularization of reincarnation in the New Age movement comes primarily from the work of someone named Dr. Michael Newton, a counselor who specialized in the practice of hypnotherapy. He put people into a state of hypnosis to bring them back into very early memories from their childhood so that the traumas and belief systems could be undone from the source. He apparently "discovered" that his patients had memories so early that they preceded birth in the spirit world, and memories that went back into past lives during which their souls had existed in other bodies. They would recall events that came before they even entered their body, which seemed compelling evidence for reincarnation.

In his books *Journey of Souls* and *Destiny of Souls* (best-sellers that have sold hundreds of thousands of copies), Newton shares case studies he has gathered from his patients over forty years to put together what has become the predominant theory of the afterlife in the New Age. Here are the nine steps of reincarnation that occur universally independent of the moral depravity and belief system of the individual:

1) **Death and departure.** When your soul disconnects from your body at death, you will be able to see your immediate surroundings. In the hypnotherapy sessions, some people allegedly report feeling peace that they finally departed, or even feeling anger as they hover over their offender and the witness events that led up to their death.

2) **Gateway to the spirit world.** A light appears in the distance and your soul becomes sucked into it almost like a vortex. People in this trance-like state of consciousness report that they remember being pulled into the spirit world after their previous life. The spirit world is not Heaven, it's just a soothing, spiritually hazy landing zone for human souls. It's the only possible destination for people whether they be Hitler or Jesus. One hundred percent of people go to a blissful spirit world. Jesus, however, tells us that not everyone goes to the same spiritual realm after death. He taught a Heaven and Hell dichotomy dozens of times in the Gospels:

> When the Son of Man comes in his glory, and all the angels with him, then he will sit on his glorious throne. Before him will be gathered all the nations, and he will separate people one from

another as a shepherd separates the sheep from the goats. And he will place the sheep on his right, but the goats on the left. Then the King will say to those on his right, "Come, you who are blessed by my Father, inherit the kingdom prepared for you from the foundation of the world…". Then he will say to those on his left, "Depart from me, you cursed, into the eternal fire prepared for the devil and his angels…". And these will go away into eternal punishment, but the righteous into eternal life. (Matthew 25:31–34, 41, 46)

3) Homecoming. Upon arriving in the spirit world, you are greeted by a host of family members in a post-death family reunion. These are not necessarily relatives from your current incarnation. They could be people you have lived with five to ten lives ago. Jesus contradicts this by saying that unsaved Jewish people will be excluded from fellowship with their ancestors because of their rejection of Him. We don't get to see people just because they are family. Ancestry means nothing as far as who we see in Heaven. The saved commune with the saved:

> I tell you, many will come from east and west and recline at table with Abraham, Isaac, and Jacob in the kingdom of heaven, while the sons of the kingdom will be thrown into the outer darkness. In that place there will be weeping and gnashing of teeth. (Matthew 8:11–12)

4) Orientation. The soul gets taken through a life review. People report seeing their entire lives as a sort of movie film, or they have a book that contains an account of all their life events. Regardless of what is in the book, there is no judgment or punishment issued, because it's meant to encourage them in what they need to work on next, not condemn them under the weight of their sin. God, in this model, is not holy and does not require moral compensation for the crimes committed against humanity. According to Scripture, the only life review unbelievers will experience is one leading to their judgment:

> Do not marvel at this, for an hour is coming when all who are in the tombs will hear his voice and come out, those who have done good to the resurrection of life, and those who have done evil to the resurrection of judgment. (John 5:28–29)

> The cowardly, the unbelieving, the vile, the murderers, the sexually immoral, those who practice magic arts, the idolaters and all liarstheir place will be in the fiery lake of burning sulfur. This is the second death. (Revelation 21:8)

5) **Transition.** Souls bypass judgment for their sins against God and find themselves at a sort of terminal area where they await transportation to the next place in the spirit world. It's a gathering place that is likened to a metropolitan center.

6) **Placement.** Souls are at different levels of evolution based on their moral character and self-awareness. Souls are divided into "clusters" or "groups" of other souls that are at the same level, ranging from groups of twenty to groups of thousands. This is when souls have fellowship and discussions with like-minded people who can bring them up to the next level of their evolution. Jesus says there is only one soul group in Heaven: the souls saved by faith in His finished work (John 3:16, John 14:6). There is no division based on soul development for saved persons, for we are all part of the corporate body of Christ:

> There is one body and one Spirit—just as you were called to the one hope that belongs to your call—one Lord, one faith, one baptism, one God and Father of all, who is over all and through all and in all. (Ephesians 4:4–6)

7) **Life selection.** This is where you choose a new life for yourself based on the lessons you want to live. You know in advance the general kind of life you will be getting into, so you assign to yourself a set of life events you believe will be advantageous to the development of your soul.

For example, you may pick a life in which you are the victim of parental abuse so you can push yourself to a higher degree of self-dependence to compensate for your parents' actions. Or perhaps you choose to be a rape victim, a child slave worker, or a homeless person. Rather than coming into the world to conquer the forces of sin in the world, you come into the world to cooperate with the forces of sin since lessons require suffering.

In this model, the development of your soul requires the presence of sin in other people around you. Jesus died to do away with sin. He came to destroy the works of the devil (1 John 3:8), which people involved in the New Age movement happen to believe are helpful for the development of wisdom. If sin against us helps long-term soul development and Jesus came to put away sin by His death (Hebrews 9:26) and take away the sins of the world (John 1:29), then the mission of Jesus is a thorn in the side of human enlightenment. Jesus came to put an end to what the New Age movement believes is a key ingredient for the expansion of human consciousness. The idea of life selection implies that the sin-inducing work of Satan in the Garden of Eden was ultimately productive for humanity. Jesus is missing the mark by trying to end something that helps us "evolve."

It also implies that maybe we shouldn't try to prevent activities such as child abuse. After all, perhaps a child willfully chose that life in advance and our interference might impede upon the lessons he or she is trying to learn by being sexually abused by their relatives. In other words, our intervention may spoil the purpose of someone's incarnation. This philosophy implies that the maturity of a child's soul will be violated if we protect it against the abuse it has chosen to receive. We may be unknowingly sinning against people by helping them. This has a terrible moral application.

8) Choosing a new body. You choose what kind of body earthly you want to have, whether it be deformed, disabled, or ordinary.

9) Rebirth. You enter a new womb, ready to take on your second or thousandth incarnation. The goal is to reach such a degree of enlightenment that we bypass the cycle of death and rebirth and no longer need to reincarnate. The means by which we leave this cycle is through realizing God-consciousness in our life just as Jesus did. We then graduate to the level of a spirit guide, spirit-world teacher, or Ascended Master.

So how did this Mr. Newton accumulate so many case studies that seemed to confirm one another? The origin of the material from his patients is easy to explain: Confirmation bias was in place prior to the therapy sessions. Patients went in believing and hoping they would have their minds guided into a hidden, subconscious memory bank, making them more likely to fabricate information as they went along. The vast majority of people who seek out "past-life therapy" believe that such a practice is valid and worth their money, making them more inclined to make the most out of their session.

If people are in an altered state of consciousness, believing they will be guided by someone (whom they've paid) who claims to be an expert, they are prone to mistaking their own daydreams or wishful fantasies as "memories." We also must take into account the suggestibility of the mind when a person is in a hypnotic state, and how easy it is to use the power of suggestion and language to guide a person's subconscious mind into believing, speaking, or acting a certain way. This is even truer when combining this with a prior disposition, desire, and payment to have such "memories" in the first place.

If we add the possibility of supernatural influence on the minds of people who are in an altered state of consciousness having yielded to something that is sinful in the eyes of God, we can easily imagine that demons may be projecting thought-forms into the minds of these susceptible people, giving them the impression that the thoughts in their heads are personal memories that belong to their history. In reality, they are mental projections being pushed into the spirit of the person by the principalities they have yielded to in their desire to engage in spiritism. There are both natural and supernatural explanations for this phenomenon that are, at the very least, jointly sufficient to account for the material.

A secondary view on the afterlife is that the consciousness of each person dissipates into the universe and is absorbed in the field of Universal Consciousness. The quantum energy of our souls is released from our bodies and recycled into the cosmos, since energy (including mental energy) can neither be created nor destroyed. Stuart Hameroff summaries this theory of consciousness: "Let's say the heart stops beating, the blood stops flowing, the microtubules [of the brain] lose their quantum state. The quantum information within the microtubules is not destroyed, it can't be destroyed, it just distributes and dissipates to the universe at large."[273]

The Bible, however, renders any view of the afterlife that does not include a final everlasting judgement impossible. Jesus is the authority on what happens after our physical body dies, and he tells us that we retain full awareness and face eternal judgement before God having to give an account for the moral crimes we have committed. The language used in Scripture excludes the possibility of a second chance:

And many of those who sleep in the dust of the earth shall awake, some to everlasting life, and some to shame and everlasting contempt. (Daniel 12:2)

They will suffer the punishment of eternal destruction, away from the presence of the Lord and from the glory of his might. (2 Thessalonians 1:9)

And the smoke of their torment goes up forever and ever, and they have no rest, day or night, these worshipers of the beast and its image, and whoever receives the mark of its name. (Revelation 14:11)

Then he will say to those on his left, "Depart from me, you cursed, into the eternal fire prepared for the devil and his angels..." And these will go away into eternal punishment, but the righteous into eternal life. (Matthew 25:41, 46)

The journey of souls as taught by Jesus ultimately places each person before the throne of God where he or she faces two eternal destinations. It is not a long list of potential destinations, but two possible dwelling places that await the soul at the final decree of Yahweh. The "wages of sin" is death, not reincarnation (Romans 6:23). We die once and once only, then face the judgment of our God, to whom we all must give an account.

Didn't Jesus Say John the Baptist Was Elijah Reincarnated?

Despite such straightforwardness in Scripture, some New Age teachers, such as Elizabeth Clare Prophet, insist that Jesus Himself taught reincarnation.[274] Justification for this comes from what Jesus says about John the Baptist being Elijah. On the surface, it may appear that Jesus is indicating the possibility of a soul rebirthing into another physical body:

For all the Prophets and the Law prophesied until John, and if you are willing to accept it, he is Elijah who is to come. (Matthew 11:13–14)

But I tell you that Elijah has already come, and they did not recognize him, but did to him whatever they pleased. So also the Son of Man will certainly suffer at their hands. (Matthew 17:12)

The theosophical foundation Share International states:

Elias, according to Jesus himself came back to earth in the personality of John the Baptist.... There is here no equivocation, no polemic, but the words are from the Master himself.[275]

If we allow the Bible to give context to itself, we see that this is metaphorical hyperbole for John the Baptist coming in the prophetic spirit of Elijah. We know this for two primary reasons. The first is that Scripture tells us in what context John was called Elijah, and it had nothing to do with actual incarnation:

> And he will go before him in the spirit and power of Elijah, to turn the hearts of the fathers to the children, and the disobedient to the wisdom of the just, to make ready for the Lord a people prepared. (Luke 1:17)

This says John will go before Jesus in the spirit and power of the Old Testament prophet. It does not say he is the Old Testament prophet. Jesus was saying that Elijah had already come, because John the Baptist had come in the same spirit, anointing, and power as Elijah. Similarly, we can deliver a speech in the spirit and power of Martin Luther King or fight a boxing match in the spirit and power of Rocky Balboa, but this doesn't mean we are literally incarnations of said people. We can do things in the spirit and power of lions, eagles, or gorillas. It's a metaphorical reference to method, attitude, anointing, ability, etc., not a literal reference to us being animals reincarnated.

A second reason we know John was not Elijah reincarnated is that John tells us specifically that he is not Elijah:

> And this is the testimony of John, when the Jews sent priests and Levites from Jerusalem to ask him, "Who are you?" He confessed, and did not deny, but confessed, "I am not the Christ." And they asked him, "What then? Are you Elijah?" He said, "I am not." (John 1:19–21)

John the Baptist says he is not Elijah. If he really was Elijah, he would be lying in this verse. We can only guess what the prooftexts would be from the 22 percent of professing Christians in that study who believe in reincarnation. Assuredly, their beliefs are not rooted in Scripture.

The New Age concept of the afterlife extends beyond the examples we have addressed, but the majority rest upon some doctrine of reincarnation combined with the absence of eternal judgment. It may lift a burden off of people's shoulders to feel as though their moral choices are inconsequential to their eternal fate, but the appeal of a worldview doesn't make it true. It may temporarily smooth over the stain of sin that knocks on the back door of a person's conscience or remedy the pain of losing loved ones, but there is simply no positive reason to believe in reincarnation.

This may not make us feel butterflies inside at times, but we can't judge a worldview based on its utility or its psycho-emotional consequences. Everything needs to be filtered and interpreted in light of God's revealed Word. If we are going to allow the words of Jesus to dictate our beliefs, and if we are going to believe He had more insight than we do on the nature of reality, we have no choice but believe that one death is followed by eternal judgment.

Everything in the Bible You've Never Heard about the Afterlife

Reincarnation might seem appealing to some at first partly because there certainly seems to be a type of boredom Christians feel when considering the afterlife. Many Christians are still under the assumption that spiritual life after physical death will find us perched on clouds playing harps and wearing white robes. Other who have moved past childish visions of Heaven do not consider the topic much during day-to-day life. However, it is a fact: We all will die. None of us knows exactly when it will happen. Death is completely unknown.

The Bible actually has quite a bit to say about death, Heaven, and Hell, yet not much of these topics is taught in mainstream churches. While it is important to know how we should be living our lives, it is at least equally important to understand that the choices we make now ring out to eternity. In the afterlife, we will deal with the benefits and consequences of our decisions in this life.

Eternity vs Infinity

There is a big difference between eternity and infinity. Most Christians understand that we are given eternal life if we put our faith in Jesus. However, most think that means we will be in Heaven forever. While the concept of this is true, "forever" isn't technically the right word. "Forever" equals infinity, yet "eternity" is something different.

Infinity is the concept of something such as time going on and on without an end. It is an attribute. The attribute, not the thing itself, is what is "never-ending." "Infinity" is a term we use to classify an abstract concept rather than to describe what something is. For example, I could say a certain block of wood is five feet long. The block is wood, yet "five feet long" is the abstract concept I attach to it. Infinity, like measurements of length, is an abstract concept and doesn't really exist in nature apart from human understanding.

Eternity is unlike infinity. Eternity is the ultimate is. Eternity is a state of being outside of time itself. This is how God has no beginning or end, yet is the beginning and the end. He is outside of time. He exists in a realm where our concepts of time are insufficient to describe any attribute of Him in a literal sense. When we are given eternal life, it means we get to exist outside of time too. We get to exist in a realm where time doesn't apply; we are outside of it. We are not held to the same level as God, of course; we will always be subservient to Him—yet we are invited to exist within the state of eternity with Him.

While this sounds strange, confusing, and probably exciting, it is only the beginning of what the Bible has to teach us about the life to come. Many more mysteries are ahead. Scripture gives us a way to crack the surface and get a general sense of some of these things, but even on the surface it is unusual and impossible to fully comprehend. However, this is what makes the biblical understanding of the afterlife so exciting. There is always something new to learn.

Celestial Flesh

The Apostle Paul gives us a strange description of different kinds of flesh in his letter to the Corinthians:

> All flesh is not the same flesh: but there is one kind of flesh of men, another flesh of beasts, another of fishes, and another of birds. There are also celestial bodies, and bodies terrestrial: but the glory of the celestial is one, and the glory of the terrestrial is another. There is one glory of the sun, and another glory of the moon, and another glory of the stars: for one star differeth from another star in glory. So also is the resurrection of the dead. It is sown in corruption; it is raised in incorruption: It is sown in dishonour; it is raised in glory: it is sown in weakness; it is raised in power: It is sown a natural body; it is raised a spiritual body. There is a natural body, and there is a spiritual body. And so it is written, The first man Adam was made a living soul; the last Adam was made a quickening spirit. Howbeit that was not first which is spiritual, but that which is natural; and afterward that which is spiritual. The first man is of the earth, earthy; the second man is the Lord from heaven. As is the earthy, such are they also that are earthy: and as is the heavenly, such are they also that are heavenly. And as we have borne the image of the earthy, we shall also bear the image of the heavenly. (1 Corinthians 15:39–49, KJV)

Here, Paul differentiates between physical, biological flesh, and celestial flesh. He concludes by telling us that, after physical death, if we find our salvation in Jesus Christ, we will inhabit a body consisting of this celestial flesh. But what exactly is celestial flesh?

Most times when we think of a celestial, or spiritual, body, we might think of something ethereal—not really made of anything. We tend not to think of something physical or biological in any way. To a certain point, that is broadly what Paul is getting at here, but the truth is much richer than that.

In Paul's day, Gentiles (Greco-Roman culture) and Jews in the area believed gods had bodies. They were not thinking of bodies made of flesh and blood, but neither were they thinking that gods were only spirits. When gods would interact with people on Earth, they would take on a form that humans could interact with. This theme presents itself throughout Greek and Roman mythology, and even shows up in the Old Testament Book of Genesis:

> And the Lord appeared unto him in the plains of Mamre: and he sat in the tent door in the heat of the day;
> And he lift up his eyes and looked, and, lo, three men stood by him: and when he saw them, he ran to meet them from the tent door, and bowed himself toward the ground. (Genesis 18:1–2, KJV)

The idea of gods or even of the one, true God of Israel having access to a body was nothing new. Paul's teaching to the Corinthians draws from the common belief in embodied deities/*elohim*. It also illustrates Paul's belief that Christians would one day inhabit the same kind of celestial flesh that the *elohim* inhabit. This celestial flesh is also the same flesh the resurrected Jesus' body was made of.[276]

This realization is incredibly profound for the average Christian. After we die and become like Christ, we not only won't sin anymore; we will inherit the type of celestial flesh Jesus took on after the resurrection and we will become conformed to Jesus (Romans 8:29). In all ways, we will become so much like Him that we will behave and react like Him.

Of course, we will still be individuals. I (Josh) tend to think of this in terms of parents and children. Certain traits occur in children that are directly inherited from their parents. All children have flesh and blood just like their parents. Children, like their parents, have hearts, brains, and lungs—as well as many other sorts of biological functions that make up their physical bodies. They all work the same. The child is so much like the parent that, biologically, they behave and react just like the parents. If either parent or child is cut, he or she bleeds. If either laughs, he or she produces the same type of sound. Both interact with the world in the same way because, biologically, they are basically the same. The child is born conformed to the physical and biological image of the parents. Yet, while all this is true, the child is still an individual. The child is not a clone of the parent, but is an individual who is created as conformed to the parent.

This is an example, though not a direct, one-to-one comparison, of what the spiritual bodies we inherit will be like. Instead of being focused on the physical, however (flesh, blood, etc.), our spiritual bodies will be focused on spiritual things. We will have the same type of celestial flesh as Jesus, but even more, we will be spiritually conformed to His likeness as well. We will behave and react like Jesus in all ways while still maintaining individuality, just as a child compared to his or her parents.

This does not mean we will have the same status as Jesus. God is eternal; we are created. We are His true image, but He still reigns with all power and authority. We will not be the same as God; we will still forever be children of our Father. However, we will inherit celestial flesh and a conformity to the perfection of Jesus Christ.

But our citizenship is in heaven, and from it we await a Savior, the Lord Jesus Christ, who will transform our lowly body to be like his glorious body, by the power that enables him even to subject all things to himself. (Philippians 3:20–21, ESV)

Kings and Priests

We are told in Scripture that we, as Christians, in the next life, will reign over the earth, become priests, and judge angels:

> The one who conquers and who keeps my works until the end, to him I will give authority over the nations, and he will rule them with a rod of iron, as when earthen pots are broken in pieces, even as I myself have received authority from my Father. And I will give him the morning star. (Revelation 2:26–28, ESV)

> And they sang a new song, saying, "Worthy are you to take the scroll and to open its seals, for you were slain, and by your blood you ransomed people for God from every tribe and language and people and nation, and you have made them a kingdom and priests to our God, and they shall reign on the earth." (Revelation 5:9–10, ESV)

> Or do you not know that the saints will judge the world? And if the world is to be judged by you, are you incompetent to try trivial cases? Do you not know that we are to judge angels? How much more, then, matters pertaining to this life! (1 Corinthians 6:2–3, ESV)

This begs the question: Whom will we be ruling? If we are all to reign over the Earth, who exactly will we be reigning over? It does stand to reason that if we are to be tasked with judging the fallen angels, we might hold rulership over some, if not all, the benevolent angels as well.

What exactly that will entail is up to debate, but that raises another question: Will some glorified humans reign over other glorified humans? There does seem to be a hierarchal structure of the citizens in Heaven based on certain rewards for how we've lived, which we will delve into a bit more in the next section. This is not salvation itself, but it is what we have done after we receive salvation. What have we done for Christ, and what did we do only for ourselves?

Death, Hell, and the Lake of Fire

The book of Revelation describes the Great White Throne Judgment that occurs just prior to all of creation being restored to the original way God intended:

> Then I saw a great white throne and him who was seated on it. From his presence earth and sky fled away, and no place was found for them. And I saw the dead, great and small, standing before the throne, and books were opened. Then another book was opened, which is the book of life. And the dead were judged by what was written in the books, according to what they had done. And the sea gave up the dead who were in it, Death and Hades gave up the dead who were in them, and they were judged, each one of them, according to what they had done. Then Death and Hades were thrown into the lake of fire. This is the second death, the lake of fire. And if anyone's name was not found written in the book of life, he was thrown into the lake of fire. (Revelation 20:11–15, ESV)

The Lake of Fire is for any rebellious entity, including human beings, whose names are not written in the Book of Life, meaning those who never submitted to Christ and received salvation through Him. That part is pretty self-explanatory; however, a strange statement appears in verse 14: "Death and Hades [Hell] were thrown into the lake of fire." Is this literal or metaphorical?

Sometimes, it seems, Hell can be a spiritual entity. That might seem odd and likely inspires questions: How can a place be a person? Is it representative? Is it a metaphor? These are the types of questions that can come up when considering certain Bible verses, such as Job 28:22, which states, "Destruction and death say, We have heard the fame thereof with our ears."

The word for "death" used here comes from the word maveth, which means "death, dying, Death (personified), realm of the dead."[277] We can see that maveth can talk about an idea, location, or personification. All we need to do is take it in proper context.

First, when trying to learn something from the Book of Job, we have to be careful to consider who is speaking. Job has some friends who frequently state their false ideas that misrepresent God. At the end of the book, God rebukes those friends for this behavior. We need to keep this in mind so we don't inadvertently adopt the same skewed beliefs as Job's friends. Now, this is not to say there is false teaching in the Bible. We can look at it this way: It is true that they said those things, but what they said is not true. In the verse mentioned earlier, however, Job is speaking, so there is no cause for concern.

Since personified actions are attributed to Death in Job 28:22, I (Josh) tend to take the more personified approach in interpretation. I go even a step farther than that. Personifying an idea seems to denote a more metaphorical way of looking at it. Giving something personified attributes that it does not have helps us gain better understanding of the idea. An example of this is the term "table legs." A table does not have literal, biological legs, but we use the term to describe the function of the appendages below the tabletop, making the concept easier to understand. I don't believe this is the type of thing we are looking at in Job 28:22.

Many times, we are told verses such as this are metaphorical. However, taking this approach with a broad stroke across the Bible causes more confusion than it answers questions. We must consider everything in context. In Job 28:22, very literal and direct language is used. Destruction and Death are "speaking." They refer to the action of hearing. They even go as far as to claim they have ears. It seems to me that we are dealing with two spiritual entities here. To show this further, we can look at the original language used to describe Destruction.

The word used for "destruction" in this verse comes from the word *abaddown*, meaning "place of destruction, destruction, ruin, Abaddon."[278] For most of us, that sounds familiar. Speaking of the locusts released from the bottomless pit, Revelation 9:11 states: "And they had a king over them, which is the angel of the bottomless pit, whose name in the Hebrew tongue is Abaddon, but in the Greek tongue hath his name Apollyon."

We are told specifically that Abaddon in an angel, the angel of the bottomless pit. In the original language of Job 28:22, we find the same word. This further shows that, at least in this passage, Death and Destruction refer to spiritual beings.

Another example we can look at is Job 26:6, which states: "Hell is naked before him, and destruction hath no covering."

The personification here is a bit more difficult to pick out, but it is there if we know how and where to look for it. First, we can identify who/what is being addressed. The word for "hell" is *sheowl*, meaning "sheol, underworld, grave, hell, pit."[279] The word for "destruction" is the same as we looked at earlier.

At first glance, this verse seems to speak of a place and an idea. We normally think of Sheol as the abode of the dead and of destruction as a state of being. Most times, these are correct interpretations. Here, however, I believe we have the same entity called Abaddon and an entity called Sheol. There are times when Sheol refers to a spiritual entity just the same as Destruction can refer to the angel of the bottomless pit.

We can show this by looking at the claims made about these two beings. First, the text says that Hell is "naked." The word for "naked" here comes from the word *arowm*, meaning "naked, bare." Either we are talking about a more physical idea of nakedness or about a bareness or emptiness. When we think of Hell (or more accurately, Sheol), do we picture it as empty? How can Sheol be the abode of the dead if there are no dead in it?

We can think of Abaddon (destruction) in the same way. If this was not talking about the spiritual entity named Abaddon, but about a state of being, how does the idea of destruction not having a covering make any sense? Some have put forth the idea that this is speaking of the bottomless pit itself, that the entity Abaddon shares a name with the place he inhabits. If Abaddon was just another name for the bottomless pit, then is it true that the bottomless pit has no covering? Consider Revelation 9:1–2, which states:

> And the fifth angel sounded, and I saw a star fall from heaven unto the earth: and to him was given the key of the bottomless pit.
> And he opened the bottomless pit; and there arose a smoke out of the pit, as the smoke of a great furnace; and the sun and the air were darkened by reason of the smoke of the pit.

For the bottomless pit to be opened, it must originally be closed. Clearly, the bottomless pit does have a covering of some kind. Job 26:6 is not talking about the bottomless pit. So, if Job 26:6 is not talking about a location or idea and is referring to spiritual entities, what is the verse trying to say? It may have something to do with rebellion. Once someone (human or angel) rebels against God, he or she is without a "covering." This goes all the way back to the time of the Garden of Eden. In the Book of Genesis, when Adam and Eve sinned, they realized they were naked. Prior to sin entering the world, Adam and Eve had a type of covering over them. Whether literal or metaphorical, I cannot say, but when Adam and Even sinned, the covering was gone. This is why God had to make them new coverings from animal skins.

This applies directly to Job 26:6. If Adam and Eve lost their covering when they sinned against God, it stands to reason that the angels lost a type of covering when they fell from Heaven. This is an example of "as above, so below." The Fall of Adam and Eve can be looked at as a shadow of the rebellion in Heaven, and the same consequence applied. This gives a whole new meaning to the idea of Sheol being naked and Abaddon having no covering. This concept of the fallen angels losing their original covering is referenced in Jude 1:6, which states, "And the angels which kept not their first estate, but left their own habitation, he hath reserved in everlasting chains under darkness unto the judgment of the great day."

The word for "habitation" comes from the word *oiketerion*, meaning "a dwelling place, habitation, of the body as a dwelling place for the spirit."[280] Whatever original covering the angels had before they fell was a dwelling place for their spirit. They lost their covering, which is why Sheol and Abaddon were referring to rebellious spiritual beings in Job 26:6. In context, this conclusion makes the most sense.

The idea that a spiritual being can share a name with a location or attribute should not be cause for confusion. In Mark 5:9, the demon horde is called "legion" because it is made up of many. It was named (whether by themselves or by someone else) after an attribute.

We even see shadows of this within humanity. When we look at the meanings of the names of the first people born in Genesis, we find that they were named after an attribute they had or would fulfill in the future. We also find many examples of locations named after the person or people group that first settled there. For an interesting study of this, compare the name of Magog in Ezekiel 38 with the children of Japheth in chapter 10 of Genesis. Also look into the names of the children of Abraham with his third wife, Keturah, in chapter 25 of Genesis as compared to Ezekiel 38; specifically Sheba and Dedan.

> This seems to be what we are looking at in Revelation 6:8, which states: And I looked, and behold a pale horse: and his name that sat on him was Death, and Hell followed with him. And power was given unto them over the fourth part of the earth, to kill with sword, and with hunger, and with death, and with the beasts of the earth.

It is difficult to tell because, in the original Greek, the words are different, but I believe these are the same two spiritual entities we looked at earlier. Death and Hell do not refer to locations in this verse. If so, the verse would lose all meaning. We even learn the eternal fate of these spiritual beings in Revelation 20:14, which states, "And death and hell were cast into the lake of fire. This is the second death."

Normally, we are told that the idea of death and the place of Hell are thrown into the Lake of Fire. How can an idea be thrown into a literal place? How can one literal place be thrown into another literal place? This interpretation loses credibility when thinking about it logically. If we are to believe in a literal Lake of Fire, does it make sense to believe the references to Death and Hell are metaphoric?

In my humble opinion, the spiritual entities named Death and Hell are cast into the Lake of Fire. They have these names because they have something to do with the idea of death and the location of Hell. What those exact connections are, I have no idea other than pure speculation. Perhaps, down the road and with further study, an answer will present itself.

This concept is sprinkled throughout the Bible. Many times we are told a place or idea is being referenced when, in fact, a spiritual entity is a much better fit. If we don't let the fact that certain people/entities are named after attributes and locations throw us, we will have a much easier time interpreting the meanings of many seemingly cryptic passages. Sometimes words will be referring to an actual location. Other times they will be addressing an idea or attribute. Yet other times, they will refer to a literal entity. All we must do is take everything we read in context and allow the Bible to interpret itself.

The Final Judgment for Christians

As we have already seen, the final judgment for fallen angels and anyone rebellious toward God is the Lake of Fire. However, for Christians, it doesn't just end at "we get to go to Heaven and get new bodies." Paul describes a different type of judgment:

For no one can lay a foundation other than that which is laid, which is Jesus Christ. Now if anyone builds on the foundation with gold, silver, precious stones, wood, hay, straw—each one's work will become manifest, for the Day will disclose it, because it will be revealed by fire, and the fire will test what sort of work each one has done. If the work that anyone has built on the foundation survives, he will receive a reward. If anyone's work is burned up, he will suffer loss, though he himself will be saved, but only as through fire. (1 Corinthians 3:11–15, ESV)

In this passage, how much is literal and how much is poetic or meta-phorical? It's difficult to tell. However, either way, the same message is still taught.

I (Josh) like to look at it this way: Imagine that after this life, you are standing in front of Jesus. All of your deeds—both what you did for yourself and what you did to serve Jesus—are represented as a stack of wood, hay, and straw. You assume there are probably some jewels and gold in there, too. All of a sudden, a huge fire comes down and burns all the wood, hay, and straw, leaving behind only the things you did for Jesus: the only things that could not be burned. You look down in surprise to see a pile of gold and jewels small enough to fit in the palm of your hand.

You walk up to that small pile, your deeds for Jesus throughout your entire life, and you scoop them up. You approach Jesus on His throne. You see the scars in His hands and on His feet: the evidence of what He has done for you with His life. You hold out your hand to Jesus, present Him with your small handful of jewels and gold, and the only thing you can muster to say is the honest, yet tragic confession, "I love you this much."

Again, whether Paul's teaching to the Corinthians is a literal judg-ment or not, the teaching is still the same: What we do with our lives on Earth matters. Our decisions have eternal rewards and consequences. It is far better to serve Jesus than ourselves.

The Defeat of Leviathan, New Jerusalem, and Restoration of All Creation

We get quite a bit of detail in the Book of Revelation about the final state of reality. When reading the following passage, keep in mind what we discussed earlier regarding Leviathan and the role of the sea in terms of the chaotic nature of our present reality:

> Then I saw a new heaven and a new earth, for the first heaven and the first earth had passed away, and the sea was no more. And I saw the holy city, new Jerusalem, coming down out of heaven from God, prepared as a bride adorned for her husband. And I heard a loud voice from the throne saying, "Behold, the dwelling place of God is with man. He will dwell with them, and they will be his people, and God himself will be with them as their God. He will wipe away every tear from their eyes, and death shall be no more, neither shall there be mourning, nor crying, nor pain any-more, for the former things have passed away." And he who was seated on the throne said, "Behold, I am making all things new." Also he said, "Write this down, for these words are trustworthy and true." And he said to me, "It is done! I am the Alpha and the Omega, the beginning and the end. To the thirsty I will give from the spring of the water of life without payment. The one who con-quers will have this heritage, and I will be his God and he will be my son. But as for the cowardly, the faithless, the detestable, as for murderers, the sexually immoral, sorcerers, idolaters, and all liars, their portion will be in the lake that burns with fire and sulfur, which is the second death." (Revelation 21:1–8, ESV)

Notice that verse 1 says "the sea was no more." This is because the sea was an image of chaos. At this time, the great sea dragon of chaos Leviathan is finally defeated forever. Nothing ever again will interfere with God's plan for us, the Earth, and all of reality. Nothing again will interfere with our direct, face-to-face relationship with our Father. Nothing will ever go wrong again.

> And I saw no temple in the city, for its temple is the Lord God the Almighty and the Lamb. And the city has no need of sun or moon to shine on it, for the glory of God gives it light, and its lamp is the Lamb. By its light will the nations walk, and the kings of the earth will bring their glory into it, and its gates will never be shut by day—and there will be no night there. They will bring into it the glory and the honor of the nations. But nothing unclean will ever enter it, nor anyone who does what is detestable or false, but only those who are written in the Lamb's book of life. (Revelation 21:22–27, ESV)

Again, we are promised a perfect, Edenic world to inhabit. However, as in the previous passage, we are reassured that only those who have their names written in the Book of Life will be able to enter. The rest will only have the Lake of Fire.

Do not allow yourself to pass from this life without making sure your name is in the Book of Life. Do not allow yourself to suffer the Lake of Fire. Instead, see the worth and value in investing your into the person of Jesus Christ. You don't have to know everything; no Christian has perfect theology. All you need is a belief in Jesus. Call upon His name and be saved. Be a part of the promise that is to come.

> Then the angel showed me the river of the water of life, bright as crystal, flowing from the throne of God and of the Lamb through the middle of the street of the city; also, on either side of the river, the tree of life with its twelve kinds of fruit, yielding its fruit each month. The leaves of the tree were for the healing of the nations.
>
> No longer will there be anything accursed, but the throne of God and of the Lamb will be in it, and his servants will

worship him. They will see his face, and his name will be on their foreheads. And night will be no more. They will need no light of lamp or sun, for the Lord God will be their light, and they will reign forever and ever.

And he said to me, "These words are trustworthy and true. And the Lord, the God of the spirits of the prophets, has sent his angel to show his servants what must soon take place."

"And behold, I am coming soon. Blessed is the one who keeps the words of the prophecy of this book." I, John, am the one who heard and saw these things. And when I heard and saw them, I fell down to worship at the feet of the angel who showed them to me, but he said to me, "You must not do that! I am a fellow servant with you and your brothers the prophets, and with those who keep the words of this book. Worship God."

And he said to me, "Do not seal up the words of the prophecy of this book, for the time is near. Let the evildoer still do evil, and the filthy still be filthy, and the righteous still do right, and the holy still be holy."

"Behold, I am coming soon, bringing my recompense with me, to repay each one for what he has done. I am the Alpha and the Omega, the first and the last, the beginning and the end."

Blessed are those who wash their robes, so that they may have the right to the tree of life and that they may enter the city by the gates. Outside are the dogs and sorcerers and the sexually immoral and murderers and idolaters, and everyone who loves and practices falsehood.

"I, Jesus, have sent my angel to testify to you about these things for the churches. I am the root and the descendant of David, the bright morning star."

The Spirit and the Bride say, "Come." And let the one who hears say, "Come." And let the one who is thirsty come; let the one who desires take the water of life without price. I warn everyone who hears the words of the prophecy of this book: if anyone adds to them, God will add to him the plagues described in this book, and if anyone takes away from the words of the book of this prophecy, God will take away his share in the tree of life and in the holy city, which are described in this book. He who testifies to these things says, "Surely I am coming soon."

Amen. Come, Lord Jesus.

The grace of the Lord Jesus be with all. Amen. (Revelation 22, ESV)

SPACE AND BEYOND
Extraterrestrials in the New Age

ONE OF THE BIGGEST ATTRACTIONS of New Age spirituality is what it teaches about extraterrestrials. These teachings are a big part of what drew in the authors of this book (Josh and Steven) to New Age practices years ago. It is generally believed that the Bible has nothing to say about aliens or UFOs. This, however, is untrue. First, let's look at what New Age teaches about aliens and why it is so influential and tempting.

Alien Species and Teachings

New Age usually takes embraces an odd combination of the biological categorization of supposed alien beings and the spiritual acceptance of their teachings. While the alien biology is generally regarded as vastly different from ours, yet similar in some ways, the aliens' spiritual teachings are understood as perfectly in line with New Age. They usually teach a mishmash of gosticism, Jewish and Eastern mysticism, and "new thought" emphasizing the divinity of man. Why is this? Wouldn't it be reasonable to assume, if aliens exist and they look different from us, that their belief system would be wildly different as well? Why would beings millions of light years away travel all the way here just to tell us they agree with Deepak Chopra?

It's a happy coincidence that the ones who embrace New Age philosophy just so happen to make contact with aliens who believe exactly what they do. They may have lizard eyes and feathers on their back, but they sure spend a lot of time reading Blavatsky.

But what if they are not who they say they are? What if these beings do exist in some sense, but they are not actually extraterrestrials from another planet? What if, instead of merely pointing us to other spiritual entities, they are spiritual entities themselves? If this was the case, we would be able learn more about their true motivations from what they are teaching instead of merely focusing on their appearances.

Within New Age, there is a wide array of beliefs regarding which species of alien comes from which star system and what their primary message is Also, these beliefs morph over time because they are influenced by a mix of pop culture and the testimonies of alleged alien abductees. As it stands at the time of this writing, here is a general consensus of some of the recognized species and belief systems of aliens from a New Age perspective:

Species: Grey Aliens (AKA Grays, Zeta Reticulans)
Origin: Zeta Reticuli
Appearance: 3–4 feet tall, almond-shaped eyes, gray skin, large head, slender body
UFO Association: Saucer, sphere, or triangular-shaped
Myth Association: Fairies
Claims: They are here for cloning and genetic manipulation in order to procreate their own race.
Abilities: Mind control, intelligence, telepathy, advanced technology

Species: Nordics (AKA Pleiadians, Space Brothers)
Origin: Pleiades

Appearance: 5–7 feet tall, blond or red hair, blue or green eyes, relatively human looking

UFO Association: Sphere or cigar-shaped craft

Myth Association: Hopi legends, angels

Claims: They are here to share spirituality, emotional wisdom, peace, harmony, and care for Earth.

Abilities: Telepathy, appearing in dreams, advanced technology

Species: Reptilians (AKA Reptoids, Lizardmen)

Origin: Draco Star System

Appearance: 6–8 feet tall, snake-like heads, brown/green/red/ white skin, webbed hands

UFO Association: Saucer

Myth Association: Chinese dragons, Islamic Djinn, sometimes biblical serpent

Claims: Want control over other aliens, including humans, Earth, and resources

Abilities: Psychic manipulations, dreams, shapeshifting

Species: Mantis Aliens (AKA Mantids, Insectoids)

Origin: Draco Star System

Appearance: 6–7 feet tall, triangular heads, usually dark brown, very similar to praying mantises

UFO Association: Cigar-shaped

Myth Association: Native American and African mythology, specifically from the Khoisan tribe

Claims: Human protection (especially children), control of Earth, human DNA harvesting

Abilities: Shapeshifting, holographic projection, mind control, inducing paralysis

Species: Blue Avians (AKA Sphere Alliance)

Origin: Unknown

Appearance: Bird head, blue feathers, humanoid, yet birdlike
UFO Association: Spherical craft
Myth Association: Ancient Egypt (Ra/Thoth mythology),
    Sumerian (Abgal), Hindu (Garuda)
Claims: Want to teach how to spiritually ascend through peace,
    love, understanding, self-work
Abilities: Telekinesis, teleportation

Ironically, none of them are interested in telling us how they got here and what we can do to travel through vast distances of space like they apparently do. They won't talk space travel, but they will tell us how to doubt the New Testament. Anyone who studies contact material, from novice to expert, will be able to tell you that these entities have an anti-Christ agenda undergirding their teachings. They are specifically interested in changing how humanity thinks about the person of Jesus, which is a strange motive to consider traveling such a long distance. Needless to say, their anti-Bible agenda speaks to their spiritual origin.

Ancient Astronaut Theory

Television shows such as *Ancient Aliens* promote what is called "Ancient Astronaut Theory." This theory states that aliens visited humanity long ago, taught early man any number of skills, including architecture, then left with a promise to return someday. Early mankind mistook these alien beings as gods and angels and wrote religious texts telling about them. However, with our modern, scientific, twenty-first century worldview, we can see that these beings were nothing more than flesh-and-blood extraterrestrials from other planets.

To support their claims, ancient astronaut teachers point to seemingly impossible architectural feats achieved by ancient humans, such as Baalbek and the Nazca Lines. They also point to religious texts that seem to describe spacecraft, such as the vimanas of the Sanskrit Mahabharata or the wheels-within-wheels construct of the book of Ezekiel in the Bible. Much like New Age theology, however, these are nothing more than misinterpretations of ancient religious texts and pseudo-archaeology.

Much debunking has been accomplished by many noted researchers, such as Chris White (*Ancient Aliens Debunked*) and ancient language scholar Dr. Michael Heiser.[281, 282] More specifically, here are some quick facts that *Ancient Aliens* conveniently leaves out for its audience:

- *Ancient Aliens* asserts that for some things like the Great Pyramid or Pumapunku, we have no mainstream consensus on how these structures were made. They also say experts don't know why some cultures drew certain cave drawings or made idols that looked slightly like aliens. These issues have all been sufficiently answered in academic journals and peer-reviewed publications. The problem is, this material is generally not made available to the public, requires exclusive subscriptions, and can cost hundreds of dollars per volume. Experts are not bewildered; their answers just aren't always published at the local bookstore.

- There is no ancient text in the history of the ancient world that attributes these beings as coming from another planet. Dr. Michael Heiser, in a recent interview I (Steve) did with him, reiterated this point as someone with a PhD in Semitic languages who is professionally familiar with ancient near-eastern and Mesopotamian texts. No culture claimed these beings were actually extraterrestrials coming from another planet.

- Most of the ancient cultures mentioned in *Ancient Aliens* believed these "gods" wanted human blood sacrifice. Pre-dynastic Egypt, Incans, Sumerians, Babylonians, Aztecs, Mayans, and other such cultures all practiced ritual blood sacrifice to these entities we are told are flesh and blood extraterrestrials. If these are our cosmic brothers and sisters, how come everyone they visited believed they were interdimensionals to be contacted and appeased by human sacrifice?

- The vast majority of people on the program (almost without exception) have no actual credentials in any relevant field of study. In other words, they aren't even qualified to speak on these matters. The six most popular speakers on the show are Erich von Däniken, David Childress, Jason Martell, Robert Bauvall, Nick Redfern, and Giorgio A. Tsoukalos. Only Giorgio graduated college. What was his degree? A bachelor's in sports information and communication. In other words, they literally have no idea what they are doing in this field of study. The few others on the show who hold degrees (such as David Wilcock) still haven't received education in any relevant field of study. They are, by nature, ignorant of proper historical and archeological procedure, and are isolated from contemporary academia on these issues.

The Impossibility of Interstellar Space Travel

One big question arises when considering aliens traveling to Earth from other worlds: How are they getting here? Most assume they can travel through space incredibly fast or are utilizing bends in spacetime called "wormholes." The former is outright impossible and the latter, while technically on the far, outer reaches of possibility, is still incredibly unlikely. Since we do not have a working interstellar spacecraft to examine, we must go by our own current understanding of physics to construct a working assumption about the likelihood of space travel outside our solar system.

First, there are problems with the idea of just going really, really fast. There is a universal speed limit: the speed of light. A "light year" does not reference a span or time, but rather a distance. It is the distance light can travel in one Earth year, and is measured this way to put into perspective how far away things actually are in the universe. For example, the star closest to us is Alpha Centauri, which is 4.3 light years away from Earth.[283] This means that if you were traveling at the speed of light, it would take you less than four and a half years to get there. At first this may seem like good news, but there are problems.

According to our own technology, we aren't close to reaching anywhere near light speed. For example, it would take the NASA Voyager 1 probe around forty thousand years to reach Alpha Centaur if it continued to travel about thirty eight thousand miles per hour, which is about 4.36 light years away (or twenty five trillion miles)We are nowhere near to accomplishing the speed it would take technologically to reach a place like this—nor could our bodies handle the g-forces of travelling such speeds.

Second, there is a problem with time itself. When you start traveling at or near light speed, time itself slows down. This happens no matter how fast you travel, even if you are just driving your car; however, the effect is so minimal it goes unnoticed. However, if you were to travel at the speed of light, time for you would actually stop. Now, this is just in relation to you and anyone else you're traveling with. The rest of the universe, however, is different. While time would be running normally to anyone you left behind, according to your perspective, time in the universe would be speeding up. Time stops for what is traveling at light speed, while it speeds up in the rest of the universe. Again, this effect is only noticed by the one traveling at light speed.

So, the issue is that at exact light speed, things get weird. Time stops for the traveler, yet speeds up infinitely to the rest of the outside universe. This means, at the exact point of hitting light speed, the traveler would reach the end of time, whenever that is. Since, as far as we know, human beings cannot live in an environment outside of time, this would likely kill the traveler (it would be impossible to reach this speed anyway, which we will look at a bit later). So, let's say instead the traveler is only going about 99 percent of light speed. There is still an issue. By the time the traveler reached Alpha Centauri, he would be so far in the future that

Alpha Centauri probably wouldn't exist anymore. Even if it did, everyone on earth the traveler knew would be long dead. There would be no way to then go back in time and report his findings. The faster in space you travel, the faster in time you travel as well.

The third and last issue we will look at (though there are many more) is the problem of mass. The faster you travel in space, the faster you travel in time, but also the more your mass increases. At light speed, you would hit infinite mass, which is physically impossible. Also, the more mass you acquire, the more fuel you would need to keep increasing speed. Infinite mass means infinite fuel. This, for lack of better words, is doubly impossible.

The reason this is the case is because mass is not substance, as we tend to think of it. Mass instead is an interaction with a quantum field. This quantum field is known as the "Higgs field." Photons, the particles of light, do not interact with the Higgs field at all. This is how a photon can be massless. This is also how a photon can travel at the speed of light and not be subject to the increasing mass problem. Similar to how a block of wood doesn't interact with the magnetic field from a kitchen magnet, photons do not interact with the Higgs field and therefore do not have mass.

We, however (as well as any spacecraft we could ever construct), absolutely do have mass. We interact with the Higgs field every day at every second. The faster you travel, the more you interact with the Higgs field, meaning the more mass you have. The increased interaction doesn't *cause* the extra mass. The increased interaction *is* the extra mass. This is why no object that interacts with the Higgs field can travel at the speed of light. Light speed would mean infinite mass. However, long before reaching infinite mass (which, again, is impossible), the particles making up your body would reach such a high amount of mass that they would all collapse into miniature black holes, which would then combine into one larger black hole the size of you, your spacecraft, and anything else traveling at a high speed with you. At some point, you would reach a speed that would be physically impossible to maintain on a subatomic level. However, you would likely have died long before that point anyway.

While these are only three reasons light speed travel is impossible, there are many more, such as high-speed collisions with dust particles (at high enough speeds, this could destroy an entire spacecraft with ease).[284] Usually, in order to get around this, some people bring up the idea of wormholes. The theory is, if you concentrate enough energy into a single point, you can bend spacetime to create a shortcut to a faraway place, drastically cutting your travel time into a manageable fraction. However, this, too, is incredibly presumptuous.

While not impossible, this mode of travel is incredibly unlikely. For a wormhole to be traversable, it would have to be stabilized. An unstable wormhole is basically a black hole. Black holes certainly do bend spacetime (as far as we know), but not in any way that would be helpful. Similar to the infinite speed and infinite mass problems of light speed travel, you run into the same issues with a black hole.

If Bob and Sally were floating in space near a black hole and Bob fell in yet Sally didn't, their experiences would be completely different. Sally would see Bob fall in to a certain point, then Bob's movements would seem slower and slower until he would eventually stop, seemingly frozen in time, forever. Sally could watch Bob for the rest of her life, but she would not see any change. For Bob, however, as he fell closer and closer to the back hole, he would see Sally's movement going faster and faster. If Sally stayed there her entire life, he would see her age faster and faster. To Bob, Sally would be dead of old age in a matter of mere moments. As he falls deeper into the black hole, Bob would see the universe itself aging. Stars would be moving faster and everything would be expanding more, then he would start to see the lights in the sky dim out. He would essentially be traveling faster and faster forward in time. He and the black hole would see the end of the universe and time. Then, tragically, they would both die together.

With this kind of extreme force, it would take an equally extreme force to counteract and stabilize the wormhole. Some have proposed an idea of the black hole spinning fast enough to counteract the gravitational effects. However, the spinning would have to be near light speed, meaning any particles traveling within would become more massive and become their own black holes, which would destabilize the entire thing yet again. If one could harness all the energy in the universe, possible such a feat could be accomplished, but again, even this is highly unlikely. Even if it was possible, it certainly would not be convenient. Think of it this way: All the energy of our own sun does not create a black hole, let alone a wormhole. Therefore, a spacecraft with the power to create and stabilize a wormhole would have to create and store more energy than a star (incredibly more). It is just not reasonable to assume this is the case. To quote physicist Michio Kaku:

> However, with the wormhole and multiply connected spaces, we are probing the very limits of Einstein's theory of general relativity. In fact, the amount of matter-energy necessary to create a wormhole or dimensional gateway is so large that we expect quantum effects to dominate. Quantum corrections, in turn, may actually close the opening of the wormhole, making travel through the gateway impossible.[285]

The Interdimensional and Extradimensional Hypotheses

Two other theories are commonly brought up to explain where alien beings might come from: the interdimensional and extradimensional hypothesis (IDH and EDH). Granted, usually when these terms are used, they are referring to the same thing. Most times, they are used interchangeably to refer to beings originating outside of our three dimensions of space and one of time. However, it can be of benefit to look at what these terms technically mean so as to not confuse one with the other.

Wikipedia defines the IDH as such:

The interdimensional hypothesis (IDH or IH), is an idea advanced by Ufologists such as Jacques Vallée that says unidentified flying objects (UFOs) and related events involve visitations from other "realities" or "dimensions" that coexist separately alongside our own. It is an alternative to the extraterrestrial hypothesis (ETH).[286]

"Interdimensional" seems to denote capability while "extradimensional" denotes origin. For example, if humans were to discover a way to travel between dimensions, we could be considered an "interdimensional" species, or beings with interdimensional capabilities. If an entity originates from a higher dimension than our own, it would be considered an "extradimensional" being. EDH states that UFOs and their pilots, at least some of them, originate from a higher dimension than the three of space and one of time in which we currently reside.

Even from a scientific point of view, this makes more sense. Many people have reported seeing UFOs that seem to be solid, yet are said to change shape. Sometimes these craft will split into more than one, only to later combine back into one. Granted, many of these sightings could very well be mirages or misunderstood naturalistic phenomena. However, giving the benefit of the doubt, let's assume these things are behaving exactly as they are described. What is happening?

Strangely enough, this can be explained through an understanding of higher spatial dimensions. What makes this compelling is that most people observing these strange phenomena do not have a deep understanding of quantum physics, yet they describe something exactly like what would be expected if an object with more than three spatial dimensions were to breach our three-dimensional physical space.

The best way to explain this is to imagine a two-dimensional universe called Flatland inhabited by two-dimensional beings called Flatlanders. Flatland has the directions of left, right, forward, and backward, but not up or down. Flatlanders have no concept of the third dimensions, so up and down are completely foreign to them.

Imagine if you were to drop a ball through Flatland. What would the Flatlanders see? They would see a point in space in front of them appear out of nowhere. As the three-dimensional ball fell through Flatland, they would see that point grow into a circle, then the circle would shrink into a point. As the ball fell out of Flatland, Flatlanders would see the point disappear, seemingly the same way it appeared.

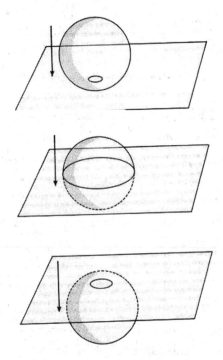

Ball dropping through Flatland

The Flatland example helps explain what an object of four spatial dimensions would look like if it breached our 3D space. If a 4D ball (called a "hypersphere") were to fall through our space, we would first see a point appear out of nowhere. It would grow into a sphere, then shrink back down into a point. After that, it would disappear. It is exactly the same as what the Flatlanders would see, only you would add one dimension.

Given the extreme limitations of interstellar space travel, the EDH provides a much more plausible hypothesis. Instead of these things being from other planets, perhaps they are from other dimensions. If they are extradimensional, this could explain why some people report seeing these being shape-shift. This could explain how their supposed spacecraft are able to disappear. Perhaps it is not godlike technology, but just a breach of a higher dimension. With the EDH, no high technology is required. Just like you could drop a ball or stick a finger into Flatland, a being of a higher dimensions could enter ours without need to go through a portal, wormhole, or extreme interstellar travel.

The problem many more scientifically minded people have with this is that it sounds an awful lot like we're talking about a spirit realm. Typically, however, New Agers do not have an issue with this, and many have embraced the EDH. However, instead of taking the biblical approach of these entities being demons and angels, they have instead adopted the New Age interpretation of Ascended Masters and Spirit Guides. If we look at the motives of these spiritual/extradimensional beings, we can show that they are more in line with malevolence rather than benevolence.

Demonic Origins of Alien Abductions

Many noted UFO researchers accept the EDH as the most likely candidate for explaining what these things are. Among them are Jacques Vallee and J. Allen Hynek. In fact, in a paper published in the *Journal of Scientific Exploration*, Jacques Vallee gave a few reasons he believes UFOs are not extraterrestrial in origin.[287] In writing this, Vallee was coming from a secular worldview. He was not proposing anything from a Christian perspective. Vallee drew his conclusions based on the evidence he collected from various witnesses and other sources. The entire paper is fascinating and pretty spectacular, given that the result goes against the grain of the mainstream view. Vallee mentions five very good reasons against the idea that UFOs are extraterrestrial in nature. I (Josh) will only mention a couple here; however, I suggest checking out the entire paper on your own.

One of the strongest points Vallee makes is the aliens' physiology. They generally appear humanoid, meaning they have a head, a body, two arms, and two legs, and are bilaterally symmetrical. Vallee suggests the fact that something like this would happen under the current understanding of Darwinian evolution (should one believe in it) should stretch our understanding of biology past the limits. In other words, given all of the factors Vallee lays out, it would be next to impossible for something so similar to evolve on a different planet than our own. If we consider this logically, Vallee has a point. How many humanoid creatures exist on our own planet compared to all creatures that do not haveg a humanoid appearance?

Another point Vallee brings up is abduction reports. A majority of abductees claim that, while aboard a spacecraft, aliens have performed intrusive and painful medical procedures on them. These procedures are usually tortuous, to the point of leaving physical abrasions that are visible the next day. While many times, the abductees' memory is "wiped clean," it is said that hypnosis enables some of these memories to be retrieved—though this view is controversial and unproven.

Vallee observes that today, on our planet and in our culture, medical advances are available that allow us to perform the same medical procedures without causing any pain. Medications like anesthesia can be used to ensure the person does not suffer and will not remember what happened. These procedures can be done without leaving the types of scars such as the abductees report. They can even be done with a minimal number of tools, meaning the person having the procedure done would not have to leave his or her house.

Given this, Vallee questions why technologically advanced extraterrestrials would need to take the individual aboard a spacecraft, subject the person to all sorts of torturous experiences, and leave evidence to show that something had happened—yet, most times, without the memory. If ETs are technologically advanced enough to get here from another planet, why are they lagging so far behind in the medical field?

Perhaps it makes more sense to consider that these beings are extradimensional entities such as demons or angels who require no such extensive technology to travel here. Perhaps they are malevolent enough to not care about the well-being of those they abduct and want to leave just enough evidence behind, enough times with enough people, to plant the idea in the minds of the general public that these things are happening. These beings seem to enjoy showing that their level of technology is more advanced than our own, yet they seem to be lacking in certain areas, such as their medical field, that are not benefitting them directly.

If these beings are strictly malevolent, they would not care about making the abductees comfortable. They would only care to progress their technology to suit their own needs, which seems to be the case with the alien abduction phenomenon.

An interesting fact in alien abduction research is that calling out to the name of Jesus has been the only repeatable method of interrupting the abductees experience as it is happening. Alienresistance.org is a website consisting of decades worth of research into demonic nature of these "alien" beings, citing contact material, abductee cases, and other examples of close encounters that clearly establish a sinister spiritual origin. It also contains over one hundred testimonies of people who have stopped alien abductions, nightmares, sleep paralysis, and unwanted OBEs through nothing more than calling upon the name of Jesus.

The anti-Christ messaging, the physical and psychological abuse, their desire to receive human blood from cultures they "visited" in the past, and their fear of the name of Jesus Christ created a very strong case that we are dealing with demonic extra-dimensional entities. This begs the question: If aliens are in fact demons or angels, is there a way they can be correlated to the Bible in a way that makes sense in light of modern contact phenomenon? In fact, there is.

Aliens in the Bible

One of the most influential revelations that has helped bring people out of New Age or secular ufology into the Bible is the realization of what the sixth chapter of Genesis means. This has been covered heavily by Christian authors and theologians; however, there very well could be people brand new to the idea. Keep in mind, the connection between Genesis 6 and the modern UFO/alien abduction phenomenon is not held by all, yet it is still worth considering. If you are interested in aliens yet have never heard of the Nephilim in the Bible, this is the section for you.

Sons of God

There are many interpretations concerning the identity of the "sons of God" from biblical Scripture. Some have called them sinful men, descendants of Cain, demons, and even aliens from another planet. To unravel this mystery, let's first look at Genesis 6:1–2, which states:

> And it came to pass, when men began to multiply on the face of the earth, and daughters were born unto them, That the sons of God saw the daughters of men that they were fair; and they took them wives of all which they chose.

This verse does not directly tell us who the "sons of God" are. To define the "sons of God," we must compare Scripture with Scripture. The term is defined twice in the Book of Job. We read in Job 1:6:

> Now there was a day when the sons of God came to present themselves before the Lord, and Satan came also among them.

Then we read in Job 38:4–7:

Where wast thou when I laid the foundations of the earth?
declare, if thou hast understanding. Who hath laid the measurements thereof, if thou knowest? Or who hath stretched the line
upon it? Whereupon are the foundations thereof fastened? or
who laid the corner stone thereof; When the morning stars sang
together, and all the sons of God shouted for joy?

This is a great example of how we can allow the Bible to define itself
for us. Comparing Scripture with itself gives us a clear understanding of
who these "sons of God" are: They are angels. Two main facts support
this. First, they presented themselves before the Lord. Second, they were
present at the creation of the world. This could only refer to angels. It
doesn't specify their standing with God, whether good or bad; it only
identifies what they are.

The Fallacy of the Sethite Theory

One misinterpretation of Scripture has been floating around the
Church, even to the point that it is being taught in seminaries, that has
caused quite a bit of confusion. It is called the Sethite theory. There are
many variations, but the theory basically states that the "sons of God"
mentioned in Genesis 6:2 were not angels, but were the male descendants of Seth. The "daughters of men" mentioned in the same verse
were the ungodly female descendants of Cain. The theory states that
descendants of Seth mated with the descendants of Cain and produced
the "giants."

To make the Sethite theory fit, we would have to twist the meaning
of the Scriptures, even in the original Hebrew, that define angels (Job
38:4–7), giants (Genesis 6:2–4), and man (Genesis 6:1–7). The Sethite
theory just does not add up when it is compared to the rest of the Bible
without completely rewriting the Scriptures themselves. This is dangerous because it keeps the believer away from the truth.

Giants

When we look at Genesis 6, we find that angels saw the daughters of men and took them for wives. Genesis 6:4 we read:

> There were giants in the earth in those days; and also after that, when the sons of God came in unto the daughters of men, and they bare children to them, the same became mighty men which were of old, men of renown.

The word "giants" is translated from the Hebrew word nepil, meaning "bully" or "tyrant," which comes from the word *napal,* meaning "to fall."288 Isaiah 14:12 uses the same word, *napal,* for our English word "fallen" to describe Satan. A common word used today for these fallen tyrants, or giants, is Nephilim. The New International Version Bible refers to these beings as Nephilim, whereas the King James Version refers to them as "giants." In our modern vernacular, the word is the most common and recognizable word referring to the giant offspring of the fallen angels and human women.

Interestingly, the definition of *napal,* "to fall," can also mean "cast down, die, fall, fallen, inferior, be lost, perish, rot, throw down," among others. The Nephilim were fallen, inferior, and lost beings that perished with no hope of salvation. They were not fallen in the sense that the angels who created them were fallen. The angels once had a high estate in Heaven, but disobeyed God and then became fallen. The Nephilim, on the other hand, were fallen right from the start. They were not men created with a hope of redemption. They were born fallen. In a spiritual sense, they were dead upon creation.

If the Nephilims' souls did not have the ability to have eternal life and were dead upon creation, what would happen to their souls when they died? It is possible that what we know today as "demons" are the disembodied spirits of the dead Nephilim. If the souls and spirits of the Nephilim were not created by God and could not achieve eternal life, there would be nowhere else to go when they died. According to Scripture, the souls and spirits of dead Nephilim would not initially go to Hell upon death before the resurrection and Judgment. Speaking of unsaved people at the Judgment, Jesus stated in Matthew 25:41:

> Then shall he say also unto them on the left hand, Depart from me, ye cursed, into everlasting fire, prepared for the devil and his angels.

Though unsaved humans take part as well, Hell was originally created for the devil and his angels. This would suggest that the dead Nephilim would be cursed to remain on the Earth until the Judgment. They would be what we refer to today as "demons." Since angels do not die, however, the fallen angels would continue to exist with Satan, who reigns as the prince of the power of the air until the Judgment (as we read Ephesians 2:2). This shows that demons and fallen angels are different altogether.

It is well documented in the Bible that demons (or devils, unclean spirits, etc.) like to possess people and take control of their physical bodies if they can. Fallen angels, on the other hand, have a type of body that is far superior to our human bodies, as we will discover a little later in this chapter. This seems to mean that fallen angels have no immediate need for a physical human body. Of course, there are certain exceptions to this in special circumstances, such as Satan possessing the body of Judas, but we do not see this as typically as we do with demons. If demons are the disembodied spirits of the Nephilim, it explains why they would want to possess humans in the first place.

Also, before the account of the Flood in Genesis, there is no mention of devils or evil spirits of any kind. There is only mention of fallen angels, heavenly angels, and man. The Bible is not clear about what evil spirits are and where they come from, but one thing is clear: Different

Hebrew words are used to distinguish evil spirits from fallen angels. If demons and fallen angels are not the same, as the Hebrew language seems to indicate, there would be nothing else for demons to be other than spirits of dead Nephilim.

Fallen Angels and Flesh Bodies

So now we know that when the fallen angels commingled with human women, the Nephilim were born. From the descriptions in the Bible, such as in Genesis and the story of Goliath, among others, we learn that these Nephilim were giants, exceedingly strong, and barbaric. The fallen angels who committed the act that led to the creation of the Nephilim were in direct violation of God's Law. We read about it in the Genesis 6 account, but there is also a familiar verse in the New Testament that may help shed more light on how unacceptable this was to God. Speaking of people at the resurrection, Jesus said in Matthew 22:30:

> For in the resurrection they neither marry, nor are given in marriage, but are as the angels of God in heaven.

There is a common misconception regarding this verse. Usually the last part, "of God in heaven," is left out. This verse is sometimes used to say that all angels in existence have never and will never take part in marriage. Such a statement is a mistake and a misinterpretation. This verse explains an attribute of only "the angels of God in heaven"— not of every angel. The angels that took part in the unholy union with human women are not angels of God nor do they reside in Heaven anymore. The angels in Heaven have never committed this terrible sin. In ages past, when certain angels decided to marry women and have children, they fell from Heaven and thus became what we refer to as "fallen angels." We can read more about this in Jude 1:6–8:

And the angels which kept not their first estate, but left their own habitation, he hath reserved in everlasting chains under darkness unto the judgment of the great day. Even as Sodom and Gomorrah, and the cities about them in like manner, giving themselves over to fornication, and going after strange flesh, are set forth for an example, suffering the vengeance of eternal fire. Likewise also these filthy dreamers defile the flesh, despise dominion, and speak evil of dignities.

Many interesting things are going on in this passage. At first, we learn about the fallen angels and how their sin of mating with humans, or "going after strange flesh" compared with Sodom and Gomorrah, resulted in God locking them in chains until the Judgment, when they will suffer the "vengeance of eternal fire." The basic understanding of this passage gives us some interesting descriptions, but when we look at the Greek words used, we gain a much deeper insight.

Let's start at the beginning with the words "first estate." The word "first" comes from the Greek word arche, meaning a high rank, such as to be first in position of political power. The word "estate" comes from the Greek word *peri*, which can mean a locality. From this we learn that the angels did not keep their highest-ranking location. The highest-ranking location an angel can have, or exist in, is Heaven. The angels left Heaven.

Now, let's look at the next part of the verse: "but left their own habitation." The word "habitation" comes from the Greek word *oiketerion*, meaning a residence, such as a family household. This is saying that certain angels left their heavenly family (God and the other angels) in Heaven, which was their home. These angels forsook God and the other heavenly hosts by leaving Heaven and coming to Earth. Their actions on Earth led them to be bound in chains and awaiting their judgment of everlasting fire. Also, if we look at 2 Corinthians 5:2, Paul speaks about being "clothed upon with our house which is from heaven." When we read the entire chapter, it is clear that "house" is another word for a body.

It is possible that the fallen angels not only forsook God and Heaven, but also forsook their heavenly spiritual bodies for a type of physical body they could use to operate within our physical dimension.

We can see here what actions led to the angels' judgment. This passage compares what they did to the sins of Sodom and Gomorrah. It says they were "giving themselves over to fornication, and going after strange flesh." The word "strange" comes from the Greek word *heteros*, meaning "another, the other, or different." This is saying that the fallen angels were fornicating with flesh that was different from their own, meaning humans. There are a lot of theories of how this could be possible, but apparently the fallen angels have some sort of physical bodies at their disposal. There are places in the Bible that mention angels having the appearance of men and even having physical attributes. For example, Jacob wrestled with an angel in Genesis 32:24, which I and many others believe was the preincarnate Jesus, and even Jesus Himself had a type of physical body after He was resurrected. So, it seems that, at least in some way and some form, certain angels can have a type of physical body. Even the fallen angels had this type of physical body and were able to mate with human women. Of course, while saying a "type of physical," we must acknowledge that it is very different from a human body.

This can make sense when we think of what we are. Humans are really spiritual beings, soul and spirit, that have been put into physical bodies so we can operate within physical reality. Our physical bodies are a type of vehicle for our souls and spirits to exist as intended within this dimension. It makes sense that if another type of spiritual being, like an angel, wanted to operate in our physical dimension, he would need a type of physical body, too. This body would be different from ours, as we were created lower than the angels (Hebrews 2:7). The angel's body would be more powerful and able to do things that the human body cannot. The "flesh" of the angel's body would be different from human flesh.

Generations and Bloodlines

Going back to where we left off in Genesis, we read in Genesis 6:9:

> These are the generations of Noah: Noah was a just man and
> perfect in his generations, and Noah walked with God.

Interesting here is that there two different Hebrew words are used
for our English word "generations." The first time it is used in this verse
is the Hebrew word *toleda*, meaning "family descent." The second time,
the Hebrew word *dor* is used, meaning "a revolution of time, or an age."
The word "perfect" comes from the Hebrew word *tamim* and means
"without blemish, complete, and undefiled." Going back to the Jude
passage, the word for "defiled" also means "corrupt," as in corrupted
flesh.

Genesis 6:9 mentions Noah's descendants, then it says he was a just
man, then it states that he was uncorrupted in all his revolution of time.
If only Noah was perfect, then by deduction the rest of the world was
blemished, or defiled, or corrupted. In Jude, we learned that the fallen
angels corrupted the human flesh by mating with them. It seems that
Genesis 6:9 is telling us that Noah and his descendants were the only
people in the world who were completely uncorrupted.

The rest of the world had been corrupted by mating with the fallen
angels and the Nephilim. Noah's entire bloodline, beginning with Adam,
was completely pure and perfect, meaning that no one had ever mated
with a fallen angel or a Nephilim. Noah's perfectly human bloodline was
the same one that Jesus Christ would be born through. That is why God
only saved Noah and his family from the Flood. Satan's plan was to corrupt the Savior's bloodline.

Jesus Himself was without blemish, so He had to have been born
through a perfectly human bloodline. Satan tried to corrupt the entire
world and knew if he could do that, the Savior could not be born. Satan

was nearly successful until God stepped in, preserved the last uncorrupted bloodline by means of the worldwide Flood, and destroyed all corruption Satan had wrought upon the earth.

Future Prophecies

We know there was an original influx of Nephilim before the worldwide Flood destroyed them all. Is it possible there will be another influx of Nephilim and, if so, could we possibly be seeing it within our lifetime? This has been the focus of much study in the field of Bible prophecy, though opinions are split on the issue.

In Luke 17:26—30, Jesus said the last days would be as the days of Noah and Lot, and then He lists some examples. The main point Jesus was making is that the world will not see His return coming until the moment it happens. The people of the world will not be expecting it. For those not remaining watchful and not spiritually prepared for it, by the time He does return, it will be too late. Their fate will be sealed. While this is a very clear and direct teaching, there are those who believe it is possible that there is a hidden truth, or a hint, found within this passage concerning end-time prophecy.

Of all of God's unexpected judgments Jesus could choose from, He used the days of Noah and Lot as His examples. We know that Noah's days were unique because of the presence of the Nephilim. We read in 2 Peter 2:4–7:

> For if God spared not the angels that sinned, but cast them down to hell, and delivered them into chains of darkness, to be reserved unto judgment; And spared not the old world, but saved Noah the eighth person, a preacher of righteousness, bringing in the flood upon the world of the ungodly; And turning the cities of Sodom and Gomorrah into ashes condemned them with an overthrow, making them an ensample unto those that

after should live ungodly; And delivered just Lot, vexed with the filthy conversation of the wicked.

We see much similarity between this passage and the Jude 1:6–8 passage referenced earlier. This passage is talking about Noah and Lot. This passage, like Jude 1:6–8, begins with talking about the angels that sinned. It even calls them examples. Some have noted it is possible that Jesus used the days of Noah and Lot to describe the end days because of the Nephilim and these two passages can be used to back it up. Also consider that in the account of Lot, whether they knew it or not, the people of Sodom were trying to have sexual relations with angels. They may have seen the angels that were sent for Lot as mere mortal men, but Scripture isn't completely clear. Either way we look at it, they were angels, and the people of Sodom were trying to have sexual relations with them.

Some have proposed that during the last days, the fallen angels will yet again attempt this unholy union with human women and produce Nephilim, more than likely through genetic manipulations rather than through direct sexual relations. When we look at this subject from a present-day perspective, the most tempting correlation to this would be the alien abduction phenomenon. However, on the other side of the argument, there are those who say this plays no role in Bible prophecy. A good argument can be made by seriously considering the success of this alien deception without the need for a worldwide revealing of UFOs and supposed alien beings. However it plays out, we can examine these arguments today to show that the alien abduction and UFO phenomena are demonic in nature rather than extraterrestrial. If speaking of demons and fallen angels, the Bible certainly does discuss this. If speaking in terms of modern-day Nephilim, opinions are split. However, it is still good to understand both sides of the argument to develop an informed opinion.

There are a lot of variations, but the basic alien/Nephilim/last days theory is pretty simple. It states that the alien abductions and activity people have been reporting are not actually caused by aliens from another planet, but by fallen angels from another dimension, which have a type of physical body and possibly technology that surpasses ours of today. The fallen angels lie, saying they are aliens from another planet to deceive people and change their worldview. These fallen angels posing as aliens have told various abductees that they created all humanity and religions, there is no God or Jesus, and they have come to usher in a new, enlightened age of peace for humanity. People have also claimed that the beings are trying to breed with humans by various methods of cloning and gene manipulation to create a type of super race to further their agenda.

Those who subscribe to this theory believe that these hybrids are modern-day Nephilim. It has been brought up that if Satan wanted to deceive the whole world into worshiping him and his minions, and if he has the capability to do so, this would be the way to go about it. Just imagine how the world would change if alien spacecraft came down and made contact. When the world is looking at so-called reality right in their faces, who would deny anything the alien beings had to say? If something like that were to actually happen, it would not be not be outside the realm of possibilities to imagine that the entire world would be handed over to Satan and the fallen angels. However, again, there are others who say this is already happening without the need for a mass revelation of UFOs across the Earth. Just look at the success and mass appeal of *Ancient Aliens*.

Be Prepared but Not Obsessed

We know Satan is the prince of the power of the air (Ephesians 2:2). We know he will come with signs and lying wonders, and to those who will believe him, God will send a strong delusion (2 Thessalonians 2:7–11). We know that men's hearts will fail them because of what they will see in the sky (Luke 21:26) and that, if it is possible, even the very elect could be deceived (Matthew 24:22–24). Can we really put anything past Satan, his angels, and their combined evil? Are there any lengths they would not go to in order to deceive mankind? Do we know the limit of their power?

Regardless of what does end up taking place, we serve a God far more powerful than anything or anyone else. We are not given a spirit of fear, but of power, love, and a sound mind (2 Timothy 1:7). We may not know every detail of the truth that awaits us in the future, but God does, and as long as we are in good standing with Him through Jesus, we have nothing to fear. We are saved, and Satan holds no power over us. We have comfort in the fact that, no matter what happens, we are safe. Even when we die, we are safe. God has us, and nothing can take us out of His hands (John 10:27–30 and Romans 8:37–39). We never have to be afraid.

Since none of us know the full future, it is important to remain prepared for what may come. At the same time, we do not want to become obsessed with the future because we do not know for sure what will happen. The important thing is to compare any theory with Scripture before subscribing to it. Many unbiblical theories are out there, and it can be easy to be deceived—or at least distracted for a while—if we accept certain ideas as truth without checking God's Word first.

If there is a contradiction between a theory and Scripture, we simply have to throw the theory out and find a new one, unless we are willing to forsake God's eternal truth for an interesting story. With eternity on the line, we cannot afford to be wrong about something if it has spiritual implications on our lives. Nor can we afford to be asleep if an alien disclosure is part of Satan's plan to lead humanity away from the cross. Be vigilant, have a strong foundation in the Bible, and know God the best you can. If you will draw near to Him first, He will draw near to you (James 4:8). In any pursuit of truth, do your own research, test what you are learning against Scripture, and follow God's direction. He has a path for you, and while it may not always appeal to your flesh like Ancient Aliens or Sci-Fi fantasy novels, following His path will always lead you to the truth. With the potential emergence of alien-related deceptions in the final days, need His truth now more than ever.

10

NEW AGE INFILTRATING THE CHURCH

THE NEW AGE MOVEMENT MUST be addressed not only because of its pervasiveness in our culture, but also because of how it is beginning to influence the Church. It is sneaking in the back door of Christianity even though it is often wrapped up in a bow of Christianese to make it indistinguishable from ordinary Christianity to the ordinary churchgoer. We are not just talking about New Age mentalities, but full-on occult practices being embraced in the Church as a means of discipleship and evangelism outreach. They can be hard to sniff out if you don't have a background in the New Age, but a good measuring stick by which to assess the appropriateness of a practice is to hold it up against the light of Scripture.

The Bible, and the Bible alone, is to be our rule of faith and practice as believing Christians. *Sola scriptura* ("Scripture alone") was a driving principle of the Protestant Reformation, and we would do best to remember the sufficiency of the sixty-six books breathed out by God for teaching, correction, and training in righteousness. We don't need to reinvent the wheel for the sake of cultural relevance. We don't need to water down, adjust, or bend the Word of God. It is firmly fixed in the heavens (Psalm 119:89) as something exalted above His own name

(Psalm 138:2). If something is not in the Bible, we should be suspicious of it at the very least. If it is in opposition to the teachings of the Bible, we should reject it immediately. If it seems to be hovering in a gray area, we need to see if there are any indirect biblical principles we can apply.

This is not a matter of heresy hunting; it's a matter of making sure the sheep of Christ are fed nothing except the bread of God. The spirit-man of each person doesn't need anything else. If the Word of God is sufficient for faith and practice, why risk corrupting ourselves by adding to it? Galatians tells us that "a little leaven leavens the whole lump" (5:9), meaning it's better that we err on the side of caution when something doesn't seem to agree with Scripture. If, in fact, demonic activity can oppress someone who is currently saved and peel them away from that which accords with sound doctrine (Titus 2:1), we can gradually descend into shipwrecking our faith (1 Timothy 1:19) as a result of another spirit luring us away the simplicity that is in Christ (2 Corinthians 11:3).

New Age and Christianity do not mix, and they don't need to. We don't have a moral obligation from God to incorporate Eastern philosophy into Church or blend occult thought with orthodox thought. If something does not line up with the Word of God, we should leave it outside the Church, not Christianize it to become more inclusive and seeker-friendly to those with a different spiritual orientation. Paul said it best:

> I imply that what pagans sacrifice they offer to demons and not to God. I do not want you to be participants with demons. You cannot drink the cup of the Lord and the cup of demons. You cannot partake of the table of the Lord and the table of demons. (1 Corinthians 10:20–21)

It's not worth ruining our relationship with God or preventing another person from entering a proper relationship with God for the sake of being trendy, alternative, or inclusive. If a practice clearly belongs to another religion, we are wise to hold fast to God's warning that seducing spirits lead to apostasy (1 Timothy 4:1).

Pray for the Teachers, Expose the Teaching

When it comes to exposing heresy within Christianity, some in the Church have fallen into the habit of calling more attention to a certain Christian leader or teacher rather than to the error itself. This approach is generally not effective, unless absolutely necessary. We must ask ourselves: Do we want the actual truth to be known by the Church, or do we want it to be known that we have better theology? Do we want people to actually know how to think through false theology so they can identity it themselves, or do we want to simply identify a single person as being in error?

There certainly are destructive teachings being taught today. There certainly are leaders within the Christian Church who should not be there. Furthermore, there are some who claim the name of Christ in positions of influence while rejecting the essentials of the faith. There also is certainly no one with perfect theology. Attacking a teacher because of a secondary disagreement is reductive, but of course this comes with limits. We have to distinguish a difference in opinion under the umbrella of orthodoxy from an actual heresy. A heresy is a belief which stands opposed to primary and secondary essentials of the Christian faith. Things such as the deity of Christ, monotheism, salvation by faith and not works, by grace and not merit, the death and resurrection of Jesus for human sin, and the virgin birth are non-negotiable truths revealed in Scripture. However, some things are simply out of the scope of what we are able to know with certainty, and to therefore call someone a "false teacher" over a topic that is non-primary and open to multiple different interpretations is to mistake an in-house discussion for a heresy.

For example, the belief in the operation of the "gifts", a pre-Trib Rapture, or a Calvinistic model of human salvation can be technically held without infringing upon the essentials. There are lines of Scripture that seem to go both for and against each of these positions. Touching such secondary issues that don't impact the essentials of the Christian worldview, we might not have the ability to know from Scripture whether an idea is certainly true or certainly false yet. So when we are talking about "heresy", what we mean is not teaching that doesn't agree with our interpretation of the text (as a lot of our beliefs about God may happen to be erroneous), but a teaching that blatantly contradicts one of the essentials of the faith

Even if a teacher is in agreement with the essentials, notable error can still be present where we have a pretty good idea that it opposes the word of God. We might not be certain, but it's enough to raise a red flag. In the case of something that is not a "heresy" but is most likely wrong, how do we go about communicating this in a way that will be effective in ministry?

There are certainly times when bringing a teacher's name into the conversation can be helpful. If a notable error is prevalent in the church, it can be helpful, in showing people how to disarm the false teaching, to refer to some Christian leaders who may adhere to it. For example, it is far more effective to say, "This teaching is wrong because of (reasons x, y, and z); this teaching is popular because even (famous Christian teacher) teaches it" rather than saying "(famous Christian teacher) should be avoided at all costs, is a heretic (even though it's technically not heresy),and should not be teaching because he (or she) teaches people (possible error x, y, and z)."

People, however, are not like an idea in the sense that a person can be both correct and incorrect in some areas. While there may be notable errors in their theology, that doesn't mean there is nothing of value they offer to the body of Christ. People are never 100 percent right and are almost never 100 percent wrong in all their theology. (I suppose this could happen, but I don't think it is very common.) A person usually has some combination of correct and incorrect theology. Even John Calvin once said no theologian is more than 80 percent correct. It is safe to say that we are at least 20 percent wrong in our theology, and if this is the case, we would naturally appreciate someone to demonstrate to us why that 20 percent is wrong rather than demonizing us, as a person, for being in error. We want our idea to be addressed, not our person to be addressed. This applies, of course, to ideas about which there is wiggle room for disagreements and error while holding to the essentials of the faith, and it applies to notable concerns that still technically fall within orthodoxy. This is when we should expose the teaching first and the teacher only if necessary. If we were denying the deity of Christ salvation by faith for example, we ought to be addressed specifically if we persist in this error while teaching other Christians.

So the questions we should be asking are: Is someone's teaching within orthodoxy or is it contrary to one of the essentials of the faith Is it probably untrue even though it still affirms all of the primary and secondary essentials of the faith? Or is it definitely off base while affirming the primary and secondary essentials? We need to train ourselves to look at matters case by case and carefully assess which of these three categories the teaching falls into, instead of crying "wolf" every time we see an assertion that is moderately suspect.

Because people themselves cannot be reduced to "correct" and "incorrect," it's beneficial to look at the actual issue in question. In any determination, the issue or idea should take precedence over the person who is teaching it for the purpose of ministry effectiveness.

We can consider the effectiveness of this approach on a larger scale. Let's say you have a teacher who is teaching something that is not "heresy," but is biblically unlikely and potentially dangerous. You can warn your friend about the teacher and tell him to stay away from the teacher at all costs. All you have done is taught your friend to avoid one person. What if another person teaches the same error? Your friend will be unequipped with what he needs to know, for he has only been taught to avoid a specific teacher and not the teaching. Now let's say you warn your friend about the error itself and show him the biblical reasons for why he should avoid this teaching at all costs. Then, no matter who is teaching it, your friend won't be taken in by the heresy (provided you have convinced him). He can avoid the heresy no matter who is teaching it or how it is being taught. This concept is similar to "give a man a fish, he'll eat for a day, but teach a man to fish, he'll eat for the rest of his life." I say, warn a man about a teacher, he'll avoid one person, but warn a man about bad theology, he'll avoid the theology no matter who is teaching it.

That said, there are times when it is helpful, when warning about a non-heretical error, to use teachers as an example. (To be honest, this is rare and most often unnecessary.) If you explain the bad teaching well enough, the person you are warning will be able to recognize it wherever it may pop up. The danger of bringing in a name is that it transforms the focus from an abstract idea to a specific person, and almost undoubtedly and perhaps even subconsciously, the person you are warning will focus on the person or people you brought up rather than the doctrine. People end up hating the teacher without really being able to articulate the theology they teach or provide reasons for why they think such theology is wrong, and instead get comfortable with have a passionate disdain toward the person themselves. It's just human nature. A specific person is a lot easier for us to picture and hold in our minds than an abstract idea or doctrine.

Additionally, we never know what kind of influence we might have with these teachers, no matter how famous and untouchable they seem to be. I often think of the viral videos in which someone attends a megachurch service then, part of the way through the sermon, stands up and shouts at the pastor, causing a scene. What does this accomplish? Are they really "heretics," or do they just underemphasize or overemphasize certain doctrines in their teaching? Its great click-bait online, sure, but no actual ideas are exchanged. No thoughtful debates are had. Nobody in the audience really understands what is going on. No one has learned anything.

Instead of circulating a cheap viral video with no context or thorough teaching being provided, how much more influential would it be if that attendee exposed the teaching itself online, teaching his audience what the Bible really says about this particular teaching? What if he or one of his viewers actually got the chance to speak with the megachurch pastor at some point and present those arguments to him? What if the video reached someone close to the megachurch pastor? What if the argument was so compelling that the megachurch pastor decided to abandon his teaching and use his enormous influence to teach more truthful theology? That has the potential for true change. A wrong idea has no potential for ever becoming right. A person who is wrong about an idea, however, has a chance to change his or her mind and exchange the wrong idea for the right one.

This is why prayer is so incredibly important for those in teaching roles. If we really care about what is being taught, not only do we have to expose false teachings (ranging from minor probably-false teachings to overt heresies), but we also have to pray for all Church leadership for a revelation of the truth. Sometimes, a teacher needs to be personally addressed and removed from the teaching role and, if God deems that necessary, then it will happen. However, how much better would it be if the teacher comes to the truth and uses his platform for what God wants, perhaps even exposing the very doctrine he once held to? It has happened before. While we need to be diligent to expose any error being taught within the Church, we also need to be diligent in prayer for those in teaching positions, especially if they are teaching something that is harmful to Christians.

Before we are even in a place where we can correct false teachings or teachers, we need to be able to distinguish false doctrines from biblical ones. We need to arm ourselves with the truth of God's Word. Some teachers within the Church may fall victim to some of the false doctrine and dangerous practices outlined in this chapter, but that doesn't mean we have to. New Age theology is infiltrating the Church right now disguising itself as a progressive spirituality. While some of practices don't technically require one to believe anything outside of orthodoxy, some of them do. They range from being spiritually harmful to potentially deadly to damnable. This is why it is useful not for us to be able to identify a few false teachers, but entire schools of thought. This way, we can know from the Bible what ideas and dangerous teachings (and heresies) we should avoid.

In our day and age, it is increasingly important for us to know the difference between New Age beliefs/practices and biblically based Christianity. These are not "in-house" discussions, these are biblically false and dangerous ideas that have crept their way into our churches via human error and demonic influence. These are not topics that theologians have been disagreeing upon for centuries that fall under the umbrella of orthodoxy, they are ideas and practices that don't even appear on the map of historic Christianity. While some of their practitioners may technically hold to the essentials of the faith, these teachings and practices have the potential to ruin a person's walk with God, invite demons into his or her life, or completely shipwreck his or her faith.

Christalignment

A new spiritual service being offered is something called "Christalignment," which offers a range of healing modalities from prophetic henna tattoos to energy impartations and spirit-life meditations. It seeks to minister to those lost in the New Age movement and the occult, but it's concerning that its methods border on what the Bible classifies as spiritism and divination. As Christalignment adherents say on the organization's website:

> We practice a form of supernatural healing that flows from the universal presence of the Christ. We draw from the same divine energy of the Christ spirit, as ancient followers did and operate only out of the third heaven realm to gain insight and evelation.[289]

The sentence stating that we draw from the "divine energy of the Christ spirit" seems to imply these people are attempting to contact energy and not a person. It's important to make a distinction between "divine energy" and personhood of the Spirit of God. We don't draw from a field, stream, or flow of divine energy; we have fellowship with the person of the Holy Spirit. The Spirit is a person like you and I, only disembodied and bearing the full nature of God. Jesus calls the Holy Spirit a "He" all the time in Scripture. He will dwell in us (John 14:16–17), He will teach us all things (John 14:26), He will bear witness about Jesus (John 15:26), He will convict the world (John 16:8). He speaks (Acts 8:29, Acts 13:2, 1 Timothy 4:1), He has a will of His own (1 Corinthians 12:11) and a mind of His own (Romans 8:27, 1 Corinthians 2:11). We draw healing power from a person (Jesus) through a person (Holy Spirit), not from a divine energy.

This seems to come through again when the proponents of Christalignment describe the artists they use for one of their services as "intuitive readers themselves and artists able to connect with spirit."[290] "Connect with spirit" with a lowercase s is something I (Steve) heard over and over in the New Age movement. It means to be in touch with the all-pervading spiritual current of the Cosmos. Or, it means to be in touch with the consciousness of the universe. This kind of language does not belong in the Church and is confusing to the outside world. People in the New Age movement may assume from this lingo that Christalignment offers the same things they already receive, only this time, "the Christ Spirit" is incorporated somehow. If the ministry and each of its "readers" and "seers" agree that the Holy Spirit is a person, public clarity on this point is necessary. People have a right to know who (not what, but who) they are contacting.

Christalignment's primary service is the use of "destiny readings," which involve sitting across a table from a client with a bunch of cards face down. There are four types of cards: color cards, animal cards, psalm cards, and destiny cards. The client is asked to pick whatever card he or she feels drawn to. At ten dollars a reading, clients are then led through intuitive card-choosing and card interpretation to receive ministry from the "Spirit of Truth" or "the Christ Spirit."[291] The ministry founder has said:

Psalm readings are similar to tarot in that cards are counted out according to your birth date date and year. Only three cards are used and these will represent your past, present, and future.[292]

The website was changed, however, after the Christian community began asking why a tarot-like service was being offered by professing Christians. The quote on the website was changed at the end of 2017, though the original can still be seen online.[293] Another old quote on the site makes a comparison to tarot cards:

We believe they are more predictive and higher than most tarot, and can address a current life question that you may have. Card readings with Christalignment are always followed by the reader taking the client into an encounter in the highest realm.[294]

What is "they"? Are the cards more predictive, or is Jesus more predictive? Why compare cards to tarot if it's Jesus and Jesus alone running the show? One color-reading session is available online and involves a client being asked to choose one of eight colored stones sitting atop cards on a table.[295] The person is asked to choose a stone that he or she feels "led to choose that feels highlighted to them." Three cards underneath the stone are picked up and held, and the client is asked to pick a card that has the color he or she chose.

The client is then asked to close his or her eyes and visualize being in a kitchen with a table in it. On the table is a gift wrapped in paper of the same color as the one chosen. The client is then asked to visualize opening the gift to see what's inside. The client claims to see a dove that has light in its eyes and a plant in its beak. The plant is blooming and growing.

Then the readers asks "the Spirit" what else "the Spirit" wants to show. The client responds by saying the dove represents somebody, and the plant represents the client being held. The client, asked how it feels to be the plant in the dove's mouth, replies "comforted." After pausing for a moment, the Christalignment worker asks, "So what else is there about the dove? Let's ask the Spirit of Truth."

The sequence of events goes as follows: Intuitive stone-picking > intuitive card-picking > visualization of an event > performance of an action while visualizing and communicating what the client sees > asking the Spirit for more clarity on what this means. Lowercasing the "s" in Spirit (as on the website) is the only thing differentiating this sequence of events from classic pagan card reading available from any intuitive reader in the world. It is methodologically indistinguishable from the practices Yahweh put the death penalty on in the Old Testament. Swapping out "spirit" for "Spirit" does not make a practice Christian. Incorporating the name of Christ into "intuitive readings" does not mean something is approved by the Lord.

> When you come into the land that the Lord your God is giving you, you shall not learn to follow the abominable practices of those nations. There shall not be found among you anyone who burns his son or his daughter as an offering, anyone who practices divination or tells fortunes or interprets omens, or a sorcerer or a charmer or a medium or a necromancer or one who inquires of the dead, for whoever does these things is an abomination to the Lord. And because of these abominations the Lord your God is driving them out before you. (Deuteronomy 18:9–12)

We are commanded to "abstain from every form of evil" (1 Thessalonians 5:22). Card reading is a form of evil because it seeks to create a man-made bridge between man and God to receive divine insight. The real bridge is a repentant faith in Christ, and the divine insight has been revealed in the written Word of God. The Bible is filled with an ample amount of divine wisdom available to all people at all times. If the Holy Spirit wants to show us something particular to our lives, He will do that without operating through a patently pagan practices.

Yes, God can bring special words in season for individuals, but that doesn't give us permission to rephrase biblical terms and commit a form of idolatry by using cards in place of God and His Word. It is sad that people in the New Age movement are looking for a word from God in an intuitive reading involving "animal cards" or "prophetic stones" instead of one of the sixty-six books in the Bible.

"All Christalignment team members operate only out of the third heaven realm. That means that we are all hearing from Christ spirit. This ensures safety for you and a way higher level of accuracy."[296] The "third heaven" is mentioned a single time in Scripture by Paul in 1 Corinthians 12:1–4. Paul described it as a realm where he had a vision that may have been either within or without his body. There is no talk in the whole Bible about believers operating out of the third heaven. Not a single person. Paul had one supernatural experience there, and while he was there, "he heard inexpressible words, not being permitted to man to speak" (v. 4).

This realm was so heavenly and sacred that Paul was not allowed to communicate what he saw in the third heaven—yet Christalignment can share wisdom from the third heaven at the drop of a hat? If they are really operating out of the third heaven, why are they allowed to share wisdom that Paul himself wasn't allowed to share

And they are in their body as the claim to be accessing the third heaven. Paul's only experience of the third heaven was so transcendental and mind-boggling that he didn't even know if he was inside his body. Nothing in Scripture allows what they are saying to be even theoretically possible. The fact that an entire ministry is claiming to be operating from a realm mentioned once in the Bible is dangerously misleading to its clients and the Body of Christ.

You don't just operate from a heavenly realm because you make a mental decision to do so. Saying you are operating from the third heaven doesn't mean you are actually operating from the third heaven. Simply put, there is nothing biblical about using cards in "intuitive readings" or about thinking you can access the third heaven any time you decide to.

Card Use: Incompatible with Christianity

Cards in and of themselves are just graphics with words printed on them. The problem is not the desire to have a beautiful picture with verses on it in the shape of the card; the problem is using this card as a substitute for going to God directly. Creating modalities to attempt to contact God is paganism. It's no different than tarot cards, runes, pendulums, or any other form of intuition-based readings that rely upon communication with "spirit."

Jesus told us to pray to the Father directly. He gave words of knowledge to people such as the woman at the well directly from the Father. He did not tell us to write down verses on a bunch of papyri, cut them into rectangles, and have the unsaved pay to pick whatever card they feel "drawn" to, ask them to visualize an image based on that card, and guide them through a visualization exercise telling his followers how much more accurate these papyri were than tarot cards. The intentions of Christian card use may be noble, but they contradict everything the Bible says about how we are to approach God.

Drawing close to God, poverty of spirit, humbleness, asking God for wisdom and the Holy Spirit, coming to God with a repentant heart, sowing to the Spirit in worship and prayer, reading the Scriptures, plugging in to a local church body, confessing our sins to God: These are some of the mandates God has put in place by which we may hear from Him more readily. Intuitive card readings show up nowhere in biblical history, except maybe the cultures God commands we be distinct from:

> Therefore go out from their midst, and be separate from them, says the Lord, and touch no unclean thing; then I will welcome you. (2 Corinthians 6:17)

I (Steve) have had the privilege of seeing Doreen Virtue come to Jesus within the last year and a half. She was a New Age teacher of two decades with more than publications, an all-time best-selling author for

the major New Age publishing house called Hayhouse.Famously known
for the angel card decks she used in intuitive readings as a medium,
she would ask to hear from "spirit" or the "angels" when giving advice
to her clients, which is not much different than what is going on with
Christalignment.

Because of legalities, the divination cards are still available in major
book chains, even though she has fully repented of them and been fired
from Hayhouse for saying that using them is abominable to God. It has
created quite the stir online within the New Age community, even more
so now that she does Bible studies with the same people she used to give
readings to.

I asked her to offer some commentary on intuitive card readings
now that she has left the New Age and uses the Bible as her final authority. Here's what she said:

> At one time, I was considered "the queen of oracle cards" which
> were designed to give people answers and guidance—or so I
> believed at the time. Everything changed once I read the en-
> tire Bible, and I learned how God wants us to go directly to
> him for our answers and guidance (James 1:5). The Bible also
> says that psychic practices are detestable to God (Deuteronomy
> 18:10–12).
>
> At first, I tried to walk in both worlds of New Age and Chris-
> tianity. I rationalized that if I prayed to God while shuffling the
> oracle cards, that would make divination okay. But I soon real-
> ized that New Age and Christianity are like oil and water. How
> can they mix? After all, New Age is all about glorifying yourself
> and Christianity is about glorifying God (Isaiah 47:8–15).
>
> So I stopped using cards, and I immediately experienced
> spiritual warfare. This showed me that the devil was behind
> cards, and he was angry that I was going to God for answers
> (Ephesians 6:10–12). Now when I see a deck of cards, it's like

looking at a deck of cigarettes: deadly and toxic. Since I was raised in a New Age family, I previously had no idea that cards were an instrument of the devil, until I studied the Bible and stopped using them. Today, I still see people, and even some churches, trying to rationalize blending cards with Christianity like I used to do. They are opposites that can never intersect, and I pray that everyone—especially churches—avoids the prowling lion of cards and other new age instruments.

Angel Boards

In yet another example of how New Age and occultism borrow Christian terms to push their own teachings, there are now "angel boards" used to contact supposed angels and spirit guides. Essentially, they are dressed-up Ouija boards. However, for Christians who are upset by Ouija boards yet still want to experiment with contacting spirits, the New Age and occultism have developed a way.

For readers who aren't familiar with a Ouija board, it is a flat board featuring all the letters of the alphabet, the numerals 0 through 9, and the words "yes," "no," "hello," and "goodbye." It also comes with a piece of wood or plastic called a "planchette." The idea is for one or more people to touch the planchette while audibly asking questions to any spirits who might be listening. If a spirit is listening, it is believed the planchette will move around the board to spell out a response.

The Ouija board was commercially introduced to the world by businessman Elijah Bond on July 1, 1890.[297] Originally designed to be a parlor game, it was popularized by spiritualist Pearl Curran as a tool of the occult and divination during World War I.[298] It was believed the dead could contact the living at the camps, and a "talking board" (similar to a Ouija board) was used to enable faster communication with spirits.[299]

Angel boards (sometimes called "spirit boards") are basically the same as Ouija boards. The only differences are Christian terminology ("angels") and decoration (typically, angels and clouds are painted on the board in soft pastel colors). People endorsing angel boards generally try to disassociate them from Ouija boards. For example, here is one question-and-answer on the Amazon page of a popular angel board:[300]

> Question: Can you talk to angels?
> Answer: yes...........if you buy a Spirit board........be sure to get angelic protection from Michael the archangel and other angels of yourchoice [sic]. NEVER get a [sic] Ouija board. You will be sorry what you may open your life to. Always say a prayer of protection when you use any Spirit board

One thing that initially interested me in New Age was the idea that I (Josh) could incorporate it with my Christianity. Of course, this is only because my faith was incredibly weak and my understanding was nearly nonexistent. This board is exactly what would have been tempting for me to try. I knew enough to stay away from Ouija boards, but I absolutely would have been foolish enough and gullible enough to try an angel board had they existed and had I been aware of them at the time. There are many in that situation now.

The problem is, a demon or fallen angel doesn't care whom a person is calling. Spiritual entities aren't bound by the rules that belief systems like occultism and New Age like to think they are. Spirits, much like us humans, are free agents and, to a certain extent, they can do as they please. Human beings have no authority over spirits, only Jesus does. Apart from operating in Christ (which would cause you to flee from such practices in the first place), you have no right or power over demonic entities that you invite into your life. Because of this, an angel board is nothing more than a Ouija board in Christian disguise. Don't be fooled by the fake Christian terminology.

Yoga in the Church

An article in *Time* magazine describes how "a fast-growing movement that seeks to retool the 5,000-year-old practice of yoga to fit Christ's teachings. From Phoenix, Ariz., to Pittsburgh, Pa., from Grand Rapids, Mich., to New York City, hundreds of Christian yoga classes are in session. A national association of Christian yoga teachers was started in July, and a slew of books and videos are about to hit the market."[301]

Entire Christian yoga ministries are built out with curriculum, DVD training videos, online classes, and yoga instructor training programs costing as much as $6,500.[302, 303] Yoga is in our churches as both a practice and a business. In speaking of "yoga," it's important to define what type of yoga we are talking about. Raja yoga is the general type of yoga that we are referring to, which emphasizes the mind-body relationship. Under the umbrella of raja yoga, there are Kundalini yoga, tantra yoga, and hatha yoga. The first two are overtly demonic and do not pose a realistic threat to the Church. The type of yoga people practicing in the Church is hatha yoga, in which the goal is to prepare the mind and body for meditation through posturing, breathing, and shifting focus away from thought.[304]

Hatha yoga:

...uses the body as a ground for spiritual techniques to prepare the practitioner to unite with the Absolute. The body is merely a tool in this process. Although one may become more fit and flexible from doing yoga, that is not the goal of yoga, which is part of a complex spiritual system. Pranayama (breathing techniques) and the asanas (specific positions) are designed to enhance and induce meditative states in which one can transcend mental fluctuations and bypass rational thinking. Hatha yoga teaches how to control the body and the senses so that the yogin (yoga student) can control the mind (Raja Yoga). Gradually, the body and mind are filled by the Atman (Pure or Supreme Universal Self) and "through the death of the body, as it were, is the resurrection of the Higher Self accomplished."[305]

We have to first understand that yoga is not a physical practice with a spiritual component. It is a spiritual and religious practice with a physical component. To say yoga is just a matter of posture, breathing, and stretching is like saying that taking communion at Church is just a matter of eating a snack or that getting baptized is simply a matter of rinsing off. Subhas R. Tiwari, a professor at the Hindu University of America with a master's degree in yogic philosophy, unapologetically clarifies the theistic implications of yoga for those who practice it in the Church:

> The simple, immutable fact is that yoga originated from the Vedic or Hindu culture. Its techniques were not adopted by Hinduism, but originated from it…. The effort to separate yoga from Hinduism must be challenged because it runs counter to the fundamental principles upon which yoga itself is premised, the yamas (restraints) and niyamas (observances). These ethical tenets and religious practices are the first two limbs of the eight-limbed ashtanga yoga system which also includes asana (postures), pranayama (breath control), pratyahara (sense withdrawal), dharana (concentration), dhyana (meditation) and samadhi (contemplation/ Self Realization). Efforts to separate yoga from its spiritual center reveal ignorance of the goal of yoga…it was intended by the Vedic seers as an instrument which can lead one to apprehend the Absolute, Ultimate Reality, called the Brahman Reality, or God.[306]

Even the Merriam-Webster Dictionary defines yoga as "a Hindu theistic philosophy teaching the suppression of all activity of body, mind, and will in order that the self may realize its distinction from them and attain liberation."[307] The goal of all types of yoga is moksha, a state of union with the spirit of Brahman, the Universal Supreme Self.

According to this philosophy, the self is inseparable from God because God is the impersonal substance of reality (see chapter on Pantheism). Therefore, when we self-realize, we enter paripurna-brahmanubhava, a union with Brahman.

Yoga is not about becoming more blissful, more loving, more reflective, or more balanced. While these things may come as a result of practicing yoga, in its roots, the practice is one of self-transcendence and unity with Brahman. It's about recognizing that the "self" is an illusion. Unity with the Supreme Self (Brahman)—not even stillness of mind— is the goal of yoga. In Hindu philosophy, samadhi describes a meditative state of consciousness achieved as a result of dhyana, the meditative practice of a state of oneness with surroundings and sense without identifying it. It is essentially meditation with no object of reference.

When you reach a state of *samadhi*, you can distinguish between illusion (*maya*, or unconsciousness) and reality (the truth about the Atman, the Self), and stillness of mind acts as a stepping stone to a state of *moksha*. *Samadhi* is the final state before reaching *moksha*, union with God. It's not the end game. Stillness of mind is the means to end of God-consciousness. As Hindu yoga teacher Pattabhi Jois describes yoga, "The essence of yoga is to reach oneness with God." He goes on to say:

> But using it [yoga] for physical practice is no good, of no use— just a lot of sweating, pushing, and heavy breathing for nothing. The spiritual aspect, which is beyond the physical is the purpose of yoga. When the nervous system is purified, when your mind rests in the atman [the Self], then you can experience the true greatness of yoga.[308]

The word "yoga" itself means "union" in reference to the unity between the individual self and the Universal Self, or "between one's individual consciousness and the Universal Consciousness. Therefore Yoga refers to a certain state of consciousness as well as to methods that help one reach that goal or state of union with the divine."[309]

As we have already established, we are not God. We are humans made by God, and we are fallen. "You are that, God himself; Meditate this within yourself," says the Vivekachudamani. "Ye shall be as gods" said Satan to Eve. Yoga is Hinduism by definition, and Hinduism echoes Satan's first lie. More troubling is that some yoga poses are named after Hindu gods. In addition to the Hindu theistic goals of yoga, some positions are meant to honor and invoke the properties of false deities. Famous yogic guru B. K. S. Iyengar says that some yoga positions "are also called after gods of the Hindu pantheon and some recall the Avataras, or incarnation of Divine Power."[310]

Virabhadra, Vasistha and Vishvamitra, Vasistha, Vishvamitra, Astavakra, Hanuman, and other positions are designed to align the mind-body relationship in hopes of embodying the attributes of Hindu gods and goddesses (or other divine creatures or human sages). To facilitate their properties, to hallow them as divine beings, and to become absorbed into their essence is the purpose of these poses.

Some stretching positions such as the Surya Namaskar (sun salutation) and the Chandra Namaskar (moon salutation) were invented for the worship of celestial bodies. The point is, yoga is not stretching; it is Hinduism. The positions people exercise during yoga were never intended to be stretches. They are positions intended to shift human consciousness toward God-consciousness and pay reverence to objects and entities other than the Triune God along the way.

The Bible tells us to abstain from things offered to idols (Acts 15:29), which would include postures named after pagan deities, and that our bodies are to be a living sacrifice to the One True God (Romans 12:1–2). Yoga creates an idol out of God by reducing Him to an impersonal force, and then builds a practice around bringing man into unity with this force through postures directed toward other idols. It's idolatry as a means to more idolatry with the ultimate goal of helping man step into his own divinity.

It is easy to at least speculate that paying homage to false gods and yielding to a self-glorying Hindu practice is a gateway to demonic oppression. As with anything involving the power and presence of demons, supernatural ability tends to follow. In yogic traditions, there are siddhis, paranormal attainments acquired through correct practice of yoga and meditation. Some primary and secondary siddhis include the following:

- Having absolute lordship over everything (*Istva*)
- Getting where and what you want at all times (*Prapti*)
- Moving the body wherever your mind intends (*Manojavah*)
- Shape-shifting to whatever form you want (*Kamarupam*)
- Leaving your body and going into the bodies of other people (*Parakaya Pravesanam*)
- Dying at will (*Svachanda Mrtyuh*)
- Seeing and participating in what the gods are doing in the supernatural worlds (*Devanam saha krida anudarsanam*)

Mainstream yogic philosophy equates the practice of yoga with the acquisition of supernatural powers that the Bible would attribute to the principalities and powers of Ephesians 6. Other siddhis are flat-out impossible, such as being able to see into your past life or your future life. We only live one life, and after this comes judgment (Hebrews 9:27). If yoga is producing visions of past lives, there are only two potential sources of origin. Either the person is hallucinating and needs to be diagnosed psychologically, or the person is being influenced supernaturally to see things that aren't really there. Evidence that they are being influenced supernaturally through the practice of yoga comes from the "Kundalini syndrome."

The Kundalini syndrome is a condition some yoga practitioners experience through stretching and breathing techniques. The Kundalini serpent is believed to be a coil of energy in the base of the spine that works its way up through the seven chakras (or energy systems) of the body, resulting in spiritual and psychological transformation.[311] As this coiled, serpentine energy fully opens all the energy systems of the body, creating a free flow of cosmic energy, people experience a "Kundalini awakening" wherein they enter an expanded state of consciousness.

Kundalini awakenings, however, come with side effects that appear to mirror psychosis, causing symptoms such as depression, insomnia, and identity confusion.[312] One yoga journal testifies of the emergence of new psychotic illness in some people who attend certain yoga courses, causing psychiatrists to become increasingly apprehensive about recommending yoga to their patients.[313] Other symptoms include pressure in the head, visions, whole-body sexual stimulation, pains in back and neck, intense feelings of head, and involuntary jerks and movements.[314]

This seems to validate the idea that demonic power enters people, causing mental and physical disarray. And all this is done through "stretching" and "breathing," which should better be understood now as practicing Hinduism. If you yield your body as an instrument to other religious systems, you are consenting to the influence of whatever demonic kingdom is over that system. If you take a step onto the other side of the fence where a mean dog might live, you might get bit. Siddhis and the Kundalini syndrome bear witness to demonic presence in the practice of yoga. Any spiritual consequences inherent in the practice of yoga are only amplified when we consider that most yoga classes usually involve one of the following:

- The burning of incense (originally used as offerings to the gods)
- Chanting and prayer (sometimes of the names of gods or goddesses)
- Meditation
- Shrines or altars
- Music intended to alter brain waves and shift awareness

This said, people who practice yoga in churches most likely are not combining yoga with any of the aforementioned practices and are generally just looking to stretch and feel better physically. But even if a person practices yoga in a neutral setting, we already have enough to think about. If yoga is methodological Hinduism intended to bring people into a realized state of self-divinity, and if yoga is named after gods and goddesses with the intention of becoming one with their attributes/ essence, and if supernatural siddhis and the Kundalini syndrome are known side effects of proper yogic practice, this seems to be the most direct parallel to the first lie in the Garden of Eden out of every other practice in history. Not only is the lie the same; there seems to be a transference of demonic power and influence resulting in paranormal abilities and psychological disarray.

When we consider that scientific studies have shown ordinary stretching practices to be just as effective in treating back pain and promoting health living than yoga,[315] we are better off to stand firm on biblical practice and methodology and flee from the appearance of evil. There is no precedence in early Church history for a Christianized version of Hinduism in the Body of Christ, and there is no justifiable reason coming from Scripture for us to start endorsing and accepting this now.

Karma

A subtle way New Age principles have infiltrated Christendom is through the concept of karma. Christians are quick to embrace an idea that our sins will find us out and that we will reap destruction if we sow into the flesh; that a person will reap some kind of negative consequences for living an immoral life. "Sure, I believe in karma. It's the principle of sowing and reaping," they may say. This is not what karma is. Karma is a spiritual principle rooted in the Eastern concept of reincarnation, wherein a person accumulates negative moral debt in their lives that they have to pay off in a future incarnation. Professor of comparative religion, Dr. Gavin Flood, summarizes it in the following way:

Karma is a Sanskrit word whose literal meaning is "action." It refers to the law that every action has an equal reaction either immediately or at some point in the future…. In Hinduism karma operates not only in this lifetime but across lifetimes: the results of an action might only be experienced after the present life in a new life…. The goal of liberation (moksha) is to make us free from this cycle of action and reaction, and from rebirth.[316]

Karma comes from a theological system that tells us we are to live out our futures as a ransom for the crimes we committed in our past or even a previous life. Bad karma needs to be alleviated through enlightenment and the suffering of evil as we atone for our evils on the Wheel of Karma.

There is a huge bundle of karma that we have accumulated over many births, and this is called Sanchita Karma. Of this, the portion that is responsible for our present birth, and all that we face in it, is called Prarabdha Karma. Our cycle of births and deaths continues because of our karma, until we become God realised and are freed from this cycle.[317]

Christians are innocently unaware that they are referring to Hindu theology when they say they believe in karma, but even the general carry-over principle that we receive in this life—the due recompense for the bad things we do—comes from Eastern philosophy and not from Scripture. It's a layman's understanding of the Indic teaching of karma. It is a perfect example of how New Age has pervaded the thought of our culture (and the Christians in it) so much that we begin to tacitly accept Eastern philosophy over the Word of God.

There is a general sowing and reaping principle in Scripture that states if we sow to our flesh, we reap spiritual death and spiritual destruction (every time), broken relationships (usually), and other kinds of consequences, but we do not necessarily have returned to us the evil we put out in the world. Life will get messy depending on the severity of our moral bankruptcy, but there is no mysterious force in the universe or deity outside the universe making sure we are going to receive in this life the measure of evil that we put out.

Many people live greedy lives and die never experiencing poverty in return for their greed. Many people commit secret adultery and continue on in their marriages without their actions ever coming to light or being returned to them in the form of a cheating spouse. Many corrupt politicians around the world will never know what it's like to be part of an oppressed class. It's simply not true that what goes around comes around. I (Steve) have never had anything inflicted back on me even remotely close to the type and measure of evil I took part in before I came to Christ, and nothing in the Word of God makes me think I ever will.

"What goes around comes around" is a Hindu teaching that rests upon the idea of a force in the universe that balances the scales of good and evil in the world. There is no such force. The belief that sin causes suffering is undeniable. The idea that morally broken people often create their own downfall is agreeable. The belief that if you are hard on people, they will be harder on you is inevitable. However, the idea that there is a force, law, or deity making sure we are going to have returned to us in this life the evil we put out into the world opposes the doctrines of sin and judgment.

In Christ, 100 percent of our moral failures were atoned for sufficiently on the cross, meaning God won't make us suffer for something His Son already suffered for. Jesus gave His life as a ransom for us (Mark 10:45), meaning that our moral debt is paid in full. Every record of debt that stood against us was nailed to the cross (Colossians 2:14). Jesus got what we deserved, and there is no judgment against us by God or the "universe" for previous sins (Romans 8:1). Outside of Christ, payment for moral corruption comes after this life in the final judgment (Matthew 25:31–46, 2 Thessalonians 1:9). The Lord's vengeance is placated for those who are saved (Romans 5:9) and delayed until eternal judgment for those who remain in sin (Revelation 21:8).

To believe that "what goes around comes around" as a Christian is to believe that Jesus did not atone for some of our sins, and that God is holding those sins against us, judging us by returning such evil (despite there being no crime left to pay for). Jesus was already judged for all of our iniquities and chastised for the sake of our forgiveness (Isaiah 53), so there are no longer any vices on our record that we must pay off by enduring evil. Jesus endured it for us.

As we have seen in an earlier chapter, a study from the Pew Research Center found that roughly 24 percent of professing Christians believe in reincarnation.[318] Since this implies karma, at least that many professing Christians plus whatever percentage rejects reincarnation yet subscribes to "what goes around comes around" believe in karma. A very conservative estimate of that number would be 9 percent, meaning we can speculate that about 33 percent of professing Christians believe in an Eastern concept of good and evil that undermines the entire function of the very Savior they claim to believe in.

As harmless as it may seem, the idea of "what goes around comes around" implies a false view of God's judgment against the unbeliever and denies the penal substitution and atonement of Christ's death for the sin of the believer. It is interesting to watch the global mind slowly conform to the general principles of Eastern religions so much that we don't even know or question where they came from. This karmic principle lingers in the back of the thought-life of Christians and arguably represents the intuitions of a fair chunk of the Church, despite having its origin entirely in Hinduism.

Mother Earth and Panentheism

Pope Francis recently wrote a letter called "Encyclical Letter Laudato Si of the Holy Father Francis on Care for our Common Home" to raise concern regarding pollution, climate change, and resource management. Without entering a theological discussion on how Catholicism fits under the umbrella of Christianity, the encyclical contains some disturbing concepts that have no place in the mind of a believer in Jesus:

> Everything is related, and we human beings are united as brothers and sisters on a wonderful pilgrimage, woven together by the love God has for each of his creatures and which also unites

us in fond affection with brother sun, sister moon, brother river and mother earth.[319]

Jesus said to call no man on Earth "father" because we have one Father who is God (Matthew 23:9), but He failed to mention Mother Earth as our only mother in the next sentence. Overlooking the inherently pagan notion that we need to be "united" with the Earth and the moon (a theme sprinkled all throughout the encyclical), no verse identifies the Earth as being feminine or sentient. The concept of "Mother Earth" first shows up in the twelfth or thirteenth centuries, but hits on a much more ancient, pagan idea of personifying the Earth as a feminine goddess. The Earth is personified as Gaia in Greek mythology, Terra in Roman mythology, Prithvi in Indic mythology, and Pachamama in Incan religions, to name a few examples.

The ancient world is replete with examples not only of fertility gods and goddesses overseeing certain aspects of nature, but also of nature itself having its own deity. The Bible contains no examples, yet the Pope introduces an entire letter with this idea to invoke empathy in the reader. The attribution of a motherly persona and spiritual identity to an unconscious planet is a form of idolatry, as the Bible says that some have "exchanged the truth about God for a lie and worshiped and served the creature rather than the Creator, who is blessed forever! Amen" (Romans 1:25).

If Jesus tells us not to call our actual father our "father," how much more would He oppose us calling a rock our "mother"? The encyclical not only speaks of the Earth as a feminine deity (something universally expressed in New Age circles), it attributes credit to this "mother" rather than to God for the blessings of life we enjoy on earth: "Our very bodies are made up of her elements, we breathe her air and we receive life and refreshment from her waters."[320]

Compare this language with that used to describe the Greek goddess Gaia in *Cassell's Dictionary of Classical Mythology*: "Mother Nature heals, nurtures and supports all life on this planet, and ultimately all life and health depend on Her."[321]

The God of the universe, not the mechanisms He put in place, is the ultimate Author and Sustainer of life. The cloud is not worthy of glory or reverence for raining on our crops. Nor is a pond worthy of adoration because it contains fish. We don't owe thanks to our fuel lines for giving our cars engine gasoline; we owe thanks to the men and women who created companies to provide this service. We don't thank "Mother Earth" for sustaining us; we thank God. The difference between these two is idolatry and obedience: "Therefore, my beloved, flee from idolatry" (1 Corinthians 10:14).

While we certainly have a degree of responsibility from God to be good stewards of His created world, we shouldn't revere the Earth as its own deity. It's a material space rock under the curse of God. He will one day destroy it in judgment in preparation for a New Heaven and a New Earth. Saving the planet is not on God's agenda; saving people is. Time will tell how this kind of language may be used to shape a one-world, "green" economic system in our future.

It may be tempting to think of the Earth in a divine manner if we misunderstand God's omnipresence. He is present in all places at all times, but in what sense? God upholds all creation metaphysically speaking, therefore His power is present in every point of space. He has knowledge of every square inch of the material world, therefore, His mind touches all points of space. He is sovereign, so He is active in every event in the universe in some sense. However, He is not the substance of reality or spread out in space like a gas. He is present everywhere in a variety of ways, without actually being inside everything as an indwelling substance.

The idea that God is both transcendent in Heaven but also present as the indwelling substance of all being is a theology called panentheism, which is simply refuted by Scripture. God is immutable, meaning He is changeless (Malachi 3:6). He is the same yesterday, today, and forever (Hebrews 13:8). If God was present within every molecule of the natural world, then He would be constantly changing as the molecules change. If He was present within every square inch of space, then He would be expanding as space is expanding. Despite the obvious theological error in equating God's omnipresence with indwelling every particle, Pope Francis still speaks in this encyclical of the universe as something that carries the presence of God inside it:

> All-powerful God, you are present in the whole universe and in the smallest of your creatures.... Father, we praise you with all your creatures. They came forth from your all-powerful hand; they are yours, filled with your presence and your tender love. Son of God, Jesus.... Today you are alive in every creature in your risen glory.[322]

The idea that Jesus Christ is alive in His risen glory in the cockroach on my bathroom floor is not only hilariously inaccurate, it's borderline heresy. Jesus made the cockroach (Colossians 1:16), supernaturally upholds the cockroach by the Word of His power (Hebrews 1:3), and sees the cockroach when it dies (Matthew 10:29). But Jesus is not inside the cockroach, and neither is the Father.

The Pope is presenting a type of theology that puts the presence of divinity in the natural world and uses this to catapult an idea of a suffering mother. The Earth is an unconscious "it," not a pseudo-conscious, quasi-divine "her." The talk of Mother Earth and a false understanding of God's omnipresence reflect a culture pervaded with paganism whose backbone has become that of New Age substance, and these concepts have worked their way into the Church from the highest levels of religious influence.

New Age Principles Claimed by the Church

A new trend we are seeing in the Church is the willingness to fully adopt New Age concepts and teachings out of a desire to recover whatever element of truth may be deeply hidden. Convinced that "there are precious truths hidden in the New Age that belong to us Christians,"[323] many Christian influencers and even pastors have begun endorsing the following beliefs practices:

- Opening up portals with your minds for angels and energies of Heaven to come through
- "Spirit-traveling" out of body
- Practicing "spiritual smell," "spiritual taste," and such
- Engaging in guided meditations
- Going through guided visualizations into one of the "Heavens"
- Using tuning forks and "sacred sounds" for energetic alignment
- Manifesting one's own destiny through visualization
- Believing that thoughts emit metaphysical vibrations and frequencies that create reality
- Practicing telepathic communication to put thoughts and images into another's mind

One work written by a group of professing Christians, including two who are senior pastors of a high-profile megachurch in America and another who is a senior associate leader, includes the following troubling statements. The first comes from a chapter attempting to mesh the New Age's loose and abused understanding of quantum mechanics with Christianity:

> Quantum physics implies that everything that exists, even atoms and subatomic particles, has a form of consciousness (sometimes called a "mind") and is interconnected through a universal consciousness (the One Mind).[324]

Quantum physics does not imply that protons have consciousness, nor does it suggest a field of universal consciousness. This is simply a false statement negated by the vast majority of experts in any relevant field of study.

This lays foundation for the next chapter, which attempts to use the infamous "observer effect" in which the wave function of a subatomic particle collapses in the presence of the observer in order to justify how we, as Christians, can call things into existence out of nothing:

"Popping a qwiff" is a physics term for the transformation of a wave into a particle by the intent of the observer. In other words, everything exists as a formless, wave-like state with the possibility of becoming a particle of solid matter. Then, by the act of observation, the wave-function is "collapsed" and the selected reality comes into actual existence. All realities only exist in probability until a particular reality is selected. If this is true, it means we can bring into existence whatever reality we have chosen by "popping that qwiff."[325]

This segment is titled "Popping Qwiffs by Faith" and offers a horrendous interpretation of the observer effect. The observer effect only demonstrates a relationship between the presence of observation and the behavior of a subatomic particle. Our minds seem to have an influence of subatomic particles when they are under inspection from a human observer. But this says nothing about a person's intent having any relevance to the behavior of a subatomic particle. Observation—not intent, declaration, prayer, or faith—caused the wave function of an electron to collapse. That is the first error.

The second error is that the observer effect doesn't say anything about people being able to influence a whole atom, a molecule, an object, or an event. Faith calls things and events into being because we serve an omnipotent God, not because an electron behaves differently when we look at it in a lab. The problem is that when people who are unqualified to make scientific observations not only observe the phenomenon but interpret it and create a whole new ontology and world philosophy around the unqualified interpretation. Some people simply don't know what they are talking about. Thankfully, qualified scientists do, and they reject these New Age interpretations. Unfortunately, some of the Church is siding with New Age teachers rather than with the qualified professionals.

This false understanding of quantum mechanics is then applied with the functioning of miracles and presence of blessings. Because consciousness has a mysterious relationship to the quantum world, miracles apparently happen through "faith and intent" interacting with the quantum world rather than the power and sovereignty of God who dwells in us. It's not my faith that heals another person, it is the Lord who provides healing through the medium of faith (Matthew 10:1). If "faith" healed, it wouldn't matter who or what my faith is in. Faith is the medium of healing; God is the provider of healing. It's God who heals through faith, not faith itself that heals. It is not my intention that will provide me with blessings; it is a Father who gives good gifts to His children who provides me with blessings (Matthew 7:11). Using New Age interpretations of quantum mechanics to answered prayer falsely attributes a natural cause to products of faith and prayer instead of a supernatural cause:

> Every good gift and every perfect gift is from above, coming down from the Father of lights, with whom there is no variation or shadow due to change. (James 1:17)

Borderline blasphemy taught in this work is the statement that Jesus performed miracles by accessing the zero-point quantum field in the universe. The zero-point field is what remains in a vacuum of empty space with no matter or molecules; it's a sea of fluctuating quantum energy.

> Jesus has redeemed everything [and] we need to know what this power is, this "sea of quantum light" that undergirds everything…. We truly have the power within us to move many, many mountains. Jesus healed the sick, cast out demons, raised the dead. We have the same power within us. And we also have power all around us, undergirding our universe.[326]

Jesus died on the cross to redeem everything so we could learn that this special "power" is a sea of quantum light? Jesus tells us where He received his power, and He did not cast out demons and raise the dead through the power of the zero-point field:

Do you not believe that I am in the Father and the Father is in me? The words that I say to you I do not speak on my own authority, *but the Father who dwells in me does his works.* (John 14:10, emphasis added)

The idea that Jesus harnessed quantum power from nature to facilitate His miracles steals glory from the Father, is unscientific, is unbiblical, and encourages a false worldview of the supernatural that puts emphasis on human ability to manipulate the universe through special knowledge rather than on the divine person of the Holy Spirit:

Not by might, nor by power, but by my Spirit, says the Lord of hosts. (Zechariah 4:6)

The chapter goes on to talk about how ultrasonic waves dolphins emit positively alter human magnetic fields and shift the vibrational frequencies of their body, insinuating this is evidence that God wants us to use the information about sound and vibration from the New Age to heal ourselves. Remember, this material features and is endorsed by some of the most influential figures in the Church today.

A red flag should be that the ideas of universal consciousness, sacred sound, and harnessing hidden powers of nature are held by the pagan nations God wars against in the Old Testament, but never by the prophets or apostles. A major selling point of New Age spirituality is that it is the "lost wisdom of the ancients," but this "wisdom" is nowhere to be found in Scripture or among the people of God historically speaking, and these "ancients" were always enemies of God.

No men or women of God have ever cared about these things in the Bible or early Church. The only people who cared are the people whom God destroyed and told us not to be like. If anything, these ideas resemble the teachings of fallen angels to mankind in the Book of Enoch more than anything else (sorcery, alchemy, etc.). If these are really "God's truths" that He wants us to know so badly, why doesn't He reveal anything to us about it in His Word? There are a couple of major reasons:

- These ideas are false. God didn't reveal them to us because there is nothing to reveal.
- These ideas are rooted in small pieces of truth, but are sinful and dangerous. God didn't reveal these matters to us because acting upon them requires us to commit sins of sorcery, witchcraft, idolatry, divination, and magic, etc. For example, it may be true that if I take a five-gram dose of psilocybin mushrooms, I will receive release from a certain degree of existential anxiety, but I will have transgressed God's commandment to be sober, thus stand condemned before Him as a guilty sinner awaiting judgement. I may also open myself up to other spirits and be deceived of a false worldview while under an altered state of consciousness. Perhaps the manipulation of my own biology and mind with sound, light, and vibration is against the will of God and therefore was not revealed in Scripture.

When we encounter a teaching or practice that looks patently New Age and yet we remain on the fence about it, we should run in the opposite direction. The Apostle Peter wrote two thousand years ago that we already have everything we need for life and godliness in the written Word and in Christ (2 Peter 1:3). We do not need anything else. Sifting through the New Age movement is doubly as dangerous when our only source of reference is people who are already misinterpreting matters without the guidance of the Word of God or the Holy Spirit. New Age teachers themselves, the only ones presenting these "hidden truths" to the public, have a host of New Age assumptions that go into their observation, interpretation, and presentation of information. We cannot trust them to be the ones with the truth, nor could we trust them to present it unbiasedly and objectively even if they did have it.

Plainly put, most Christians have no idea how to interpret light from dark in the fine print of publications like this because they have not spent five, ten, or twenty years engulfed in New Age content to be able to recognize it. They aren't equipped through experience to navigate the slight deceptions cloaked in "common sense" that can lead to being sub-dued by another spirit or acting and thinking in opposition to the Word of God. Rather than encouraging the Church to look for a diamond in a place they have never sifted through before that may not be there in the first place, we should keep our eyes off the ways of the New Age move-ment and on the sufficiency of Jesus Christ, in whom are hidden all the treasures of wisdom and knowledge (Colossians 2:3).

Baptist Labyrinth Meditation Prayer

The labyrinth is a single, intricate path that leads to the center of a design then back out. A prayer labyrinth is used to inspire prayer, mediation, and spiritual awareness. For centuries, prayer labyrinths have been used in Catholic cathedrals. Yet, in recent years, there has been a resurgence in popularity of prayer labyrinths in New Age, the Emergent Church, Neopaganism, and even in the Baptist church.

This modern resurgence of prayer labyrinths is supported and endorsed by groups such as The Labyrinth Society and Veriditas (The World-Wide Labyrinth Project). From the Veriditas website, the group's stated purpose is "to transform the Human Spirit" using "the Labyrinth Experience as a personal practice for healing and growth, a tool for com-munity building, an agent for global peace and a metaphor for the blos-soming of the Spirit in our lives."[327] According to Veriditas, walking the prayer labyrinth includes purgation (releasing), illumination (receiving), and union (returning).

Purgation happens as a person walks toward the center of the labyrinth and sheds the distractions of life while opening the heart and mind. Illumination occurs at the center of the labyrinth, in which the person is to receive whatever spiritual enlightenment is available through prayer and meditation. The last stage, union, happens as the person exits the labyrinth and invokes joining God, a higher power, or the healing forces at work int he world.

The labyrinth, in various forms, can be found throughout ancient pagan religions. Mosaics of labyrinths can even be found on the floors of Freemason lodges. Now, Christianity has joined the trend. In an article entitled "Labyrinth Transforms Prayer Life, Baptists Say," *Baptist News Global* reported on a growing trend in the Baptist church.

The article states:

The ancient practice which involves walking a maze while praying has become more popular among Baptists as Christians in general are adopting more eclectic spiritual disciplines.[328]

Rita Martin, one who practices this ritual, is described in the article as well:

Martin said she has "always been a pray-er" but now sees her mind often drifted off during normal prayer times.

The labyrinth "is a very good tool to keep your mind on track and to concentrate on what you're praying for, and why you're praying and just communing with God."

Martin said her Baptist upbringing offered no opposition to the practice, especially after she realized the leavening effect it's had on her spiritual life overall.

"I'm thinking, why have we never done this before?"

Martin's Baptist upbringing offered no position on this practice and she is left wondering why they had not done it before. I (Josh) would question why this was encouraged in the first place. Unbelievably, this isn't just one obscure Baptist church somewhere. It is a growing trend. Another article describes the restoration of the prayer labyrinth at a different Baptist church.[329]

> "It needs to be used," church member Marie Allen said. "It's a beautiful space and it's meaningful."

The article describes how the labyrinth is different than a maze. The labyrinth has one entry/exit point and one path. Church members follow the path until it meets a dead end in the center, then they turn around and return to the starting point. This journey is used for personal reflection and prayer.

> "I've seen people reach that center point and just start sobbing," said Sandy Londos, another church member who worked on the labyrinth. "Other times, I've seen people get to the center and just (exhale)."
>
> "When I would go through the labyrinth, I would say to myself, 'Stay on the path, stay on the path,' and that became not only a mantra but also a metaphor for things that were going on in my life," Rick Allen said.

While on the surface this might seem harmless or even beautiful, the idea of the labyrinth is not rooted in Christianity but in ancient mythologies. Greek mythology states the labyrinth was set up with a Minotaur in the center.[330] The story tells us King Minos prayed to Poseidon for help to become the most powerful king. Poseidon then sent him the "Cretan Bull," which was perfect and snow white. Minos kept the bull rather than sacrificing it to Poseidon, offering a substitute bull. As a punishment, Poseidon had Aphrodite cause the wife of Minos, Pasiphae, to fall in love with the white bull. Pasiphae then committed adulterous acts with the white bull (Zeus in disguise), and the result was a terrifying half-bull, half-man abomination. This was the Minotaur. The Minotaur required human flesh and was too difficult to control, so Minos, by direction of the Delphi Oracle, commissioned Daedalus to create a huge labyrinth to imprison the monster. From time to time, humans were sent in to the labyrinth as a type of sacrifice to the Minotaur. Later, Theseus (the demigod son of Aegeus and Poseidon) managed to enter the labyrinth and kill the Minotaur.

With churches taking on the mystical practice of walking the labyrinth in prayer, it is evident the enemy is plunging the Church into further deception. Of course, this isn't the first time this has happened, considering the yoga, angel prayer, and everything else discussed throughout this chapter.

If we don't perform due diligence to learn about these issues, we will fall into deception. We need to stay informed so we don't become tricked into worshiping the serpent. As Hosea 4:6 states:

> My people are destroyed for lack of knowledge: because thou hast rejected knowledge, I will also reject thee, that thou shalt be no priest to me: seeing thou hast forgotten the law of thy God, I will also forget thy children.

Contemplative Prayer

Contemplative prayer focuses on shifting and balancing a person's internal world rather than outward communication with God. It's more about adjusting one's interior mental state with the awareness of God as opposed to reaching out to God Himself with dialog. The goal is to rise above ordinary consciousness and dissolve the false self into the presence and awareness of the Divine through contemplation, since God "is known in pure consciousness rather than by some subject-object knowledge."[331]

One champion of contemplative prayer says that this type of prayer is meant to lead us to a place "in which the knower, the knowing, and that which is known are all one. Awareness alone remains. The one who is aware disappears along with whatever was the object of consciousness. This is what divine union is."[332]

This kind of prayer is oriented more towards a self-created shift in consciousness than it is in communication with God, and it's gaining popularity in Christian mysticism as well as evangelicalism. Popularized by a group of Roman Catholic monks named William Meninger, M. Basil Pennington, and Abbot Thomas Keating, contemplative prayer is carried out in what is called a "centering prayer."

Pennington outlines the steps of centering prayer as follows:[333]

- Sit comfortably with your eyes closed, relax, and quiet yourself. Be in love and faith to God.
- Choose a sacred word that best supports your sincere intention to be in the Lord's presence and open to His divine action within you.
- Let that word be gently present as your symbol of your sincere intention to be in the Lord's presence and open to His divine action within you.
- Whenever you become aware of anything (thoughts, feelings, perceptions, images, associations, etc.), simply return to your sacred word, your anchor.

The first step encourages us to "quiet" ourselves. Of the over thirty-one thousand verses in the Bible, not a single one tells us to quiet ourselves. Stillness of mind has no correlation to connection with God in Scripture. We are told by Jesus not to be fearful and anxious over tomorrow because it's unproductive (Matthew 6:24–35), but we aren't instructed anywhere to silence our mind to enter into union with God. You can't love God with all your mind if your mind is empty.

We are to "meditate" on the Word of God and person of Christ in terms of self-reflection, but we aren't to empty our mind in hopes that the absence of mental chatter is somehow flattering to the Father. Paul says "whatever is true, whatever is honorable, whatever is just, whatever is pure, whatever is lovely, whatever is commendable, if there is any excellence, if there is anything worthy of praise, think about these things" (Philippians 4:8).

The only verse in the Bible remotely close to a command to quiet ourselves is one which has been famously hijacked by the New Age community: "Be still, and know that I am God" (Psalm 46:10). The word "still" is translated from rephah which means "to let go, to relent, or to cease striving," and this command was given in reference to the sovereignty of Yahweh over natural disasters (v. 2–3) and war (8–9).[334] The raging nations (v. 6) coming against His people were reminded that God is the One who breaks the bows, burns the chariots, and makes peace on the earth (v. 9). Yahweh is speaking here to the enemies of the people of Israel whom He will be victorious over, telling them that their efforts are futile and that they should be still and recognize Him as God:

> God's goal for his choosing of Zion is that out of it the word might go forth to the peoples of the whole world, bringing them all to live in godly peace with one another (Isa. 2:1–5). This will be the means by which he makes wars cease (Ps. 46:9). Since the address in v. 10, be still, and know, is plural, readers should imagine God speaking these words to the nations, among whom he will eventually be exalted.[335]

"Stop fighting against me and my people, because I am a sovereign God" is much different than "empty your mind to have communion with me." This is not to say this verse couldn't be a reference to God telling His people to relax in the face of their adversaries, but it is most certainly not a reference to mindfulness in the sense of emptying one's mind of all thought.

The second step is to choose a "sacred" word. There are no sacred words in Christianity. Sacredness is the property the Triune God and anything he imparts anointing to (such as the Ark of the Covenant). But the word "ark" is not sacred. The word "love" is not sacred. The word "God" is not even sacred. The One to whom the proper title of "God" belongs is sacred, but the syllable itself has no intrinsic divinity.

The idea that some words are sacred is not found in the Bible, but in Hinduism under the title of "mantra." A mantra is a sacred utterance that has the ability to produce higher levels of spiritual awareness in a person through repetition.[336] Phrases such as Aum Namah Shivaya are intended propel one into a transcendent state of awareness, which happens to be the apparent goal of contemplative prayer through the use of English words.[337] Using a mantra to shift one's consciousness is an overt New Age practice that has no business in a Christian's life, whose God is supposed to be Yahweh and not the alteration of his or her mind.

The third step is to let this word be gently present in our being. We are encouraged to focus on a "sacred word," not on the person of Jesus. Even at this point, notice that no vertical connection is made between man and God. Man is still in the vain, selfish business of modifying his own internal states for his own pleasure. He is not ministering unto the Lord, asking God for wisdom, worshiping God, or talking with Him. Instead, he is pursuing a personal experience in his own mind. God is a means to an end of his own psychological pleasure.

It's also noteworthy that bringing consciousness to things like breath, mental objects, and sensations in an attempt to shift a person's psychology is not prayer. Prayer, properly defined, "is communication with God in worship."[338] A repeated word is not evidence of our "sincere intention" to be in the presence of the Lord. A broken, repentant, contrite spirit is (Psalm 51:17). A godly sorrow over sin is (2 Corinthians 7:10). A fear of the Lord and His commandments is (Ecclesiastes 12:13).

We are additionally told to bring our attention back to the sacred word (our anchor) when other thoughts come up. Our anchor is not a person, our anchor is a word. Rather than allowing the Holy Spirit to guide our thoughts in prayer and worship, we are told to dogmatically set our attention on one word and not allow anything to pull us away from it. The New Age and Eastern practice of mindfulness "is the practice of maintaining a nonjudgmental state of heightened or complete awareness of one's thoughts, emotions, or experiences on a moment-to-moment basis."[339]

This type of prayer is the textbook definition of mindfulness.

Contemplative prayer holds the same assumptions about nature of man, God, and prayer as the New Age movement, because it is rehashed mindfulness. It maintains that God is knowable in a state of non-dual awareness, that thought is the barrier between man and God in relationship, that a shift in our consciousness somehow equates to a relationship with a transcendent person, etc.

As we have seen in other chapters, this is incompatible with what the Bible says about man being separated from God through wicked works, and that the blood of Jesus (not mindfulness) is what brings us into fellowship with God. A three-page journal article on contemplative prayer written by an ex-professional astrologer accurately summarizes the difference between biblical prayer and contemplative prayer (CP):

Nowhere in the Bible is prayer a technique or a way to go beyond thinking. Creating a whole theology of prayer apart from the Bible is dangerous, precisely because we are entering an area fraught with subjectivism, truth based on experience, and therefore, an area where we can be deceived. CP teachers tell us that prayer is listening to and having "divine union" with God, but the Bible presents prayer as words and thoughts. CP tells us to focus inward, but the Bible admonishes us to focus outward on the Lord. CP is a misnomer, since it is neither contemplation nor prayer as found in the Bible.[340]

Additional Teachings from Another Jesus

Unfortunately, it is not uncommon for professing Christians to claim to receive direct, word-for-word messages from Jesus in ways that resemble channeling and automatic writing. While in deep prayer or a trance-like moment of stillness, they claim to hear the Lord speaking to them they begin to write the words down in the form of best-selling "Christian" books speaking in the place of Jesus.

These books contain new language that Jesus didn't use a single time in His earthly ministry, language that reflects New Thought churches and New Age lingo. Phrases such as "divine force," "divine mind," "sense-life," "spiritual plane," "material plane," "spirit sounds," "material manifestation," and "divine alchemy" are apparently used by the risen Jesus.[341],[342]

This kind of language was not used by Jesus, anyone who knew Jesus, or anyone who knew anyone who knew Jesus. It does not sound like words that would come from the Jesus described in Matthew, Mark, Luke, or John. Nor does it sound like the Jesus described in Acts, in 2 Corinthians, or Revelation, where He says nothing remotely close. Jesus Christ is the same yesterday, today, and forever (Hebrews 13:8). If it doesn't sound like Jesus did yesterday, why should we assume it's Jesus at all? Why must we assume this is Jesus if He sounds more like a New Age teacher than Jesus of Nazareth?

This hits on an issue we see creeping into the Church from the New Age movement: New methods of hearing from Jesus that are indistinguishable from "channeling," "automatic writing," and "overshadowing" are understood in the occult. The Lord apparently speaks verbatim to or through an individual apart from His revealed Word while they are in an altered state of consciousness for the purpose of bringing forth new doctrine and revelation

Jesus is not a person we channel, He's a Lord we follow. There is a difference between the Holy Spirit giving us a word as we sit under one of His appointed offices (such as a pastor), or the Spirit bringing Scripture to life in a way that is specific to our situation, and sitting in silence with a pen for an hour waiting to be verbally taught doctrine by Jesus.

One is God confirming the already-revealed Word in a personal way, the other is additional revelation to the firmly fixed Word of God.

One is new light on old revelation, and one is new revelation. There is a difference between receiving a prophetic word over your life or the life of someone else and receiving new and elaborated doctrine from Jesus Himself. There is no indication from Scripture that it is possible to receive any kind of new and improved doctrinal teaching from Jesus:

> Long ago, at many times and in many ways, God spoke to our fathers by the prophets, but in these last days he has spoken to us by his Son, whom he appointed the heir of all things, through whom also he created the world. (Hebrews 1:1–2)

"Has spoken" is past tense, meaning that God has already communicated the necessary doctrine through the ministry of Jesus and that no man has a right to speak doctrinally on behalf of God in addition to the final words given by Jesus. "The force of the expression in Hebrews is to characterize the Son as the one through whom God spoke his final and decisive word."[343]

The Bible contends that the "faith" Jude describes was "once for all delivered to the saints" (Jude 1:3). The apostolic teachings of Jesus had already been established in the early Church when Jude wrote this, and the point of this verse was to ward off false teachers who wanted to claim they had personal revelation from God in addition to those whom God appointed to speak through.

"The faith" to which Jude refers is the body of definable Christian truth known as "the pattern of sound teaching" in the writings of Paul (2 Timothy. 1:13). This body of truth was "once for all entrusted to the saints." Christians are not continuously or periodically being given new basic truths, as the false teachers had to claim, especially when their teachings conflicted with the previous teachings of Jesus and the apostles."[344]

We should be extremely careful when reading material that claims to be delivered by Jesus, and doubly so when the material offers new and improved teachings that don't appear in Scripture and that use words that we find nowhere in early Church history. As our Western culture becomes so desensitized to the idea of channeled material such that it is available in virtually every major bookstore, Christians might be deceived into thinking Jesus operates through saints the same way that demons operate through sinners. Thankfully, God tells us that anyone who adds to the Word of God is not doing so by the Spirit of God:

> You shall not add to the word that I command you, nor take from it, that you may keep the commandments of the Lord your God that I command you. (Deuteronomy 4:2)

> Everything that I command you, you shall be careful to do. You shall not add to it or take from it. (Deuteronomy. 12:32)

> Do not add to his words, lest he rebuke you and you be found a liar. (Proverbs 30:6)

> I warn everyone who hears the words of the prophecy of this book: if anyone adds to them, God will add to him the plagues described in this book. (Revelation 22:18)

Near-Death Experiences That Defy the Gospel

Near-death experiences (NDEs) are experiences people have outside of their body after physical death, often involving alleged trips to the afterlife before their bodies are resuscitated. A fair deal of what New Agers believe about the afterlife comes from the work of Dr. Raymond Moody on near-death experiences, the popular website Near-Death.com, a handful of primary published testimonies of near-death experiences that became best-sellers, and the in-between life memories recorded by Michael Newton.

While most stories about near-death experiences have not been of interest to the Church, a handful of best-selling books about near-death experiences sometimes line the shelves of Christian bookstores despite being antithetical to the gospel. Since we know that God is not a man that He should lie (Numbers 23:19), the account given in the Bible is the measuring stick by which we assess the validity of near-death experiences.

Jesus Christ is the standard of truth (John 18:37) and the embodiment of truth (John 14:6) who became to us wisdom from God (1 Corinthians 1:30). Since Jesus is the God-ordained authority on all matters of truth, if someone claims to die and have an experience outside their body that blatantly contradicts the words of Jesus, we can confidently conclude one of the following:

- They didn't actually die but simply had a dream, hallucination, or vision (possibly guided by a demon) causing them to think they had died. Theoretically, this could be caused by the release of DMT (*Dimethyltryptamine*) from the serotonin receptors in the brain, causing wild hallucinations and a dream-like state of consciousness before death is actually finalized. It could be the flickerings and hallucinations of a dying brain that hasn't fully died.
- They actually died, experienced nothing as their spirit remained in their body, and had a dream, hallucination, or vision in the multiple-second transition phase of consciousness setting back in. Brain scans reveal that hours of dreaming can take place in a matter of minutes or even seconds of earth time, even though the subject experiences a rich, vivid, lasting experience. Additionally, it's possible that the consciousness was demonically influenced and had a guided dream or vision as they were in an vulnerable state of being in between unconscious and conscious.
- They suffered some level of disjointed memory impairment causing them to generate and comprise new memories that

didn't actually take place in their experience, possibly as a subconscious survival-based response to alleviate and nullify psycho-emotional trauma.

- They actually *did* die and for some reason God allowed them to have a demonically driven experience outside of their body while their physical body was dead. Similar to how an argument can be made for demonic deception during actual out-of-body experiences in the form of astral projection, perhaps demonic deception during near-death experiences is something God would permit to occur for morally sufficient reasons. They were deceived out of the body, just like you can be deceived in your body. Having an OBE doesn't guarantee your experience is deception-free.

- They didn't die and hovered in an intermediary state between consciousness and unconsciousness, where they encountered a sense of stillness and serenity as their sensory experience began to shut down. Anyone going into diabetic shock, for example, can testify of seeing bright white lights or stars as their brain becomes impaired by altered blood-sugar levels. If this were combined with a slipping into unconsciousness and the sensory experience beginning to fade out, they may feel profound rest accompanied by glowing white lights. Imagination may fill in some gaps.

- They didn't experience anything of the sort and are simply making this us. This, to me, is probably the least likely of the options, but it still a far better explanation than Jesus being incorrect. If I have to pick between Jesus and a person who claims to have seen Shiva in Heaven after they got hit in the head with a brick, I am going to go with Jesus 100 percent of the time. I will not rest the eternal destiny of my soul on the ability of a person to retain what he or she believes are memories while the person's brain was biologically impaired.

One popular near-death experience detailed in Proof of Heaven can be located in some Christian bookstores, and involves the story of a man who experience multiple levels of the afterlife while he was in a coma with a severe case of bacterial meningitis. He claims to have experienced Heaven, despite the fact that:

- There was no mention of Heaven being eternal (Matthew 25:46).
- There was no Jesus or Yahweh in Heaven (Acts. 7:55–56).
- There was no throne of God in Heaven (Revelation 4).
- There was no worship in Heaven (Revelation 4).
- He didn't come back believing or teaching the Gospel.
- He didn't come back ministering to us about Jesus.
- He didn't come back affirming the God of the Bible.
- He didn't come back believing in eternal Hell.

He did, however, pair up with a variety of New Age institutions promoting transcendental meditation, centering prayer, and sacred acoustics. He also spoke at the Theosophical Society, the esoteric mystery school started by Luciferian Helena Blavatsky, whom we have already looked at. If this really was God granting this experience, we would expect this man to have the wherewithal to stay away from organizations that endorse the enemy of God. Here are some of the things he believes after his experience as revealed by his speeches at the Theosophical Society:

- "We come back in multiple incarnations in our ascendence towards that oneness. Any friction between schools of religious thought are false boundaries."[345]
- "If someone has a near-death experience as a Christian, they might describe this beautiful all-loving light body as Jesus. If they are a Muslim, they might describe this beautiful all-loving light body a Muhammad. A Buddhist might see Buddha."[346]

- "You can do no wrong.... As long as we realize that we reap what we sow. If we hand out pain and suffering to others as part of the lessons we're trying to learn, we're gonna end up making amends in this incarnation, or having to live through the pain and suffering on their behalf in the life review. There is no need for an eternal Hell...We are eternal spiritual beings through multiple incarnations...I promise you, there is a tremendous amount in original Christianity that supports reincarnation."[347]

A major way New Age thought is infiltrating the Church is through best-selling NDEs about Heaven that Christians innocently mistake as legitimate. This, in part, may be a reason such high numbers of professing Christians believe in reincarnation. Their local Christian bookstore might happen to shelve works that endorse it. We need to be more vigilant about the material we read, and we should test every story and teaching against the Word of God:

Beloved, do not believe every spirit, but test the spirits to see whether they are from God, for many false prophets have gone out into the world. By this you know the Spirit of God: every spirit that confesses that Jesus Christ has come in the flesh is from God, and every spirit that does not confess Jesus is not from God. This is the spirit of the antichrist, which you heard was coming and now is in the world already. (1 John 4:1–3)

The best thing we can do is compare everything with the Word of God. If it doesn't line up, we ought to reform our beliefs and practices and move on for the good of the Kingdom.

11

MINISTERING TO THE
NEW AGE MOVEMENT

I (JOSH) CANNOT SAY THAT my experience is going to be equal to that of every New Ager out there, but as a former New Ager, in hindsight, I can see what I was thinking and why New Age was so appealing to me. As stated earlier, I was raised in Christianity. However, unbeknownst to me at the time, my understanding of Christianity and the Bible was extremely shallow. It was based more on Church tradition than on the original, first-century Jewish understanding of Scripture. Because of this, I had questions that were left unanswered. I also believed I knew everything there was to know of importance in the Bible. The sermons themselves were more about how to be a good person and operate as a Christian in our modern society rather than anything resembling deep biblical theology. In short, I was bored.

We are more than just body; we are also soul and spirit. Because of this, if a church is going to strip away the supernatural aspect of the Christian faith, there are going to be Christians who will starve spiritually and go somewhere else to be fed. That is what I believe happened to me. In saying this, I take 100 percent responsibility for my own poor choices. I certainly did not go out of my way to research if my newly found New Age theology was wrong. I really thought I knew better than what any Christian would be able to tell me. I thought I was enlightened. In truth, I was living in total spiritual darkness.

I was replacing a good relationship with God with mystical experiences and astral projection. I believed this ability made me unique. I had been brought up in an incredibly broken home, so New Age was giving me the sense of worth I had been denied as a child. New Age played to all the worst parts of me that had been developed through the tough times of my childhood. It allowed me to take my own lack of self-worth and turn it into selfishness, my want for love into greed, my trauma into a victimhood mentality, my fear into substance abuse, and my depression into a lack of faith. New Age did not help any of my problems; it only turned them into subtler and unrecognizably ugly character flaws.

Rededicating my life to Christ, however, shone a light that cut through all the darkness and showed me how flawed, fragile, and ignorant I was. While this sounds uncomfortable (believe me, in the short term, it was), ultimately, it was best. For the first time, I could begin to see myself through Christ's eyes instead of my own. My own eyes were used as filters so I could see myself in a fake but positive light. The eyes of Christ were pure and double-edged. On one hand, I could see how filthy, pathetic, and ugly I had become. However, I could also see how Christ loved me anyway. Jesus was the source of all the love, care, and security I had been craving my whole life. All I had to do was allow Him to help me.

Since that time, I have found what I thought to be impossible. I found genuine love. I discovered true acceptance. I genuinely enjoy being myself. I take pride in my work. I find great joy in continuing to learn about and improve myself. I don't only feel, but know, that I am special because I have the Holy Spirit living within me, and I don't ever have to be alone again. I have found amazing brothers and sisters in Christ who understand all of these things as well. It is a family that keeps growing as we continue to love and learn together. Truly, there is no substitute.

What New Agers Are Looking For

I (Josh) really think, at the core, New Agers mainly want to be understood, respected, and cared for, and to feel worthy. Like everyone else, they just want to be loved. Unfortunately, a big factor in why people turn to New Age is they are trying to fill a hole of spirituality that we all have. For some, this hole was made deeper during childhood when their family didn't love them the way they should have. For others, the hole is shallow and subtle, but still there is a nagging feeling it needs to be filled. Whatever the case, people go to New Age because there is something unfulfilled in their lives. They are not enemies. They only need to be introduced to Jesus.

It is tempting, as Christians, to take the moral and theological high ground from New Agers and talk down to them, mock them, or use sarcasm to win an argument. This is ineffective and, in many cases, is the attitude that has driven so many people to New Age in the first place. All Christians should ask: *Do I want to win an argument or do I want to win a soul?*

If you take the time to care about how best to reach New Agers, while they might be hostile at first, they eventually appreciate your effort, because you are showing them a type of caring the world generally denies. If you listen to what they have to say about New Age, you will better understand their thought processes and motivations. You can use that to have a more open conversation. You don't have to condone or agree with what they are doing, but neither do you have to be insulting. Understand that the eternal fate of their soul is at stake and recognize that no one is beyond hope. If Jesus can save an astral-projecting, drug-using, self-centered egomaniac like I was, He can save anyone. They just might need a little help getting there.

The Love of God

New Agers esteem love above all else. Ram Dass once said, "I'm interested in only being love."[348] Many followers got into New Age in the first place because they were looking for love and community. Love, to the postmodern, New Age thinking, is evidence that a person is operating in the truth. Those who are unloving are trapped in ego and cannot have the truth. If they feel unloved during the conversation, they, like most people, shut down and become unwilling to listen to what any Christian has to say. We don't want to be unloving people talking about an unloving God to people who value love above anything else. Instead, we should be quick to emphasize the amazing things our God has to say about them.

They are made in the image and likeness of God (Genesis 1:26). They were knit together in their mother's womb by God (Psalm 139:13). They are fearfully and wonderfully made (Psalm 139:14). God has a plan and purpose for their life (Jeremiah 29:11). Jesus died for them out of love to bring them back into relationship with the Father (John 3:16). The sacrifice of Jesus for their sins means that their life is extremely valuable in the eyes of God. Something underneath all their brokenness and sin was worth the blood and body of Jesus to the Father. This incredible goodness and kindness of God toward us as broken people leads us to repentance (Romans 2:4). God is willing to forgive them, give them a new spiritual rebirth, be in relationship with them, and spend eternity in Heaven with them because of His great love for them.

When we communicate to New Agers, should do so in the spirit of gentleness (2 Timothy 2:24–26). They will not want to hear from us if their community is able to love better than we are. We should have the advantage because our God is love (1 John 4:8), so all we have to do is represent Him. If we want to win the New Age movement for Jesus, we can't allow it to out-love us. Frankly, it is embarrassing when those without the Holy Spirit (Jude 19) exhibit more peace, love, and joy than those who have the God of the universe living inside them.

The Holiness of God

The New Age movement wholly rejects the notion of judgment and holiness in the discussion of God's nature. New Agers need to be aware that they have an outstanding debt of justice with a righteous God that they can't pay back on their own. The fundamental issue is that God is a morally perfect being. This means He is fair and just in all matters pertaining to morality and will hold us accountable. :The LORD is righteous in all his ways" (Psalm 145:17). Since God is holy, His will for our lives is that we live up to His standard of righteousness. He wants us to live holy lives that reflect His character for His good and for ours: "For I am the Lord your God. Consecrate yourselves therefore, and be holy, for I am holy" (Leviticus 11:44). Or, as Jesus says, "You therefore must be perfect, as your heavenly Father is perfect" (Matthew 5:48).

We are made in the image of God, and part of that means we are ingrained with this sense of right and wrong, and our conscience alarms us when we sin. In addition to His general revelation to us in conscience, He has also given us special revelation in Scripture. The Ten Commandments, for example, are some of the most basic of God's moral commands that reflect His holy nature.

The Law of God as an expression of the holiness of God is a great place to engage with someone in the New Age movement, because everyone understands that a perfectly loving being must be perfectly good, and a perfectly good being must be perfectly fair. If we can agree that a loving God must be fair, we can help them recognize their need for a Savior.

Just as a good, fair judge in court must hold a criminal morally accountable for his crimes, our crimes must be punished by God who is judge of all (James 4:12). A criminal can't be released from murder charges because he is sorry and will try his best not to murder again. Any judge who wants to keep his job will sentence the murderer to prison, even if he regrets his criminal actions. Likewise, a moral judge will not acquit the murderer on the grounds of his own good deeds. Volunteering at the homeless shelter several years ago does not make the murderer innocent of his crime.

When God punishes sin, He acts consistently with His own nature. Thankfully, all of our sin was transferred to Christ and judged by the Father on the cross (Colossians 2:14, Isaiah 53:4–12). But if the atoning death and resurrection of Jesus for our sins has not been applied to us by faith, what do we do with our moral guilt before a holy God? How is the problem of our sin dealt with?

Asking New Agers questions like the following can be helpful:

- "Do you believe that if a perfectly holy God exists, He would have to hold you accountable for sins, even if He didn't take pleasure in doing it?"
- "How could a holy God who can't even look upon sin (Habakkuk 1:13) allow people like you and me into Heaven?"

The holiness of God has the ability to awaken people from believing that God is whoever they define Him to be, because the Law of God bears witness with their conscience that they have fallen short of His glory. Their own consciences testify of a holy, personal God who is the foundation of moral values and duties. A friendly discussion on the holiness of God helps bring these suppressed intuitions to light and confronts the individual with the truths about God that they have not allowed themselves to see

The Person of the Holy Spirit

Something I (Steve) wish had been emphasized more during my Christian upbringing is the subject of the person and ministry of the Holy Spirit. We may be handcuffed in our ability to show that Jesus is the only way in a limited demonstration of apologetics, but we must assure the New Ager that we can all *know* He is the only way through the inner witness of the Holy Spirit. The Holy Spirit is the third person of the Trinity, a personal agent bearing the fullness of the divine nature who indwells believers the moment they receive Jesus through faith (Galatians 3:2, Ephesians 1:13–14).

He dwells in us (John 14:16–17); He teaches us (John 14:26); He bears witness about Jesus (John 15:26); He convicts us of sin, righteousness, and judgment (John 16:8); and He bears witness with our spirit that we are the children of God (Romans 8:17). Following Jesus is not about white-knuckle gripping your life and biting your lip to avoid doing all the things you want so you can go to Heaven. It's about being supernaturally born again by the Spirit of God (John 3:3–6) so that we have a new heart and a new mind that is gradually transformed by the indwelling Spirit through a process called sanctification (2 Corinthians 5:17; 2 Corinthians 4:16):

> I will sprinkle clean water on you, and you shall be clean from all your uncleannesses, and from all your idols I will cleanse you. And I will give you a new heart, and a new spirit I will put within you. And I will remove the heart of stone from your flesh and give you a heart of flesh. And I will put my Spirit within you, and cause you to walk in my statutes and be careful to obey my rules. (Ezekiel 36:25–27)

The faith of Christians is ultimately grounded in the inner witness of the Holy Spirit who immediately confirms to them the truth of the Gospel. This is why Christians are so fervently convinced of their faith.

Apologetics and evidence may serve as dual-warrant for our faith, but are epistemically rooted in the Spirit of God who lives inside us. We have direct access to God, and our belief in Him becomes fundamental. Walking with Jesus is a supernatural, living, vibrant, Spirit-filled experience (which most New Agers are unaware of).

Members of the New Age movement are thirsty for supernatural experience and don't feel they can have that within a church, by reading the Bible, or through worship, prayer, and fasting. The Holy Spirit is so helpful and crucial to the life of a Christian that Jesus said it was better for Him to leave this Earth so that the Holy Spirit could be sent to us (John 16:7). What an under-expressed tool in evangelism—that people Jesus didn't just die to get us into Heaven, but that He died to get Heaven inside of us.

Those in the New Age need to know that all supernatural experience they crave can be found in a relationship with Jesus, and that everything they experience in the New Age is a counterfeit of the supernatural walk available to everyone through the blood of Jesus. Christianity is a supernatural relationship with three divine persons—not with one person or two persons, but three persons. If we leave any of these out, we offer an incomplete picture of the gospel and miss the very elements New Agers long for.

Christianity Is Different from Every Other Religion

One thing that makes Christianity different from every other religion in the world is that it maintains that we are supernaturally transformed (regenerated), saved (justified), and brought back into right-standing with God (reconciled) through faith and faith alone. Every other religion involves works and a constant striving to earn the approval of and relationship with God. Those in the New Age movement are continuously told to do the following to have a spiritual life:

- Raise your vibration.
- Practice mindfulness.
- Balance and cleanse your *chakras*.
- Meditate and practice yoga to self-realize.
- Use crystals, psychedelics, *reiki*, and other "tools" for spiritual development.
- Contemplate and study secret divine knowledge such as sacred geometry and alchemy.
- Practice magik and divination.
- Try to astral project and lucid dream to explore higher realms.
- Maintain positive dominant thoughts since you attract what you put out.
- Be loving to people to work off bad karma from past lives.
- Disidentify from the thought, emotion, and ego.
- Study Buddhism, Hinduism, Sikhism, Taoism, and other wisdom traditions.

After they have done all this, they have to do it all over again in a potentially infinite number of incarnations. There is a never-ending laundry list of things to do to achieve a state of enlightenment. A mountain of ascension with no visible peak is what everyone in the New Age movement is spending time, money, effort, blood, sweat, and tears trying to climb. The New Age followers are told that maybe one day, they will graduate to a higher level of spiritual being where they will then have a new list of works to do in the spirit world to carry on the process of ascension. It's a works-based system wherein liberation and relationship to "God" is contingent upon the ability to perform, explore, and follow through with practice and study.

However, here is what the Bible says:

- "Now to the one who works, his wages are not counted as a gift but as his due. And to the one who does not work but believes in him who justifies the ungodly, his faith is counted as righteousness" (Romans 4:5).

- "For by grace you have been saved through faith. And this is not your own doing; it is the gift of God, not a result of works, so that no one may boast" (Ephesians 2:8–9).
- "Truly, truly, I say to you, whoever believes has eternal life" (John 6:47).
- "Because, if you confess with your mouth that Jesus is Lord and believe in your heart that God raised him from the dead, you will be saved" (Romans 10:9).

Christianity is the only system of faith and worship that maintains that a person is made entirely right with God through faith and faith alone. We are "justified," which means that we are declared innocent and righteous through nothing more than sincerely believing. We are then brought back into supernatural relationship with God on the basis of Christ's substitutionary work on the cross in our place where He bore our sin (2 Corinthians 5:21). Since everything was taken care of in the representative life of Jesus (Romans 5:19), even moral works of righteousness do not contribute to our salvation: "For we hold that one is justified by faith apart from works of the law" (Romans 3:28).

Those in the New Age movement are longing for spiritual freedom, but they are, ironically, stuck in a works-based salvation that constantly has them striving toward higher consciousness. What if Jesus accomplished everything necessary in His death and resurrection to take care of all our sin and grant us eternal life in Heaven through faith?

What if God loves you and took care of everything so that all you have to do to be saved is believe and receive with a repentant heart? Jesus came to set us free from ourselves, sin, religious deception, and the unbearable weight of the Law. We can now rest from our works as God rested from His (Hebrews 4:9–10) because we have been restored back to God through faith. Christianity is the only religion in the world that offers eternal salvation from the power and penalty of evil as an absolutely free gift. Contrasting salvation by faith with the never-ending process of ascension is a wonderful way to impart a sense of grace and hope to the hearer. We can truly be saved right now by faith alone and have everything we seek in Jesus, or we can never be actually be saved (but graduate to the next step in our "evolution") by karmic alleviation, ascension, and self-realizing through a potentially infinite amount of time and live.

Jesus Is the Only Way

Jesus very clearly says He is the only way to the Father. He doesn't say adopting His morals is the way, He doesn't say imitating His life is the way, and He doesn't say embodying His state of consciousness is the way. As much as we need to have compassion on those lost in the New Age movement, we must stand strong on what Jesus meant when He claimed that nobody has access to God apart from Him: "Jesus said to him, 'I am the way, and the truth, and the life. No one comes to the Father except through me'" (John 14:6).

This verse needs to be contextualized by others for us to understand what Jesus meant by coming "through" Him. This simply means that faith in Him as the Messiah is the only way we can have access to God:

- "Whoever believes in him is not condemned, but whoever does not believe is condemned already, because he has not believed in the name of the only Son of God" (John 3:18).
- "I told you that you would die in your sins, for unless you believe that I am he you will die in your sins" (John 8:24).
- "Whoever believes and is baptized will be saved, but whoever does not believe will be condemned" (Mark 16:16).

The number of verses in the New Testament specifying Jesus as the only path to God are too numerous to list (1 Timothy 2:5). It's simply not enough to say, "Well, everyone has his or her own path"; "Everyone has his or her own truth"; or, "We all have our beliefs."

He believed He was the only way. He either is, or He isn't. The New Ager must be able to give an intellectually viable answer for why Jesus claimed that faith in Him is the only path to salvation. Why would Jesus claim He is the only way if He really wasn't? If Jesus is right, everyone else is wrong, and He is worthy of our life's worship. If He is wrong, we need a good explanation for why God raised a lying lunatic from the dead.

To reduce the ministry of Jesus to pluralism is historically untenable given what He actually said in the biographies we have of Him, and to deflect to postmodern rhetoric is evasive. Jesus Christ claimed to be the only way to God, and all who followed Him claimed He was the only way to God. When we present the exclusive Messianic claims of Christ to those in the New Age movement, it forces them to consider more thoughtfully the person of Jesus. A Jesus who is one of many ways does not provoke urgency, but a Jesus who is the only possible way out of the judgment of Hell might jolt a person's conscience back into self-honesty.

CONCLUSION

IT IS OUR (JOSH AND STEVE) hope that this book has been eye opening and helpful. The most important question is this: What are you going to do with the information? If you are currently involved with New Age people or practices, you should consider Christianity. If you recognize the massive holes in New Age philosophy and would like to learn more about how you can saved, we will show you how. If you are already a Christian, but you might want to know how to witness to someone in the New Age movement, this will help as well. While accepting Jesus and getting saved is the most important decision a person can make, we have also included information about how to break free from the spiritual bondage and demonic oppression that can take place through occult affiliation.

Occult Objects in Your House Give Demons Legal Ground

A biblical case can be made for the idea that occult items give demons and principalities a foothold into your life. Since our battle is not against flesh and blood, but against "the spiritual forces of evil in the heavenly places" (Ephesians 6:12), we must get used to the idea that this is more than just a formulaic biblical principle. It's a spiritual reality active in the world, especially regarding people who are submitting to these spiritual forces of wickedness and consenting to have them involved in their life through occult practices.

Consider the possibility that principalities have been assigned to these items as overseers of occult practice just like certain demons are involved in child sacrifice (Psalm 106:37) and divination (Acts 16:16). Is it possible that associating with these activities, even in a loose and seemingly innocent sense can cause us to be oppressed by the same kinds of spirits that oppressed people in Scripture?

As we have seen in chapter 1, the Bible equates idol worship with demon worship in Revelation 9:20, Leviticus 17:7, and Deuteronomy 32:17, which states:

> They sacrificed to demons that were no gods, to gods they had never known, to new gods that had come recently, whom your fathers had never dreaded.

Paul likens the presence of idolatry to sitting at the table with demons and drinking the cup of demons (1 Corinthians 10:20–22).

The only way I could be accused of sitting with demons as an idolator is if idolatry puts me into some kind of a relationship with demons. Therefore, it may follow that idols in our homes (which itself is a form of idolatry) might cause us to sit at the table of demons (or at least, pretty close to it). After all, they are statues of foreign gods and goddesses referencing spiritual powers the Bible labels as demons.

If the presence of spiritual idolatry is actually spiritual adultery with demons in the spirit realm (1 Corinthians 10:20–22), is it possible that the presence of spiritual adultery in my house enables me to be influenced by them, at least to a degree? Could it be that the object themselves bridge the natural and the spirit world where demons are seeking to manifest their power through these objects? If this is a possibility, then occult objects may contribute to oppression, distortion, or spiritual health by virtue of the beings the objects refer to in the spirit realm.

Let's be clear: The idols contain no actual power (Jeremiah 10:5). They have no independent will, agency, rationality, personhood, or anything of the sort. But by virtue of what they are associated with in the spirit, they carry a different spiritual oppression and may give demons access into our lives—not because of the object itself, but because of what it's connected to.

When we think about it, occult tools are made for supernatural interaction oriented towards witchcraft, spiritism, sorcery, or contact with beings in the spirit. They aren't just symbols or décor; they are a medium for spiritual forces to infiltrate the natural realm and advance their kingdom on earth. They are the tools of demons to strengthen people in spiritual delusion by acting as a doorway to the demonic realm. As Satan masquerades himself as an angel of light, demons can as well, and by doing so, they create a certain atmosphere through the presence of the object that matches the feeling of the worldview they are trying to deceive people into believing.

There is a reason some objects and books feel inherently evil, pagan, astral and floaty, or Hindu: because demonic powers are tricky and create a spiritual signature that matches the general "feeling" that confirms that worldview. A principality can create the heavy spiritual haziness and false peace that comes through Hindu mysticism or the earthen, organic, enchanting sensation that comes from pagan Earth worship.

It's almost as if occult materials can create certain energetic signatures in the spirit that carry a resonance and feeling that match the lies they are trying to teach you. You are more likely to be influenced by pantheistic teachings if you are in a Hindu temple, because the temple has a general atmosphere that, frankly, most people have the ability to pick up on. A Satanic temple feels different from a Buddhist monastery, which feels different from a psychic fair, which feels different from a Theosophical conference. We can sense the spiritual difference between an altar used for child sacrifice and a bag of apples, or a witchcraft museum and a pail of water. Our spirit tends to pick up on such things.

These objects were considered hallowed and sacred to ancient cultures for a reason, and it's not just because of what they represented. They believed the objects were a literal bridge connecting them to the gods. Is it possible that the presence of occult objects in your life makes you guilty of the sin of idolatry and seats you at or close to the table of demons? Could this result in consequences such as an unsound mind; ambiguous thoughts regarding Jesus; unclear thinking; disorientation; a heaviness or haziness in certain rooms in your house; a spiritual urge to go deeper into the occult; nightmares; spiritual attacks; manifestations in your house; and poor spiritual discernment?

These are not only possible outcomes, but they are likely. An interesting Scripture, Acts 19:19, states that when people who practiced magic arts repented to follow Jesus, they burned all their scrolls worth fifty thousand pieces of silver. Notice that the people got rid of the scrolls permanently. They didn't redistribute them to other sorcerers and they didn't try to recycle them back into the satanic kingdom.

Here is a list of items that should be thrown out or burned:

- **Books.** Occult books, New Age books, Gnostic books, Esoteric books, Transcendentalist books. Hindu books, Buddhist books, yoga books—any that advocate reincarnation, the use of crystals, the activity of aliens, universalism, pantheism, the use of drugs, spiritism, sorcery, magic, mysticism, channeling, "spiritual awakening," a false version of Jesus, Atlantis, Theosophy, etc. I would also include fiction books such as those in the Harry Potter series, as they do nothing except normalize the abominations God punished with the death penalty in the Old Testament. Better forms of entertainment are out there that don't glorify the satanic kingdom.

- **Card decks.** Tarot cards, angel decks, ascended master decks, fairy and elf decks, fortune-telling decks, magic card decks—anything of the sort.
- **Idols and statues.** Buddha statues, Hindu idols, and figurines of dragons, fairies, elves, pagan gods, and Greek mythology figures, etc.
- **Crystals.** Crystal balls, crystal wands, crystal jewelry, crystal stones.
- **Clothing.** Any items featuring pagan symbolism, all-seeing eyes, witchcraft symbolism, esoteric images, etc.
- **Music.** Meditation music, chanting, music with occult, satanic, or esoteric themes. Music that is "conscious" usually mixes political and social awareness with New Age philosophy.

In addition, tapestries, jewelry, posters, movies and DVDs, trinkets, masks, dream catchers, incense, sage, and other such items all play a role in opening up your spirit to being oppressed. In my experience (Steve), these types of materials kept an extra set of blinders on me after I came to Christ. They stunted me from being able to walk in complete spiritual victory because my soul was still constantly associated with occult objects that surrounded me. My house was full of occult paraphernalia right after I came to the Lord, and the result was a demonic stir in my house that was legitimately frightening. That simmered down once I rid my life of everything that belonged to the wrong kingdom; more spiritual peace and mental clarity set in immediately.

Spiritual Warfare and Deliverance

Ultimately, it's all about Jesus. It is important to understand that, without Jesus, you have no power over the enemy. With the authority of Jesus, you can cast out the enemy. If we wish to operate within His authority, we must know we have a responsibility to live in accordance to Jesus' teachings. Rebelling against God only invites the enemy into your life. It's also important to remember that our true enemy is not other people. Our true enemy is spiritual in nature:

> For we do not wrestle against flesh and blood, but against the rulers, against the authorities, against the cosmic powers over this present darkness, against the spiritual forces of evil in the heavenly places. (Ephesians 6:12, ESV)

All of the things listed above are spiritual. People aren't the problem. It is better to think of unbelievers as prisoners of a war they don't even know or believe exists. It is up to us to teach them so they can remove themselves from the bondage of deception with the help of Jesus Christ. Jesus does all the work; all a person has to do is believe on Him trusting that He knows best. The rest of Ephesians 6 gives us a great blueprint for how to live out each day:

> Therefore take up the whole armor of God, that you may be able to withstand in the evil day, and having done all, to stand firm. Stand therefore, having fastened on the belt of truth, and having put on the breastplate of righteousness, and, as shoes for your feet, having put on the readiness given by the gospel of peace. In all circumstances take up the shield of faith, with which you can extinguish all the flaming darts of the evil one; and take the helmet of salvation, and the sword of the Spirit, which is the word of God, praying at all times in the Spirit, with all prayer and supplication. To that end, keep alert with all perseverance, making supplication for all the saints, and also for me, that words may be given to me in opening my mouth boldly to proclaim the mystery of the gospel, for which I am an ambassador in chains, that I may declare it boldly, as I ought to speak. (Ephesians 6:13–20, ESV)

Josh's Personal Experiences of the Supernatural Reality of the Christian Walk

Many times, people enter New Age practices for a spiritual experience without realizing that it is absolutely possible within Christianity to have a vibrant supernatural walk with Jesus. The difference is, in New Age, the individual initiates the activity from the wrong kingdom, resulting in a weaker perverted spiritual experience. In Christianity, it is up to God to determine who will receive a spiritual experience and what it will be. Sometimes they can be as extravagant as a dream, vision, word of knowledge, or powerful encounter with the presence of Jesus, but most often they are not as overt yet incredibly helpful. Sometimes, for example, it will simply be a pull or alarm in our spirit urging us to go in one direction versus the other when making a decision in our lives

There have been two times in my life when I thought I had a genuine visionary and auditory supernatural experience after rededicating my life to Jesus. I will share one of them here. Before describing this experience, I must make clear that this is completely subjective. I can't prove to anyone that it is true, nor do I have any interest in doing so. People have said in the past that this could have just been a dream or something else, and I am open to that possibility. I would never want to use this or any other experiences to create some kind of new doctrine. This was very personal, and was really just meant for me. The only thing readers should take away from this account is that I personally believe these types of experiences from God are possible. No one should try to initiate this type of experience or create some new interpretation or belief about any Bible passages because of what I am sharing here.

That said, once, shortly after I rededicated myself to Christ, I was feeling a lot of doubt about my salvation. For some reason, I was worried that if I died, I would go to Hell. I didn't have a logical reason for feeling this way, yet the sensation persisted. I prayed to God about my lack of faith. I asked Him for a sign that I was actually saved while apologizing that I didn't have the faith to believe it.

Later that night, I was lying in bed reading a book, completely awake, the lights on, when I suddenly because to hear a voice. It wasn't external; it seemed to be coming from inside. The voice started very quietly and slowly began to get louder. I realized the voice was singing. I was hearing a single voice singing from within me that I wasn't exactly hearing with my physical ears. Needless to say, this is difficult to explain, but it wasn't alarming at the time it occurred. It lasted a few moments, then the voice faded away.

At the time, I was just beginning to learn how to use Strong's Concordance. I had heard of angels singing, but what I heard was not a choir of angels. I had never heard of Jesus or God singing, but I used the concordance to see if any Bible verses described such a thing. I found one:

The Lord thy God in the midst of thee is mighty; he will save, he will rejoice over thee with joy; he will rest in his love, he will joy over thee with singing. (Zephaniah 3:17, KJV)

When I read this, I had no idea what the verse was originally about— nor had I ever even heard of the Book of Zephaniah. However, to me, the personal message was clear: I had been worried about my salvation, and this verse said "He will save." I had heard God's voice inside of me, and this verse said "God in the midst of thee is mighty." My fear of not being saved had stemmed from my feelings about all the bad things I had done against God, yet this verse said "He will rejoice with joy and joy over thee with singing." My fears were laid to rest and I knew God had answered my prayer.

That said, clearly, that wasn't anything close to the verse's original meaning. This is why I remain cautious in saying that I do not want to contribute to a doctrine that says any Bible verse can mean whatever the person reading it wants it to mean. I believe that if this was truly from God and not any other explanation, I was extremely young in my faith and this is exactly the type of thing that would have spoken to me and made sense. Similar to how a parent might teach a child using a metaphor to explain a higher truth in a way they can understand, I believe God was speaking to me in a way I would understand at that time. God will not give us new doctrinal revelation, but He will sometimes shine a new light on old revelation for us personally. The point was not to tell me what Zephaniah 3:17 meant literally, but to use it in a supernatural experience to assure me I did not need to worry about my salvation.

Steve's Supernatural Reality of Walking with Jesus

I can say with full integrity that being in relationship with Jesus has been the most supernatural and transcendental experience of all the years I was in the New Age movement. During a period of my life when I was studying and practicing astral projection, I felt so close to the astral realm in my waking life that I felt as though my spirit was actually somewhere else as my body and soul remained in the astral.

While I am not having out-of-body experiences like I used to (but I have experienced what I could consider a dream from God, visions and words of knowledge), there are times when I feel closer to Heaven than I do to Earth because of how built up my spirit-man is in the presence of God. The Spirit fills us more and more as we surrender more of ourselves to the Lord and sow into the spirit through worship, prayer, obedience, and fasting. God places no cap on how intimate we can be with Jesus. If we want to get so close to Him that our life becomes so supernaturally infused with the Spirit of God that we don't recognize anything around us, we can decide to pray two hours a day as we fast for a week and begin to walk in those deeper levels of intimacy.

My exploration of Jesus all started when my sin started catching up with me as I was in a season of writing articles for the largest New Age website in the world. I also had my own successful website that was getting hundreds of thousands of views a day and making me tens of thousands of dollars a month. I was fully convinced of my worldview at the time. I was successful by the world's standards—especially for being in my early 20s, but my sin and brokenness were out of control. I was being exposed in my relationships and in my field of work, and every- thing was hitting me in the face at once. I didn't even know the extent to which I was broken, but looking back, it was greater than I realized at the time. I was too depraved, too psychologically enslaved, too beat up from my past, and too infected by my sin.

This is when I decided to stop suppressing my spiritual intuitions about Jesus and give Him a chance by actually seeking Him out. So what did I do? Not much. I said a prayer (with my Christian parents), I went to a church service that night, and then went back to posting New Age-esque articles and living in sin. I had some slightly new orientations towards sin and spiritual things, but nothing changed. I simply wanted to give Jesus more of a chance than I previously had, since blocking Him out had clearly done me no good.

This time, I was open and not closed. I wasn't going to make excuses for my apostasy or explain away Jesus as something that He never claimed to be. I wasn't going to be a coward and hide from the God I knew existed deep down, or keep pushing off the inevitable. I was going to be open to Jesus however He is and whomever He is— the Jesus who revealed Himself in the New Testament.

A few weeks later, I had to come to terms with the people I had hurt, so I decided to fall on my face before Him, just weeping to Him, hoping He would hear me and forgive me. I was not only hurt, but completely twisted and distorted in my heart and thinking. My life was in ruins, as were my psychology and emotions.

I was telling God I was sorry, I was giving in, I needed Him, I needed a sign from Him, and that I was finished being the lord of my own life. This was the first time I had ever really repented and pushed into Him. I was just done with being the god of my own life, and I wanted Him as He truly was

When I did this, the spiritual atmosphere started to change. It wasn't a minor change, or a change of emotion, but a change in the spirit around me. Things were simply not the same around me in the spirit. His presence started to fill the atmosphere and the horizon, and the air became thick and heavy with His Spirit and glory. It was a personal, divine, authoritative presence engulfing me and permeating the atmosphere all around me. I could not stand up. I tried and I couldn't. I couldn't do anything except break more taking in the full weight of who He is. I knew it was Jesus, but didn't know He could be known this way. The Jesus of Scripture. The Jesus whom I had suppressed in unrighteousness. I was interacting with His Spirit, and it was absolutely undeniable.

My spirit and mind were coming into alignment with the reality of who He is—and let me just say this: When we come into his presence, all doubts fade away. It's done. Whatever you think you knew goes out the window. You know the truth and it's right in front of you. You know He is Lord of everything, especially of you. You know everything in creation is under His feet. You know He is sovereign.

You know He loves you and has deep concern for you. But for me, what stuck out was how I knew exactly where I stood in relation to Jesus, and where He stood in relation to the world.

He was King; I was a sinner. The universe was subject to Him. I knew that it was this way. I was overwhelmed with the feeling that He was God over me and everything around me. Jesus is Lord. It is just that simple. Jesus is Lord.

He stood over everything in creation, and everything in creation seemed to pay Him honor in that moment. The wind through the leaves and the sounds of the crickets seemed to point to Him and glorify Him, which really did a number on me, because I was able to see how nature seemed to respond to His presence. This is why I tell people I encountered Jesus, because I did. It may sound strange or unbelievable, but this is the best way I can describe what happened. I was confronted with the Lord, as hundreds of millions had been before me. He revealed Himself to me, and has tangibly lived inside me ever since. He has not left me since that day.

His Spirit inside me caused me to forsake all my old beliefs and practices, quit my job, and sell my mansion to live in my parents' basement for the next two and a half years in ministry. His Spirit inside me convinced me that the Bible was the Word of God when I made a living denying all of its fundamental teachings. I didn't believe the Bible was divinely inspired until the Spirit of God first filled me and bore witness to me that it was.

I remember lying in bed reflecting on the presence I felt inside me shortly after my conversion experience. I could sense a personal presence within and upon me where there once had been nothing, and it was self-verifying and self-authenticating. I remember thinking, "How does nobody in the New Age movement know this is possible? I have to tell them about this!" Striking to me was the supernatural component to a Christian's walk. The Creator of Heaven and Earth is personal and comes to live inside us in a way that can be tangibly known and experienced. I couldn't believe I had missed it this whole time.

I legitimately feel God inside my spirit every single day so tangibly and so vividly that I would give my life for it, and will if I ever have the privilege of doing so. The Holy Spirit has interacted with me powerfully so many times beyond what I am able to put into words, but even when I am not pressing in, I still feel Him with me. It's about truth, not feelings, but when we are in the truth we have encounters with the living God. The point is, God has made every spiritual experience available to us in Christ Jesus, and as we draw near to Him, He draws near to us. Jesus is alive. The Spirit He puts inside of us is alive—and then our spirituality becomes supernaturally led by the One who made us. It's supernatural relationship with a living, divine person, and it's what every person was made for.

How To Be Saved

When God created Adam and Eve as the first people in the Garden of Eden, they lived in obedience to God's commandments and were without fault—until, that is, they transgressed His command by eating from the tree they were told not to eat from. They believed Satan's lie that special knowledge that came from eating the fruit of the tree would elevate them to the level of the gods. When they ate from the tree, they were punished by God in the form of guilt, spiritual death, and curses upon their lives. They were severed from their relationship to God, and later died physically as a result of the curse that sin had brought. Since they were our representatives before God, we have inherited the consequences of their sin and were born in fallen bodies in a fallen world.

Just like Adam and Eve, we are sinners who transgress the law of God. Some of the most common examples of sins we commit include sexual immorality, cheating, abusing and mistreating other people, vanity, envy, gossiping, idolatry, drug abuse, covetousness, witchcraft, divination, etc. When we do things we shouldn't do, we sin. When we fail to do the things we should do, we sin.

But we can also sin in the privacy of our own thoughts. God sees everything, and His moral standard extends to our thoughts, fantasies, and attitudes:

> You have heard that it was said to those of old, "You shall not murder; and whoever murders will be liable to judgment." But I say to you that everyone who is angry with his brother will be liable to judgment. (Matthew 5:21–22)

> You have heard that it was said, "You shall not commit adultery." But I say to you that everyone who looks at a woman with lustful intent has already committed adultery with her in his heart. (Matthew 5:27–28)

> None is righteous, no, not one; no one understands; no one seeks for God. All have turned aside; together they have become worthless; no one does good, not even one. Their throat is an open grave; they use their tongues to deceive. The venom of asps is under their lips. Their mouth is full of curses and bitterness. Their feet are swift to shed blood; in their paths are ruin and

misery, and the way of peace they have not known. There is no fear of God before their eyes. for all have sinned and fall short of the glory of God. (Romans 3:10–18, 23)

The Bible says that in our sinful condition, we are:

...following the course of this world, following the prince of the power of the air, the spirit that is now at work in the sons of disobedience—among whom we all once lived in the passions of our flesh, carrying out the desires of the body and the mind. (Ephesians 2:2–3)

We live in sin like a fish lives in water. Our sin runs right down to the core of our hearts. We are not bad people with good hearts; we are bad people with bad hearts. We are not as bad as we can be, but let's face it, we royally mess up all the time. It is not as though sin is a cosmetic problem wherein some surface stains need to be cleaned up a little bit with *chakra* cleansing or self-work. Our hearts themselves are hardened, depraved, and infected with sin.

- "For out of the heart come evil thoughts, murder, adultery, sexual immorality, theft, false testimony, and slander" (Matthew 15:19).
- "The heart is deceitful above all things, and desperately sick; who can understand it?" (Jeremiah 17:9).
- "The hearts of the children of man are full of evil, and madness is in their hearts while they live" (Ecclesiastes 9:3).

Our heart itself is the fountainhead of all the sin we commit. We don't need behavior modification, we need a supernatural heart transplant. We need to be cured and healed from the sickness that sin has brought upon us when it entered into the world through Adam, because this sin has separated us from God:

- "The face of the LORD is against those who do evil" (Psalm 34:16).
- "But your iniquities have made a separation between you and your God, And your sins have hidden His face from you so that He does not hear" (Isaiah 59:2).
- We are "alienated (from God) and hostile in mind" (Colossians 1:21).
- We are "dead in the trespasses and sins" (Ephesians 2:1, 5).
- We are "alienated from the commonwealth of Israel and strangers to the covenants of promise, having no hope and without God in the world" (Ephesians 2:12–13).

And as liars, thieves, blasphemers, idolaters, adulterers, and murderers at heart, we will be found guilty of breaking God's Law. As diviners, witches, mediums, and sorcerers, we have committed cosmic treason against the Creator of Heaven and Earth. We have chosen sin over God, and as lawbreakers we will be sentenced to eternal Hell apart from the presence of all things that are good:

- "But as for the cowardly, the faithless, the detestable, as for murderers, the sexually immoral, sorcerers, idolaters, and all liars, their portion will be in the lake that burns with fire and sulfur, which is the second death" (Revelation 21:8).
- "They will suffer the punishment of eternal destruction, away from the presence of the Lord and from the glory of his might" (2 Thessalonians 1:9).

Jesus, however, was sent into the world to bear the sins you and I committed so that God's judgment toward us could be transferred to Jesus. Jesus existed eternally in Heaven from the very beginning alongside the Father, sharing the full divine nature and being of God. All of the attributes that God the Father has, Jesus has. He left Heaven and took on a human nature being conceived of the Holy Spirit in the virgin

Mary, yet retained the divine nature He had from eternity. Jesus was therefore truly man and truly God in His identity, and when He walked this earth, He kept all 613 commandments of the Old Testament that God had commanded mankind to follow. He lived a perfect life to fulfill the righteous requirements of the Law that we fail to abide by. He was then crucified on a cross as our representative and substitute, paying the price for the sins you and I have committed.

Jesus Christ willfully laid down His life for His sheep out of perfect love for us, so that we can be pardoned of our sins against God. Your moral debt was passed off on to the head of Jesus, and the Father inflicted in Christ the spiritual death and suffering that would have been ours if we had gone to Hell:

> Surely he has borne our griefs and carried our sorrows; yet we esteemed him stricken, smitten by God, and afflicted. But he was pierced for our transgressions; he was crushed for our iniquities; upon him was the chastisement that brought us peace, and with his wounds we are healed. All we like sheep have gone astray; we have turned—every one—to his own way; and the Lord has laid on him the iniquity of us all. He was oppressed, and he was afflicted, yet he opened not his mouth; like a lamb that is led to the slaughter, and like a sheep that before its shearers is silent, so he opened not his mouth. By oppression and judgment he was taken away; and as for his generation, who considered that he was cut off out of the land of the living, stricken for the transgression of my people? And they made his grave with the wicked and with a rich man in his death, although he had done no violence, and there was no deceit in his mouth. Yet it was the will of the Lord to crush him; he has put him to grief; when his soul makes an offering for guilt, he shall see his offspring; he shall prolong his days; the will of the Lord shall prosper in his hand. Out of the anguish of his soul he shall see and be satisfied; by his

knowledge shall the righteous one, my servant, make many to be accounted righteous, and he shall bear their iniquities. Therefore I will divide him a portion with the many, and he shall divide the spoil with the strong, because he poured out his soul to death and was numbered with the transgressors; yet he bore the sin of many, and makes intercession for the transgressors. (Isaiah 53:4–12)

He himself bore our sins in his body on the tree, that we might die to sin and live to righteousness. By his wounds you have been healed. (Peter 2:24)

He is the propitiation for our sins, and not for ours only but also for the sins of the whole world. (1 John 2:2)

In this is love, not that we have loved God but that he loved us and sent his Son to be the propitiation for our sins. (1 John 4:10)

If you are reading this right now and don't know Jesus Christ as your Lord and Savior, we love you enough to say that you are still under the weight of your sin, guilty before God. If you die in your sin, you will be held accountable for your moral crimes by a holy God, and you will not enjoy eternal fellowship with Him. God is loving, but He is also just and will not be blink at sin.

So how do we go from being isolated from God because of sin to having the atoning death and resurrection of Jesus applied? If Jesus died to save us, how do we become saved? We are saved by believing on the Lord Jesus Christ with a sorry, repentant faith that has turned from sin to the cross. We contribute nothing to our own salvation.

Contrary to the New Age mentality of works-based ascension, we don't have to embody Christ Consciousness in order to have relationship with God. We don't need to have 51 percent good karma to graduate to the next spiritual level. And we certainly don't have to be cleaned up spiritually before Jesus will save us. We come as we are with a sorry, repentant heart and a desire to change, and we put our faith fully in Christ for our salvation. The lie of the New Age movement is that salvation is liberation from suffering and is accomplished through self-realization. The reality is that salvation is freedom from the penalty and power of sin through faith in Jesus who accomplished it all for us.

- "For God so loved the world, that he gave his only Son, that whoever believes in him should not perish but have eternal life" (John 3:16).
- "For this is the will of my Father, that everyone who looks on the Son and believes in him should have eternal life, and I will raise him up on the last day" (John 6:40).
- "Then he brought them out and said, 'Sirs, what must I do to be saved?' And they said, 'Believe in the Lord Jesus, and you will be saved, you and your household'" (Acts 16:30–31).

We have to be sincerely sorry over our sin, sincerely turned away from the direction of that sin to Jesus, and then sincerely believe on Jesus as our Savior. We should not merely be aware of the gospel, not merely agree with the facts about the gospel, and not merely combine this awareness with a desire to be better people. We turn toward Jesus and trust Him alone. Our own works don't save us; Jesus saves us through faith:

- "He saved us, not because of works done by us in righteousness, but according to his own mercy, by the washing of regeneration and renewal of the Holy Spirit" (Titus 3:5).
- "...who saved us and called us to a holy calling, not because of our works but because of his own purpose and grace, which he gave us in Christ Jesus before the ages began" (2 Timothy 1:9).

We are saved by a repentant faith that means it. Every other religion in the world tells us we can be made right with God by balancing the scales, by trying earn God's approval with good works. But according to the gospel, all we need to do to be made right with God is believe on the Lord Jesus Christ. This is why the Bible calls salvation a free gift over and over:

- "...justified by his grace as a gift, through the redemption that is in Christ Jesus, whom God put forward as a propitiation by his blood, to be received by faith" (Romans 3:24–25).
- "For the wages of sin is death, but the free gift of God is eternal life in Christ Jesus our Lord"—(Romans 6:23).

Salvation is God's merciful gift from His Fatherly love. It's a gift of grace. If it was of works, it wouldn't be a gift. There is no grace available in New Age theology. There is a never-ending cycle of Samsara (Sanskrit word that means "wandering" or "world," signifying the cycle of death and rebirth to which life in the material world is bound), keeping us in a state of lesson-learning and karmic alleviation into future lives.

Jesus tells us that salvation cannot be merited, earned, or achieved; it can only be received by faith. We change our minds about our sin and the person and work of Jesus, we turn in our hearts from wanting to follow after our sin, we look toward Jesus with a sincere desire to be forgiven, and we trust in Him. When we do so, we are saved, and some amazing things take place.

Forgiveness

Our sins are removed from us. Our record of sin is washed clean by the blood of Jesus (1 John 1:7), and we are totally forgiven by God (Ephesians 1:7; Colossians 1:14). He takes our sin, removes it from our account, and cleanses us from the stain it has left on our souls.

- "The next day he saw Jesus coming toward him, and said, 'Behold, the Lamb of God, who takes away the sin of the world!'" (John 1:29)
- "Repent therefore, and turn back, that your sins may be blotted out" (Acts 3:19).
- "As far as the east is from the west, so far does he remove our transgressions from us" (Psalm 103:12).
- "Though your sins are like scarlet, they shall be as white as snow; though they are red like crimson, they shall become like wool" (Isaiah 1:18).
- "The blood of Jesus his Son cleanses us from all sin" (1 John 1:7).
- "For if the blood of goats and bulls, and the sprinkling of defiled persons with the ashes of a heifer, sanctify for the purification of the flesh, how much more will the blood of Christ, who through the eternal Spirit offered himself without blemish to God, purify our conscience from dead works to serve the living God"—(Hebrews 9:13–14).

Our record of sins has been wiped clean, our conscience has been wiped clean, and He remembers our sins no more. We are no longer held liable and culpable for the sins we have committed because Christ took those sins for us. We don't have to pay it off in the next life. We don't have to pay for in through suffering during a life review. They have been imputed to Christ and done away with in His death and resurrection, so that when God sees us, He no longer sees us in our sin because our sin was extinguished in Christ. We are forgiven our debt fully and completely.

Justification

When we believe on the Lord, we become justified. To be justified means to be declared righteous before the throne of God. This is a legal term that has to do with where we now stand in God's heavenly courtroom. It has to do with a change of positioning, relationship, and status between us and the Law of God. When we are justified, we are pronounced to be just before God in a legal and judicial sense. We don't become righteous in and of ourselves when we have faith, but we are counted as ones who keep the whole law blamelessly. Our status before God changes from lawbreaker to law-keeper. This is the most important aspect of salvation—that we, as unrighteous sinners, are pronounced "just" by faith in Jesus Christ.

God sent Jesus as our representative and substitute "in order that the righteous requirement of the law might be fulfilled in us.... For Christ is the end of the law for righteousness to everyone who believes" (Romans 8:4, 10:4). The grounds of our justification is Jesus' obedience, not our own obedience, spiritual development, degree of enlightenment, or special knowledge.

So when we believe on Him, a great exchange takes place. Christ takes our sin, and in exchange He gives us His own righteousness. The righteous standard of the Law is fulfilled in those who believe on Jesus because God counts those who have faith with the very righteousness of Jesus. Everything the Law requires of us is fulfilled in us through faith. Just like God laid our sins upon Jesus, He now lays the righteousness of Jesus upon us. Just like Jesus was counted among the transgressors (Isaiah 53:12), we are counted to be righteous (Isaiah 53:11). Our sins get applied to Jesus, who was judged as if He were us, and His righteousness gets applied to us as if we had lived the life of Christ.

This idea of transference of life-record is the message New Agers need right now. They don't need all these life-cycles, suffering, and methods of karmic alleviation through enlightenment. They need the righteousness of someone else. When we believe on Jesus, we are cloaked in the robe of His righteousness, so that we have all the righteousness necessary to be able to stand before God. We are pardoned of the liability of our sins and declared legally righteous before His throne because God has imputed the righteousness of Jesus to our account:

- "...and be found in him, not having a righteousness of my own that comes from the law, but that which comes through faith in Christ, the righteousness from God that depends on faith" (Philippians 3:9).
- "For our sake he made him to be sin who knew no sin, so that in him we might become the righteousness of God" (2 Corinthians 5:21).
- "Out of the anguish of his soul he shall see and be satisfied; by his knowledge shall the righteous one, my servant, make many to be accounted righteous" (Isaiah 53:11).
- "For in it the righteousness of God is revealed from faith for faith, as it is written, 'The righteous shall live by faith'" (Romans 1:17).
- "Therefore, as one trespass led to condemnation for all men, so one act of righteousness leads to justification and life for all men. For as by the one man's disobedience the many were made sinners, so by the one man's obedience the many will be made righteous"—(Romans 5:19).

Christ, as our representative, has made all who believe in Him to be counted righteousness before the judgment seat of God. Notice that these verses about the righteousness from God that is not our own say the righteousness is accounted to us by faith. This is because the righteousness of Jesus becomes legally ascribed to us, so that we stand before God as if we have the life-record of Jesus. Romans 3:22 talks about "the righteousness of God through faith in Jesus Christ for all who believe."

Yet we know that a person is not justified by works of the law but through faith in Jesus Christ, so we also have believed in Christ Jesus, in order to be justified by faith in Christ and not by works of the law, because by works of the law no one will be justified. (Galatians 2:16)

"Abraham believed God, and it was counted to him as righteousness." The wages to the one who works are not counted as a gift but as his due. And to the one who does not work but believes in Him who justifies the ungodly, his faith is counted as righteousness, just as David also speaks of the blessing of the one to whom God counts righteousness apart from works:

> Blessed are those whose lawless deeds are forgiven, and whose sins are covered; blessed is the man against whom the Lord will not count his sin...For we say that faith was counted to Abraham as righteousness. (Romans 4:3–8, 9)

> What shall we say, then? That Gentiles who did not pursue righteousness have attained it, that is, a righteousness that is by faith; but that Israel who pursued a law that would lead to righteousness did not succeed in reaching that law. Why? Because they did not pursue it by faith, but as if it were based on works.... For, being ignorant of the righteousness of God, and seeking to establish their own, they did not submit to God's righteousness. For Christ is the end of the law for righteousness to everyone who believes. (Romans 9:30–32, 10:3–4)

When we believe on Jesus, we are counted to be not only innocent as if we have never done anything wrong, but perfectly righteous as if we had done everything right. We are granted all the perks of being enlightened (such as eternal life in Heaven, spiritual life, refreshment, rebirth, etc.) while not having done anything to earn this result. He wore our sin; we now wear His righteousness. This righteousness cannot be added to or taken away from. It does not come with holes in it waiting to be filled in with our own efforts. It is complete and sufficient for salvation.

All the righteousness we need to enter into Heaven is supplied to us through faith alone in Jesus Christ alone, who cloaks us in His own righteousness the moment we repent and put our trust in Him. God did this "so that he might be just and the justifier of the one who has faith in Jesus" (Romans 3:26).

We can enter Heaven on the basis of Christ's righteousness and approach the throne of God and be judged as if we had lived the perfect life of Christ.

Regeneration

When we believe on the Lord, God does a supernatural work inside us, resurrecting us from spiritual death to spiritual life. We become supernaturally born again by the Spirit of God, meaning a new nature is birthed in us, causing us to walk in the newness of life. A heart once calloused and hardened because of sin is now refreshed with the resurrection life of Jesus. This is the closest analogy to the New Age idea of higher consciousness and enlightenment, only we are given this spiritual transformation as a gift from the Spirit of God.

> I will sprinkle clean water on you, and you shall be clean from all your uncleannesses, and from all your idols I will cleanse you. And I will give you a new heart, and a new spirit I will put within you. And I will remove the heart of stone from your flesh and give you a heart of flesh. And I will put my Spirit within you, and cause you to walk in my statutes and be careful to obey my rules. (Ezekiel 36:25–27)

> Blessed be the God and Father of our Lord Jesus Christ! According to his great mercy, he has caused us to be born again to a living hope through the resurrection of Jesus Christ from the dead. (1 Peter 1:3)

Truly, truly, I say to you, unless one is born again he cannot see the kingdom of God.... That which is born of the flesh is flesh, and that which is born of the Spirit is spirit. (John 3:3, 6)

And you, who were dead in your trespasses and the uncircumcision of your flesh, God made alive together with him, having forgiven us all our trespasses. (Colossians 2:13)

Even when we were dead in our trespasses, made us alive together with Christ—by grace you have been saved. (Ephesians 2:5)

Therefore, if anyone is in Christ, he is a new creation. The old has passed away; behold, the new has come. (2 Corinthians 5:17)

Whoever believes in me, as the Scripture has said, "Out of his heart will flow rivers of living water." (John 7:38)

He supernaturally changes from the inside out, curing us of our infected hearts, refreshing our minds, and giving us a new spiritual nature that is born by the Spirit of God. And remember, all of this spiritual benefit has already been paid for by the blood and body of Jesus on your behalf. Special knowledge, self-awareness, and the alteration of human consciousness cannot attain or earn the supernatural transformation God wishes to give to all people. It's imparted to us through a repentant faith.

Reconciliation

As a result of our justification, we are then brought into communion with God as our Heavenly Father. We are reconciled with God, and now have access to fellowship with Him. Though we were once separated by our sin, He walks alongside us as a Father. He receives us as His children and adopts us into His Kingdom as sons and daughters, restoring us to proper relationship with Him:

> For in him all the fullness of God was pleased to dwell, and through him to reconcile to himself all things, whether on earth or in heaven, making peace by the blood of his cross. And you, who once were alienated and hostile in mind, doing evil deeds, he has now reconciled in his body of flesh by his death, in order to present you holy and blameless and above reproach before him. (Colossians 1:19–22)

> For you did not receive the spirit of slavery to fall back into fear, but you have received the Spirit of adoption as sons, by whom we cry, "Abba! Father!" (Romans 8:15)

> But to all who did receive him, who believed in his name, he gave the right to become children of God. (John 1:12)

> "I will be a father to you, and you shall be sons and daughters to me, says the Lord Almighty." (2 Corinthians 6:18)

> For in Christ Jesus you are all sons of God, through faith. (Galatians 3:26)

God not only justifies us and looks at us now as if we were the righteousness of His Son, He treats us as if we were the righteousness of His Son by counting us as one of His children. Once we were enemies of God, now we are walking in relationship with Him. We were once darkness, and now we are light. We were once strangers of God, we are now fellow heirs with Christ. We have passed from condemnation into reconciliation with God by faith in Jesus. The vibrant spiritual life every looks for in the New Age is now possible by a restored relationship between us and the Father.

Sanctification

He then sanctifies through the indwelling of the Holy Spirit, meaning that we are led through a gradual process of being set apart from our sin and conformed to the image of Jesus. In one sense, we are sanctified the minute we believe on Jesus because we have been forgiven and regenerated, set apart from the consequences of our sin and given a new heart. But in addition to this, God begins to supernaturally change us by infusing us with righteousness day by day, renewing our minds, maturing us in the faith, and training us how to renounce ungodliness.

If the Spirit of him who raised Jesus from the dead dwells in you, he who raised Christ Jesus from the dead will also give life to your mortal bodies through his Spirit who dwells in you. (Romans 8:11)

...and have put on the new self, which is being renewed in knowledge after the image of its creator. (Colossians 3:10)

For by a single offering he has perfected for all time those who are being sanctified. (Hebrews 10:14)

Now may the God of peace who brought again from the dead our Lord Jesus, the great shepherd of the sheep, by the blood of the eternal covenant, equip you with everything good that you may do his will, working in us that which is pleasing in his sight, through Jesus Christ. (Hebrews 13:20–21)

So we do not lose heart. Though our outer self is wasting away, our inner self is being renewed day by day. (2 Corinthians 4:16)

God starts a work in you which He will continue to complete, transforming you as a person and causing you to grow in love and obedience toward Him. We also begin to be healed from our past traumas and wrongs by the Spirit of God, as the Father now treats us as His children. And as any good Father, God longs for us to be made whole and well.

> Lest they should see with their eyes and hear with their ears and understand with their heart and turn, and I would heal them. (Matthew 13:15)

> The thief comes only to steal and kill and destroy. I came that they may have life and have it abundantly. (John 10:10–11)

> But for you who fear my name, the sun of righteousness shall rise with healing in its wings. You shall go out leaping like calves from the stall. (Malachi 4:2)

And one day after this life is over, we will receive glorified bodies and live on into eternity. There will be no more suffering, pain, disease, or sin. We will share in the inheritance of Christ, and we will rule and reign with Him forever in the Kingdom of God wherein righteousness dwells.

> But, as it is written, "What no eye has seen, nor ear heard, nor the heart of man imagined, what God has prepared for those who love him." (1 Corinthians 2:9)

The Gospel is not just about what God has saved us from, it's also about what God has saved us for. It's not just that we can be pardoned from our sin, it's that we can be reconciled with God, restored as people, and pass over into His Kingdom. But you must believe on the Lord. You must put your faith in Christ, or else the atonement will not be applied to you, and you will stand before God under the weight of your sin. Remember, you cannot be saved from your sins by being a good person, by meditating, by using psychedelics, by special knowledge, by self-awareness, by good works, by going to church, by being under the umbrella of a Christian household, or by having been baptized when you were a child. Nothing any New Age guru under the sun can offer you can bring you back to the God who made you. You, personally, must repent and believe on Jesus as your Lord and Savior; otherwise you will die in your sins:

> I told you that you would die in your sins, for unless you believe that I am he you will die in your sins. (John 8:24)

> Whoever believes in him is not condemned, but whoever does not believe is condemned already, because he has not believed in the name of the only Son of God. (John 3:18)

> But as for the cowardly, the faithless, the detestable, as for murderers, the sexually immoral, sorcerers, idolaters, and all liars, their portion will be in the lake that burns with fire and sulfur. (Revelation 21:8)

Be reconciled to God today. If you hear His voice, do not harden your heart. God loves you and has more for you in store than the never-ending pursuit of self-improvement and "enlightenment" can provide. God has more for you than living in guilt, shame, and condemnation. God has more for you than brokenness and addiction. God certainly has more for you than the empty promises of ascension and liberation offered to you by teachers in the New Age movement.

Prayer of Salvation

For those who do not know the Lord yet, I would like to lead you right now in a prayer of salvation that you can repeat out loud with me wherever you are. But remember this: You are not saved by reciting a prayer. You are saved by being sincerely sorry of your sin, sincerely changing your direction from sin to Jesus, and sincerely trusting on the Lord for your salvation.

Fix your heart upon the Lord right now, and recite this from your own heart:

Jesus, I recognize that I am a sinner in need of salvation. I recognize that I am deserving of God's judgment. Please have mercy on me. Forgive me of the sins I have committed. I believe that you died and rose for my sins so that I could be saved. I believe that you took my place on the cross. I put my trust in you and you alone for my salvation. I put my faith in you and declare you to be Lord and Savior of my life. I turn from all beliefs and practices that stand opposed to you and want to walk with you now. Wash me clean, give me a new heart, and give me power over the sin that remains in my life. I ask all of this in your name, Jesus. Amen.

If you prayed that just now with a repentant, believing heart, you have passed from death to life and are now a child of God in Christ Jesus. The atonement has been applied to you. No more endlessly trying to evolve through self-work. No more striving toward the peak of an infinitely tall mountain. No more doubt about your value, your purpose, or your eternal destiny. You have been reconciled with God. You have been made a new creation and have taken your first step through the gates of eternal life. You are loved, you have infinite value to God, and He wants to lead you into complete and total spiritual victory as you follow His Son.

And you were dead in the trespasses and sins in which you once walked, following the course of this world, following the prince of the power of the air, the spirit that is now at work in the sons of disobedience—among whom we all once lived in the passions of our flesh, carrying out the desires of the body and the mind, and were by nature children of wrath, like the rest of mankind.

But God, being rich in mercy, because of the great love with which he loved us, even when we were dead in our trespasses, made us alive together with Christ—by grace you have been saved—and raised us up with him and seated us with him in the heavenly places in Christ Jesus, so that in the coming ages he might show the immeasurable riches of his grace in kindness toward us in Christ Jesus. For by grace you have been saved through faith. And this is not your own doing; it is the gift of God, not a result of works, so that no one may boast. For we are his workmanship, created in Christ Jesus for good works, which God prepared beforehand, that we should walk in them. (Ephesians 2:1–10)

About the Authors

Josh Peck and Steven Bancarz, who years ago were both heavily involved in New Age practices, teachings, and beliefs, left the New Age to pursue Jesus Christ and Christianity. Since that time, they have both worked within their own ministries to expose the fallacies of the modern New Age movement. Bancarz and Peck met in April of 2016, shortly after Bancarz released his first testimony video about leaving the New Age for Jesus (receiving over half a million views) and also shortly after Peck began working in full-time ministry at SkyWatchTV. Since that time, Josh Peck has been submitting articles for Steven Bancarz's popular website, Reasons For Jesus (ReasonsForJesus.com). This book is the first writing and authoring collaboration between Peck and Bancarz.

NOTES

1. Research Release in Faith & Christianity, March 27, 2018. Accessed at: https://www.barna.com/research/half-churchgoers-not-heard-great-commission/.
2. "Teachings & Blogs." Ascended Masters and The Hearts Center Community, www.heartscenter.org/TeachingsBlogs/AscendedMasters/MessagesfromJesus/tabid/1121/Default.aspx#.Ws5LSS-ZOL8.
3. Liu, Joseph. "Many Americans Mix Multiple Faiths." Pew Research Center's Religion & Public Life Project. December 08, 2009. Accessed January 19, 2018. http://www.pewforum.org/2009/12/09/many-americans-mix-multiple-faiths.
4. Lipka, Michael, and Claire Gecewicz. "More Americans now say they're spiritual but not religious." Pew Research Center. September 06, 2017. Accessed January 19, 2018. http://www.pewresearch.org/fact-tank/2017/09/06/more-americans-now-say-theyre-spiritual-but-not-religious/.
5. Masci, David, and Conrad Hackett. "Meditation is common across many religious groups in the U.S." Pew Research Center. January 02, 2018. Accessed January 19, 2018. http://www.pewresearch.org/fact-tank/2018/01/02/meditation-is-common-across-many-religious-groups-in-the-u-s/.
6. "Alternative Healthcare Providers in the US: Market Research Report." Alternative Healthcare Providers in the US Market Research | IBISWorld. Accessed January 19, 2018. https://www.ibisworld.com/industry-trends/market-research-reports/healthcare-social-assistance/ambulatory-health-care-services/alternative-healthcare-providers.html.
7. "2016 Yoga In America Study." Yoga Alliance. January 2016. Accessed January 19, 2018. https://www.yogaalliance.org/

Portals/0/2016%20Yoga%20in%20America%20Study%20
RESULTS.pdf.
8. "Psychic Services in the US: Market Research Report." Psychic
Services in the US Market Research | IBISWorld. Accessed January
21, 2018. https://www.ibisworld.com/industry-trends/specialized-
market-research-reports/consumer-goods-services/personal/psychic-
services.html.
9. "Celestine Prophecy Author Unveils a Twelfth Insight: An Interview
with James Redfield." BellaSpark. Accessed January 19, 2018. http://
bellaspark.com/articles/entry/celestine-prophecy-author-unveils-a-
twelfth-insight-an-interview-with-james/.
10. "Rhonda Byrne Biography | The Secret — Official Website." The
Official Website of The Secret. Accessed January 19, 2018. https://
www.thesecret.tv/about/rhonda-byrnes-biography/.
11. "List of best-selling books." Wikipedia. January 14, 2018.
Accessed January 19, 2018. https://en.wikipedia.org/wiki/
List_of_best-selling_books.
12. Conversations With God, Book 4: Awaken the Species
(9781937907495): Neale Donald Walsch: Books.
Accessed January 19, 2018. https://www.amazon.com/
Conversations-God-Book-Awaken-Species/dp/193790749X.
13. Ross, Tim. "Belief in God is part of human nature — Oxford study."
The Telegraph. May 12, 2011. Accessed January 21, 2018. http://
www.telegraph.co.uk/news/politics/8510711/Belief-in-God-is-part-
of-human-nature-Oxford-study.html
14. Dawkins, Richard. "River Out of Eden: A Darwinian View of Life"
(1995).
15. Walsh, R. & Vaughan, F. "On transpersonal definitions." Journal of
Transpersonal Psychology, 25 (2) 125–182, 1993.
16. The Editors of Encyclopedia Britannica. "Python." Encyclopedia
Britannica. April 28, 2008. Accessed January 29, 2018. https://www.
britannica.com/topic/Python-Greek-mythology.
17. Plutarch, Defect. orae. 414e
18. O'Toole, R. F. (1992). Slave Girl at Philippi (Person). In D. N.
Freedman (Ed.), The Anchor Yale Bible Dictionary (Vol. 6, p. 58).
New York: Doubleday.

19. Guyer, M. S. (2016). Philippian Slave Girl. In J. D. Barry, D. Bomar, D. R. Brown, R. Klippenstein, D. Mangum, C. Sinclair Wolcott, W. Widder (Eds.), The Lexham Bible Dictionary. Bellingham, WA: Lexham Press.

20. Crowley, Aleister. Magick in Theory and Practice. Albatross Publishers, 2018. Chapter 13.

21. Crowley, Aleister, and Israel Regardie. Magick without Tears. Falcon Press, 2001. Chapter 81.

22. James A. Eshelman, The Mystical and Magical System of the A A . Los Angeles: College of Thelema, Dec 1993 (1st hardcover edition 2000), Chapter 11. Crowley, Aleister, One Star in Sight.

23. "Satanic Astral Temple." Satan's Den, 29 July 2012, zalbarath666. wordpress.com/satanic-magick/satanic-astral-temple/.

24. Bancarz, Steven. "Astral Projection Unveiled: The Demonic 'Astral' Realm." Reasons for Jesus, 15 Oct. 2016, reasonsforjesus.com/astral-projection-exposed/.

25. "Testimonies of Freedom." Alien Resistance, www.alienresistance. org/stop-alien-abduction/testimonies-of-freedom/.

26. "Alien Resistance HQ—UFOs and the Bible? Stop Alien Abduction Info." Alien Resistance, www.alienresistance.org/.

27. Francis E. Peters Greek Philosophical Terms: A Historical Lexicon, 1970, p. 42.

28. Diogenes Laertius, Lives and Opinions of Eminent Philosophers.

29. Ibid.

30. Schenke, Hans Martin. ""The Phenomenon and Significance of Gnostic Sethianism" in The Rediscovery of Gnosticism. E. J. Brill 1978

31. Clement of Alexandria, Stromata III.9.63.

32. "Michael Heiser —Gnosticism and Early Christianity." YouTube, YouTube, 30 Apr. 2016, www.youtube.com/watch?v=HOD5sINobq8.

33. Burnham, Josh. "Sethian Gnosticism and the Female: A Synthesis." Academia.edu, www.academia.edu/7074728/Sethian_Gnosticism_and_the_Female_A_Synthesis.

34. P. T. Raju (2006), Idealistic Thought of India, Routledge, page 426 and Conclusion chapter part XII.

35. Lochtefeld, James G. (2002). The Illustrated Encyclopedia of Hinduism. The Rosen Publishing Group. p. 122.

36. Stephen Philips (1998), Routledge Encyclopedia of Philosophy: Brahman to Derrida (Editor; Edward Craig), Routledge, pages 1–4

37. Gavin Flood (1996), An Introduction to Hinduism, Cambridge University Press, pages 84–85

38. Radhakrishnan, S., The Principal Upanisads, HarperCollins India, 1994, page 77.

39. Deussen, Paul and Geden, A. S. The Philosophy of the Upanishads. Cosimo Classics (June 1, 2010). P. 86.

40. Richard King (1995), Early Advaita Vedanta and Buddhism, State University of New York Press, page 64

41. David Lorenzen (2004), The Hindu World (Editors: Sushil Mittal and Gene Thursby), Routledge, pages 208-209

42. Sharma, Arvind (2000), Classical Hindu Thought: An Introduction, Oxford University Press

43. "Book of Jasher, Chapter 9." Laotzu's Tao and Wu Wei: Title Page, www.sacred-texts.com/chr/apo/jasher/9.htm.

44. Goodrick-Clarke 2004, p. 8; Lachman 2012, pp. 137–138.

45. Lachman 2012, p. 156.

46. Lachman 2012, pp. 159–160.

47. Campbell 1980, p. 33; Washington 1993, p. 52.

48. Campbell 1980, p. 35; Meade 1980, p. 179; Washington 1993, p. 52; Lachman 2012, p. 152.

49. Lachman 2012, p. 171.

50. Hammer 2001, p. 121

51. Ibid.

52. Blavatsky 1888b, p. 471.

53. Blavatsky 1888b, p. 200.

54. Blavatsky 1888b, p. 195.

55. Bevir 1994, p. 765; Goodrick-Clarke 2004, p. 18; Santucci 2006, p. 184.

56. New Age Encyclopedia 1990, pp. 458–461.

57. New Age Encyclopedia 1990, ix, xxxviii.

58. Blavatsky, Helena. The Secret Doctrine. Vol. 2, Theosophical University Press, 1888. pg. 229. https://www.theosocicty.org/pasadena/sd/sd-hp.htm.

59. Ibid., pg. 234.
60. Ibid., pg. 243.
61. Ibid., pg. 377.
62. Ibid., pg. 513.
63. Bailey 1951 p.1. From the Preface by Foster Bailey.
64. Mills, Joy, 100 Years of Theosophy, A History of the Theosophical Society in America, 1987, p. 62
65. "Lucis Trust." Wikipedia, Wikimedia Foundation, 10 Apr. 2018, en.wikipedia.org/wiki/Lucis_Trust.
66. Initiation, Human and Solar. Copyright 1922 by Alice A. Bailey. First Edition. Lucifer Publishing Co., 135 Broadway, New York City.
67. Hutton 1999, p. 175; Dyrendal 2012, pp. 369–70.
68. Hutton 1999, p. 175.
69. van Luijk 2016, p. 309.
70. High Priest, Magus Peter H. Gilmore. "The Magic Circle / Order of the Trapezoid."
71. Faxneld & Petersen 2013, p. 79.
72. "Contemporary Religious Satanism." google.com.
73. Anton LaVey, quoted in Church of Satan, B. Barton, p.107.
74. Ibid.
75. Ministries, Joy of Satan. "Satanic Witchcraft Index." Esmeralda Santiago's Biography, www.angelfire.com/empire/serpentis666/Satanic_Witchcraft_Index.html.
76. Ministries, Joy of Satan. "Information Concerning the Mind." Esmeralda Santiago's Biography, www.angelfire.com/empire/serpentis666/TheMind.html.
77. "Satanic Meditation." Esmeralda Santiago's Biography, www.angelfire.com/empire/serpentis666/Satanic_Meditation.html.
78. Heselton 2012a, p. 39.
79. Bracelin 1960, p. 19; Heselton 2012a, p. 40.
80. Bracelin 1960, pp. 19–20; Heselton 2012a, pp. 40–41.
81. Bracelin 1960, p. 121; Heselton 2012a, pp. 59–62.
82. Bracelin 1960, p. 35; Heselton 2012a, pp. 66–67.
83. Heselton 2012a, p. 72.
84. Bracelin 1960, pp. 45–48; Heselton 2012a, pp. 74–76.

85. Heselton 2012a, pp. 196–198.
86. Heselton 2012b, pp. 327–332.
87. Bracelin 1960, p. 171; Valiente 2007, p. 57; Heselton 2012b, pp. 341–362.
88. Heselton 2012b, pp. 494–503.
89. Lamond 2004, p. 19; Bourne 1998, p. 29.
90. Gardner's Passing, thewica.co.uk/Gardners death.htm.
91. Valiente 2007, p. 44.
92. "New Page 2." Modern Witchcraft, www.thewica.co.uk/Ggrave. htm.
93. "Maitreya (Theosophy)." Wikipedia, Wikimedia Foundation, 15 Apr. 2018, en.wikipedia.org/wiki/Maitreya_(Theosophy).
94. M. Lutyens pp. 20–21
95. M. Lutyens pp. 276, 285.
96. Jayakar, "Krishnamurti" p 203.
97. See On Krishnamurti, by Raymond Martin, Wadsworth, 2003, for a discussion on Krishnamurti and the academic world.
98. "Core of the Teachings." Search Results - J. Krishnamurti Online, www.jkrishnamurti.org/about-core-teachings.
99. York, Michael (1995). The Emerging Network: A Sociology of the New Age and Neo-Pagan Movements. Rowman & Littlefield. p. 60.
100. "The Edgar Cayce Predictions." Alamongordo Prophecies, 30 Aug. 2014, www.alamongordo.com/the-edgar-cayce-predictions/.
101. "Spirit Science 12 - The Hidden Human History Movie." YouTube, 1 Feb. 2012, youtu.be/U8NNHmV3QPw?t=8m28s.
102. Bancarz, Steven. "Proof The New Age Is Satanic (Fixed)." YouTube, 17 May 2016, youtu.be/DtkGgtExLcY?t=13m40s.
103. Melchizedek, Drunvalo. The Ancient Secret of the Flower of Life. Vol. 2, Clear Light Trust, 2000. pg. 191 http://www.tachyon-aanbieding.eu/Documentation/Ancient Secret of The Flower of Life (vol.2).pdf.
104. Ibid., pg. 194.
105. Ibid., pg. 197.
106. Ibid. pg. 198.
107. Melchizedek, Drunvalo. The Ancient Secret of the Flower of Life.

Vol. 1. pg. 2. http://www.tachyon-aanbieding.eu/Documentation/ Ancient Secret of The Flower of Life (vol.1).pdf.

108. Ministries, Joy of Satan. "High Ranking Gods and Crowned Princes of Hell."Esmeralda Santiago'sBiography, www.angelfire.com/ empire/serpentis666/DEMONSI.html.

109. "Keys to the Ancient Ones Part II: The Meaning of Azag-Thoth." Warlock Asylum International News, 17 Aug. 2009, warlockasyluminternationalnews.com/2009/08/06/ keys-to-the-ancinet-ones-part-11-the-meaning-of-azag-thoth/.

110. Szandor, La Vey Anton. The Satanic Bible. Avon Books, 2005. pg. 144, 146.

111. Blavatsky, Helena. Isis Unveiled , Vol. I: Science, New York, Trow's Printing and Bookbinding Company, 1877, p. 554, xxxiii.

112. "Ningishzidda by Sasha Lessin, Ph. D. (Anthropology, U.C.L.A.)." Enki Speaks, 20 Jan. 2018, enkispeaks.com/ ningishzidda-by-sasha-lessin-ph-d-anthropology-u-c-l-a/.

113. "Anunnaki Computers—Sasha Lessin, PhD (Anthropology, U.C.L.A.)." Enki Speaks, 15 Nov. 2017, enkispeaks.com/ computers-of-the-anunnaki-by-sasha-lessin-ph-d-anthropology-u-c-l-a/.

114. Kinnaer, Jacques. "Human Sacrifie." The Ancient Egypt Site, www. ancient-egypt.org/from-a-to-z/h/human-sacrifice.html.

115. "Ningishzidda by Sasha Lessin, Ph. D. (Anthropology, U.C.L.A.)." Enki Speaks, 20 Jan. 2018, enkispeaks.com/ ningishzidda-by-sasha-lessin-ph-d-anthropology-u-c-l-a/.

116. "Ningishzidda." Library of Halexandria, www.halexandria.org/ dward376.htm.

117. The Necronomicon. Avon Books. http://alleeshadowtradition.com/ pdf/necronomicon2.pdf.

118. Britannica, The Editors of Encyclopaedia. "Sir Leonard Woolley." Encyclopædia Britannica, 10 Apr. 2018, www.britannica.com/ biography/Leonard-Woolley.

119. Digitization Project - Penn Museum & British Museum. "The Digital Resource for the Excavation of Ur." Ur Online, www. ur-online.org/about/6/.

120. "Bear Witness." Merriam-Webster, Merriam-Webster, www.
merriam-webster.com/dictionary/bear witness.

121. David, Marian. "The Correspondence Theory of Truth." Stanford
Encyclopedia of Philosophy, Stanford University, 10 May 2002,
plato.stanford.edu/entries/truth-correspondence/.

122. "True | Definition of True in English by Oxford Dictionaries."
Oxford Dictionaries | English, Oxford Dictionaries,
en.oxforddictionaries.com/definition/true.

123. Bakewell, Charles M. Pragmatism: a New Name for Some Old
Ways of Thinking. Harvard University Press, 1907.

124. Hookway, Christopher. "Pragmatism." Stanford Encyclopedia of
Philosophy, Stanford University, 16 Aug. 2008, plato.stanford.edu/
entries/pragmatism/#PraPra.

125. Bertrand Russell, A History of Western Philosophy (Forage Village,
MA: Simon and Schuster, 1945), pg. 817

126. "Smoking & Tobacco Use." Centers for Disease Control and
Prevention, Centers for Disease Control and Prevention, 20 Feb.
2018, www.cdc.gov/tobacco/data_statistics/fact_sheets/fast_facts/
index.htm.

127. "What We Resonate with Is What Is Aligned with Our Energy, Path
and Purpose." Enlightening Life, 7 Oct. 2013, enlighteninglife.
com/resonate/.

128. Moreland, J. P., and William Lane Craig. Philosophical Foundations
for a Christian Worldview. Intervarsity Press, 2017. pg. 130–131.

129. "What Is the New Age Movement?" Teal Swan, Admin, 2 June
2016, tealswan.com/teals-blog/what-is-the-new-age-movement/.

130. The Law of One Session 10, L/L Research, www.lawofone.info/
results.php?s=10

131. Simmons, Robert, et al. The Book of Stones: Who They Are &
What They Teach. Heaven & Earth Publishing, 2015.

132. Heid, Markham. "You Asked: Do Healing Crystals Actually Work?"
Time, Time, 5 Oct. 2017, time.com/4969680/do-crystals-work/.

133. Palermo, Elizabeth. "Crystal Healing: Stone-Cold Facts About
Gemstone Treatments." Live Science, 23 June 2017, www.
livescience.com/40347-crystal-healing.html.

134. Hitchens, Christopher. "The Fanatic, Fraudulent Mother Teresa."
     Slate Magazine, Slate, 20 Oct. 2003, www.slate.com/articles/news_
     and_politics/fighting_words/2003/10/mommie_dearest.html.
135. October 1951, as noted in McElheny 2004, p. 40: "That's what
     a helix should look like!" Crick exclaimed in delight (This is the
     Cochran-Crick-Vand-Stokes theory of the transform of a helix).
136. June 1952, as noted in McElheny 2004, p. 43: Watson had
     succeeded in getting X-ray pictures of TMV showing a diffraction
     pattern consistent with the transform of a helix.
137. "Photo 51." Wikipedia, Wikimedia Foundation, 27 Apr. 2018,
     en.wikipedia.org/wiki/Photo_51.
138. "New Age Medicine." New Age Medicine, www.
     drgarciaquantumhealing.com/.
139. Pemberton, Lisa (July 16, 2006). ""Behind the gates at Ramtha's
     School." The Olympian. Retrieved November 20, 2009.
140. Ron Hogan (2005-09-05). ""New Age: What the Bleep? Categories
     conflate, confound, connect." Publishers Weekly. Archived from the
     original on 11 August 2007. Retrieved 2007-12-28.
141. Gorenfeld, John (2004-09-16). "'Bleep' of faith." Salon. Retrieved
     2017-12-12.
142. Benedicta Cipolla ""Bleep' Film Challenges Traditional Religion,
     Attracts Following," beliefnet.com. Accessed 2007-12-30.
143. "'What the #$*!' makes 'Bleep' so popular." *Fort Worth Star
     Telegram*. 2005-01-22.
144. Randall, Lisa. Knocking on Heaven's Door: How Physics and
     Scientific Thinking Illuminate the Universe and the Modern World
     (1st ed.). New York: Ecco. p. 10. ISBN 978-0-06-172372-8.
145. Kuttner, Fred; Rosenblum, Bruce (November 2006). "Teaching
     physics mysteries versus pseudoscience." *Physics Today*. American
     Institute of Physics. 59 (11): 14. Bibcode:2006PhT....59k..14K.
     doi:10.1063/1.2435631.
146. Wilson, Elizabeth (2005-01-13). "What the Bleep Do We
     Know?!"American Chemical Society. Retrieved 2007-12-19.
147. "The minds boggle." The Guardian Unlimited.
148. Bhagavata Purana, 12.2.16–17.

149. Blavatsky, Helena Petrovna. Isis Unveiled: a Master-Key to the Mysteries of Ancient and Modern Science and Theology. Theosophy, 1975.

150. Gilbert, Derek P., et al. The Day the Earth Stands Still: Unmasking the Old Gods behind ETs, UFOs, & the Official Disclosure Movement. Defender, 2017.

151. Day, J. (1992). Leviathan. In D. N. Freedman (Ed.), The Anchor Yale Bible Dictionary (Vol. 4, p. 295). New York: Doubleday.

152. "Enuma Elish." Laotzu's Tao and Wu Wei: Title Page, www.sacred-texts.com/ane/enuma.htm.

153. Lincoln, A. T. (1990). Ephesians (Vol. 42, p. 96). Dallas: Word, Incorporated.

154. "Pantheism." Merriam-Webster, Merriam-Webster, www.merriam-webster.com/dictionary/pantheism.

155. Mander, William. "Pantheism." Stanford Encyclopedia of Philosophy, Stanford University, 7 July 2016, plato.stanford.edu/entries/pantheism/.

156. Radin, Dean I. The Conscious Universe: the Scientific Truth of Psychic Phenomena. HarperOne, 2009.

157. Goswami, Amit. Physics of the Soul: the Quantum Book of Living, Dying, Reincarnation, and Immortality. Hampton Roads Publishing Company, Inc., 2013.

158. Robinson Jeffers, in a letter to Sister Mary James Power (1 October 1934); published in The Wild God of the World : An Anthology of Robinson Jeffers (2003), edited by Albert Gelpi, p. 189; also partly quoted in the essay ""Robinson Jeffers, Pantheist Poet" by John Courtney.

159. Maharishi Mahesh Yogi (1976). Creating an ideal society. Rheinweiler, Germany: Maharishi European Research University Press. Pg. 123.

160. https://www.mum.edu/wp-content/uploads/2014/07/hagelin.pdf, Pg. 59.

161. Hawking, S. 1996. The Nature of Space and Time. p. 20.

162. Vilenkin, A. 2006. Many Worlds in One. p.176.

163. Penrose, R. 1981. "Time-Asymmetry and Quantum Gravity" in Quantum Gravity 2, ed. p. 249.

164. Ibid.
165. Ellis, G. 1988. "The Anthropic Principle: Laws and Environments" in The Anthropic Principle: Proceedings of the Second Venice Conference on Cosmology and Philosophy.
166. Davies, P. 1988. The Cosmic Blueprint: New Discoveries in Nature's Creative Ability To Order the Universe. P.203.
167. Fred Hoyle, "The Universe: Past and Present Reflections." Engineering and Science, Nov 1981. pp. 8–12
168. Craig, W. Transcript: Fine-Tuning Argument.
169. McFadden, J. (2013). "The CEMI Field Theory Closing the Loop" (PDF). Journal of Consciousness Studies. 20: 153–168.
170. Jeffrey Gray (2004). Consciousness: Creeping up on the Hard Problem. Oxford University Press. ISBN 0-19-852090-5.
171. Hiroomi Umezawa. Advanced Field Theory: Micro, Macro and Thermal Physics (1993). American Institute of Physics.
172. "John Hagelin, Ph.D on Consciousness 1 of 2." YouTube, YouTube, 8 Dec. 2007, www.youtube.com/watch?v=OrcWntw9juM.
173. Ehrman, Bart. "Freedom From Religion Foundation Lecture." YouTube, 14 Aug. 2014, youtu.be/VAhw2cVRVsA?t=51m46s.
174. Ehrman, Bart D. "Did Jesus Exist?" The Huffington Post, TheHuffingtonPost.com, 20 May 2012, www.huffingtonpost.com/bart-d-ehrman/did-jesus-exist_b_1349544.html.
175. Hoffman, R. Joseph. "Mythtic Pizza and Cold-Cocked Scholars." The New Oxonian, 25 Apr. 2012, rjosephhoffmann.wordpress.com/2012/04/23/mythtic-pizza-and-cold-cocked-scholars/.
176. "Facts and Friction of Easter." Brisbane Times, Brisbane Times, Mar. 2008 www.brisbanetimes.com.au/news/national/facts-and-friction-of-easter/2008/03/21/1205602592557.html?page=3.
177. "Bart Ehrman vs. Reginald Finley—Existence of Jesus." YouTube, 19 Sept. 2014, youtu.be/9qZfXVntEl4?t=6m31s.
178. Habermas, Gary R., and Mike Licona. The Case for the Resurrection of Jesus. Kregel Publications, 2004. Pg. 233
179. "Freedom From Religion Foundation Lecture." YouTube, 14 Aug. 2014, youtu.be/VAhw2cVRVsA?
180. "Ancient Buddhist Scrolls from Gandhara." UW News, 2016. www.washington.edu/uwpress/search/books/SALANC.html.

181. Willemen, Charles, transl. (2009), Buddhacarita: In Praise of Buddha's Acts, Berkeley, Numata Center for Buddhist Translation and Research, p. XIII.

182. Maier, Paul. "Did Jesus Really Exist?" NAMB, www.namb.net/apologetics/did-jesus-really-exist?pageid=8589952895.

183. McGrath, James F. "Review of Bart Ehrman, Did Jesus Exist? Part One." Faith on the Couch, Patheos, 10 Apr. 2012, www.patheos.com/blogs/religionprof/2012/04/review-of-bart-ehrman-did-jesus-exist-part-one.html.

184. Bailey, Alice. Initiation, Human and Solar. Lucis Publisihing Company, 1972. Pg. 12–13

185. Ibid., pg. 19.

186. Ibid., pg. 56.

187. "Maitreya and Jesus." Share International, Apr. 1999, www.share-international.org/maitreya/Ma_jesus.htm.

188. Creme, Benjamin. The World Teacher For All Humanity. Share International Foundation, 2007. Pg. 7.

189. Ibid. pg. 120.

190. Bailey, Alice A. Externalization of the Hierarchy. Lucis Press Ltd, 1972. http://www.auricmedia.net/wp-content/uploads/2015/12/The-Externalization-of-the-Hierarchy.pdf.

191. Szandor, La Vey Anton. The Satanic Bible. Avon Books, 2005. Pg. 162.

192. Rudhyar, Dane. The Magic of Tone and the Art of Music. Shambhala, 1982. Pg. 69.

193. Greer, John Michael. The New Encyclopedia of the Occult. Llewellyn Publications, 2013. Pg. 418.

194. Michaels, Kim. Jesus, Lucifer and Sanat Kumara, www.ascendedmasteranswers.com/spiritual-topics/dark-forces/288-jesus-lucifer-and-sanat-kumara.

195. Bailey, Alice. Initiation, Human and Solar. Lucis Publishing Company, 1972. Pg. 56.

196. Creme, Benjamin. The Awakening of Humanity. Share International Foundation, 2008. Pg. 70.

197. Biema, David Van. "Deepak Chopra on Jesus." Time, Time Inc., 13 Nov. 2008, content.time.com/time/arts/article/0,8599,1858571,00.html.

198. Tolle, Eckhart. A New Earth: Awakening to Your Life's Purpose. Penguin Books, 2016. Pg. 46.

199. Tolle, Eckhart. The Power of Now: A Guide to Spiritual Enlightenment. Namaste Publishing, 2004. Pg. 68.

200. A Course in Miracles: Workbook for Students, Manual for Teachers. Course in Miracles Society, 2008. Pg. 87.

201. Walsch, Neale Donald. Conversations with God Book 2. Hampton Roads, 1997. Pg. 25–26.

202. Chopra, Deepak. The Third Jesus: How to Find Truth and Love in Today's World. Rider, 2009. Pg. 139.

203. "'Christ Consciousness'–Oprah Winfrey." YouTube, Sam Botta, 4 Mar. 2013, www.youtube.com/watch?v=C8Ubaw-rZdg.

204. Chopra, Deepak. The Third Jesus: How to Find Truth and Love in Today's World. Rider, 2009. Pg. 36.

205. Osho. Philosophia Perennis. Vol. 2, Osho Online Library. Ch. 11. http://www.osho.com/iosho/library/read-book/online-library-seeking-becoming-within-34423188-61c?p=57a2ec179850c5df292f0cec4cee9c09.

206. Swanson, James. A Dictionary of Biblical Languages with Semantic Domains: Greek New Testament. 2nd ed., 2001.

207. Bullinger, Ethelbert W. A Critical Lexicon and Concordance to the English and Greek New Testament, Together with an Index of Greek Words and Several Appendices. 5th ed., revised. Pg. 49.

208. Biema, David Van. "Deepak Chopra on Jesus." Time, Time Inc., 13 Nov. 2008, content.time.com/time/arts/article/0,8599,1858571,00.html.

209. Darecki, Yanush. "'Ye Are Gods'." Yogananda on Meditation, yogananda.com.au/sc/new_testament_ye_are_gods_j10-34.html.

210. West, Brandon. "You Are God: The True Teachings of Jesus." The Mind Unleashed, 5 Nov. 2015, themindunleashed.com/2015/11/you-are-god-the-true-teachings-of-jesus.html.

211. Calvin, J., & Pringle, W. Commentary on the Gospel according to John. 2010. Vol. 1, p. 419. Bellingham, WA: Logos Bible Software.

212. Lutts, Andy. Human Origins: The Elohim, www.salemctr.com/newage/center31.html.

213. "The Mighty Elohim." Great White Brotherhood of Ascended Masters, www.ascension-research.org/elohim.html.

214. Blavatsky, H. P. Isis Unveiled: a Master-Key to the Mysteries of Ancient and Modern Science and Theology. Vol. 1, J.W. Bouton, 1889. Pg. 589.

215. "Genesis 1:1 (KJV)." Blue Letter Bible, www.blueletterbible.org/ lang/Lexicon/Lexicon.cfm?strongs=H430&t=KJV.

216. Heiser, Michael. "So What Exactly Is An Elohim." The Divine Council, www.thedivinecouncil.com/What is an Elohim.pdf.

217. Heiser, Michael. "Should The Plural אלהים of Psalm 82 Be Understood as Men or Divine Beings?" The Divine Council, www. thedivinecouncil.com/What is an Elohim.pdf.

218. Michael S. Heiser, "Divine Council," in Dictionary of the Old Testament: Wisdom, Poetry & Writings (ed. Tremper Longman III and Peter Enns; Downers Grove, IL; Nottingham, England: IVP Academic; Inter-Varsity Press, 2008), 112.

219. Heiser, Michael. "Old Testament Godhead Language." The Divine Council, www.thedivinecouncil.com/OTGodheadLanguage.pdf.

220. Heiser, Michael S. The Unseen Realm: Recovering the Supernatural Worldview of the Bible. Lexham Press, 2015.

221. Heiser, Michael. "Chapter 4: God Alone." *More Unseen Realm*, www.moreunseenrealm.com/?page_id=10.

222. Tolle, Eckhart. The Power of Now: A Guide to Spiritual Enlightenment. Namaste Publishing, 2004. Pg. 69.

223. Chopra, Deepak. The Third Jesus: How to Find Truth and Love in Today's World. Rider, 2009. Pg. 40.

224. Singh, Jagbir. "The Resurrection of Christ within You." The Concept of Shakti: Hinduism as a Liberating Force for Women, www.adishakti.org/_/resurrection_of_the_christ_within_you.htm.

225. Hinnells, John R. Mithraic Studies: Proceedings of the First International Congress of Mithraic Studies. Manchester Univ. Press, 1975. Pg. 173.

226. Hastings, James. Encyclopedia of Religion and Ethics. Vol. 8, T & T Clark, 2003. Pg. 757

227. Gordon, Richard. Image and Value in the Greco-Roman World. Aldershot: Variorum, 1996, pg. 96.

228. Hesiod, Theogony, 940 ff (trans. Evelyn-White) (Greek epic C8th or 7th B.C.)

229. Habermas, Gary. Historian Vs Mythicist: Is Jesus A Copy Of Pagan Gods? Faith Under Fire, 6 Mar. 2017, www.youtube.com/watch?v=HCqaVSQkFdQ.

230. Wilkinson, Richard. Complete Gods and Goddesses of Ancient Egypt, Thames and Hudson. 2003. p. 146.

231. Dunand Françoise, and Christiane Zivie-Coche. Gods and Men in Egypt: 3000 BCE to 395 CE. Cornell Univ. Press, 2004.

232. Ludemann, Gerd. The Resurrection of Christ: A Historical Inquiry, Prometheus Books, 2004. pg. 50.

233. Crossan, John Dominic. Jesus: A Revolutionary Biography, HarperCollins, 1991. Pg. 145.

234. Ehrman, Bart. The Historical Jesus Part 1: Transcripts and Guidebook (Great Courses). The Teaching Company, 2000. Pg. 162.

235. Did Jesus Exist? The Historical Argument for Jesus of Nazareth, HarperOne, 2003. Pg. 230.

236. Ehrman, Bart D. "Did Jesus Exist?" The Huffington Post, TheHuffingtonPost.com, 20 May 2012, www.huffingtonpost.com/bart-d-ehrman/did-jesus-exist_b_1349544.html.

237. Smith, Jonathan Z. "Dying and Rising Gods," in Encyclopedia of Religion, Macmillan 1987, Vol. 3, page 521.

238. Mettinger, Tryggve N.D. The Riddle of Resurrection: "Dying and Rising Gods" in the Ancient Near East. Stockholm: Almqvist & Wiksell International, 2001. Pg. 221.

239. Robinson, John. Can We Trust the New Testament? Grand Rapids: Eerdmans, 1977. Pg. 36

240. Ehrman, Bart. The New Testament: A Historical Introduction to the Early Christian Writings. Oxford University Press, 2007. 3rd edition. p. 229.

241. Craig, William Lane. "The Evidence for Jesus." Reasonable Faith, www.reasonablefaith.org/writings/popular-writings/jesus-of-nazareth/the-evidence-for-jesus/.

242. Dunn, James. Jesus Remembered: Christianity in the Making. Eerdmans, 2003. pg. 185.

243. Stanton, Graham. The Gospels and Jesus. Cambridge University Press, 2004. pg. 192.

244. Keener, Craig. Will the Real Historical Jesus Please Stand Up? The Gospels as Sources for Historical Information about Jesus. 2010. http://www.bibleinterp.com/articles/keener357924.shtml

245. Bishop, James. "The General Reliability of the Gospels." James Bishop's Theological Rationalism, 4 Aug. 2016, jamesbishopblog. com/2016/08/03/the-general-reliability-of-the-gospels/.

246. Wallace, Dan. Fragments of Truth. Film. Faithlife, 2018.

247. Bruce, F. The New Testament Documents: Are They Reliable? 1960.

248. Moss, J. A Manual of Classical Bibliography. 1825. p. 526.

249. Habermas, Gary. Answers from Dr. Gary R. Habermas—Online Resource for the Resurrection of Jesus Christ, www.garyhabermas. com/qa/qa_index.htm.

250. Pesch, Rudolf. Das Markusevangelium, 2 vols., Herders Theologischer Kommentar zum Neuen Testament 2 (Freiburg: Herder, 1976–77), Vol. 2. pg. 519–20

251. Bruce, F. Ibid. pg. 9–10.

252. Craig, William Lane. Reasonable Faith: Christian Truth and Apologetics. 2008. 3rd edition. Pg. 336.

253. Habermas, Gary. Answers from Dr. Gary R. Habermas - Online Resource for the Resurrection of Jesus Christ, www.garyhabermas. com/qa/qa_index.htm.

254. Barry, J. D. The Lexham Bible Dictionary. "Jews in the New Testament." Lexham Press, 2016.

255. Cohen, Shaye. "He Was Born, Lived, and Died as a Jew." PBS, Public Broadcasting Service, www.pbs.org/wgbh/pages/frontline/ shows/religion/jesus/bornliveddied.html.

256. Whipps, Heather. "Who Was Jesus, the Man?" Live Science, 10 Apr. 2009, www.livescience.com/3482-jesus-man.html.

257. Habermas, Gary. "The Empty Tomb of Jesus." North American Mission Board, www.namb.net/apologetics/ the-empty-tomb-of-jesus?pageid=8589952861.

258. Habermas, Gary. "Recent Perspectives on the Reliability of the Gospels." Answers from Dr. Gary R. Habermas - Online Resource for the Resurrection of Jesus Christ, www.garyhabermas.com/ articles/crj_recentperspectives/crj_recentperspectives.htm.

259. Allison, Dale. Resurrecting Jesus: The Earliest Christian Tradition and Its Interpreters. Bloomsbury Publishing, 2005 pg. 283–284.

260. Ludemann, Gerd. What Really Happened to Jesus: A Historical Approach to the Resurrection. Westminster John Knox Press, 1996. Pg. 80.

261. Sanders, Ed Parish. The Historical Figure of Jesus. Penguin Books, 1993. Pg. 280

262. "The Bahá'í Faith." The Seven Valleys and the Four Valleys | Bahá'í Reference Library, www.bahai.org/.

263. Tolle, Eckhart. A New Earth, Awakening To Your Life's Purpose. Pg. 10, 45–46 https://www.apnamba.com/Ebooks-pdf/A new Earth.pdf.

264. Harper, Jennifer. "84 Percent of the World Population Has Faith; a Third Are Christian." The Washington Times, 23 Dec. 2012, www.washingtontimes.com/blog/watercooler/2012/dec/23/84-percent-world-population-has-faith-third-are-ch/.

265. Taylor, Justin. "How Much Do You Have to Hate Somebody to Not Proselytize?" The Gospel Coalition, 18 Nov. 2009, www.thegospelcoalition.org/blogs/justin-taylor/how-much-do-you-have-to-hate-somebody-to-not-proselytize/.

266. Fresco, Koi. "Was Jesus Christ a Buddhist?! (Discovering The Truth)." YouTube, 17 July 2016, www.youtube.com/watch?v=lPBPgtHMUsE.

267. Hanson, James. "Was Jesus a Buddhist?" The Zen Site, www.thezensite.com/non_Zen/Was_Jesus_Buddhist.html.

268. "A Basic Buddhism Guide: Differences From Other Religions." Do Buddhist Believe in God?, www.buddhanet.net/e-learning/snapshot01.htm.

269. Tolson, Jay. "Q And A: Deepak Chopra." U.S. News & World Report, 12 June 2007, www.usnews.com/news/blogs/faith-matters/2007/06/12/q-and-a-deepak-chopra.

270. Bhagwan, Dada. "Is Reincarnation True?" Dadabhagwan, www.dadabhagwan.org/path-to-happiness/spiritual-science/science-of-death/is-reincarnation-true/.

271. Liu, Joseph. "Many Americans Mix Multiple Faiths." Pew Research Center's Religion & Public Life Project, 9 Dec. 2009, www.pewforum.org/2009/12/09/many-americans-mix-multiple-faiths/.

272. Ibid.

273. "Stuart Hameroff Brain Quantum Computer." *YouTube*, YouTube, 26 Nov. 2012, www.youtube.com/watch?v=jjpEc98o_Oo. 'Is Life After Death Possible? 'Through the Wormhole, Discovery Science Channel, hosted by Morgan Freeman, interview with Stuart Hameroff. Season 2, Episode 1. 2011.

274. "Reincarnation—The Continuity of Existence—Life After Life." *The Summit Lighthouse*, www.summitlighthouse.org/inner-perspectives/reincarnation/.

275. Miller, Jeanine. "Reincarnation and Karma in the Bible by Jeanine Miller." Visit to the Weeping Madonna Icon in Toronto, by Connie Hargrave; Share International Archives, www.share-international.org/archives/agelesswisdom/aw_jmreincarn.htm.

276. *The Naked Bible Podcast*, www.nakedbiblepodcast.com/naked-bible-88-what-is-the-spiritual-body-paul-talks-about-in-1-cor-15/.

277. "Hebrew Lexicon :: H4194 (KJV)." Blue Letter Bible. Accessed 7 Dec, 2013.http://www.blueletterbible.org/lang/Lexicon/Lexicon.cfm?Strongs=H4194&t=KJV.

278. "Hebrew Lexicon :: H11 (KJV)." Blue Letter Bible. Accessed 7 Dec, 2013.http://www.blueletterbible.org/lang/Lexicon/Lexicon.cfm?Strongs=H11&t=KJV.

279. "Hebrew Lexicon :: H7585 (KJV)." Blue Letter Bible. Accessed 7 Dec, 2013.http://www.blueletterbible.org/lang/Lexicon/Lexicon.cfm?Strongs=H7585&t=KJV.

280. "Greek Lexicon :: G3613 (KJV)." Blue Letter Bible. Accessed 7 Dec, 2013.http://www.blueletterbible.org/lang/Lexicon/Lexicon.cfm?Strongs=G3613&t=KJV.

281. "Ancient Aliens Debunked—(Full Movie) HD." *YouTube*, 30 Sept. 2012, youtu.be/j9w-i5oZqaQ.

282. "Biblical Scholar | Author | Semitic Languages Expert." *Dr. Michael Heiser*, drmsh.com/.

283. Space.com. "Alpha Centauri's Earth-like Planet by the Numbers." *CBS News*, CBS Interactive, 17 Oct. 2012, www.cbsnews.com/news/alpha-centauris-earth-like-planet-by-the-numbers/.

284. Regis, Ed. "Interstellar Travel as Delusional
     Fantasy [Excerpt]." *Scientific American*, 3 Oct.
     2015, www.scientificamerican.com/article/
     interstellar-travel-as-delusional-fantasy-excerpt/.
285. Kaku, Michio. Hyperspace: a Scientific Odyssey through Parallel
     Universes, Time Warps, and the Tenth Dimension. Anchor Books,
     1995. p. 231
286. "Interdimensional Hypothesis." *Wikipedia*, Wikimedia Foundation,
     10 Apr. 2018, en.wikipedia.org/wiki/Interdimensional_hypothesis.
287. Jacques F. Vallee, *Five Arguments Against the Extraterrestrial Origin of
     Unidentified Flying Objects,* Journal of Scientific Exploration, Vol. 4,
     No. 1, pp. 105-117, 1990, Pergamon Press plc. Printed in the USA.
288. "H5303 - n phiyl – Strong's Hebrew Lexicon (KJV)." Blue Letter
     Bible. Web. 18 May, 2018. https://www.blueletterbible.org//lang/
     Lexicon/Lexicon.cfm?Strongs=H5303&t=KJV.
289. "About." *Christalignment*, www.christalignment.org/.
290. "Our Cards Lead The Way" *Christalignment*, www.christalignment.
     org/destinyreadingcards.
291. "Christalignment Destiny Readings." *YouTube*, 8 Aug. 2017, www.
     youtube.com/watch?v=9YDXPcSv9ZM.
292. Hodge, Jen. "Christalignment Destiny Readings". www.
     christalignment.org/destinyreadingcards. Changed Dec 17, 2017.
293. "Christalignment - Our Cards Lead The Way." *Polybius
     at the Clickto Network,* Fox News, web.archive.org/
     web/20171213060600/http://www.christalignment.org/
     destinyreadingcards.
294. Ibid.
295. "Bethel Now Endorsing 'Christian Tarot Cards' After All."
     Pulpit & Pen, 19 Dec. 2017, pulpitandpen.org/2017/12/19/
     to-be-edited-bethel-tarot-cards/.
296. "Our Services." *Christalignment*, www.christalignment.org/
     what-we-offer-at-dandenong.
297. United States Patent and Trademark Office. "US Trademark
     Registration Number 0519636 under First Use in Commerce."
     http://tsdr.uspto.gov/#caseNumber=71546217&caseType=SER
     IAL_NO&searchType=statusSearch.

298. Brunvand, Jan Harold. American Folklore: an Encyclopedia. Routledge, 1998.

299. McRobbie, Linda Rodriguez. "The Strange and Mysterious History of the Ouija Board." *Smithsonian.com*, Smithsonian Institution, 27 Oct. 2013, www.smithsonianmag.com/history/the-strange-and-mysterious-history-of-the-ouija-board-5860627/?no-ist.

300. Stokes, Anne "Spirit Guide Angel Board" https://www.amazon.com/Spirit-Guide-Angel-Board-Stokes/dp/B00U2NOQ6Y/.

301. Cullen/Mahtomedi, Lisa Takeuchi. "Stretching for Jesus." *Time*, Time Inc, 29 Aug. 2005, content.time.com/time/magazine/article/0,9171,1098937,00.html.

302. "Holy Yoga." *Holy Yoga*, holyyoga.net/.

303. "Yahweh Yoga" Yahweh Yoga, yahwehyoga.com/.

304. "Hatha Yoga." *Yoga Journal*, 3 Apr. 2017, www.yogajournal.com/yoga-101/types-of-yoga/hatha.

305. Fuller, J.F.C. Yoga for All, Bombay, India: D. B. Taraporevala Sons & Co. Private Ltd., 1993. pg. 51.

306. Tiwari, Subhas. "Yoga Renamed Is Still Hindu." *Hinduism Today Magazine*, www.hinduismtoday.com/modules/smartsection/item.php?itemid=1456.

307. "Yoga." Merriam-Webster, www.merriam-webster.com/dictionary/yoga.

308. "Yoga Hindu Origins." *Hindu American Foundation (HAF)*, www.hafsite.org/media/pr/yoga-hindu-origins.

309. Bharati , Swami Jnaneshvara. "Modern Yoga versus Traditional Yoga." Yoga Meditation, www.swamij.com/traditional-yoga.htm.

310. Iyengar, B.K.S., Astadala Yogamala (Collected Works) Volume 2, Allied Publishers, 2016. Pg. 46.

311. "Yoga Style Profile: Kundalini Yoga." *Yoga Journal*, 6 Apr. 2017, www.yogajournal.com/yoga-101/spotlight-on-kundalini-yoga.

312. Isaacs, Nora. "Is a Kundalini Awakening Safe?" Yoga Journal, 6 Apr. 2017, www.yogajournal.com/yoga-101/safe-awaken-snake.

313. Bharadwaj B. Proof-of-concept studies in Yoga and mental health. Int J Yoga 2012;5:74.

314. "Kundalini." *Wikipedia*, Wikimedia Foundation, 31 May 2018, en.wikipedia.org/wiki/Kundalini.

315. JAMA and Archives Journals. "Yoga and stretching exercises beneficial for chronic low back pain, study finds." ScienceDaily. 24 October 2011. www.sciencedaily.com/releases/2011/10/111024164710.htm.

316. Flood, Gavin. "Religions—Hinduism: Hindu Concepts." BBC, 24 Aug. 2009, www.bbc.co.uk/religion/religions/hinduism/concepts/concepts_1.shtml#h4.

317. "The Karmic Wheel." The Hindu, 25 Dec. 2012, www.thehindu.com/features/friday-review/religion/the-karmic-wheel/article4239678.ece.

318. Liu, Joseph. "Many Americans Mix Multiple Faiths." Pew Research Center's Religion & Public Life Project, 9 Dec. 2009, www.pewforum.org/2009/12/09/many-americans-mix-multiple-faiths/.

319. Bergoglio, Jorge. "Encyclical Let6ter Laudato Si' of the Holy Father Francis on Care for Our Common Home." Vatican Online, 2015, w2.vatican.va/content/francesco/en/encyclicals/documents/papa-francesco_20150524_enciclica-laudato-si.html#_ftn1.

320. Ibid.

321. March, Jennifer R. Cassell Dictionary of Classical Mythology. London: Cassell, 1998. Pg. 324.

322. Ibid.

323. Franklin, Judy. Physics of Heaven. Destiny Image Incorporated, 2016. Chap. 2

324. Ibid., Chap. 12.

325. Ibid., Chap. 13.

326. Ibid., Chap. 1.

327. "Welcome! " Veriditas—New to the Labyrinth?, www.veriditas.org/.

328. "Labyrinth Transforms Prayer Life, Baptists Say—Baptist News Global." Baptist News Global, 7 May 2014, baptistnews.com/article/labyrinth-transforms-prayer-life-baptists-say/#.WwXR9FMvyM4.

329. rdennis@wacotrib.com, REGINA DENNIS. "Prayer Labyrinth Restored near Lake Shore Baptist Church." WacoTrib.com, 26 Nov. 2013, www.wacotrib.com/news/religion/prayer-labyrinth-restored-near-lake-shore-baptist-church/article_bc6d8ab6-98b6-53d2-8f0b-24cd8284dd2e.html.

330. Kern, Hermann (2000). *Through the Labyrinth*. Munich, London, New York: Prestel. p. 34. ISBN 3791321447.

331. M. Basil Pennington, Centered Living: The Way of Centering Prayer NY: Image, Doubleday. 1988, pg. 95.

332. Thomas Keating, *Open Mind, Open Heart* (Rockport, MA: Benedict's Monastery, 1992) pg. 74.

333. Pennington, Fr. M. Basil. "Centering Prayer: Refining the Rules." Review for Religious, 45:3, 386-393.

334. Swanson, J. (1997). Dictionary of Biblical Languages with Semantic Domains: Hebrew (Old Testament) (electronic ed.). Oak Harbor: Logos Research Systems, Inc.

335. Crossway Bibles. The ESV Study Bible (p. 994). Wheaton, IL: Crossway Bibles. 2008.

336. "Mantra." *EncyclopÄ¦dia Britannica*, Encyclopedia Britannica, Inc., 21 June 2013, www.britannica.com/topic/mantra.

337. Sadhguru. "Mantras Explained: How a Mantra Can Lead to Transformation." Isha Yoga, 27 Jan. 2015, isha.sadhguru.org/us/en/wisdom/article/mantras-explained-mantra-to-transformation.

338. Ferguson, S. B., & Packer, J. I. (2000). In New Dictionary of Theology (electronic ed., p. 526). Downers Grove, IL: InterVarsity Press.

339. "Mindfulness." Merriam-Webster, www.merriam-webster.com/dictionary/mindfulness.

340. Montenegro, Marcia. "Contemplating Contemplative Prayer: Is It Really Prayer?" *Christian Answers for the New Age*, www.christiananswersforthenewage.org/Articles_ContemplativePrayer3.html.

341. Montenegro, Marcia. "Jesus Calling: Channeling A False Christ." *Reasons for Jesus*, 4 Apr. 2017, reasonsforjesus.com/jesus-calling-channeling-a-false-christ/.

342. Young, Sarah. Jesus Calling (Nashville: Thomas Nelson, 2004), XI pg.

343. Lane, W. L. (1998). Hebrews 1–8 (Vol. 47A, p. 11). Dallas: Word, Incorporated.

344. Baker, W. H. (1995). Jude. In Evangelical Commentary on the Bible (Vol. 3, p. 1191). Grand Rapids, MI: Baker Book House.

345. Theosophical Society. "Eben Alexander on the Essential Message of 'Proof of Heaven.'" *YouTube*, 29 Apr. 2015, www.youtube.com/watch?v=3_IrT8wqwBs.

346. Theosophical Society. "Eben Alexander—Synthesis of Science and Spirituality: The Arc of Human Destiny over Millennia." *YouTube*, 18 Sept. 2014, www.youtube.com/watch?v=NpjX9aHcjAo.

347. Theosophical Society. "Eben Alexander: A Neurosurgeon's Journey through the Afterlife." *YouTube*, 27 Aug. 2014, www.youtube.com/watch?v=qbkgj5J91hE.

348. Dass, Ram. "Being Love." Ram Dass, 5 June 2013, www.ramdass.org/being-love/.